Poland's Solidarity Movement and the Global Politics of Human Rights

In the historiography of human rights, the 1980s feature as little more than an afterthought to the human rights breakthrough of the previous decade. Through an examination of one of the major actors of recent human rights history – Poland's Solidarity movement – Robert Brier challenges this view. Suppressed in 1981, Poland's Solidarity movement was supported by a surprisingly diverse array of international groups: US Cold Warriors, French left-wing intellectuals, trade unionists, Amnesty International, even Chilean opponents of the Pinochet regime. By unpacking the politics and transnational discourses of these groups, Brier demonstrates how precarious the position of human rights in international politics remained well into the 1980s. More importantly, he shows that human rights were a profoundly political and highly contested language, which actors in East and West adopted to redefine their social and political identities in times of momentous cultural and intellectual change.

ROBERT BRIER is a historian focusing on the intersection of international relations and intellectual history in the late twentieth century. He was Senior Researcher at the German Historical Institute in Warsaw from 2008 to 2015 and taught International History at the London School of Economics from 2015 to 2018.

Human Rights in History

Edited by

Stefan-Ludwig Hoffmann, University of California, Berkeley

Samuel Moyn, Yale University, Connecticut

This series showcases new scholarship exploring the backgrounds of human rights today. With an open-ended chronology and international perspective, the series seeks works attentive to the surprises and contingencies in the historical origins and legacies of human rights ideals and interventions. Books in the series will focus not only on the intellectual antecedents and foundations of human rights, but also on the incorporation of the concept by movements, nation-states, international governance, and transnational law.

A full list of titles in the series can be found at:
www.cambridge.org/human-rights-history

Poland's Solidarity Movement and the Global Politics of Human Rights

Robert Brier

CAMBRIDGE
UNIVERSITY PRESS

University Printing House, Cambridge CB2 8BS, United Kingdom

One Liberty Plaza, 20th Floor, New York, NY 10006, USA

477 Williamstown Road, Port Melbourne, VIC 3207, Australia

314–321, 3rd Floor, Plot 3, Splendor Forum, Jasola District Centre,
New Delhi – 110025, India

79 Anson Road, #06–04/06, Singapore 079906

Cambridge University Press is part of the University of Cambridge.

It furthers the University's mission by disseminating knowledge in the pursuit of
education, learning, and research at the highest international levels of excellence.

www.cambridge.org
Information on this title: www.cambridge.org/9781108478526
DOI: 10.1017/9781108565233

© Robert Brier 2021

This publication is in copyright. Subject to statutory exception
and to the provisions of relevant collective licensing agreements,
no reproduction of any part may take place without the written
permission of Cambridge University Press.

First published 2021

A catalogue record for this publication is available from the British Library.

Library of Congress Cataloging-in-Publication Data
Names: Brier, Robert (Historian), author.
Title: Poland's solidarity movement and the global politics of human rights /
　Robert Brier.
Description: Cambridge, United Kingdom ; New York, NY : Cambridge
　University Press, 2021. | Series: Human rights in history | Includes
　bibliographical references and index.
Identifiers: LCCN 2020058319 (print) | LCCN 2020058320 (ebook) |
　ISBN 9781108478526 (hardback) | ISBN 9781108460491 (paperback) |
　ISBN 9781108565233 (epub)
Subjects: LCSH: NSZZ "Solidarność" (Labor organization) | Human
　rights–History–20th century.
Classification: LCC HD8537.N783 B75 2021 (print) | LCC HD8537.N783
　(ebook) | DDC 323.09/048–dc23
LC record available at https://lccn.loc.gov/2020058319
LC ebook record available at https://lccn.loc.gov/2020058320

ISBN 978-1-108-47852-6 Hardback

Cambridge University Press has no responsibility for the persistence or accuracy
of URLs for external or third-party internet websites referred to in this publication
and does not guarantee that any content on such websites is, or will remain,
accurate or appropriate.

For Pati, Ella, Vincent, and Paulina

Contents

Acknowledgments		*page* ix
Note on Geographical Regions		xiii
Note on Cited Primary Documents		xiv
List of Abbreviations		xv
	Introduction	1
1	The Rise of Dissent in Poland	19
2	Dissent and the Politics of Human Rights	39
3	The Principle of Noninterference as Laid Down in the Helsinki Final Act: The Polish Crisis, the Cold War, and Human Rights	66
4	The End of the Ideological Age: Human Rights and *Ostpolitik*	91
5	Solidarity, Human Rights, and Anti-Totalitarianism in France	107
6	The "Bedrock of Human Rights": US Labor, Neoconservatism, and Human Rights	127
7	Letters from Prison: The Prisoner of Conscience and the Symbolic Politics of Human Rights	147
8	Lech Wałęsa, the Symbolism of the Nobel Peace Prize, and Global Human Rights Culture	173
9	General Pinochecki: Poland, Chile, and the Global Politics of Human Rights Culture	186

vii

viii   Contents

10 Human Rights and the End of the Cold War   200

Epilogue   217

Bibliography   233
Index   260

Acknowledgments

This book is the product of over a decade of research and writing. One of the most satisfying aspects of seeing it published is the ability to thank all those people and institutions who helped me along the way.

A work of history is always only as good as the sources it draws on. This book, therefore, would have been impossible without the professional support of the archivists at the Archiv der sozialen Demokratie, the Archiv Grünes Gedächtnis, the Archives du Secrétariat Confédéral CFDT and the Archives de la CGT-Force Ouvrière (who also kindly ignored my terrible spoken French), the Archiwum Akt Nowych, the Archiwum Instytutu Pamięci Narodowej, the Ośrodek KARTA, the Charles E. Young Research Library at UCLA, the George Meany Memorial Archive, the Hoover Institution, the International Institute for Social History, the National Archives of the UK, the National Security Archives of George Washington University, and the Ronald Reagan Presidential Library. I am also particularly grateful to Seweryn Blumsztajn, Eric Chenoweth, Jacek Czaputowicz, Marcin Frybes, Irena Grudzińska, Irena Lasota, Karol Sachs and Krystyna Vinaver, Aleksandr Smolar, and Elisabeth Weber all of whom took the time to share their memories with me and make personal collections of documents available. Friedhelm Boll, Andrzej Friszke, Idesbald Goddeeris, Patryk Pleskot, and Bernd Rother provided invaluable support in identifying and navigating crucial collections, as did Andrea Chiampan, Greg Domber, Wanda Jarząbek, and Christie Miedema who also became friends along the way.

I did the vast majority of the research and writing that led to this book from 2008 to 2015, while working at the German Historical Institute (GHI) in Warsaw, first as a postdoctoral visiting fellow and then as a senior researcher. I could not possibly have asked for a better place to work at. The GHI provided an outstanding professional framework as well as indispensable funding. More important, though, was the intellectual companionship, support, and warmth I received from the outstanding colleagues I had the privilege to work with. For that, I am deeply indebted to Eduard Mühle, the GHI's director from 2008 to 2013, to his successor Miloš Řezník, to deputy director Ruth Leiserowitz, as well as to Dariusz Adamczyk, Stephan Böhm, Helge von Boetticher, Jens Boysen, Hanna Chrobocińska, Mareike Hirsch, Izabella Janas, Artur Koczara, Maciej Kordelasiński, Stephan Lehnstädt, Krzysztof Machaj, Anna Novikov, Maren Röger, Grażyna Ślepowrońska, Katrin Stoll, Piotr Szlanta, Grischa Vercamer, Krzysztof Zdanowski, and Dorota Zielińska. I also gratefully acknowledge the financial support from the Foundation for Polish-German Cooperation, which provided the postdoctoral scholarship for my first sixteen months at the GHI, and the Gerda Henkel Foundation for a much needed travel grant.

I finished working on this manuscript while teaching at the London School of Economics' Department of International History from 2015 to 2018. I had the great privilege to teach exceptionally bright students there, while the department, with its intellectually vibrant and internationally diverse faculty, proved an excellent place to think and write about international history. I would like to thank Kristina Spohr as well as Matthew Jones and Janet Hartley for welcoming me to the department. I am also particularly grateful to Molly Avery, Bastiaan Bouwman, Tanya Harmer, Nataliya Kibita, N. Piers Ludlow, Tommaso Milani, Jeppe Mulich, Daniel Strieff, and Eline van Ommen for many stimulating discussions on international history, the Cold War, and human rights, especially at the department's research seminar and the White Horse afterward.

My thinking on the topics discussed in this book has benefitted tremendously from presentations I gave at numerous convention panels, conferences, workshops, and research colloquia. I would like to thank the organizers of these events for inviting me and the attendants for their remarks. Some of them were very critical, others encouraging, all were extremely helpful. In the course of attending these events and of organizing some of them myself, I met many people whose advice, criticism, and encouragement helped me sharpen and deepen my thinking about human rights, the Cold War, intellectual history, and dissent and thus made a major contribution to this book. Just as importantly, they often provided company and friendship. In particular, I would like to thank Agnes Arndt, Arnd Bauerkämper, Paul Blokker, Tim Buchen, Winson Chu, Hella Dietz, Jan Eckel, Barbara Falk, Mateuzs Fałkowski, and everyone at the Research Group "New Approaches to the Solidarity Movement," Steven Jensen, Michal Kopeček, Patrick W. Kelly, Padraic

Acknowledgments

Kenney, Barbara Keys, Piotr Kosicki, Rasmus Mariager, James Mark, Ned Richardson-Little, Brian Porter-Szűcs, Jakub Szumski, Jan Skórzyński, Sarah Snyder, David Tompkins, Barbara Walker, Marcin Zaremba, and anyone I may have forgotten.

I would also like to thank Samuel Moyn and Stefan-Ludwig Hoffmann for including the book in their series. I am deeply grateful to Mark Bradley who encouraged me to get in touch with them, whose scholarship was a tremendous source of inspiration, and who provided invaluable support and most helpful feedback on the manuscript.

The comments of the two anonymous readers were much appreciated and helped sharpen and deepen the argument of this book. Michael Watson's and Emily Sharp's terrific editorial work and unending patience were similarly instrumental in bringing my project to fruition.

None of the chapters listed below has been published previously. Earlier and much abbreviated versions of some of the arguments made in Chapters 3–6 have been published as "Poland's Solidarity as a Contested Symbol of the Cold War: Transatlantic Debates after the Polish Crisis," in Ken Weisbrod and Kiran-Klaus Patel, eds., *European Integration and the Atlantic Community* (New York: Cambridge University Press, 2013); "The Helsinki Final Act, the Second Stage of *Ostpolitik*, and Human Rights in Eastern Europe: The Case of Poland," in Rasmus Mariager et al., eds., *Human Rights in Europe during the Cold War* (London, New York: Routledge, 2014); "Beyond the 'Helsinki Effect': East European Dissent and the Western Left in the History of the 'Long' 1970s," in Rasmus Mariager, et al., eds., *The "Long 1970s": Human Rights, East-West Détente, and Transnational Relations* (London: Routledge, 2016). Some of the materials on which Chapters 2 and 8, respectively, are based were used to inform different arguments in "From Civil Society to Neoliberalism and Armed Intervention? Reflections on the Human Rights Legacy of '1989.'" *European Remembrance and Solidarity Studies* 3 (2014), 165–188; "The Court of World Opinion: Eastern Europe and Latin America in the Late Modern Global Public of Human Rights," in Valeska Huber and Jürgen Osterhammel, eds., *Global Publics: Their Power and Their Limits, 1870–1990* (Oxford: Oxford University Press, 2020).

Finally, I would like to thank my family. I would never have been able to work as an academic historian without the love and support my parents gave me, without the optimism, humor, and appreciation for *Bildung* they instilled in me, nor without the many spirited discussions we have had over the years. I am also deeply grateful to my siblings Barbara and Christoph, their partners Nat and Kathrin, and my nieces and nephews for their love and support. For over twenty-five years, Bernhard Schütz has been the best friend anyone could have.

By far my greatest debt, however, is to my wife Patricia. Through her love, companionship, patience, and many sacrifices she has contributed more than anyone else to the completion of this project. More importantly, it is she and the family we started who give real meaning to what I do. I lovingly dedicate this book to her and to our children Ella, Vincent, and Paulina.

Note on Geographical Regions

Throughout the text, the term "Eastern Europe" refers to the formerly Communist dominated part of Europe, while "Western Europe" denotes the non-Communist part. Thus, Austria, Greece, and Turkey were West European countries even though they lie partly or fully East of countries like the former states of the GDR and Czechoslovakia. The term "Central Europe" denotes the cultural and geographical region comprising the Baltic states, Poland, the current Czech Republic, Slovakia, and Hungary.

Note on Cited Primary Documents

This book draws on published and unpublished primary sources coming from five different countries, each with its own system of referencing sources. Document descriptions have been adapted to the form used in British and US historical monographs only where possible. Most document descriptions have been left in their original form as have been the places where they have been found (*Mappe* in German archives vs. *File* in American ones). This way, everyone working in these archives should be able to identify the cited documents. Wherever archivists paginated documents in an archival unit, these page numbers are given in the footnotes using the abbreviation "fol." (folium/folia). Abbreviations used in the footnotes for archives and their holdings can be found in the bibliography.

Abbreviations

AFL-CIO	American Federation of Labor and Congress for Industrial Organizations
ASFP	Association Solidarité France-Pologne
CDM	Coalition for a Democratic Majority
CFDT	Confédération française democratique du travail
CGT	Confédération générale du travail
CPSU	Communist Party of the Soviet Union
CSCE	Conference on Security and Cooperation in Europe
CSS	Committee in Support of Solidarity
DGB	Deutscher Gewerkschaftsbund
EC	European Community
ICCPR	International Covenant on Civil and Political Rights
ICESCR	International Covenant on Economic, Social, and Cultural Rights
ICFTU	International Confederation of Free Trade Unions
ILO	International Labour Organization
KOR	Komitet Obrony Robotników (*Committee to Defend the Workers*)
KSS "KOR"	Komitet Samoobrony Społecznej "KOR" (Committee for Social Self-Defense "KOR)
NATO	North Atlantic Treaty Organization
NED	National Endowment for Democracy
NSC	National Security Council
NSZZ	Niezależny Samorządny Związek Zawodowy (*Independent Self-Governed Trade Union*)
PAC	Polish American Congress
PATCO	Professional Air Traffic Controllers Organization
PRL	Polska Rzeczpospolita Ludowa (People's Republic of Poland)
PZPR	Polska Zjednoczona Partia Robotnicza (*Polish United Workers' Party*)
RFE	Radio Free Europe

xvi   List of Abbreviations

RL	Radio Liberty
ROPCziO	Ruch Obrony Praw Człowieka i Obywatela (*Movement to Defend Human and Civil Rights*)
SB	Służba Bezpieczeństwa (*Security Service; under Communism, a division in the Ministry of the Interior responsible for state security, intelligence and counterintelligence and thus for the surveillance of the domestic opposition and the émigré groups in the West*)
SDUSA	Social Democrats U.S.A.
SPD	Sozialdemokratische Partei Deutschlands
TKK	Tymczasowa Komisja Koordinacyjna (*Provisional Coordinating Commission;* Solidarity's underground leadership between 1982 and 1987)
UDHR	Universal Declaration of Human Rights
UN	United Nations
UNCHR	United Nations Commission on Human Rights
USIA	United States Information Agency
WCL	World Confederation of Labour

Introduction

No text has a more prominent place in the global human rights imagination than the Universal Declaration of Human Rights (UDHR). Its adoption on December 10, 1948, an influential account has it, forever transformed the "moral terrain" of international relations.[1]

Yet when the UN celebrated this very moment 10 years later, the general mood was one of resignation about a human rights project "deep frozen" by the geopolitics of the Cold War. In 1968, two years after the adoption of two international human rights covenants, the UN even organized an International Year of Human Rights to commemorate the UDHR's adoption, culminating in the First World Conference on Human Rights. Held in Tehran, dominated by authoritarian states, the conference left the UDHR's few remaining admirers desperate about the future of human rights in the world.[2]

Over 20 years later, in August 1988, a town in the suburbs of Poland's ancient capital of Cracow called Nowa Huta, witnessed a celebration of the UDHR which could not have been more different from the proceedings in Tehran. A group of social activists had braved the country's still repressive regime to organize an international conference in and around a Catholic parish church. Over 800 people from Europe, the Soviet Union, and the Americas attended the meeting. Convened under the patronage of Nobel Peace Laureate Lech Wałęsa, its plenary sessions featured addresses and letters by veteran members of the Soviet bloc's dissident movement. Its resolutions and speeches all dismissed the principles of sovereignty and noninterference as excuses of tyrannies and dictatorships, calling for a global social movement holding states accountable to human rights norms. Outside the church, young peace

---

[1] Mary Ann Glendon, *A World Made New: Eleanor Roosevelt and the Universal Declaration of Human Rights* (New York: Random House, 2001), xv.

[2] Samuel Moyn, *The Last Utopia: Human Rights in History* (Cambridge, MA: Harvard University Press, 2010), 126–129; Roland Burke, "Human Rights Day after the 'Breakthrough': Celebrating the Universal Declaration of Human Rights at the United Nations in 1978 and 1988," *Journal of Global History* 10 (2015), 1.

2 Poland's Solidarity Movement & the Politics of Rights

activists from around Central Europe shared experiences and sold their movements' buttons and T-shirts at tables lining the church walls. Representatives of Western human rights groups like the International Helsinki Federation and Freedom House had come, as had the chairmen of the world's two largest non-Communist labor federations. West German pacifists rubbed shoulders with US Cold War liberals while listening to a talk by a Chilean human rights lawyer.[3]

The conference's festive atmosphere was reinforced by its gray backdrop. Founding Nowa Huta in 1949, Poland's Communist rulers had wanted to create a socialist model city, an urban utopia anticipating the creation of a new society. As the Cold War wore on, however, urban planners abandoned the neoclassic architecture of revolutionary socialism for the architectonic hallmark of really existing socialism – cheap panel-built high-rise settlements whose dark facades testified to the ecological havoc wrought by Nowa Huta's namesake steel mill.[4]

Yet exciting though it must have been for those attending the conference, an emergent new historiography of human rights suggests that the meeting of 1988 was a mere coda to developments from over a decade earlier. The conclusion much of this literature gravitates toward is that in the years around 1977 human rights were suddenly catapulted from a long dormant or even stillborn project into the global phenomenon they have been ever since.[5] Reconstructing the experiences, struggles, and

---

[3] Padraic Kenney, *A Carnival of Revolution: Central Europe 1989* (Princeton, NJ: Princeton University Press, 2002), 236–237; Eric Chenoweth, "Poland Today: Democracy Aborning," *Freedom at Issue* (November–December 1988). For the participants see "Lista zagranicznych uczestników," not dated; see also Petr Uhl, letter to the participants of the Human Rights Conference, dated August 11, 1988, Maximo Pacheco, "Obecna sytuacja w dziedzinie praw człowieka w Chile," undated translation of speech manuscript, Jerzy Turowicz, "Prawa człowieka," undated speech manuscript, all in Ośrodek KARTA, Warsaw, Archiwum Opozycji, (hereafter: KARTA), AO IV/191; "A Resolution of the International Human Rights Conference in Cracow – August 1988," Archiv Grünes Gedächtnis (hereafter: AGG), Petra-Kelly-Archiv (hereafter: PKA), Mappe 461.

[4] Katherine Lebow, *Unfinished Utopia: Nowa Huta, Stalinism, and Polish Society, 1949-56* (Ithaca, NY: Cornell University Press, 2013).

[5] The now classic formulation of this thesis is Moyn, *Utopia*. For two of the finest studies applying this thesis to the United States and Latin America respectively see Barbara Keys, *Reclaiming American Virtue: The Human Rights Revolution of the 1970s* (Cambridge, MA: Harvard University Press, 2014); Patrick William Kelly, "Sovereignty and Salvation: Transnational Human Rights Activism in the Americas in the Long 1970s" (PhD thesis, University of Chicago, 2015). See also Jan Eckel and Samuel Moyn, eds., *The Breakthrough: Human Rights in the 1970s* (Philadelphia, PA: University of Pennsylvania Press, 2013); Joe Renouard, *Human Rights in American Foreign Policy: From the 1960s to the Soviet Collapse* (Philadelphia, PA: Universiry of Pennsylvania Press, 2016); William Michael Schmidli, *The Fate of Freedom Elsewhere: Human Rights and U.S. Cold War Policy toward Argentina* (Ithaca, NY: Cornell University Press, 2013). For two major studies

Introduction

beliefs of a wide array of people from Europe and the United States and pushing the narrative of human rights history beyond the human rights moment of the 1970s, this book suggests a different interpretation.

In its colorful internationalism, political diversity, and defiance of a repressive regime, I will show, the gathering in Nowa Huta aptly reflected a wider transnational network of activists working for human rights in Poland and elsewhere in the Soviet bloc. When we look at the contemporary history of human rights through the prism of their experiences, a picture emerges which is characterized not by a single breakthrough of human rights – whether in the 1970s or after – but by their repeated reinvention, their continuous adaptation to new circumstances. More than once, Western governments were willing to abandon their pledges to uphold human rights. Those who did support East European dissidents were still figuring out what human rights were and what kinds of communities – "dissidence," "the Left," "the US," "the West," "the international community" – could be built around them. A politics of human rights is at the center of this book – an ongoing struggle over the meaning of human rights and their role in legitimating domestic and international order.

Human Rights History beyond the 1970s

This book makes four contributions to the historiography of human rights. First, it argues that we need to rethink the way in which the history of human rights has come to be written. The new historiography of human rights has convincingly demonstrated that the sudden popularity of human rights during the 1970s was not the inexorable outcome of seeds planted in antiquity or the Enlightenment. It was the result of a reinvention of human rights in a time of ideological change and political crisis. Yet convincing though these findings are this new historiography also tends to be characterized by what Mark Bradley has usefully called a "take-no-prisoners competitive sweepstakes" between different chronologies, a desire to pinpoint the moment, decade, person, cause, or state

representing a different approach centered respectively around different "human rights vernaculars" and "multiple chronologies" see Mark Philip Bradley, *The World Reimagined: Americans and Human Rights in the Twentieth Century* (Cambridge, MA: Cambridge University Press, 2016); Jan Eckel, *Die Ambivalenz des Guten: Menschenrechte in der internationalen Politik seit den 1940ern* (Göttingen: Vandenhoeck & Ruprecht, 2014); for studies on the relationship between anti-colonialism and human rights, see Roland Burke, *Decolonization and the Evolution of International Human Rights* (Philadelphia, PA: University of Pennsylvania Press, 2010); Fabian Klose, *Human Rights in the Shadow of Colonial Violence: The Wars of Independence in Kenya and Algeria* (Philadelphia, PA: University of Pennsylvania Press, 2013).

that turned human rights into the moral lingua franca of our time.[6] As a result, the broader implications of the human rights moment of the 1970s for the history of human rights before or after this time are usually only stated in sweeping terms rather than demonstrated.[7] Having set out to overcome ahistorical origin stories, we have come dangerously close to writing one ourselves.

The events described in this book, by contrast, bring to light how contingent, at times even accidental, the rise of human rights was and how tenuous their position remained even after their seeming breakthrough. In the late hours of December 12, 1981, the Polish government imposed martial law on the country to save the Communist system from imminent collapse. Fifteen months earlier, in August 1980, a nationwide strike movement had forced the authorities to allow the creation of the independent trade union Solidarność, or Solidarity. Within months it evolved into a mass movement of 9 million people demanding democracy and human rights.

In the previous years, human rights had exploded onto the world stage. Repression in Chile had become a global cause célèbre, Jimmy Carter had pledged an absolute commitment to human rights, Amnesty International had won Nobel Prize fame. On August 1, 1975, the superpowers and almost all European countries had come to Helsinki to sign the Final Act of the Conference on Security and Cooperation in Europe, or CSCE. These "Helsinki Accords" set out provisions to foster East–West economic cooperation but also obliged its signatories to respect human rights – a fact that the Dutch and US governments would turn into a central issue of East–West relations.[8]

---

[6] Mark Philip Bradley, "American Vernaculars: The United States and the Global Human Rights Imagination," *Diplomatic History* 38 (Jan. 2014), 1, 4. Even studies critical of narratives focused on the 1970s adhere to the historiography's approach of locating a point of origin. See, for instance, the otherwise brilliant study by Steven L.B. Jensen, *The Making of International Human Rights: The 1960s, Decolonization and the Reconstruction of Global Values* (Cambridge, MA: Cambridge University Press, 2016). Sarah Snyder has recently suggested to see the "long 1960s," the period from 1961 to 1977, as the decade in which human rights originated.

[7] Tellingly, the one study that does go significantly beyond the 1970s, Jan Eckel's *Ambivalenz des Guten*, rejects the idea that there is one breakthrough decade.

[8] On the CSCE, see Sarah B. Snyder, *Human Rights Activism and the End of the Cold War: A Transnational History of the Helsinki Network* (Cambridge, New York: Cambridge University Press, 2011); Hermann Wentker and Matthias Peter, eds., *Die KSZE im Ost-West-Konflikt: Internationale Politik und gesellschaftliche Transformation 1975-1990* (München: Oldenbourg, 2012); for a still much cited work see Daniel C. Thomas, *The Helsinki Effect: International Norms, Human Rights, and the Demise of Communism* (Princeton, NJ: Princeton University Press, 2001).

Introduction 5

But despite all these developments and while a meeting to review the CSCE Final Act's implementation was taking place at that very time, the arrests of thousands of Polish activists in December 1981 failed to trigger what Daniel Thomas has called the "Helsinki effect" – the denouncement of Warsaw for violating the Helsinki Accords human rights provisions. To the contrary, whereas NATO's West European members saw events in Poland as an internal affair, shielded by the Helsinki Accords' principle of noninterference, the USA considered pulling out of the CSCE process altogether. In the face of mass repression in Poland, NATO was thrust into a crisis that very nearly derailed the human rights aspect of the CSCE process.

If the suppression of Solidarity was eventually framed as a human rights issue that obliged the West to respond, it was largely thanks to a rather strange and almost accidental coalition – the transnational network which the conference in Nowa Huta reflected so vividly. Two of its most outspoken members were the celebrated French philosopher Michel Foucault and the anti-Communist US trade union boss Lane Kirkland. If they made for rather strange bedfellows, the list of Solidarity's Western supporters also included US president Ronald Reagan and West German peace activist Petra Kelly, Pope John Paul II and Italian Communist leader Enrico Berlinguer. A broad variety of actors from Europe and the USA, from East and West came together in a campaign to support Solidarity – secular ex-Marxists and devout Catholics, French left-wing intellectuals and their US neoconservative counterparts, international trade unionists and early neoliberal thinkers, Western politicians of all stripes, peace and human rights activist.

But even after this coalition emerged the Polish activists and exiles could never take international support for granted. In the years after 1981, they had to navigate a transnational world of professional Cold Warriors and East European diaspora communities, human rights activists and trade union functionaries, government bureaucrats, and intellectuals. Locked up in prison, hiding underground, living on welfare support in Western countries whose languages they often did not speak, the Poles could achieve nothing without the help of people who had little or no stakes in the political struggles of Eastern Europe. Solidarity's emergence and repression briefly thrust Poland into the international limelight, but Western interest in Poland quickly waned or wandered off to other instances of human rights violations. The most precious resource for any human rights campaign – international attention – proved to be scarce and highly contested. Moving beyond the 1970s, it becomes apparent rather quickly that we need to reexamine some of the more expansive narratives based on studying this momentous decade.

Political Human Rights

If the finality of a seeming human rights breakthrough in the 1970s is one aspect that this book assesses critically, its second contribution is to the question of why human rights exploded onto the world stage in the first place. An emergent consensus suggests that the human rights moment of the 1970s was at least partly the result of the collapse of ideologies and political programs of large-scale social transformation and revolutionary change. Focused on specific and obtainable goals, the release of prisoners, or the abolishment of torture, human rights appeared to be a fresh source for political idealism – a new path to improving the world that avoided the violent pitfalls into which other such paths had led. As social activism was brought from the level of grand ideological schemes down to such basic emotions as responsibility and compassion, human rights became the center of a minimalist, even anti-political, program. This project was primarily about alleviating pain abroad not political change at home, about the human rights of people in distant countries not the civil rights of fellow citizens. Amnesty International, the foremost human rights organization of the 1970s, even forbade its activists to work for prisoners of conscience in their own countries. The "suffering stranger" emerged as a crucial symbolic figure for the Western human rights imagination of the time.[9]

This anti-political moment, I argue, waned rather quickly and it may have always been the matter of a small group of privileged Western activists. Almost everyone in the transnational campaign for Solidarity mimicked the anti-political style of Amnesty International but they all did so for more or less overtly political purposes. Chief among them was the very group who is most clearly associated with anti-politics – Soviet bloc dissidents. Despite their rejection of traditional politics and ideology, the dissidents understood their activism always in a profoundly political way – and it is difficult to see how it could have been otherwise, as I shall show below. The middle-class Americans and West Europeans who swell the ranks of Amnesty International may have been motivated by a vague sense of powerlessness in the face of worldwide injustices[10] – the dissidents *were*

---

[9] Moyn, *Utopia*, 121; Kelly, "Sovereignty," 4–5; Keys, *Virtue*, 88–89, 178–213, 270–271; Eckel, *Ambivalenz*, 394–411; on Amnesty see also Tom Buchanan, "'The Truth Will Set You Free:' The Making of Amnesty International," *Journal of Contemporary History* 37 (October 2002), 4; Kenneth Cmiel, "The Emergence of Human Rights Politics in the United States," *The Journal of American History* 86 (1999), 3; Stephen Hopgood, *Keepers of the Flame: Understanding Amnesty International* (Ithaca, NY: Cornell University Press, 2006).

[10] Eckel, *Ambivalenz*, 402.

Introduction

powerless in the face of a state that could revoke their rights at will. Setting off human rights from civil rights may have made sense in the United States – in Communist Eastern Europe, claiming one's human rights meant to become a citizen, an active participant in the collective affairs of one's countries. In the thought of the dissidents, human rights were never separated from questions of democracy and self-determination.

One of dissidence's best-known documents, the Czechoslovak Charter 77, was about the suppression of civil liberties at home, freedom of expression chief among them.[11] In Poland, the creation of a trade union was perfectly in line with a human rights activism that was as much about social self-organization as about international treaties. For the dissidents, the release of a political prisoner was no aim in itself, no substitute for broken utopian promises, but part of a wider struggle in which they sought to reclaim public discourse from a regime that suffocated it under a transparently meaningless ideological language.

The dissidents were not the only ones who do not fit the narrative of "human rights as anti-politics." American neoconservatives never made a secret out of the fact that, for them, human rights was about the political struggle between Communism and the West. Other admirers of Solidarity – French anti-totalitarian intellectuals, trade unionists, West German peace activists – shared with the Polish movement the idea that human rights were meant to empower individual human beings to associate and communicate with one another, to join forces and shape their collective lives. The most fundamental human right, labor activists argued, was freedom of association because it allowed people to establish organizations that helped them to protect all other rights. For the French anti-totalitarian intellectual Claude Lefort, freedom of opinion was the central right because he saw it as "man's right ... to step out of himself and to make contacts with others, through speech, writing, and thought." Freedom of opinion was "a freedom of relationships."[12] In these discourses, human rights were meant to be the foundation of a new form of politics. This was, to be sure, a political vision whose contours always remained vague and whose vehicles would not be parties and states but the nebulous aim of society's self-organization. Meant to empower

---

[11] "Declaration of Charter 77," English translation confiscated by the Czechoslovak authorities, probably prepared for Western correspondents, dated Jan. 1, 1977, available at www.libpro.cz/charta/docs/declaration_of_charter_77.pdf (last accessed May 2013).

[12] Claude Lefort, *The Political Forms of Modern Society: Bureaucracy, Democracy, Totalitarianism*, trans. John B. Thompson (Cambridge: Polity, 1986), 248–251, 257–258, quotations on 250, 257; see also Claude Lefort, *L'invention démocratique: Les limites de la domination totalitaire* (Paris: Fayard, 1981), 27–30.

8   Poland's Solidarity Movement & the Politics of Rights

individuals to take control of their common fate, it was a political vision nonetheless.

As this book moves the historiography of human rights into a new decade, then, it appears that Amnesty International's world-weariness, its claim to "not work against any government, only against repressive policies and practices," to being agnostic about "the merits of the views of the victims," may have resonated with the sensibilities of some Western activists but proved unworkable for those actually suffering human rights abuses.[13] It is also doubtful whether these sentiments sustained human rights discourses in the following years and into our own time.[14] While some people focused on human rights as such, many more discovered them as a means to an end – the formation of a trade union or the freedom to publish one's thoughts. Only by being coupled with such substantial aims could human rights survive and thrive beyond their 1977 moment in the limelight. Human rights' association with the worldwide promotion of Western political and economic institutions – a project born, among others, in the Reagan administration's response to the suppression of Solidarity – thus emerges as a major reason why human rights became the global moral language of our time.

Contested Icons

Human rights were also political in a less overt sense. Addressing the international community, the dissidents became icons. Through the repression they suffered, they were powerful witnesses to the moral authority of human rights, to the idea that the universal and absolute dignity of individuals should trump geopolitical considerations and utopian projects. Much like the sacred images of Byzantine spirituality, they came to be seen as reflections of the sacred core of the secular religion of human rights.

This "iconization" of the Polish dissidents greatly empowered them. Recast as "prisoners of conscience," inmates of Polish prisons acquired the moral authority to appeal to the powerful in the East and the West, even from within their cells. Receiving the Nobel Peace Prize in 1983,

---

[13] *Amnesty International Report 1981*, Oct. 1, 1981, 2. The Amnesty International reports cited throughout this book have been accessed at www.amnesty.org/en/latest/research/?contentType=2564&documentType=Annual+Report&sort=date&p=4 (last accessed June 2016).

[14] Jan Eckel's work suggests that it may not even have sufficed to sustain the work of Amnesty itself. See Eckel, *Ambivalenz*, 423–434.

Wałęsa became a larger-than-life figure whom Western political leaders treated as one of their own. But as the Polish activists became symbolic representatives of absolute values they were also divorced from the actual political goals they fought for. Iconization empowered prisoners to appeal to the international community, but also stripped them of a political identity. But precisely as universal icons, the Polish activists became even more of an empty canvass unto which Western supporters could project their own desires. Iconization inducted Solidarity into an international "pantheon" of morally unassailable causes, but also exposed it to competing interpretations according to the political beliefs of the movements' international admirers. Solidarity became a contested icon.

As icons, the dissidents gave concrete shape to the still abstract notion of human rights, showing what political projects could be based on them, and they provided legitimacy for these visions: Embracing such human rights icons allowed Western activists to reframe their projects in terms of the values that it embodied. The specific political projects Solidarity came to be associated with could not have been more different. In the United States, support for the Polish movement became enmeshed in a conflict between President Ronald Reagan, who sought to redefine the Cold War as being about the universal struggle with the modern state and traditional Cold War liberals from the American Federation of Labor and Congress of Industrial Organizations, or AFL-CIO, who wanted to salvage basic tenets of consensus liberalism by reframing them in a human rights language. In France, solidarité avec Solidarité became a vehicle for debates about a democratic socialism that avoided the perceived totalitarian potential inherent in this project.

Reconstructing these debates, Solidarity emerges as a unique case to bring out the full variety of human rights vernaculars that emerged at the time. The Polish movement defied all Western political categories. Built on a coalition of labor activists, intellectuals, and Catholic clergy, Solidarity employed the new vernacular of human rights, but it did so to frame classic labor demands; it adopted the traditional organization of a trade union, but used tactics like those of Western civil rights and social movements; it was staunchly anti-Communist, but advocated nonviolence and workers' self-management of factories. Cutting across these diverse ideas were discourses of Polish nationalism and a rather traditional Catholicism. Describing the same factories or shipyards, some international observers were struck by seeing workers who knelt confessing to a priest; others drew parallels to the founding of the Second Socialist International in 1889, Barcelona in

10   Poland's Solidarity Movement & the Politics of Rights

1936, or Paris in May 1968.[15] Where other human rights icons in the late twentieth century, such as the Soviet dissident movement or Chile, seemed to appeal to specific political groups, Solidarity was a movement whose appeal cut across traditional political divides.

The politics of meaning around Solidarity played out in both domestic and global contexts. At the United Nations, US politicians tried to turn the Polish movement into a symbolic counterweight against another global icon of human rights – Chile. While resistance to the Chilean dictatorship was a focal point of left-wing human rights activists, American neoconservatives saw in it a double standard that highlighted human rights violations among America's allies while ignoring them in the Communist world. Poland promised to change this. While these debates again reveal the ambiguities of human rights culture they also show that the Polish activists proved surprisingly savvy in using their symbolic power to further their goals, even by striking a symbolic coalition with Chilean human rights activists and thus undercutting attempts to use their cause for Cold War purposes. Activists from Eastern Europe and Latin America shaped human rights discourses as much as they were shaped by them.

Human Rights in an "Age of Fracture"

If this book argues that the seeming 1970s breakthrough of human rights was much less final than is often assumed and that human rights discourses remained much more diverse than the historiography suggests, it is not in order to argue that it was during the 1980s and in the activism of the dissidents and their supporters that human rights "really" experienced their breakthrough and came to mean what they mean today. The story of this book, in fact, is one of tragic heroes and bittersweet victories. The dissidents, trade unionists, French intellectuals, and to some extent even the American neoconservatives that are at its center all saw human rights as a means to empower citizens to organize themselves and to confront the issues that concerned them most, economic injustices chief among them. Instead, they got a neoliberal economy and the transfer of Western political institutions. The revolutions of 1989 had created a sense of "Ex Oriente Lux," a Polish intellectual recalled, the expectation that the experience of totalitarianism would enable Central and East

---

[15] Anthony Kemp-Welch, *Poland under Communism: A Cold War History* (Cambridge, MA: Cambridge University Press, 2008), 320; David Ost, *Solidarity and the Policits of Anti-Politics: Opposition and Reform in Poland since 1968* (Philadelphia, PA: Temple University Press, 1990), 10.

Introduction

Europeans to show the world the unfulfilled potential of democracy. Instead, their transition to democracy came to be framed as them fulfilling the membership criteria of the West's international institutions – NATO and the EU.[16]

The third contribution this book makes, then, is to propose to abandon the search for elusive breakthroughs and to acknowledge that the history of human rights is one of their continuous competition with other universalisms, their repeated reinvention and adaptation to new causes.[17] And precisely the question why human rights proved to be so adaptable might provide a common thread for a narrative that extends both before and beyond the 1970s. This would not be the different uses to which human rights have been put, whether they were invoked to justify welfare policies at home or alleviate suffering abroad, but the kinds of political claims they made possible.

The historiography of human rights often makes broad statements about how the 1970s shaped human rights language and practices but very few of these studies contain a definition of what human rights came to mean at the time and few engage in detailed conceptual and semantic analyses of specific ideas and discourses.[18] Once we conduct these kinds of analyses, it will become apparent that the seeming minimalism of human rights was based on a moral absolutism. To say that we have a right to something means that we are entitled to it. It is not granted to us nor is it a benefit we may or may not receive but it rightfully belongs to us. To say that we have a *human* right to something means that it belongs to us because of who we are as human beings, because of the absolute value and dignity each of us has. Human rights ground an absolute – inalienable – claim in a self-evident truth about our human identity.[19] Amnesty activists and Soviet bloc dissidents did not see the freeing of a political prisoner or the defense of freedom of expression as a consolation prize for the failure to reach utopian goals. They saw it as the defense of an absolute value whose violation could be justified neither by the

---

[16] Aleksander Smolar, "History and Memory: The Revolutions of 1989-91," *Journal of Democracy* 12 (July 2001), 3, 11, 13.

[17] This approach also returns to a vision of human rights history laid out by Stefan-Ludwig Hoffmann, "Introduction: Genealogies of Human Rights," in Stefan-Ludwig Hoffmann, ed., *Human Rights in the Twentieth Century* (Cambridge, MA: Cambridge University Press, 2011), 13–25.

[18] The laudable exceptions are Lynn Hunt, *Inventing Human Rights: A History* (New York: W. W. Norton & Co., 2007); Lora Wildenthal, *The Language of Human Rights in West Germany* (Philadelphia, PA: University of Pennsylvania Press, 2013). For a recent study providing extensive semantic and cultural analyses see Bradley, *World Reimagined.*

[19] Jack Donnelly, *Universal Human Rights in Theory and Practice*, 3rd ed. (Ithaca, NY: Cornell University Press, 2013), 7–17; see also Hunt, *Inventing*, 19–22.

12   Poland's Solidarity Movement & the Politics of Rights

exigencies of geopolitics nor the necessities of economic development, and certainly not the promise of a radiant future.

Understanding this moral absolutism of human rights claims, I argue in this book, shows that their emergence as a global norm was not only about new sources of idealism but about how a fundamental transformation of systems of knowledge and social imaginaries created what Bradley has called "conditions of possibility" under which this moral absolutism became plausible.[20] In this context, it is instructive to ask not only why human rights succeeded but why they failed to do so, not only why some people endorsed this cause but why others did not.

Polish dissidents were startled and upset when they found that some of the most well-meaning proponents of détente did not support their cause. The reason, however, was not that the latter lacked empathy with the dissidents but that theirs was a social imaginary still indebted to the world of the early Cold War. At the core of "consensus liberalism," the common ideological framework of the Western alliance in the Cold War was an understanding of historical time as an ordered process which science could decipher and thus guide the self-transformation of societies – a belief in which consensus liberalism resembled its Marxist antagonist.[21] From this perspective, the idea that politics could be about the protection of the absolute rights of every individual, everywhere, of rights that flowed from a timeless human nature was not undesirable so much as implausible.

"Liberty," to be sure, was a core value of consensus liberalism and enshrining rights, even human rights, in constitutions or the European Human Rights Convention was seen as a means of protecting this liberty. Yet consensus liberalism saw the individual as heavily embedded in larger social structures and historical processes and it focused its projects of social betterment on these structural contexts. The "cultural Cold War" the West had waged with Communism in the 1950s and 1960s had not entailed the creation of a worldwide system monitoring human rights compliance, but the propagation of the political and economic

---

[20] Bradley, *World Reimagined*, 7.

[21] Jürgen Habermas, "The New Obscurity: The Crisis of the Welfare State and the Exhaustion of Utopian Energies," *Philosophy & Social Criticism* 11 (January 1986), 2, 1–2; on consensus liberalism and the welfare state in a Cold War context see also the concept of "Westernization" which Anselm Doering-Manteuffel and his collaborators developed: Julia Angster, "'Safe by Democracy': American Hegemony and the 'Westernization' of West German Labor," *Amerikastudien/American Studies* 46 (2001), 4; Holger Nehring, "'Westernization': A New Paradigm for Interpreting West European History in a Cold War Context," *Cold War History* 4 (January 2004), 3; see also Samuel Moyn, "Die neue Historiographie der Menschenrechte," *Geschichte und Gesellschaft* 38 (2012), 4, 555–557, 568.

Introduction

institutions of the welfare state.[22] Even as some advocates of détente sought to go beyond the Cold War, the social theory underpinning their policies remained unchanged. One of their signature achievements, the Final Act of the CSCE, had not been intended by them to establish a quasi-court for human rights but to create an instrument of fostering the economic modernization of the Soviet bloc and thus the gradual evolution of its political system toward greater respect for individual rights and freedoms.

But the social thought undergirding consensus liberalism all but collapsed during the 1970s. When the American war in Vietnam and the revelations of Aleksandr Solzhenitsyn's *Gulag Archipelago* compromised both sides of the Cold War, when the youthful revolutionary hopes of "1968" were betrayed and "socialism with a human face" was crushed, and when the oil crises and environmental destruction exposed the "limits to growth," the belief in the ability of collective self-transformation – whether through social revolution or welfare legislation – began to crumble. Intellectually, the 1970s initiated, in Daniel Rodgers' apt phrase, an "age of fracture" – a time when time horizons seemed to shrink and imaginaries revolving around History, social structures, and cultures gave way to social visions centered on the disembedded individual.[23] In this context, human rights flourished not only as a moral alternative to failed utopias but also because the moral absolutism of rights claims became plausible. The conveyors of the 1988 human rights conference mentioned at the beginning could not have chosen a more apt venue to celebrate human rights than the former socialist model city of Nowa Huta – the "ruins" of a failed experiment to transform society.

As human rights claims became plausible they also became appealing, especially to the future dissidents as this book will show. As it reconstructs the experiences that turned nonconformist Polish intellectuals into dissidents, a social world will emerge whose most important trait

---

[22] Giles Scott-Smith and Hans Krabbendam, eds., *The Cultural Cold War in Western Europe, 1945-1960* (London: Frank Cass, 2003).

[23] Daniel T. Rodgers, *Age of Fracture* (Cambridge, MA: Harvard University Press, 2011). For a perceptive contemporaneous analysis of this intellectual and political change, see Habermas, "Obscurity." On the intellectual history of the time see Jan-Werner Müller, *Contesting Democracy: Political Ideas in Twentieth-Century Europe* (New Haven, CT: Yale University Press, 2011), 203–242; on the 1970s more broadly see Thomas Borstelmann, *The 1970s: A New Global History from Civil Rights to Economic Inequality* (Princton, NJ: Princeton University Press, 2011); Anselm Doering-Manteuffel and Lutz Raphael, *Nach dem Boom: Perspektiven auf die Zeitgeschichte seit 1970* (Göttingen: Vandenhoeck & Ruprecht, 2008); Niall Ferguson et al., eds., *The Shock of the Global: The 1970s in Perspective* (Cambridge, MA: Harvard University Press, 2011); Göran Therborn et al., "The 1970s and 1980s as a Turning Point in European History?," *Journal of Modern European History* 9 (2011), 1.

was arbitrariness. The few rights which citizens of the Soviet bloc enjoyed had been granted to them by a state who could revoke them at any time. Even truthful speech itself seemed impossible in a society where public life was permeated by empty ideological rituals. In this context, the idea that everyone was entitled to liberty and freedom of expression because of a timeless, absolute truth about the worth and dignity of all human beings could not but have a tremendous appeal.

Uncovering the diverse transnational discourses that crystallized around the Polish dissidents' cause, this book shows that the enduring appeal of human rights did not follow from what could be claimed with them but from how it could be claimed. If "freedom of association," the focal point of the AFL-CIO's campaign, was recognized as a human right, it ceased to be the expression of a group interest and became something to which all people were entitled because they were human beings. In this way, human rights became part of a struggle that was not only about specific political aims but also about what could legitimately be the subject of political debate. At a time when conceptual and moral worlds underwent deep changes, the moral absolutism of human rights turned them into rich sources of what Pierre Bourdieu has called "symbolic power" – the power to sustain or transform the social world by sustaining and transforming the concepts through which people think and talk about it.[24]

This struggle for symbolic power is indispensable to understanding why a transnational campaign for human rights in Poland emerged and how human rights became a global language of morality and protests. Declaring itself an ally of an iconic movement like Solidarity greatly enhanced a group's claim that its goals were not the expression of a special interest but a human right. The global iconization of domestic movements was a profoundly political process.

Rethinking Cold War Human Rights Policies

This book's fourth and final contribution is to the historiography of human rights during the Cold War, the field in which the majority of studies of dissent and Western support for it is written. Overwhelmingly, this literature focuses on dissent's contribution to the end of the Cold War. And yet in taking 1989 as its starting point, they seize upon an event that was completely beyond the horizon of the historical actors themselves. The Nowa Huta conference of 1988, celebrating the fortieth

---

[24] Pierre Bourdieu, *Language and Symbolic Power* (Cambridge, MA: Polity Press, 1991), 236; see also David Swartz, *Symbolic Power, Politics, and Intellectuals: The Political Sociology of Pierre Bourdieu* (Chicago, London: The University of Chicago Press, 2013).

Introduction

anniversary of the UDHR, took place on the very brink of the Cold War endgame. The day it ended, the Polish government began confidential talks with Solidarity leader Lech Wałęsa – the first step toward the dismantlement of the Soviet bloc. And yet for the people in Nowa Huta, the prospect that Communism might collapse any time soon was only slightly less fantastic than it had been at any point in the 20 years since activists in Moscow had first invoked human rights. The perspective from 1989 may allow us to understand what human rights activism contributed to the end of the Cold War but it does not tell us why people turned to human rights in the first place.[25] If we want to understand their struggle, we must focus on how human rights allowed them to interpret and view their immediate social reality in new ways, not on the unexpected success of their work in 1989.

What is true for the dissidents is even more important for their Western supporters. A number of excellent recent studies – most notably the work of Sarah Snyder and Gregory F. Domber – have brought out the inertia and resistance that had to be overcome to get Western governments to become active on behalf of the dissidents.[26] Yet books continue to be published which portray US human rights policies as little more than a recalibration of foreign policy toward American ideals and dissidents groups as allies of sweeping Western strategies to beat the Soviet Union.[27] The truth, however, is that the dissidents' emergence undercut the West's main approaches to East–West relations. They challenged the proponents of détente with their language of anti-totalitarianism and stark moral choices, they challenged Cold Warriors by claiming that totalitarianism could slowly be eroded from within, and they challenged both by using a familiar language in new ways – human rights. As we try to understand why Western governments and activists supported dissidents in the Soviet bloc we must avoid the temptation of reading the events of 1989 into earlier developments, of ascribing Western policies a farsightedness and consistency they simply did not have.

Though this book focuses on themes usually associated with the intellectual history of politics, it does not eschew questions of the actual

---

[25] For a similar perspective focused solely on dissent in Czechoslovakia, see Jonathan Bolton, *Worlds of Dissent: Charter 77, the Plastic People of the Universe, and Czech Culture under Communism* (Cambridge, MA: Harvard University Press, 2012), 44.

[26] Gregory F. Domber, *Empowering Revolution: America, Poland, and the End of the Cold War* (Chapel Hill, NC: University of North Carolina Press, 2014); Snyder, *Activism*.

[27] Hal Brands, *Making the Unipolar Moment: U.S. Foreign Policy and the Rise of the Post-Cold War Order* (Ithaca, NY: Cornell University Press, 2016), 24–27, 64–72, 76–77; James E. Cronin, *Global Rules: America, Britain and a Disordered World* (New Haven, CT: Yale University Press, 2014).

impact human rights had on the international relations of the late Cold War era. Much as my narrative is a cautionary and critical one, exploring as it does struggles for symbolic power, it will also show that human rights activism was effective in freeing political prisoners and transforming a repressive regime. Yet human rights became such a force for change in international relations because they enabled people in East and West to recast their political projects at a time of momentous cultural and intellectual change not because they were part of sweeping strategies to win the Cold War.

Showing how important intellectual debates and struggles over ideas are to explain an outcome as momentous as the end of the Cold War, this study will also contribute to further expanding the boundaries of diplomatic history. It features household names of contemporary international history – Willy Brandt,, Helmut Schmidt, François Mitterrand, Ronald Reagan. But it will show that their actions can only be understood once we also focus on people not traditionally associated with international history. The book's main protagonists are, first, a group of Polish intellectuals. Arrested and later socially ostracized for political reasons in 1968, some of them adopted the model of Soviet dissent to the situation in Poland thus laying the groundwork for the emergence of Solidarity which many of them advised in senior positions. Others became political exiles in the West where they established transnational contacts both among dissident groups in Eastern Europe as well between them and potential Western supporters. Among the latter, this book focuses on the two most important groups – US Cold War liberals in the Reagan administration and the AFL-CIO as well as French trade unionists and left-wing intellectuals, with Foucault and Lefort chief among them. For these two groups, support for human rights in the Soviet bloc was a major *cause célèbre* and they pushed their initially unwilling governments to exert pressures on the regime in Warsaw. They are also very clear examples for how this kind of activism was driven by the desire to recast political identities and projects.

I also focus on people who did not embrace the new vernacular of human rights. The most important person in this respect will be West Germany's ex-chancellor Willy Brandt, one of the most outspoken opponents of ostracizing Poland for its human rights violations. At the same time, this book considers the role Western journalists, transnational NGOs like Amnesty International, international trade unionists, the Norwegian Nobel Committee, and exiles from other parts of the world, especially Latin America, played in turning human rights into a global vernacular.

By thus broadening the cast of historical actors, this study adopts a research approach that is multi-archival in two senses. First, while it draws on the governmental records that have traditionally been the bread

Introduction 17

and butter of international history, it is also based on private records of non-state actors and organizations, often unsystematically stuffed into cardboard boxes kept in basements and on top of shelves, as well as in the essays and books in which intellectuals expressed their thinking more systematically. Second, it draws on archival and published sources coming from six countries and written in five languages – Polish, English, German, French, and Russian.

If the United States emerges as a central actor in these processes, this history of Western human rights policies further decenters America's role in the international system. The American contribution to the events described in this book was rarely the outcome of a systematic policy and often heavily influenced by non-state actors many of which came from outside the United States. By putting European events into the global context of human rights discourses, especially by comparing Poland and Chile, this book is also a modest contribution to decentering European history as well.

Plan of This Book

The ten chapters of this book are organized chronologically, leading from the rise of dissent in Poland during the 1970s to the fall of Communism in 1989. They also move from the local contexts in which Polish intellectuals first used human rights language through the international relations of the Cold War to the level of global human rights discourses and the emergence of the post–Cold War world.

Chapters 1 and 2 tell the story of how Polish intellectuals embraced human rights during the 1970s. Contextualizing their intellectual and political itinerary in the Soviet bloc of the 1970s, it explores how they became part of a transnational community of dissidents. Applying a creative reinterpretation of the term "totalitarianism" to their countries, they developed a politics revolving around social self-organization and based on the universal dignity and rights of all human beings. And as they applied this view to the realities of Poland, they helped pave the way for the rise of Solidarity.

Political understandings of human rights are also a central theme of Chapters 3 to 6. Chapter 3 reconstructs how human rights were revived after the "near death experience"[28] of the Polish crisis. Chapter 4

---

[28] I gratefully borrow this expression from Steven Jensen, "Defining the Social in the Global: Social Rights, International Organization, and the Evolution of International Non-Discrimination Efforts in the Age of Brown vs. Board of Education, 1950–1960," unpublished paper presented at the SHAFR 2016 Annual Meeting, June 23–25, 2016, University of San Diego.

explores the reasons for Willy Brandt's reluctance to embrace the cause of dissent by showing how his influential approach to détente and his view of the CSCE remained wedded to ideas from before the "age of fracture." Chapters 5 and 6 recount how Solidarity's respectively French and American supporters turned repression in Poland into a human rights issue while using the Polish movement's iconic status to reinvent their own political projects.

Chapters 7 to 9 explore the global politics of human rights icons. At their center is a systematic analysis of how activists or causes became human rights icons as well as the ambiguities of this process. To this end, they show how Polish activists deployed a major symbol of human rights culture – the "prisoner of conscience" – and drew on the symbolic authority flowing from the 1983 Nobel Prize for Lech Wałęsa in their appeals to the West. Thus, they translated their cause into a widely understandable language, turned the fate of Poland's political prisoners into the central issue of the country's relations with the West, and exerted pressures on their government which led to the release of all prisoners. Turned into an icon, however, Solidarity became enmeshed in a conflict at the UN Commission on Human Rights where the US government tried to turn into a symbolic counterweight to Chile.

Chapter 10, finally, explores the role of human rights activism for the fall of Communism. It demonstrates that even if human rights activism did not evolve out of a strategy to win the Cold War, it did have an important impact on how this conflict ended.

What these ten chapters confirm is that, beyond a specific semantic core, the meanings of human rights were "the unpredictable results of political contestations."[29] At its core, human rights entailed the idea that there were some goods to which human beings were entitled simply because they were human beings. Yet what these goods were and how they could and should be claimed could differ widely, depending on the social imaginaries from within which historical actors invoked human rights and on the political conflicts in which they did so. Bringing out this diversity is at the center of this book.

[29] Hoffmann, "Introduction," 4.

1   The Rise of Dissent in Poland

Soviet bloc dissent has a prominent place in histories of human rights old and new.[1] Alongside Amnesty International, the "dissidents" seem like the quintessential representatives of a movement seeking to transcend politics in the name of a universal morality. What characterized them, after all, were not their political views or ideology but their courage to express a dissenting opinion against a totalitarian leviathan. The moral purity of their acts was more important to them than the efficacy of their actions. For the dissidents, morality trumped politics – a view many of them acquired when they were repressed by a regime whose utopian faith in the omnipotence of politics they themselves had once professed.

Human rights historians, then, ascribe dissent a central place in their narratives because it seemingly embodies what is increasingly seen as the essence of human rights and thus the telos of human rights history: an anti-political attitude. The overarching aim of the following two chapters is to problematize this view both of dissent and of human rights. As they reconstruct the rise of dissent in Poland from the late 1960s to the suppression of Solidarity in December 1981, they will show that dissent was not, and could not have been, an attempt to transcend politics in the same way in which Amnesty International's activism for suffering strangers was.

There were practical reasons for why Polish dissent could not remain aloof from politics for long. In a repressive regime like Communist Poland, politics was inescapable – a point driven home, at the latest, when Solidarity's struggle to guarantee the human right to strike or form a trade union became a struggle about who gets to govern Poland. But dissident human rights activism had had a political dimension since the

---

[1] Paul Gordon Lauren, *The Evolution of International Human Right: Visions Seen* (Philadelphia, PA: University of Pennsylvania Press, 1998), 254–256; Moyn, *Utopia*, 133–141, 149–150, 160–166; Hoffmann, "Introduction," 22–23; Aryeh Neier, *The International Human Rights Movement: A History* (Princeton, NJ: Princeton University Press, 2012), 138–147; Eckel, *Ambivalenz*, 715–745.

early 1970s, well before the success of Solidarity was even only thinkable. In fact, it had always been as much about the creation of spaces of citizenship and social agency as about defending individual human beings from repression. For Polish dissidents, human rights activism and the struggle for labor rights or national independence were part of the same political project, a view shared by dissidents in other Soviet bloc countries, especially Czechoslovak Charter 77.

Dissent, then, was shaped more by the issues and discourse of its time than already a harbinger of the human rights ideas of our own. Against this background, one could argue that dissent does not deserve its central place in human rights history. But that would mean to project our own understandings backward in time and discard all those historical processes that did not bring these understandings about. It would mean, in other words, to adopt a teleological view of human rights history. A historical approach deserving of its name, in contrast, requires us to try to understand 1970s human rights discourses on their own terms. And as we do, we might learn something important about human rights in the process, namely, that what made them appealing was not that they determined a specific kind of social activism. To the contrary, human rights were appealing because of their malleability, the way they could be integrated in a wide variety of social ontologies and anthropologies and serve to legitimate a wide range of political causes.

The conceptual world within which the dissidents developed their human rights vernacular had two central features. The first was a specific anthropology based on the notion that human beings have an inalienable dignity but that they are also enmeshed in social and cultural relations outside of which they cannot truly flourish. These views were reinforced by the second feature, the view that the state-socialist societies the dissidents lived in were totalitarian systems, systems, that is, that had banished truthful speech from public discourse, thus destroying the social community by making it impossible for its members to discuss and tackle their collective concerns. The struggle to preserve individual dignity and to rebuild a social community were thus seen as one and the same thing. In this context, human rights were appealing because they simultaneously expressed the truth of human dignity and, by guaranteeing freedom of expression, opinion, association, etc., provided the means to rebuild the social community.

In reconstructing this human rights vernacular, I proceed in two steps. This chapter provides an overview of the history of Polish dissent and human rights work from the late 1960s to the early 1980s. This will provide the necessary foundation for a conceptual analysis of Polish human rights discourses in Chapter 2. Readers familiar with the history

The Rise of Dissent in Poland 21

of dissent and opposition in Poland during the 1970s might want to skip this chapter. However, it brings out a hitherto under-researched aspect of this development: the importance of the international context for the rise of dissent.

In emphasizing this international context, I diverge from two of the most important books on the history of dissent even as I draw on their insights: Barbara Falk's *The Dilemmas of Dissidence in East-Central Europe* and Jonathan Bolton's *World of Dissent*.[2] Both books made a crucial point: Dissent can only be understood from within its local context and discourses. In fact, the very term "dissent" was a Western label which nonconformist intellectuals in the Soviet bloc used "with distaste, rather ironically" and always in quotation marks, as Václav Havel wrote in 1978.[3] Yet crucial though it is to emphasize these local contexts it would be wrong to ignore that, during the 1970s, remarkably similar forms of political resistance emerged in different countries of the Soviet bloc.[4] There is mounting evidence that these similarities were the result of the transnational circulation of ideas and even direct cooperation between dissident groups, as I hope to show. It is similarly remarkable that, even as Havel underlined an ironical distance to the term "dissent," he did not simply discard it but felt that it was necessary to define it. This points to the fact that the term was important to him and his fellow intellectuals, precisely as a Western label. A national and a transnational perspective, then, are complementary, not contradictory approaches to the study of dissent.

I

The central figures of Polish dissent came from two broad social and cultural milieus. The first of them had deep roots in the social movements and political parties of the pre-Communist era. Many of its members had served in the military units of Poland's underground army during the German occupation and some had suffered repression at the hands of Poland's new Communist rulers after 1945. Traditionally, this milieu was characterized by a deep divide separating those who traced

---

[2] Barbara J. Falk, *The Dilemmas of Dissidence in East-Central Europe: Citizen Intellectuals and Philosopher Kings* (Budapest: CEU Press, 2003); Bolton, *Worlds*.
[3] Václav Havel, "The Power of the Powerless," *International Journal of Politics*, 15 (1985), 3/4, 58.
[4] For a systematic discussion of how the term "dissent" is used in this book, see Robert Brier, "Entangled Protest: Dissent and the Transnational History of the 1970s and 1980s," in Robert Brier, ed., *Entangled Protest: Transnational Approaches to the History of Dissent in Eastern Europe and the Soviet Union* (Osnabrück: Fibre, 2013).

22   Poland's Solidarity Movement & the Politics of Rights

their political lineage back to the socialist "founding father" of Poland's interwar republic, Józef Piłsudski, from those who were heirs of his political adversary, the nationalist and anti-Semite Roman Dmowski. Under Communism, however, these two groups found common cause in their rejection of the Communist system and their desire for restoring full sovereignty to Poland.[5]

It is important to note that, after the Communist party had consolidated its rule over Poland, few, if any, of the members of this milieu were engaged in active resistance to Communist rule. In fact, most of them had managed to carve out a niche for them in postwar realities, working in technical fields or in the science departments of universities. Thus, they had mostly managed to retain for themselves and their children their status as members of the Polish *inteligencja*, that is, a stratum of Polish society made up of people with university degrees who would also often claim for themselves the position of a cultural elite.[6]

But though they were not openly resisting Poland's postwar political order, it is without doubt that their attitude to Communist rule was deeply hostile. They cultivated a distinctly non-Communist identity by keeping the memory of the interwar period and the non-Communist resistance to the German occupation of World War II alive. An important point of reference for them was the memory of the so-called Katyń massacre of 1940 where the Soviet NKVD had executed over 20,000 Polish officers who had been captured in the USSR's seizure of Poland's eastern territories. Another pillar of this milieu was Poland's powerful Catholic Church with its Polish blend of religious and patriotic symbols and rites. Members of this milieu also regularly listened to the BBC's or Radio Free Europe's Polish language broadcasts and, to the extent that this was possible, were in touch with the circles of Polish political émigrés in Western Europe and the United States. Children and adolescents growing up in this milieu often went to the same schools and joined Poland's non-Communist boy scout movement.

The second milieu out of which Polish dissent emerged was the so-called Warsaw Left.[7] It comprised secular intellectuals, former

---

[5] There is no systematic historical study of this milieu. For interviews with those of its members who would work in KOR, see Justyna Błażejowska, *Harcerską drogą do niepodległości: Od "Czarnej Jedynki" do Komitetu Obrony Robotników. Nieznana historia KOR-u i KSS "KOR"* (Kraków: Arcana, 2016).

[6] On the *inteligencja*, see Andrzej Walicki, "Polish Conceptions of the Intelligentsia and Its Calling," *Slavica Lundensia* 22 (2005), 1-22.

[7] The history of this social milieu has been portrayed in two monumental volumes by Andrzej Friszke which together run 1,000 pages. This account draws heavily on these books. See Andrzej Friszke, *Anatomia buntu: Kuroń, Modzelewski i komandosi* (Kraków: Znak, 2010); Andrzej Friszke, *Czas KOR-u : Jacek Kuroń a geneza Solidarności* (Kraków:

supporters of the left wing of Poland's interwar socialist party, as well as members of the political and cultural establishment of Communist Poland. In the 1970s, people born in the mid-1940s to members of the last group would become particularly influential members of Poland's dissident community. Overwhelmingly, they came from Jewish families. Their parents had welcomed the revolutionary changes after 1945, not least because they had experienced the anti-Semitism of the interwar period and the genocidal horrors of the German occupation. Their intellectual outlook was shaped by revisionism, a humanist interpretation of Marxist thought which had emerged in the mid-1950s at Warsaw University and emphasized the role of individual human agency in social change. During the relative liberties of the de-Stalinization period, revisionism's intellectual fathers saw it as a way of laying the theoretical groundwork for a more democratic and humane, Polish variety of state socialism.

In the second half of the 1960s, the children of these internal critics of Polish Communism entered Warsaw University where they would earn the nickname "Commandos" from their peers. Invoking the Israeli special forces of the Six-Day War, the moniker alluded to the students' Jewish background but it also captured the discipline, intellectual elitism, and bravado with which they openly and publicly criticized even high-ranking party officials at the meetings of the socialist student organization. But however fierce the Commandos' criticism of Polish political reality was, it was still based on a revisionist perspective. They did not attack Communism itself so much as the ideological ossification of its Soviet-style variety. They wanted Poland's People's Republic to live up to its socialist ideals, not overthrow it.

During the first two decades of the postwar period, these two milieus – the independence group and the Warsaw Left – were deeply hostile toward each other, given their different, even antagonistic political ideals. This, however, started to change from the end of the 1960s onward. By that time, the already modest margins of intellectual liberty at Warsaw University had started to narrow further, a process that first culminated in 1966 when the Communist party expelled Leszek Kołakowski, the

---

Znak, ISP PAN, 2011). For a brilliant intellectual history see Dariusz Gawin, *Wielki zwrot: Ewolucja lewicy i odrodzenia idei społeczeństwa obywatelskiego* (Kraków: Znak, 2013). Additional important works in writing this chapter were Agnes Arndt, *Rote Bürger: Eine Milieu- und Beziehungsgeschichte linker Dissidenz in Polen (1956–1976)* (Göttingen: Vandenhoeck & Ruprecht, 2013); Jan Skórzyński, *Od Solidarności do wolności* (Warszawa: Trio, 2005); Jan Skórzyński, *Siła bezsilnych: Historia Komitetu Obrony Robotników* (Warszawa: Świat Ksiażki, 2012).

24   Poland's Solidarity Movement & the Politics of Rights

central intellectual figure of Marxist revisionism.[8] Two years later, the authorities cancelled the production of a nineteenth-century play by Poland's national poet Adam Mickiewicz at Warsaw's National Theatre for fear that it might ignite anti-Soviet sentiment.[9] When the Commandos collected and published signatures against this decision, the regime had them arrested. At the same time, it expelled their parents and academic teachers from the Communist party and Warsaw University under the pretext of a "purge" from what it claimed were "Zionist" influences. Most of the Commandos, their parents, and revisionist mentors, as well as the majority of Poland's Holocaust survivors, were pressured to leave Poland amid this more or less openly anti-Semitic campaign. Those who stayed behind were put on trial and sentenced to prison.

Yet the momentum created by the student protests could not be stopped. Students coming from Catholic and nationalist backgrounds, especially those active in Poland's non-Communist boy scout movement, took over from the Commandos and the protests spread to other universities. In most cities, the authorities could restore order only by having the police storm campuses and break up the meetings.

At the time, most of the students involved in the protests of 1968 experienced their repression as a traumatic event. In the medium term, however, the common experience of resistance and repression proved to be an important step toward a realignment of Poland's two major cultural milieus and thus toward the rise of dissent in Poland. For the Commandos, the events of 1968 meant that they finally broke with Communism. More traditionally minded students and intellectuals, on the other hand, admired the courage with which the Commandos had risked their liberty for a patriotic cause.

While the repression of 1968 lowered barriers of cooperation between Poland's two major cultural milieus, it was a global development that provided them with a language of cooperation and protest: the rise of human rights.[10] In the second half of the 1970s, they became

---

[8] The speech that led to Kołakowski's expulsion is reprinted in "Nr 185: 1966 październik 21, Warszawa – Stenogram z nagrania dźwiękowego wystąpienia prof. Leszka Kołakowskiego na otwartym zebraniu ZMS na Wydziale Historycznym Uniwersytetu Warszawskiego," in Franciszek Dąbrowski et al., eds., *Marzec 1968 w dokumentach MSW* (Warszawa: IPN, 2009), 690–692.

[9] For these events, see Piotr M. Osęka, *Marzec '68* (Kraków: Znak, 2008); Jerzy Eisler, *Polski rok 1968* (Warszawa: IPN, 2006); Marcin Kula, Piotr Osęka, and Marcin Zaremba, eds., *Marzec 1968: trzydzieści lat później*, 2 vols. (Warszawa: PWN, 1998).

[10] For a detailed sociological study of how human rights provided a common language of protest in Poland, see Hella Dietz, *Polnischer Protest: Zur pragmatistischen Fundierung von Theorien sozialen Wandels* (Frankfurt, New York: Campus, 2015).

"dissidents" – people who opposed dictatorship not in the name of their respective, often antagonistic political ideologies but in the name of universal human rights many of which Communist regimes claimed to respect.

Standard narratives of the Cold War often describe the adoption of the so-called Helsinki Accords on August 1, 1975, as the event triggering this East European encounter with human rights.[11] Signed by the United States, Canada, the Soviet Union, and almost all European countries, the Helsinki Accords concluded the Conference on Security and Cooperation in Europe, or CSCE, which had been held between 1973 and 1975 to establish a more cooperative framework for East–West relations. It did commit its signatories to uphold human rights and became an important point of reference for dissidents, especially because it established regular meetings where the Act's signatories would review its implementation. The Helsinki Accords, however, were not the first time Communist states had made a public commitment to human rights. Most of the Soviet bloc states, for instance, had been involved in the drafting of the two UN human rights pacts of 1966.[12] The CSCE, moreover, was but one of a number of factors which raised the international salience of human rights and thus created the context for the rise of dissent.

For Poland, the most important development in this respect was the emergence of Soviet dissidence. Through East European émigré groups in the West, foreign correspondents in Poland, and especially the broadcasts of Western radio stations such as Radio Free Europe and the Polish section of the BBC, Polish intellectuals were integrated into transnational networks through which texts and ideas could circulate within the Soviet bloc and between East and West.[13] Through these channels,

---

[11] Rosemary Foot, "The Cold War and Human Rights," in Melvyn P. Leffler and Odd Arne Westad, eds., *The Cambridge History of the Cold War*, vol. III (Cambridge, MA: Cambridge University Press, 2010); Snyder, *Activism*; Thomas, *Effect*.

[12] Jensen, *Making*.

[13] For detailed analyses of these various contacts, see the contributions to Robert Brier, ed., *Entangled Protest: Transnational Perspectives on the History of Dissent in Eastern Europe and the Soviet Union* (Osnabrück: Fibre, 2013); Friederike Kind-Kovács and Jessie Labov, eds., *Samizdat, Tamizdat, and Beyond: Transnational Media during and after Socialism* (New York: Berghahn Books, 2013). For studies of major Polish émigré centers and their impact on events in Poland, see Andrzej Paczkowski, "Aneks 1973–1989," *Res Publica* 4 (1990), 9; Mikołaj Tychran, "'Aneks': Pismo emigracji pomarcowej," *Studia medioznawcze*, 2 (2009), 104-120; Małgorzata Alberska, *Ośrodki emigracji polskiej wobec kryzysów politycznych w kraju (1976–1981)* (Wrocław: Arboretum, 2000); Małgorzata Alberska and Rafał Juchnowski, "Z dziejów polskiej emigracji politycznej po II wojnie światowej," in Małgorzata Alberska and Rafał Juchnowski, eds., *Polska i Polacy poza granicami kraju w polskiej polityce i myśli politycznej XX wieku* (Wrocław: Wydawnictwo Uniwersytetu Wrocławskiego, 2006); Andrzej Stanisław Kowalczyk, *Giedroyc i "Kultura"* (Wrocław: Wydawn. Dolnośląskie, 1999).

26   Poland's Solidarity Movement & the Politics of Rights

the Polish intellectuals learned about the Moscow "dissidents" (*inakomyslaščie*) and among them especially the "defenders of rights" (*pravozaščitniki* or *zakonniki*). In the Soviet Union, dissent had emerged out of protests against the regime of General Secretary Leonid Brezhnev's narrowing of the already very modest margins of artistic and intellectual liberty granted under his predecessor Nikita Khrushchev.[14]

Within this context, the mathematician Alexander Volpin established a form of political protest which Benjamin Nathans aptly described as "radical civil obedience." Rather than refusing to act according to laws deemed unjust – as in the approach of civil disobedience – Volpin demanded that the Soviet authorities respected norms they pretended to uphold anyway such as the many rights enshrined in the Soviet constitution.[15]

As for nonconformist intellectuals in Poland, 1968 was an important year for the Moscow dissidents. They held an illegal demonstration against the Soviet invasion of Czechoslovakia which marked the end of any attempt to reform Soviet-style Communism. The year 1968 also witnessed the first issue of the *Chronicle of Current Events* – a new samizdat journal but also a crucial contribution to a new genre of political literature which internationalized Volpin's tactic of civil obedience. Neither a forum to discuss Soviet history nor a revolutionary pamphlet, the *Chronicle* merely documented Soviet violations of UN human rights treaties. The authors of the *Chronicle*, moreover, cast the publication of their journal not as an act of resistance, but as a contribution by concerned citizens to upholding the UN's International Covenant on Civil and Political Rights, which Moscow had signed in 1967, and to the

---

[14] On Soviet dissent see Lyudmila Alekseeva, *Soviet Dissent: Contemporary Movements for National, Religious, and Human Rights* (Middletown, CT: Wesleyan University Press, 1985); Robert Horvath, *The Legacy of Soviet Dissent: Dissidents, Democratisation and Radical Nationalism in Russia* (London: Routledge, 2005); Robert Horvath, "Breaking the Totalitarian Ice: The Initiative Group for the Defense of Human Rights in the USSR," *Human Rights Quarterly* 36 (2014), 1; Benjamin Nathans, "The Dictatorship of Reason: Aleksandr Vol'pin and the Idea of Rights under 'Developed Socialism'," *Slavic Review* 66 (2007), 4; Benjamin Nathans, "The Disenchantment of Socialism: Soviet Dissidents, Human Rights, and the New Global Morality," in Jan Eckel and Samuel Moyn, eds., *The Breakthrough: Human Rights in the 1970s* (Philadelphia, PA: University of Pennsylvania Press, 2013); Barbara Walker, "Pollution and Purification in the Moscow Human Rights Networks of the 1960s and 1970s," *Slavic Review* 68 (2009), 2; Barbara Walker, "Moscow Human Rights Defenders Look West: Attitudes toward U.S. Journalists in the 1960s and 1970s," in György Péteri, ed., *Imagining the West in Eastern Europe and the Soviet Union* (Pittsburgh, PA: University of Pittsburgh Press, 2010).

[15] Nathans, "Dictatorship."

The Rise of Dissent in Poland 27

celebrations of 1968 as the Year of Human Rights – a UN event in which the Soviet Union had pledged to participate.[16]

Well before the Helsinki Accords had been signed, then, the Warsaw intellectuals were reading the *Chronicle of Current Events*, other writings by the Soviet dissidents – most notably Aleksandr Solzhenitsyn's *The Gulag Archipelago*, but also the Universal Declaration of Human Rights all of which reached the Commandos in Poland via Western émigré centers.[17] The courage of the Soviet dissidents deeply impressed the intellectuals in Warsaw. While the signing of the Helsinki Final Act seemed to have had little direct impact on them, they were electrified by the news that Andrei Sakharov was awarded the 1975 Nobel Peace Prize.[18]

Another important development for the emergence of Polish dissent was the increasing international salience of Amnesty International.[19] In 1974, some of the Polish intellectuals had become active on behalf of a group of nationalist Polish political prisoners who had planned to blow up a monument to Lenin. Among others by appealing to Amnesty International for support, they contributed to getting the authorities to release the prisoners.[20] In the following year, this success led to the first attempt to organize dissent in Poland by establishing a Polish section of Amnesty International.[21] While this project failed to materialize, not least because of concerns by Amnesty's London leadership, several right-wing activists became members of Amnesty, translating and distributing its newsletters and joining its campaigns against repression in Uruguay and on behalf of prisoners of conscience.[22]

While these international developments provided a crucial context for the rise of dissent in Poland, two domestic events were the main impetus to create open forms of resistance. First, in September 1975, Poland's

---

[16] English translations of the *Chronicle* are available online from Amnesty International at www.amnesty.org/en/ai_search?title=chronicle+of+current+events. The Russian original is available from the homepage of Memorial, a Russian NGO that collects the documents of Soviet dissidents. www.memo.ru/history/diss/chr/index.htm. (both accessed January 2013).

[17] "Archipelag wolnej myśli," special issue of *Aneks* 7/8 (1975); *Powszechna Deklaracja Praw Człowieka: W językach polskim, białoruskim, czeskim, litewskim, rosyjskim, słowackim, ukraińskim* (Paris: Instytut Literacki, 1974); Alexander Solzhenitsyn, *Archipelag GUŁag* (Paris: Instytut Literacki, 1974).

[18] Friszke, *Czas*, 79–81; on the impact of Soviet dissent on Polish intellectuals, see Skórzyński, *Siła*, 33; Jacek Kuroń, *Autobiografia* (Warszawa: Wydawnictwo Krytyki Politycznej, 2011), 406; Zbigniew Romaszewski et al., *Autobiografia* (Warszawa: trzecia strona, 2014), 108–111, 123–124, 185.

[19] On this aspect, see especially Christie Miedema, *Not a Movement of Dissidents: Amnesty International Beyond the Iron Curtain* (Göttingen: Wallstein, 2019).

[20] Friszke, *Czas*, 45–46.   [21] Ibid., 92.   [22] Miedema, *Movement*, 120–125, 150–156.

28   Poland's Solidarity Movement & the Politics of Rights

rulers announced a set of constitutional amendments enshrining the Communist Party's leading role and Poland's "fraternal" ties to the Soviet Union as constitutional norms. In protest, the Warsaw intellectuals signed and published an open letter demanding to scrap the amendments. While not preventing the changes to the constitution, the letter did set off an entire wave of similar protest notes from other social groups, crucially including the Catholic Church.[23]

Second, in June 1976, the Polish authorities decided to raise the prices for food thus triggering a strike involving some 80,000 workers with violent clashes erupting in two Polish cities. The Communist Party swiftly suppressed the protests, arresting hundreds of workers and sacking many more.[24] The labor protests galvanized the Warsaw intellectuals. Over the following weeks, they organized public protests, collected money and food for the families of sacked or arrested workers, provided legal aid, and signed letters of protest to Polish and international audiences. To institutionalize these activities, some of the intellectuals formed the Committee to Defend the Workers, or KOR, Poland's first dissident organization.[25]

KOR recruited its members from both the nationalist and the left-wing milieus in Warsaw. The latter, however, played a more influential role in the Committee's work and thought. Resentful of this dominance, a group of right-wing intellectuals founded their own dissident group, the Movement to Defend Human and Civil Rights, or ROPCiO, in March 1977.[26] Crucially, some of ROPCiO's leading members were the same people who had joined Amnesty International two years before, an experience they seem to have drawn on as they created their movement.[27]

---

[23] Friszke, *Czas*, 83–92.

[24] Paweł Sasanka, *Czerwiec 1976 r: Geneza – przebieg – konsekwencje* (Warszawa: IPN, 2006).

[25] "Appeal to Society and the Authorities of the PRL," September 23, 1976, in Lipski, *KOR*, 467–469. For the discussions leading up to the creation of KOR, see "Nr 1, 1976 wrzesień 13, Warszawa – Informacja operacyjna dotycząca planów utworzenia Komitetu ds. Obrony Praw Człowieka, opracowana przez inspektora Wydziału IV Departamentu III MSW mjr. Romualda Szapałasa, tajne specjalnego znaczenia," "Nr 2, 1976 wrzesień 22, Warszawa – Meldunek operacyjny dotyczący spotkania w dniu 12 września 1976 r. osób prowadzących działalność opozycyjną i planów utworzenia Komitetu ds. Obrony Praw Człowieka, opracowany przez inspektora Wydziału IV Departamentu III MSW mjr. Romualda Szapałasa, tajne," "Nr 3, [Po 23 września 1976, Warszawa] – Meldunek operacyjny dotyczący utworzenia KOR, tajne," in Łukasz Kamiński and Grzegorz Waligóra, eds., *Kryptonim "Gracze": Służba Bezpieczeństwa wobec Komitetu Obrony Robotników i Komitetu Samoobrony Społecznej "KOR"* (Warszawa: Instytut Pamięci Narodowej, 2010), 53–65.

[26] Grzegorz Waligóra, *Ruch Obrony Praw Człowieka i Obywatela 1977-1981* (Warszawa: IPN, 2006).

[27] Miedema, *Movement*.

The Rise of Dissent in Poland

These early expressions of open dissent drew heavily on the social and political practices established by the human rights movement, especially by the Soviet dissidents. Adhering to the principle of openness and legality, the names of KOR's members were published. Both the planned constitutional changes of 1975 and the repression of the workers in 1976 were condemned as violations of human rights guaranteed by Polish law and international agreements such as the Helsinki Final Act and the UN Human Rights Covenants of 1966.[28] KOR also published an *Information Bulletin*, a samizdat periodical emulating the *Chronicle of Current Events*.[29]

KOR also adopted the Soviet dissidents' approach of appealing to international audiences via Western correspondents. The flat of Jacek Kuroń, one of KOR's most active members, became an information center where news about arrests or trials was collected and passed on to Western correspondents and the émigrés, turning the rise of the KOR into the main topic of Western news coverage of Poland. Adam Michnik, a former leader of the student radicals and close friend of the intellectuals creating KOR, was in Paris in 1976. Supported by East European émigrés, he publicized the Polish events in Western Europe, meeting leading figures of West European intellectual and political life, publishing essays in Western newspapers, giving interviews, and holding press conferences in London, Paris, Cologne, and Rome.[30]

ROPCiO followed the dissident model even more closely. Its members announced the creation of their movement in a press conference for foreign correspondents in which they read out an "Appeal to Polish Society."[31] It invoked Poland's recent ratification of two major UN human rights pacts, claiming that they corresponded to the "most profound wishes of Polish society." The aim of ROPCiO was defined as monitoring that "all rights of man and of the citizen as well as his dignity" were respected.[32] At the press conference, the human rights activists explained that ROPCiO was not an organization with formal membership but a movement to which everyone who was concerned about the

---

[28] "Appeal to Society," 468; "Memoriał '59-ciu'," *Kultura* (Paris) no. 1–2 (Jan.–Feb. 1976), 235–236.

[29] Kuroń, *Autobiografia*, 409.

[30] Robert Brier, "Broadening the Cultural History of the Cold War: The Emergence of the Polish Workers' Defense Committee and the Rise of Human Rights," *Journal of Cold War Studies* 15 (2013), 4, 106–108.

[31] Waligóra, *Ruch*, 64–67.

[32] "Apel do społeczeństwa polskiego," in Grzegorz Waligóra, ed., *Dokumenty uczestników Ruchu Obrony Praw Człowieka i Obywatela w Polsce 1977-1981* (Kraków: Księgarnia Akademicka, 2005), 3–4.

state of human rights in Poland could contribute, another practice adopted from the human rights movement in the Soviet Union.[33]

A major activity of both KOR and ROPCiO consisted in documenting instances of human rights violations and in appealing to the Polish authorities and international bodies, such as the UN and the CSCE conference in Belgrade, to respect human rights.[34]

While Polish dissident intellectuals were part of a broader movement, they were the most successful representatives of it. The authorities had initially tolerated the rise of dissent. In spring 1977, however, under pressure from Soviet General Secretary Leonid Brezhnev,[35] they initiated a major crackdown. Yet before the prosecutor could even only finish his investigation, the Polish Politburo changed course again, adopting a general amnesty and ordering to release all KOR activists, despite the fact that they insisted they would continue to struggle for human rights and democracy.[36] While domestic protests, especially by the Catholic Church, played their part in bringing the amnesty about, the release of the prisoners was primarily due to the threat of Western pressures on Poland. Polish leader Edward Gierek was heavily dependent on Western credits for his economic modernization program. He was thus on friendly terms with Western politicians and had cultivated a liberal and modern image of Poland. The international publicity KOR had created around the labor unrest of 1976 and the crackdown of 1977 threatened to demolish this image.[37] Given that US president

---

[33] "Informacja o formule Ruchu Obrony Praw Człowieka I Obywatela w Polsce," in ibid., 5–6.

[34] KOR regularly issued communiques which always featured a section documenting repression. They were compiled by KOR's Intervention Bureau. The communiqués are reprinted in Andrzej Jastrzębski, ed., *Dokumenty Komitetu Obrony Robotników i Komitetu Samoobrony Społecznej* "KOR," 2nd ed. (Warszawa: PWN, 2014). The volume also reprints KOR's appeals to international bodies. For ROPCiO see the documents in Waligóra, ed., *Dokumenty uczestników*. For instance, "Oświadczenie ROPCiO, poświęcone naruszaniu praw obywatelskich w dniach 15 i 15 kwietnia 1977 r." and "Oświadczenie ROPCiO, tzw. Belgradzkie wystosowane w związku ze spotkaniem przedstawicieli Państw Sygnatariuszy Aktu Końcowego KBWE w Belgradzie," both in ibid., 10–11, 36–39.

[35] See Szyfogram Nr 3617/I, z Moskwy, dated Mar. 17, 1977, AAN, KC PZPR, XIA/1048.

[36] Friszke, *Czas*, 239.

[37] For evidence of this, see, for instance, the fact that Polish embassies in France noted how rapidly Poland's image had worsened as a result of KOR's activities. Zebranie sprawodawczo-wyborcze POP przy Ambasadzie PRL w Londynie - 2 czerwca 1977 r. Referat sprawodawczy Egzekutywy POP, not dated, AAN, KC PZPR, LXXVI-147/117. French diplomatic posts were particularly concerned about these developments. See Protokół z zebrania sprawodawczo-wyborczego POP przy placówkach polskich we Francji w dniu 17 grudnia 1976 roku , not dated, AAN, KC PZPR, LXXVI-138/24; Protokół z posiedzenia Egzekutywy P.O.P. przy polskich placówkach w Francji w dniu 3 stycznia 1977 r., dated Jan. 03, 1977, AAN, KC PZPR, LXXVI-150/1; Protokół Nr 3 z

The Rise of Dissent in Poland   31

Jimmy Carter, who had just made human rights a central theme of his presidency, was slated to visit Poland and the first meeting to review the Helsinki Accords were to open in October 1977 in Belgrade, the Politburo seemed to have decided that the best way to preempt Western pressures was to release the prisoners.[38]

In September 1977, after all workers had been released from prison, KOR's members dissolved the Committee founding a new organization, the Committee for Social Self-Defense "KOR," in its stead, though most people continued to refer to it simply as KOR. While the Committee's name shows that it adopted a broader approach to social activism than a narrow focus on human rights, KOR's work remained indebted to the human rights movement. Its aim was to "support and defend all social initiatives intended to implement human and civil rights"[39] which it hoped to achieve, among others, by demanding the full implementation of the UN human rights pacts.[40] KOR also continued to use the political practices of the transnational human rights movement, documenting repression in a dispassionate language, sending telegrams to the CSCE conference in Belgrade, cooperating with Amnesty International, and holding press conferences for Western correspondents.[41] In January

zebrania otwartego OOP przy Konsulacie Generalnym PRL, odbytego w dniu 23 marca 1977r., dated Mar. 23, 1977, AAN, KC PZPR, LXXVI-150/27.

[38] The relevant Politburo protocol does not contain minutes of the discussion preceding the decision to implement the amnesty. See Protokół posiedzenia Biura Politycznego, dated July 19, 1977, AAN, KC PZPR, Mf 2911. For a discussion of the reasons for the amnesty see Friszke, *Czas*, 237–238; see also Rakowski, *Dzienniki polityczne, 1976-1978*, 134, 221, entries dated Nov. 21, 1976 and July 20, 1977. Notably, a review of how the Western press responded to the amnesty was drawn up for Gierek. Tadeusz Łojkowski, Głosy prasy zachodniej w związku z ogłoszeniem w Polsce amnestii, dated Aug. 17, 1977, AAN, KC PZPR, XIA/817.

[39] "Oświadczenie Komitetu Obrony Robotników wydane w związku z przekształceniem się w Komitet Samoobrony Społecznej 'KOR'," Sept. 29, 1977, in Zygmunt Hemmerling and Marek Nadolski, eds., *Opozycja demokratyczna w Polsce 1976-1980: Wybór dokumentow* (Warszawa: Wydawnictwo Uniwersytetu Warszawskiego, 1994), 204–205. My translation differs slightly from the one in Jan Józef Lipski, *KOR: A History of the Workers' Defense Committee in Poland, 1976-1981* (Berkeley, CA: University of California Press, 1985), 470.

[40] "Meldunek operacyjny dotyczący spotkania działaczy KOR w dniu 17 września 1977 r., tajne," in Kamiński and Waligóra, eds., *Kryptonim "Gracze,"* 298.

[41] For appeals of KOR and its successor KSS "KOR" to the Belgrade conference see "Oświadczenie z dnia 28 października 1977 r.," "Telegram z dn. 14 lutego 1978 r. do Prezydium Konferencji do Spraw Bezpieczeństwa i Współpracy w Europie, Belgrad," for telegrams to Amnesty International see "Oświadczenie z dnia 17 października 1977 r.," "[List:] Do Amnesty International—Warszawa 10 Marca 1978 r.," "Telegram z dnia 31 Maja 1978 r. do Amnesty International i Międzynarodowej Konfederacji Wolnych Związków Zawodowych," "List do Amnesty International z dnia 21 Maja 1979," "List do Amnesty International z dnia 7 listopada 1979," in Jastrzębski, ed., *Dokumenty*, 186, 231 and 188, 238, 264, 399, 445.

32   Poland's Solidarity Movement & the Politics of Rights

1980, following a meeting between a Polish dissident and members of the Soviet dissident movement in Moscow, KOR also established a Polish Helsinki Commission to monitor the implementation of the CSCE Final Act in Poland.[42]

ROPCiO, on the other hand, did not fare as well as KOR did. In 1978, it split into two mutually hostile groups amid conflicts orchestrated by collaborators of the secret police. While both groups remained active, the competition between the two, not least for Western funds, greatly restricted their ability to work on behalf of human rights.[43]

II

As the 1970s wore on, Poland witnessed a further broadening and diversification of dissident activity. Independent student committees were set up at universities and intellectuals and academics created a Society for Academic Courses where they gave lectures on political, historical, and legal topics in private flats. On the second anniversary of the labor protests of 1976, more importantly, members of KOR on Poland's Baltic coast and in its Silesian industrial districts made the creation of Committees to Establish Free Trade Unions public. This shift toward labor activism clearly evolved out of and was shaped by dissident tactics. An appeal by the Committees "To All Working People in Poland and Trade Unions Throughout the World" put their work into the context of a "new period in the struggle for material and human rights" which were, the appeal said, guaranteed by the Polish constitution, the UN human rights pacts, and the conventions of the UN's International Labor Organization. It also ended by asking Amnesty International for support.[44]

The samizdat press of the labor activists also imitated the publications of the Soviet dissidents. Each frontpage of the *Chronicle of Current Events* featured Article 19 of the Universal Declaration of Human Rights, guaranteeing freedom of opinion and expression; the frontpage of the samizdat journal of the labor activists in Gdańsk, *The Worker of the Coast*, featured articles 2 and 3 of the International Labor

---

[42] "O powołaniu Komisji Helsińskiej w Polsce: Oświadzenie z dnia 17 stycznia 1980 r.," in ibid., 474–475.

[43] Waligóra, *Ruch*, 131–192.

[44] "To: All Working People in Poland and Trade Unions Throughout the World," in Lipski, *KOR*, 472–473. On the committees, see Leszek Biernacki, "Początki Wolnych Związków Zawodowych Wybrzeża," *Wolność i Solidarność* 5 (2013).

The Rise of Dissent in Poland 33

Organization's convention no. 87, guaranteeing the right of workers to form trade unions.[45]

Eighteen months later, the Committees published the "Charter of Workers' Rights."[46] With its demands for, among others, a general wage raise, a reduction of working hours, and greater safety at the work place as well as its call for workers to create trade unions, it diverted significantly from the narrower aims of the original dissident movement. The Charter, however, did clearly bear the marks of the latter. It was, after all, a charter of *rights*. It did not call for class struggle, much less social revolution, but characterized the hardship of Polish workers as a violation of their rights. It also had an appendix which demonstrated that the labor activists' work was legal by extensively citing the conventions of the UN's International Labor Organization (ILO) and the International Covenant on Economic, Social, and Cultural Rights.

The most active of the trade union committees was the one in Gdańsk where an illegal commemoration for a labor uprising in December 1970 had turned one Lech Wałęsa into a household name among the increasingly renitent workers.[47] Nevertheless, this kind of activism remained at the margins of the life of most of Poland's workers. The Gdańsk Committee had only a handful of members the majority of which were not even workers. If Polish workers had heard of human rights and human dignity, it was most likely not from samizdat publications but Catholic sermons.

The most important of these sermons were given in the summer of 1979 when Pope John Paul II, formerly the Archbishop of Cracow, Cardinal Karol Wojtyła, came to Poland. Following de-Stalinization, the Catholic Church in Poland had managed to claim and retain a relatively independent and powerful position in Polish society with its leader, Poland's primate Cardinal Stefan Wyszyński, even considered by many Poles as an interrex leading Poland under Communist rule. The Church, however, never incited open resistance against Communist rule, even as individual priests and parishes provided shelter and support for the emerging opposition. The impact of John Paul II's visit of 1979, moreover, is easily overestimated. Some documents from the time suggest that both the bishops and the opposition were disappointed of a turnout of Polish Catholics that was lower than had been expected. The authorities, it appears, had managed to restrict attendance of papal

---

[45] The Russian text of the *Chronicle* is available at http://old.memo.ru/history/diss/chr/index .htm (accessed April 2017). A full run of the *Worker of the Coast* (*Robotnik Wybrzeża*) is available at the archive of the KARTA foundation in Warsaw (call no. AO V/0482).

[46] "Charter of Workers' Rights," in Lipski, *KOR*, 492–500.   [47] Lipski, *KOR*, 354–356.

34   Poland's Solidarity Movement & the Politics of Rights

masses both by creating obstacles for Poles who wanted to go to the meetings and by broadcasting the visit live on TV.[48]

But while the Church's role in Poland may not have been as heroic as some accounts suggest,[49] it certainly did provide important spaces of shelter and relatively free discourse. John Paul II, moreover, may not have united his compatriots on Poland's streets and squares, he does seem to have united them in front of their TV sets. The pope's visit, moreover, had a major impact on two crucial, overlapping groups: young people and workers. The meetings with John Paul II were organized by an army of young volunteers. For them, the pope's visit may very well have been a formative event.[50] Their experience of organizing and attending the Masses powerfully underscored the pope's sermons in which he infused the abstract language of human rights and dignity into a heroic national narrative that was readily understandable to Polish society.[51] The pope's sermons also focused on human work. In 1977, before he became pope, Wojtyła had consecrated a church whose construction the fiercely Catholic steel workers of the socialist model city of Nowa Huta had wrested from the authorities.[52] Returning there as pope, he addressed the many workers in the crowds directly, recalling how he had "learned the Gospel anew" in his encounters with workers and demanding that workplace relations respected the dignity of work and human dignity.[53]

The emergence of independent labor activism and the visit of the pope were both important for the creation of Solidarity in 1980. More than anything else, however, the latter's creation was driven by the demands of

[48] "Informacja dotycząca przebiegu pielgrzymki Jana Pawła II, zachowań społecznych i działań władz, opracowana w Wydziale Administracyjnym KC PZPR dnia 10 czerwca 1979 r.," "Sprawozdanie z działań ministerstwa spraw wewnętrznych związanych z pobytem w Polsce Jana Pawła II," in Andrzej Friszke and Marcin Zaremba, eds. *Wizyta Jana Pawła II w Polsce 1979: Dokumenty KC PZPR i MSW* (Warszawa: Biblioteka "Więzi," 2005), 250–258, at 253, 272–298, 283–284; Friszke, *Czas*, 417.

[49] See, for instance, George Weigel, *The Final Revolution: The Resistance Church and the Collapse of Communism* (New York: Oxford University Press, 1992).

[50] "Nr 54: Dokument przedstawiający projekt przeciwdziałnia negatywnym dla ustroju skutkom pielgrzymki Jana Pawła II, opracowany zapewne w Wydziale Pracy Ideowo-Wychowawczej KC PZPR, brak daty [1979 r.]," in Friszke and Zaremba, eds. *Wizyta*, 300–316, at 301.

[51] For three excellent analyses of the discourse and symbolism of the papal visit, see Grzegorz Bakuniak and Krzysztof Nowak, "The Creation of a Collective Identity in a Social Movement: The Case of 'Solidarność' in Poland," *Theory and Society* 16 (May 1987), 3; Dietz, *Polnischer Protest*, 250–257; Jan Kubik, *The Power of Symbols against the Symbols of Power: The Rise of Solidarity and the Fall of State Socialism in Poland* (Pennsylvania University Park: Pennsylvania University Press, 1994), 129–152.

[52] Lebow, *Utopia*, 161–169.

[53] John Paul II, "Homily at the Shrine of the Holy Cross," Mogiła, June 9, 1979, available at http://w2.vatican.va/content/john-paul-ii/en/homilies/1979/documents/hf_jp-ii_hom _19790609_polonia-mogila-nowa-huta.html (accessed July 2015).

The Rise of Dissent in Poland   35

a Polish industrial working class, which was among the groups hit the hardest by Poland's disastrous economic situation. It was in the factories where the government's unrelenting success propaganda clashed most clearly with the reality of energy shortages, work stoppages, and an ineffective and corrupt management, thus reinforcing the sense of absurdity and cynicism many Poles encountered in their daily lives.[54]

In July 1980, these conditions had triggered a wave of industrial strikes throughout Poland. The government, however, managed to quench them by negotiating with each factory individually and granting the workers some of their demands. On the back of this first wave of protests, however, came a second one which had much more far-reaching consequences than the first. Its epicenter was the Lenin shipyards in Gdańsk. Members of the Founding Committees for Free Trade Unions had managed to join the workers there and to convince them to broaden their demands to request not only material concessions from the government but the right to form a trade union. Moreover, the activists got workers from other factories, first in Gdańsk and increasingly all over Poland, supported this demand.[55]

The Warsaw intellectuals also made a crucial contribution by keeping correspondents abreast about the strikes. Thus, they both created international awareness of the strikes, making it impossible for the government to suppress them without damaging its relations to the West, and, as Western radio stations broadcast the reporting of the foreign correspondents back into Poland, further spread news of the events on the Baltic coast. When the striking Gdańsk workers published their famous 21 demands on a large board on the Lenin shipyard walls, the strikes had already spread to other cities on the Baltic coast. By the end of August, the Politburo estimated that in all of Poland approximately 700,000 employees in over 700 work sites were on strike; the entire country was at a standstill.[56] By the end of August, the authorities conceded to the

---

[54] "Doc. nr 1. Protokół nr 8 z posiedzenia Biura Politycznego KC PZPR 3 czerwca 1980 r.: Notatka w sprawie aktualnej oceny realizacji Narodowego Planu społeczno-Gospodarczego na rok 1980 i wniosków wynikających z tej oceny," May 31, 1980, in Zbigniew Włodek, ed., *Tajne dokumenty Biura Politycznego: PZPR a "Solidarność" 1980-1981* (London: Aneks, 1992), 7–9. For a fascinating account of daily life in the late 1970s, see Marcin Zaremba, "Zimno, ciepło, gorąco Nastroje Polaków od 'zimy stulecia' do lata '80," *Working Papers on the Solidarity Movement*, http://solidarnosc.collegium.edu.pl/wp-content/uploads/2012/12/Zaremba-07-01-2013.pdf (accessed July 2015).
[55] For a detailed, day-to-day analysis of the events of August 1989, see Andrzej Friszke, *Rewolucja Solidarności 1980-1981* (Kraków: Znak, 2014), 25–73.
[56] On the intellectuals' role in passing information to foreign correspondents see Friszke, *Czas*, 548–552. On the breadth of the strike wave in late August, see "Doc. nr 13. Protokół nr 29 z posiedzenia Biura Politycznego KC PZPR 30 sierpnia 1980 r.," Aug. 30, 1980, in Włodek, ed., *Tajne dokumenty*, 90–92, at 91.

36   Poland's Solidarity Movement & the Politics of Rights

workers' central demands and in the following month the Independent Self-Governing Trade Union Solidarity was founded.

Solidarity was one of the strangest beasts ever to have stomped through Europe's political history. While its economic program was every syndicalists' dream and its tactics textbook examples of "civil obedience" and peaceful resistance, its members were staunchly anti-Communist and decorated occupied work sites with religious icons and patriotic symbols. No one embodied these various aspects more than the union's leader Lech Wałęsa. Born in Poland's countryside, he combined a devout Catholic faith with a proud labor identity. A former collaborator with Poland's secret police, he later chose the dissident's life of a social outcast. An often erratic and at times authoritarian character, he also had wit and a radiating charisma. Posing as a people's tribune, he listened to the advice of Catholic intellectual Tadeusz Mazowiecki and the Jewish medieval historian Bronisław Geremek.[57]

Whatever Solidarity was it certainly had blown the roof off of the Moscow intellectuals' cautious dissident strategy. Observing the Polish events from afar, they were both exhilarated and shocked.[58] But however profound the difference between the embattled Moscow intellectuals and Poland's muscular mass movement, Solidarity could not deny its roots in dissident activism. Most importantly, dissident activists had convinced the workers to frame their grievances in a specific way – not exclusively as

[57] The degree and length of Wałęsa's cooperation with the Polish Security Service is the matter of much controversy among Polish historians. There is a consensus that he agreed to become an informant during his interrogation as a ringleader of labor protests in December 1970 and that he was registered under the codename "Bolek." Recently uncovered evidence shows that his cooperation with the Secret Service was much more substantial than hitherto thought. The available documentation also suggests, however, that he was struck from the Service's register in 1976 after he had repeatedly refused to provide useful information and became a vocal critic of the management of the Lenin shipyard. He also rejected later attempts of the Security Service to reestablish contacts even though he had been sacked from his job in the shipyard because of his criticism. The thesis that he secretly continued to work for the Security Service after 1976 lacks evidence. "Prof. Friszke: Teczki Wałęsy to nie są śmieci," *Gazeta Wyborcza*, Feb. 23, 2016; Piotr Osęka, "Spór o teczkę Bolka: Co zmienia potwierdzenie autentyczności podpisów Lecha Wałęsy?," *Newsweek Polska*, Jan. 31, 2017. For very fine recent biographies, written before the most recent revelations, see Jan Skórzyński, *Zadra: Biografia Lecha Wałęsy* (Gdańsk: ECS, 2009); Reinhold Vetter, *Polens eigensinniger Held: Wie Lech Wałęsa die Kommunisten überlistete* (Berlin: BWV, 2012); Wałęsa's cooperation with the Security Service was first systematically discussed in a hightly politicized account by Sławomir Cenckiewicz and Piotr Gontarczyk, *SB a Lech Wałęsa. Przyczynek do biografii* (Gdańsk: IPN, 2008); for a discussion of the book's findings see Michael Szporer, *Solidarity: The Great Workers Strike of 1980* (Lanham, MD: Lexington Books, 2012), 283–286.

[58] Tatiana Kosinowa, *Polski mit: Polska w oczach sowieckich dysydentów* (Kraków, Warszawa: Instytut Książki, 2012).

The Rise of Dissent in Poland

material demands, but primarily as a struggle for the right to strike and for freedom of association, that is, for universal human rights guaranteed by international treaties and the Polish constitution.

The list of 21 demands which the strike committee published on August 17 also clearly betrayed the influence of the dissidents. The workers demanded freedom of conscience and the release of all political prisoners, freedom of expression, publication, and free access to the media as "guaranteed by the Constitution of the People's Republic of Poland," and the right to strike. Even the demand to improve the country's economic situation focused on freedom of information and access to political institutions. The strike committee in the city of Szczecin – the second largest center of protest – demanded the publication of the "Charter of Human and Civil Rights from the Conference in Helsinki."[59] After the legalization of Solidarity, moreover, the Polish dissidents drew on their experience with samizdat to help the trade union establish a burgeoning labor press. They advised it on self-organization and established contact to Western correspondents and émigrés.

Solidarity's initial approach, then, remained deeply indebted to dissent. It did not aim to overthrow the existing system, but merely demanded rights the Polish state pretended to grant anyway. Soon enough, this strategy reached its limits. Within a few months after its creation, Solidarity claimed to have over 9 million members. Able to force concessions onto the government, it came to embody hopes for fundamental political changes in Poland. The Communist party, meanwhile, struggling to manage an economic and political situation spinning out of control, went into meltdown: Some 300,000 of its members left. Around one million – a third of the party's membership – remained but joined Solidarity anyway.[60]

Solidarity, too, found itself in an increasingly difficult situation. The union's first congress – held in Gdańsk in September 1981 – was overshadowed by a deepening divide between those who wanted to stick to trade unionism and those who demanded more far-reaching political changes.[61] Social support for Solidarity, meanwhile, had been dwindling for some time: The constant conflict between government and opposition exacerbated the already catastrophic economic situation; so-called hunger marches – demonstrations against the catastrophic supply

---

[59] "Nr. 11. 1980 sierpień 22, Gdańsk – Żądania strajkujących załóg zakładów pracy i przedsiębiorstw reprezentowanych przez MKS," Aug. 22, 1980, in Bronisław Pasierb, ed., *NSZZ "Solidarność" 1980-1981* (Wrocław: Wydawnictwo Uniwersytetu Wrocławskiego, 1990), 147–149.

[60] Andrzej Leon Sowa, *Historia Polityczna Polski 1944-1991* (Kraków: Wydawnictwo Literackie, 2011), 539–544; Friszke, *Rewolucja*, 469–475.

[61] Friszke, *Rewolucja*, 569–717.

situation – had marked Solidarity's first anniversary, while the threat of a civil war or a Soviet invasion concerned many Poles. The Church, too, seemed in crisis when the pope narrowly survived an assassination attempt and Poland's charismatic Primate Cardinal Wyszyński died.

At a meeting held on December 12, 1981, Solidarity's leadership adopted a resolution that called for a nationwide referendum, effectively a vote of confidence on the government.[62] When the resolution had been passed, just after midnight on December 13, 1981, telephone lines had already been cut, police units were taking to the streets, and tanks had started to roll out of their garrisons. Over the next days, some 6,000 people, including almost the entire leadership of Solidarity, were round up and brought to detention camps. Factories and shipyards were surrounded by tanks and stormed by the riot police. Nine workers were killed and 21 wounded as military and police forces moved to "pacify" an Upper Silesian coal mine. The social experiment begun 16 months before was over.

★★★

The history of 1970s Polish dissent, the foregoing sketch has shown, greatly complicates a view of dissent as a deliberately anti-political movement that sought to permanently replace politics for the sake of a universal morality. Poland's Solidarity – a trade union-cum-political and social mass movement – did clearly evolve out of the dissidents' once narrow focus on basic rights even if the union itself cannot be classified as dissent anymore. Human rights, it turned out, was a strategy adaptable to a number of causes, including the struggle for freedom of association. But once human rights were invoked for such causes, they inevitable became political. The dissident tactic of what Benjamin Nathans aptly called "radical civil obedience,"[63] of merely demanding rights the regimes pretended to grant anyway, worked only so long as the rulers were not forced to honor their commitments to human rights. Once they did, their monopoly of power and with it the entire *modus operandi* of the Communist party state was inevitably drawn into question. Where human rights were invoked to effect domestic political changes, they led to struggles for power.

---

[62] "Document No. 77: Notes of Meeting of the Presidium of Solidarity's National Coordinating Commission, Gdańsk," Dec. 2, 1981, "Document No. 78: Solidarity NCC Presidium 'Position Taken by the National Coordinating Commission of the NSZZ,'" Dec. 3, 1981, in Andrzej Paczkowski and Malcolm Byrne, eds., *From Solidarity to Martial Law: The Polish Crisis of 1980-1981 - A Documentary History* (Budapest, New York: Central European University Press, 2007), 414–424.

[63] Nathans, "Dictatorship."

2 Dissent and the Politics of Human Rights

Human rights, the Polish experience of 1976–1981 had shown, could not supplant politics for long. Within five years, the attempt to emulate the model of the Soviet dissidents had contributed to the rise of a social mass movement, and eventually to a major domestic and international crisis. To some extent, it is difficult to imagine how things could have turned out differently. Once Poland's rulers were forced to actually implement the human rights norms they had subscribed to at the UN and in Helsinki, they had to accept a new center of power in Polish society. In repressive societies, then, human rights are always political because they always require that the rulers relinquish and share some of their power.

But in Poland, human rights activism became political for another reason. Polish dissidents, in fact, had never wanted to replace politics with a purely moral focus on human rights. True, many of them did urge Solidarity's leadership to show more restraint, but only because they were weary of how long the Polish and Soviet leadership's tolerance would last, not because they believed the movement should restrict itself to appealing to Amnesty International or the CSCE follow-up conferences. To the contrary, many intellectuals came to interpret the rise of Solidarity as the beginning of a new kind of politics, the birth of a self-governing republic, a view that was very much in line with what they had written and discussed in the decade prior to Solidarity. Most dissidents in Poland and, as I shall show below, in other parts of the Soviet bloc had always understood human rights in a profoundly political way, as a means to turn people into citizens, into active participants of their society's public life. In the Soviet bloc, human rights was not meant to replace politics but to make politics possible again.

To bring out this aspect, this chapter reconstructs how a specific human rights vernacular emerged in Poland. To do so, it will reconstruct the two main, overlapping, and mutually reinforcing ideas of the conceptual world into which Polish intellectuals integrated the notion of universal human rights: The first was their conviction that they lived in a totalitarian society. The dissidents' interpretation of the concept of totalitarianism differed from the one found in Western political science. Where Western scholars had believed that a totalitarian system's main pillar was its apparatus of repression, many dissidents held that its power derived from how it deformed public speech and saturated social life with obvious ideological lies. Thus, the system deprived people of the ability to engage in social life and shape their collective concern. Anti-totalitarian resistance, therefore, was seen primarily as a struggle to reinsert truth into public discourse.

The second core idea of Polish dissident thought was a broadly personalist anthropology. By this, I do not meant that all the dissidents were adherents of personalist philosophy, though many of them were. What I mean, instead, is that most Polish dissidents saw humans as beings who, on the one hand, had been endowed with an inalienable universal dignity that most dissidents saw as rooted in a transcendent moral order. On the other hand, dissidents saw humans as relational beings, that is, as enmeshed in social relations and cultural norms that they needed to be fully human. From this point of view, the totalitarian system both violated the universal dignity of humans and, by deforming public speech, deprived them of their social community.

Against this background, the appeal of human rights was that they seemed to point to the objective foundation for the dissidents' struggle with totalitarianism: the notion of human dignity. What made human rights appealing, in other words, was not their political minimalism but their moral absolutism. But if, as the dissidents believed, the power of totalitarianism rested on how it deformed collective speech through ideology, then the struggle for human rights was not primarily about defending one's private sphere or protecting people from repression. To be sure, those were important aims of the dissident movement. But they were means to an end: reclaiming the public sphere from the totalitarian leviathan. Expressing an unalienable human dignity, human rights were seen as a means of breaking the totalitarian system's grip on the public sphere by creating pockets of freedom where people could speak their minds freely and communicate with each other to tackle their shared concerns.

Underpinning dissident thought, then, was a "thick" understanding of human rights as rooted in notions of community and of an objective transcendent moral order. Moreover, they appeared as indissoluble from questions of collective agency and struggles for social justice. Human rights, in this view, were no anti-political alternative to comprehensive visions of social change or even to politics as such; anti-politics, it turns out, was profoundly political.

I

"Totalitarianism" was one of the most widely used terms not only of the opposition in Poland but of the entire dissident community in the Soviet bloc. This was rather ironic: As an analytical category, totalitarianism had fallen largely out of favor among Western analysts of the Soviet bloc, given how little 1970s "consumer socialism" resembled the horrors of Stalinism. The early 1970s, in fact, were a time of relative affluence in the Soviet bloc. In Poland, Communist leader Edward Gierek used Western credits to initiate a program of economic modernization, making modern consumer goods widely available and opening his country to the West.[1] And yet, when many Poles were enjoying their first Pepsi-Cola or ordering their model of the license-built Fiat 126p, a copy of *The Great Terror*, Robert Conquest's depiction of the Stalinist purges of the 1930s, circulated among independent intellectuals in Warsaw, while a Polish émigré introduced them to the political writings of George Orwell.[2]

To understand why the theory of totalitarianism appealed to these intellectuals, it is important to note that they did not partake in the modest affluence Polish society enjoyed in the early 1970s. This was especially true for the Commandos who had experienced their arrests and the anti-Semitism of the "anti-Zionist" purge as a trauma, not the defeat of a political project so much as the collapse of an entire social and cultural life world. Their parents had devoted their lives to building a society where a person's religious or ethnic background would be irrelevant, now they were pressured to leave because they were Jews.[3] When the Commandos were released from prison in late 1971, they began lives as social outcasts, shutting themselves up in a tightly knit, hermetically sealed, and greatly diminished milieu.[4] Not knowing what else to do, they continued to cultivate their style of intellectual inquiry and critical debate, but it was unclear where this was supposed to take them. The

---

[1] Andrzej Friszke, *Polska Gierka* (Warszawa: Wydawnictwa Szkolne i Pedagogiczne, 1995).
[2] Friszke, *Czas*, 42; Andrzej K. Drucki [Marcin Król], "George Orwell," *Aneks* 6(1974). On totalitarianism in Central and East European discourses see Jacques Rupnik, "Le totalitarisme vu de l'Est," in Guy Hermet, ed., *Totalitarismes* (Paris: Economica, 1984); see also Abbott Gleason, *Totalitarianism: The Inner History of the Cold War* (New York: Oxford University Press, 1995); Jeffrey C. Isaac, "Critics of Totalitarianism," in Terence Ball and Richard Bellamy, eds.,*The Cambridge History of Twentieth Century Political Thought* (Cambridge, MA: Cambridge University Press, 2003); Eckhard Jesse, ed., *Totalitarismus im 20. Jahrhundert: Eine Bilanz der internationalen Forschung*, 2nd ed. (Bonn: Bundeszentrale für politische Bildung, 1999); Alfons Söllner, Ralf Walkenhaus, and Karin Wieland, eds., *Totalitarismus: Eine Ideengeschichte des 20. Jahrhunderts* (Berlin: Akademie Verlag, 1997).
[3] Friszke, *Anatomia*, 597–736. [4] Friszke, *Czas*, 19–68; Skórzyński, *Siła*, 19–35.

42   Poland's Solidarity Movement & the Politics of Rights

only thing that was clear was that there would be no returning to the Communist project.[5]

This sense of failure and hopelessness prepared the ground for the emergence of a Russian and Central European variety of the theory of totalitarianism. One source of the concept's popularity among Polish intellectuals was that it captured the complete arbitrariness of political and social life in state socialism. To say that the state socialist systems were totalitarian, Leszek Kołakowski explained, did not mean that they applied extreme repression always and everywhere but that they *could* apply whatever form of oppression they saw fit at any time.[6] Throughout the Soviet bloc, dissidents had experienced this very painfully; during the many crackdowns in the Soviet Union, the repression after the Prague spring, or when a period of relative liberty, in the aftermath of 1956, ended in Poland with incarceration or exile in the midst of an anti-Semitic campaign.

But there was a more profound dimension to this experience of arbitrariness. Many Soviet bloc dissidents agreed that ideology had come to play a specific role in the public life of state socialist societies where a plethora of organizations pretended to represent society, while in reality merely extolling phony ideological slogans. Invocations of "eternal friendship with the USSR" – a particularly bizarre claim both in Poland and Czechoslovakia – remained a staple of public life, and for all of Gierek's focus on consumption and patriotism, the official Polish discourse revolved around the image of a dynamically developing country – a "second" Poland – on the road to a brighter, socialist future. It is doubtful that many Poles had ever taken this "success propaganda" seriously, but when Gierek's economic program collapsed under the worldwide recession of the 1970s and the success propaganda continued unabated, public life started to take on a sense of surrealism and absurdity.[7]

People living under 1970s state socialism, then, may have had greater liberties than those who had to endure the horrors of Stalinism. But they

---

[5] Among the first to reject Marxism in a rather radical way was Leszek Kołakowski who continued to exert great intellectual influence on the Warsaw Left. See Leszek Kołakowski, "My Correct Views on Everything," *Socialist Register* 11 (1974); Leszek Kołakowski, "Marxist Roots of Stalinism," in Robert C. Tucker and Włodzimierz Brus, eds., *Stalinism: Essays in Historical Interpretation* (New York: Norton, 1977); Leszek Kołakowski, *Main Currents of Marxism: Its Rise, Growth, and Dissolution*, trans. P. S. Falla, 3 vols. (Oxford: Clarendon Press, 1978). See also Gawin, *Wielki*, 280–309.

[6] Leszek Kołakowski, *Leben trotz Geschichte* (München: Piper, 1977), 265.

[7] On Gierek's success propaganda, see Marcin Zaremba, "Propaganda sukcesu: Dekada Gierka," in Piotr Semków, ed., *Propaganda PRL: Wybrane problemy* (Gdańsk: IPN, 2004); Kubik, *Power*, 31–74.

Dissent and the Politics of Human Rights 43

were nevertheless forced to live in a split reality: In private, they could speak their minds comparatively freely, unless they had come into open conflict with the regime; in public, they had to enact an ideological script that looked increasingly absurd, if not downright ridiculous. Herein, Kołakowski believed, lay the strength of what he called "Sovietization." It did not require "faith, passion, adherents and fanatics." To the contrary, it was most effective when "no one, really no one, takes the ideology of sovietism seriously ... Sovietization is created precisely as a situation in which everyone knows that nothing is and *nothing canbe* 'true' [naprawdę] in public speech, that all words have lost their original meaning and there is nothing strange about the fact that a cockroach can be called a nightingale and a parsley called a symphony. ..."[8] The fact, then, that the authorities of a totalitarian system could arrest whoever they saw fit expressed a more profound arbitrariness: the system's ability to shape the meaning of speech according to its will and thus to banish truth from public discourse.

This power, Kołakowski believed, constituted a more efficient mechanism of subjugating society than naked terror. By monopolizing all forms of social organization and deforming language, the Communist system deprived society of the very ability to express its interests and mount resistance. This mechanism, moreover, enslaved the citizens of the Soviet bloc in a way that made them complicit in their own oppression. By participating in the system's rituals, by letting its lies stand, they daily contributed to laying and sustaining the fundament for society's enslavement. This idea was first expressed in 1974 by Russian dissident Aleksandr Solzhenitsyn, in an essay widely read among the Polish intellectuals and émigrés, titled "Live not by Lies." The citizens of the Soviet Union, not the authorities, were to blame for the situation they found themselves in, Solzhenitsyn wrote shortly before he was arrested and deported to West Germany. "If we did not paste together the dead bones and scales of ideology, if we did not sew together the rotting rags, we would be astonished how quickly the lies would be rendered helpless and subside. That which should be naked would then really appear naked before the whole world."[9]

---

[8] Leszek Kołakowski, "Sprawa polska," *Kultura* 307(Apr. 1973), 6, 8.

[9] Alexander Solzhenitsyn, "Live not by Lies," *Washington Post*, Feb. 18, 1974. A Polish translation was published in *Aneks* No. 4/1974. Notably, when a Polish underground publishing house published an anthology of *Aneks'* most important articles, Solzhenitsyn's text opened the collection. See Aleksandr Sołżenicyn, "Żyć bez kłamstwa," in *"Aneks" – kwartalnik polityczny: Wybór, część I* (Warszawa: NOWa, 1980), 1–3. For references to Solzhenitsyn's text, see Jacek Kuroń, *Opozycja: Pisma polityczne 1969-1989* (Warszawa: Wydawnictwo Krytyki Politycznej, 2010), 55; Adam

44   Poland's Solidarity Movement & the Politics of Rights

This analysis of state-socialism had an important consequence for what it meant to be a dissident intellectual in the Soviet bloc: Resistance to totalitarianism was not about developing an elaborate counter-ideology to that of the socialist system. The essence of totalitarianism, after all, was not ideological fanaticism but a kind of radical relativism. Totalitarian rule did not consist in imposing doctrinal purity on society but in constantly shifting the lines between right and wrong, good and evil, truth and lie. But if this was true, even the smallest act of openly and publicly speaking the truth was a triumph over the system's attempt to banish truth from public discourse. The very work of intellectuals – bearing witness to truth in speech and writing – thus was in itself already a form of anti-totalitarian resistance. Tellingly, a 1974 essay by the Polish dissident intellectual Marcin Król praised George Orwell as the author of an unsurpassed analysis of totalitarianism for he had understood how "the political reality of dictatorship and totalitarianism ... degrades language." The defense of the clarity of language and of its ability to describe reality truthfully was thus the main way of opposing totalitarianism.[10]

Anti-totalitarian resistance, therefore, began with an individual choice, as Antoni Macierewicz, one of the leading voices among KOR's younger activists, wrote in 1976. Only individuals could resist totalitarianism, he argued, human beings who had "the courage to set themselves, their sense of good and evil" against a reality in which the definition of good and evil was made dependent on the will of the rulers. "If there is no one to accept this burden, no one to whom such a way of acting comes natural, no logical proof, no ideology will smash the Communist myth."[11]

Michnik, *The Church and the Left*, trans. and ed. David Ost (Chicago, London: Chicago University Press, 1993), 120; see also Jarosław Szarek, "Nim powstał SKS," *Biuletyn Instytutu Pamięci Narodowej* 5–6 (May–June 2007), 26; Andrzej Friszke, *Opozycja polityczna w PRL 1945-1980* (London: Aneks, 1994), 298–299. For Solzhenitsyn's influence among students and even a worker without higher education, see "Nr 49, 1977 marzec 21, Warszawa – Meldunek operacyjny dotyczący aktualnej działalności KOR w Poznaniu, opracowany przez inspektora Wydziału III Departamentu III MSW kpt. Kazimierza Dzienię, tajne," in Kamiński and Waligóra, eds., *Kryptonim "Gracze,"* 179–180, at 179.; "Nr 109, 1977 listopad, Warszawa – Notatka sporządzona na podstawie meldunków operacyjnych w sprawach założonych na osoby represjonowane za udział w wypadkach czerwcowych 1976 r. w Radomiu, tajne," in ibid., 367–375, at 370. On Solzhenitsyn's impact among emigres see Józef Czapski, "Sołżenicyn," *Kultura* 12 (1974), 3; Maciej Broński, "Archipelag," *Kultura* 3 (1974); Michał Heller, "Ziemia Gułag," *Kultura* 3 (1974); see also Adam Michnik, "Odszedł jeden z gigantów XX wieku," *Gazeta Wyborcza*, Aug. 5, 2008.

[10] Drucki [Marcin Król], "George Orwell," 10.

[11] Marian Korybut [Antoni Macierewicz], "Refleksje o opozycji," *Aneks* 12 (1976), 72.

This view of totalitarian rule resonated strongly with someone like Macierewicz who came from a family steeped in Poland's patriotic and religious traditions. Throughout their childhood, he and his peers had listened to their parents talk about nineteenth century Polish patriots, about the non-Communist resistance to the German occupation, about the execution of over 20,000 Polish officers by the Soviet NKVD in 1940, aspects of Polish history all of which were suppressed or at least not mentioned in public discourse in favor of mostly obvious government propaganda.[12] So for people like Macierewicz, the theory of totalitarianism suggested that keeping the memory of these facts alive was not a desperate act of clinging to a reality that had long since disappeared. The telling of these stories, and the commitment to truthfulness it entailed, rather, was an act of resistance against totalitarian rule, the only type of resistance that, in Macierewicz's view, was capable of undermining Communist ideology, for it struck to the very core of totalitarian rule, its aim to banish truth from public discourse.[13]

But the theory of totalitarianism was also highly appealing to the former Commandos. It allowed them to understand their arrest not as a defeat, but an epiphany – a moment when they realized the "true" nature of the system and of their own role in sustaining it. They could also recast what had hitherto been a political style as a form of political resistance in its own right. During the 1960s, the Commandos' political style of open debate, of diligent intellectual work, of contesting hierarchies and criticizing authorities had been a means to an end: the creation of democratic socialism. Having come to understand the People's Republic as totalitarian, as a system that enslaved society by deforming language, the mere holding of open debates became an end in itself, the path toward liberating society by freeing public speech from the suffocating grip of ideological language.

Before it became a moderately successful form of political activism, then, dissent was primarily a way of endowing a hopeless reality with new meaning. Coming to see state socialism as totalitarian, a form of rule based on banishing truth form public discourse, the core of what the future dissidents did as intellectuals – speaking truth to power – could be reinterpreted as the only possible way of confronting Communism. The mere publication of a samizdat journal like the *Chronicle of Current Events* was therefore just as important as its efficacy in preventing repression, for it was meant to disclose a hidden truth, to let the facts speak for themselves. Its dispassionate style expressed more than a pragmatic

---

[12] Błażejowska, *Harcerską drogą*, 17–41.   [13] Korybut, "Refleksje."

46   Poland's Solidarity Movement & the Politics of Rights

setting aside of ideological differences – it embodied a commitment to truthfulness and as such the antidote to a system based on saturating public life with obvious lies.[14]

II

This theory of totalitarianism is crucial to understand one of the major features of the dissident human rights vernacular – its strongly religious undertones. In Poland, this dimension became particularly visible during the Solidarity period with its Masses attended by thousands of workers, the public hearing of confession, and the display of Catholic icons and symbols. But religious language and symbolism had been part of Polish dissident culture well before that.

At first sight, this aspect may not seem all that surprising given the important role of Catholicism in Polish society and culture. Many of the Polish dissidents as well as the workers who would fill the ranks of Solidarity, after all, had grown up in devoutly Catholic families. But the central place of religion in Polish human rights discourses becomes more puzzling once we recognize that especially KOR, Poland's most success-ful opposition group of the late 1970s, was significantly shaped by the Commandos as well as by older left-wing intellectuals. A religious perspective came hardly natural to these activists given that in Poland religion was largely synonymous with a Catholicism that was staunchly authoritarian and conservative, even by Catholic standards. It was also nationalist, with sermons and pastoral letters claiming that only a Catholic Pole was a "true" Pole. Before the war, anti-Semitism had been rampant in Polish Catholicism, among both priests and bishops.[15] Until the 1970s, therefore, the Commandos – mostly children from Jewish Communist families – had had two main enemies: the Communist Party's Central Committee and the Polish episcopate.[16] During the 1970s, however, they revised their views of Christianity in general and

---

[14] Ann Komaromi, "Samizdat and Soviet Dissident Publics," *Slavic Review* 71 (2012), 1, 82.

[15] For a brilliant survey of the role of Catholicism in modern Polish nationalism, see Brian Porter-Szücs, *Faith and Fatherland: Catholicism, Modernity, and Poland* (New York: Oxford University Press, 2011), 258, 295–322; on the role of nationalism for Polish theology, see Czesław Bartnik, *Chrześcijańska nauka o narodzie według Prymasa Stefana Wyszyńskiego* (Lublin: Wydawnictwo KUL, 1982); for a long-term sociological account of the Church's role in creating a Polish opposition movement see Maryjane Osa, *Solidarity and Contention: Networks of Polish Opposition* (Minneapolis, MN: University of Minnesota Press, 2003).

[16] Gawin, *Wielki*, 196.

Dissent and the Politics of Human Rights   47

the Catholic Church in particular, a development which stunned those of the Commandos who had moved to the West after 1968.[17]

To some extent, the Commandos' rapprochement with Polish Catholicism had to do with how the Church changed during the 1960s and 1970s. Crucially, it embraced the notion of human rights, an idea it had previously rejected. In the encyclical *Pacem in terris* of 1963,[18] on which the Polish bishops wrote a long pastoral letter to Polish Catholics, Pope John XXIII described human rights as evolving out of the Catholic view of humans.[19] Among the Polish laity, this Catholic rights discourse was picked up by a group of progressive left-wing Catholic intellectuals. In an influential book published in 1971, one of them interpreted the political ethos of nineteenth-century Polish socialists as a possible common ground for Catholics and the secular Left. The core of this ethos, he wrote, was the belief in the dignity of the human person and in "the universality of fundamental human rights."[20]

Among both the episcopate and the laity, this newfound support for human rights also translated into practical steps to support left-wing dissidents and opposition groups. While the Polish bishops had failed to condemn the anti-Semitic campaign of 1968, they had spoken out for the protesting students and supported them when they were released from prison. Two of Commandos, for instance, could finish their studies at the Catholic University of Lublin after they had been released

---

[17] Ibid., 189–276; Jonathan Luxmoore and Jolanta Babiuch, "In Search of Faith: The Metaphysical Dialogue Between Poland's Opposition Intellectuals in the 1970s," *Religion, State and Society* 23 (1995), 1.

[18] John XXIII, *Pacem in terris* [Encyclical Letter on Establishing Universal Peace in Truth, Justice, Charity and Liberty], available at /www.vatican.va/holy_father/john_xxiii /encyclicals/documents/hf_j-xxiii_enc_11041963_pacem_en.html (accessed March 2012). The relevant council documents are Vatican Council II, *Gaudium et Spes* [Pastoral Constitution on the Church in the Modern World], available at www.vatican.va/archive/ hist_councils/ii_vatican_council/documents/vat-ii_const_19651207_gaudium-et-spes_en .html (accessed July 2015); Vatican Council II, *Dignitatis humanae* [Declaration of Religious Freedom] available at http://www.vatican.va/archive/hist_councils/ii_vatican_council/ documents/vat-ii_decl_19651207_dignitatis-humanae_en.html (accessed July 2015). On these aspects see Porter-Szűcs, *Faith*, 149–150; Bernhard Sutor, "Katholische Kirche und Menschenrechte: Kontinuität oder Diskontinuität in der kirchlichen Soziallehre?," *Forum für osteuropäische Ideen- und Zeitgeschichte* 12 (2008), 1.

[19] "List pasterski episkopatu Polski o encyklice Ojca Świętego Jana XXIII 'Pokój na ziemi," in *Listy pasterskie episkopatu Polski 1945-1975* (Paris: Éditions du dialogue, 1975), 291–295.

[20] Bohdan Cywiński, *Rodowody niepokornych* (Warszawa: Biblioteka "Więzi," 1971), 514. For the most important texts emerging from this dialogue see Adam Michnik, *Kościół - lewica - dialog* (Paris: Instytut literacki, 1977); for an extensive analysis of this dialogue, see Dietz, *Polnischer Protest*, 33–150; on the milieu of left-wing Catholic intellectuals see Gawin, *Wielki*, 194–213; Andrzej Friszke, *Oaza na Kopernika: Klub Inteligencji Katolickiej, 1956-1989* (Warszawa: Biblioteka "Więzi," 1997).

48 Poland's Solidarity Movement & the Politics of Rights

from prison.[21] The Polish bishops, moreover, joined the protests against the constitutional amendments of 1975. In the second half of the 1970s, there were even direct contacts between leading bishops like Primate Stefan Wyszyński and Cardinal Karol Wojtyła, the later pope and KOR. In 1977, the bishops appealed to the authorities to release the arrested workers and KOR activists and intervened on their behalf with the Polish government.[22] The Catholic lay intellectuals began inviting left-wing and post-Marxist intellectuals to their symposia and published some of their articles in their journals, usually under pseudonym.[23]

In part, then, the Catholic-post-Marxist rapprochement of the 1970s demonstrates the coalitional nature of human rights. If the struggle with totalitarianism was not primarily about specific political views but the right to express them freely, Adam Michnik, a leading intellectual figure of the Commandos, wrote in a long essay, the Church's demand for religious freedom was part of that struggle. The Church, moreover, could be a formidable ally, given its membership and its relative independence.[24]

The Commandos' encounter with religion, however, went beyond such a strategic alliance. Many of them began to actively search for religious inspiration and learned Christian and Jewish songs and prayers.[25] Writing shortly before the end of the Cold War, Michnik would even interpret the entire dissident experience as a "religious renaissance" in which the dissidents "lived and acted exactly ... as if God were watching over them continuously from on high, as if they were aware of the presence of God."[26] The Commandos' mentor and main strategist of KOR, Jacek Kuroń, a one-time Trotskyite and lifelong agnostic, too, conceded a "fascination with Christianity" which he called the "oxygen of European culture."[27]

The key to understanding the Commandos' embrace of religious sentiments is their specific theory of totalitarianism. In some ways, to be sure, the concept of totalitarianism had reinforced the anti-authoritarianism of the Commandos who, by the mid-1970s, had come to proudly embrace their position as social outcasts. But the Commandos' rejection of ideological master narratives had not turned them into post-modernists *avant la lettre*. To the contrary, "the Stalinist

---

[21] Friszke, *Czas*, 34.   [22] Ibid., 60–61, 94–95, 137–139.   [23] Ibid., 54–59.

[24] This is the main argument of Michnik, *Kościół*.

[25] Luxmoore and Babiuch, "Search," 90.

[26] Adam Michnik, "The Moral and Spiritual Origins of Solidarity," in William M. Brinton and Alan Rinzler, eds., *Without Force or Lies: Voices from the Revolution of Central Europe in 1989-1990* (San Francisco, CA: Mercury House, 1990), 246.

[27] Kuroń, *Opozycja*, 62.

Dissent and the Politics of Human Rights   49

and communist experience had turned us into moralists," one of them later remembered, "[... it] had taught us the dangers of moral compromise."[28] The memory of how, in 1968, an entire lifeworld had come tumbling down, the isolation during interrogation and imprisonment, the very real experience of being at the mercy of an arbitrary system and the conviction that, through their ideological blindness and moral compromises, they had been accomplices of their own oppression – all of this sent the Commandos on a quest for moral universals, for a firm, self-evident truth on which to base their individual autonomy. For some time at least, they believed they had found it in religion. What attracted the Commandos primarily to Christianity, then, was the idea of a "transcendent Moral Law," as Kuroń later remembered.[29] Their turn toward religion was, as Michnik wrote, part of a "collective return to issues of transcendence, to issues of whether there is any order that is absolutely hard and fast," it was about "the struggle for fidelity to natural law."[30]

Notably, this "religious renaissance" did not necessarily entail an uncritical embrace of organized religion or even only "mere Christianity." One of the Commando's favorite religious authors was the German Protestant pastor Dietrich Bonhoeffer whom the German authorities had executed in 1945 for his opposition to Nazi rule. In his prison writings, which were translated into Polish in the early 1970s, the Commandos encountered both an appealing person – an early dissident as it were – and the notion of a "religionless Christianity," a way of acting *as if* God existed, a theology that resonated with the Commandos' abstract understanding of religion.[31]

In a social world characterized by state arbitrariness and the pressure to publicly conform to obvious nonsense, in sum, religion seemed to provide an objective moral order beyond the reach of any secular ruler, however powerful. As such, it appeared to Polish intellectuals both left and right as a firm conceptual grounding for their attempt to regain control over the meaning of their lives and to reinject truth into public discourse.

Kuroń summarized this development in a programmatic text published just before the rise of Solidarity in which he reinterpreted the

---

[28] Luxmoore and Babiuch, "Search," 79.   [29] Kuroń, *Autobiografia*, 378.
[30] Michnik, "Origins," 246.
[31] Jacek Kuroń, "Chrześcijanie bez Boga," published under pseudonym in 1975 in *Znak*, Poland's other personalist monthly journal. Reprinted in Kuroń, *Opozycja*, 58–73. See also Michnik, "Origins," 246; on the Commandos see Luxmoore and Babiuch, "Search," 78–79, 90; Dietrich Bonhoeffer, *Wybór pism*, trans. Anna Morawska (Warszawa: Biblioteka "Więzi," 1970).

history of Poland's pre-war democratic socialists as a struggle for "the highest values of European culture – that is, Christian values." Kuroń did not deny, nor excuse, the "intolerance, chauvinism, xenophobia" that had characterized interwar Catholicism. Yet after the experience of totalitarianism, he wrote, the Polish non-Communist Left had come to adopt the values expressed in Bonhoeffer's letters, "written in a Hitlerist death cell," and the program of the Christian socialist youth in occupied Warsaw as their own.

"One has to live as if God has died," says Pastor Bonhoeffer. "One has to live as if God exists," writes the non-believing Warsaw intellectual. Searching for hope, [the Polish socialist youth organization under German occupation] found the gospel. We believe that this was their most important discovery. To deny transcendent values leads to moral relativism and then all political activity turns into a crime or, at best, into fraud and manipulation.[32]

The Polish dissidents' embrace of human rights language was very much a part of this turn toward religion. At the center of "transcendent moral law," Kuroń wrote, was the "sovereignty of the human person and from this point of view we reevaluated our vision of a social order realizing justice and freedom."[33] The term "human rights" was thus less important to the Commandos and their Catholic interlocutors than "human dignity" – the idea that human beings have a transcendent kernel which is the source of their absolute worth and universal rights.[34]

The human rights vernacular of Polish dissidents, in sum, had a clear religious dimension. It revolved around the idea that the dignity and rights of every human being were an objective truth guaranteed by a transcendent, divine order and that, as such, they were the antithesis to a system based on banishing truth from public discourse.

III

Thus far, the analysis might seem to confirm standard views of dissidents as anti-political figures who sought to substitute politics for a quest for moral purity. For Polish dissidents, after all, resistance to totalitarian rule began with an individual commitment to truthfulness, as Macierewicz had written.[35] Yet the mere fact that resistance was to begin with an individual moral choice tells us little about where this resistance was supposed to lead. Delving into this question will show that while dissent

---

[32] Kuroń, *Opozycja*, 199.   [33] Kuroń, *Autobiografia*, 378.
[34] Cf. Michael Rosen, *Dignity: Its History and Meaning* (Cambridge, MA: Harvard University Press, 2012).
[35] Korybut, "Refleksje."

began with an individual's choice to resist totalitarianism's assault on truth, it was meant to lead to profoundly political aims. To show this, this section will reconstruct the second major feature of the Polish dissidents' conceptual world – the anthropology and social ontology, underpinning Polish dissident thought.

To the extent that Polish dissident thought of the 1970s was based on a systematic and explicit philosophy, it was supplied by broadly personalist views. The most influential current of personalism evolved out of the attempts of mid-twentieth century Christian thinkers to strike a middle ground between liberal individualism and Communist collectivism. The starting point for any social and political philosophy, these thinkers held, had to be the experience of the individual human person which they saw as unique and as endowed by God with an inviolable dignity. At the same time, personalists also believed that human persons were social and inter-relational beings, that they could exist and flourish only in a community with others.[36] At the heart of personalism, in other words, was the idea that human beings were simultaneously spiritual and social beings, as the Catholic intellectual Tadeusz Mazowiecki, a leading figure of Polish personalism, explained in the late 1960s.[37]

Personalism, it seems, proved crucial for the Polish human rights movement because it helped to integrate the abstract notion of rights with concerns which had been at the center of Polish politics since the nineteenth century – nationalism and the struggle for a central place of Catholicism in social life. A powerful strain in personalism argued that the social community in which the human person flourished could not be freely chosen. Its foundation, rather, had to be God for he was the "creator of the spiritual and natural order," as the Polish bishops wrote in 1963 in their pastoral letter on "Pacem in terris."[38] Thus, they under-lined the "indissoluble link between rights and obligations," insisting

---

[36] On personalism in Poland, see Piotr H. Kosicki, "L'avènement des intellectuels catholiques: Le mensuel *Więź* et les conséquences polonaises du personanalisme mounierien," *Vingtième Siècle* 102 (Apr.–June 2009), 34; Roman Graczyk, *Od uwikłania do autentyczności: Biografia polityczna Tadeusza Mazowieckiego* (Poznań: Zysk i S-ka, 2015), 76–80; Dietz, *Polnischer Protest*, 55–79. On personalism and human rights, see Samuel Moyn, "Personalism, Community, and the Origins of Human Rights," in Stefan-Ludwig Hoffmann, ed., *Human Rights in the Twentieth Century* (Cambridge, MA: Cambridge University Press, 2011); on its relevance in Poland see Stefania Szlek Miller, "Catholic Personalism and Pluralist Democracy in Poland," *Canadian Slavonic Papers/ Revue Canadienne des Slavistes* 25 (1983), 3; for a comparative analysis of twentieth-century Catholic social thought see James Chappel, "Slaying the Leviathan: Catholicism and the Rebirth of European Conservatism, 1920-1950" (Ph.D. thesis, Columbia University, 2012).
[37] Tadeusz Mazowiecki, *Rozdroża i wartości* (Warszawa: Biblioteka "Więzi," 1970), 27.
[38] "List pasterski," 292.

52   Poland's Solidarity Movement & the Politics of Rights

among others that the correlate of a right to a life in dignity was a dignified life. They also specifically mentioned the Universal Declaration of Human Rights' right to marry and its insistence that the "family is the natural and fundamental group unit of society."[39] Tellingly, the bishops also argued that the individual rights of Polish Catholics to free exercise of religion, as guaranteed in the Universal Declaration of Human Rights and by the principles of democracy, required that the Church be given a privileged position in Poland, given its central role in Polish national life.[40]

The most prominent exponent of this personalist practice of weaving a vocabulary of individual rights and dignity into a simultaneously religious and national discourse was the later Pope John Paul II, Karol Wojtyła.[41] His first encyclical, *Redemptor hominis*, used the term "dignity" twenty seven times, stressing that "in Christ and through Christ man has acquired full awareness of his dignity, of the heights to which he is raised, of the surpassing worth of his own humanity, and of the meaning of his existence."[42] In a famous sermon he gave in the center of Warsaw in 1979, he wove this idea of Christ as the source of human dignity into an elaborate heroic vision of Polish nationhood. "It is right," he said, "to understand the history of the nation through man, each human being of this nation. At the same time man cannot be understood apart from this community that is constituted by the nation." Christ was thus for him "an ever open book on man, his dignity and his rights and also a book of knowledge on the dignity and rights of the nation."[43]

Almost identical, if less overtly Christian, views could be found in the programmatic writings of traditionalist and nationalist dissident groups in Poland. One of them, the Young Poland Movement, subscribed to the dissident approach of uniting opposition groups with different political views in the common cause of defending human rights.[44] They also conceded that other people's faith in human rights could draw from

---

[39] "List pasterski," 292–293.

[40] "Biskupi polscy do braci kapłanów," Aug. 28, 1963, in *Listy pasterskie*. 296–313, at 310–311. See also "Orędzie o prawie do nauczania religii," Aug. 28, 1963, in ibid., 317–320, at 317–318.

[41] For this discourse, see especially Porter-Szűcs, *Faith*, 347–359.

[42] John Paul II, *Redemptor hominis* [Encyclical Letter at the Beginning of his Papal Ministry], available at www.vatican.va/content/john-paul-ii/en/encyclicals/documents/hf_jp-ii_enc_04031979_redemptor-hominis.html (accessed March 2012).

[43] John Paul II, Homily given on Victory Square, Warsaw, June 2, 1979, available at _www.vatican.va/content/john-paul-ii/en/homilies/1979/documents/hf_jp-ii_hom_19790602_polonia-varsavia.html (accessed March 2012).

[44] "Deklaracja ideowa Ruchu Młodej Polski," in Hemmerling and Nadolski, eds., *Opozycja demokratyczna*, 611–626, quote on 612.

Dissent and the Politics of Human Rights 53

secular sources, even as they wrote that their faith in human rights was rooted in Christian beliefs. They also insisted that every "human person is a unique individual endowed with a set of innate and unalienable rights and freedoms" guaranteed by a growing body of international human rights treaties.[45] Yet even as they conceded these pluralist views, the activists also rejected both materialist social orders which denied man's nature as a spiritual being as well as an "individualism based on a naturalist enlightenment libertinism" because it threatened such social bonds as the family, the nation, and the state.[46] They went on to describe the nation as "one of the communities in which the human individual evolves" and though they wrote that the nation was "no absolute value but primarily a great promise for the self-realization of man in a community in which his individual agency is preserved,"[47] the remainder of the programmatic statement focused on the nation and on national independence as a necessary condition for individual liberty. Tellingly, these activists would refer to human rights and the rights of the nation in the same breath.[48]

But personalism was not only important for conservative and traditionalist thinkers. One of the centers of personalist thought in Poland was the circle of left-wing Catholic intellectuals who, by the mid-1970s, had begun to support the Commandos. In 1978, in a symposium on human rights, the aforementioned Mazowiecki, who would go on to become one of Solidarity's leading advisors, argued that the human person "realizes herself not by holding back, but through commitment, by giving, through free and conscious social engagement." Human rights, he therefore insisted, would remain dead letter unless there was a social order empowering human beings to participate actively in social life. Individual liberty and the agency of society were indissolubly linked; the struggle for human rights was always also the struggle for a just social order created by active and committed human persons.[49]

This left-wing strand of the personalist understanding of human rights resonated strongly with the philosophical past of the Commandos and of the Polish Left more broadly. After having adopted the notion of human dignity from his Christian interlocutors, Kuroń developed a left-wing personalism of sorts.[50] Following a Marxist anthropology, Kuroń believed that every human being shaped their world and thus themselves through their creative activity. Since human beings could not create their world alone, Kuroń, too, believed that personal fulfillment was possible

---

[45] Ibid., 614.   [46] Ibid.   [47] Ibid., 615–616.   [48] Ibid., 612.
[49] Tadeusz Mazowiecki, "Chrześcijaństwo a prawa człowieka," *Więź* 2 (1978), 12, 7.
[50] Friszke, *Czas*, 44.

only through active participation in social life. For him, questions of human dignity were thus intertwined with questions of solidarity and love. His anthropological credo was that *"to be human [żyć po ludzku] means to be creative [tworzyć] and to love and what is more they are in fact one and the same thing."*[51]

The respectively nationalist and post-Marxist traditions of Polish dissidents proved a crucial sounding board for the personalist understandings of human rights dominant in Poland at the time. Yet the effect of these traditions was also powerfully reinforced by the dissidents' specific theory of totalitarianism. According to the latter, as shown above, the power of totalitarianism rested on its ability to deform public language and thus to deprive the social community of its oxygen. While resistance to totalitarianism thus began with an individual moral choice, its aim was to reinject truth into public discourse and to thus rebuild the community's social life. Nourishing the national traditions and narratives which official propaganda sought to repress and cultivating Polish language were thus ways of opposing totalitarianism. Even religious rituals could appear as ways in which people communicated publicly in a way that was authentic.

As a result, questions of national identity and culture were central to the thought of both right-wing and left-wing Polish intellectuals. To be sure, the nationalist views of the members of ROPCiO were a major reason for its conflicts with the left-wing members of KOR. But questions of national identity and culture also loomed large in the writings of a liberal and cosmopolitan intellectual like Michnik. To counter sovietization, he believed, Polish culture needed a "traditionalist current" in thinking about history and culture, even as he also insisted on the need for a "radical current" which taught "skepticism and critique" and found "support in the contemporary anti-authoritarian movements in the West."[52] This insistence on the importance of national culture, then, was not necessarily at odds with Michnik's simultaneous embrace of human rights. In contrast to the obvious lies which totalitarianism imposed upon society, human rights meant a turn toward moral universals and "natural law," a normative order that followed from the "sheer factuality" of reality. In a similar vein, Kołakowski had argued that resistance to sovietization involved a return to language "just as it was," to give words their "true" meaning back.[53]

---

[51] Kuroń, *Opozycja*, 61, 67. For further evidence for a Marxist influence on his thought see ibid., 8, 57.
[52] Michnik, *Church*, 157, 161, 163.   [53] Kołakowski, "Sprawa."

In contrast to the empty ideological slogans dominating Polish public life, then, Polish literature and culture acquired an air of authenticity and truthfulness. The cultivation of national culture and language, in other words, evolved out of the same commitment to a life in truth and dignity as the adoption of human rights. The struggle for individual rights and for Polish culture, in fact, were often seen as two sides of the same coin. Individual rights like freedom of expression, opinion, and publication were meant to enable Polish society to nurture national traditions, fill blank spots in collective memory, and give the Polish language its "true" meaning back, thus reconstructing an active community that would provide the context for individual autonomy.

In Poland, in sum, Catholic and post-Marxist intellectuals shared a "deeper" or "thicker" understanding of human liberty than the dry language of human rights activism suggests. Individual autonomy was thinkable only within a community of human persons, and freedom meant the freedom to create the social world together with them.[54] Manifesting one's individual autonomy from the state was, as Jerzy Szacki has shown, "inseparable from the desire to participate in a community" – the dissidents' individualism was a "collective individualism."[55]

IV

Though dissent began with an individual moral choice, then, it did not end there. To the contrary, its aim was to rebuild the connecting tissue of society – a public discourse committed to truthfulness. Even as Polish dissent mimicked the work of the Helsinki Committees in Moscow and of Amnesty International, it was neither of the two.[56] In fact, understanding KOR and ROPCiO as a Helsinki monitoring group would mean to miss how Central European dissidents "vernacularized" the human rights discourse in a way in which monitoring human rights compliance was no aim in itself, but the starting point for a broader democratization

---

[54] Kuroń, *Opozycja*, 75.

[55] Jerzy Szacki, *Liberalism after Communism* (Budapest, New York: Central European University Press, 1995), 85.

[56] For a still widely read study reducing dissent largely to Helsinki monitoring see Thomas, *Effect*. The view of KOR as a Helsinki monitor can even be found in otherwise excellent work on dissent and human rights. See, for instance, Foot, "Cold War"; Friederike Kind-Kovács, *Written Here, Published There: How Underground Literature Crossed the Iron Curtain* (Budapest, New York: Central European University Press, 2014), 354–355; Jacques Rupnik, "The Legacies of Dissent: Charter 77, the Helsinki Effect, and the Emergence of a European Public Space," in Friederike Kind-Kovács and Jessie Labov, eds., *Samizdat, Tamizdat & Beyond: Transnational Media during and after Socialism* (New York: Berghahn Books, 2013); Snyder, *Activism*, 67–71.

56   Poland's Solidarity Movement & the Politics of Rights

of society, for the creation of spaces of citizenship and political participation. Struggling for their human and civil rights they wanted to reclaim the public space from the deformed language of totalitarianism. This section is devoted to documenting how this understanding of human rights led to a distinct practice of rights activism which was different from Amnesty International's approach of focusing primarily on protecting people from incarceration and torture.

Seeing civil rights as human rights and vice versa, the protest of Polish dissidents had always had a positive thrust and an overtly political dimension. The first open expression of dissent in Poland, after all, had been directed against changes in the country's constitution. The first letter of protest against this decision said that since the Polish government had "solemnly confirmed the Universal Declaration of Human Rights" in Helsinki, these "fundamental liberties" should now be introduced to Polish life, in order to begin "a new era in the history of the nation and in the life of individuals."[57]

This political thrust of human rights activism was particularly prominent in the work of ROPCiO, the group which, ironically, copied the practices of the international human rights movement more faithfully than KOR. When its members decided to create a human rights organization, they drew up a long internal memorandum to outline their views. It did enumerate individual liberty as well as the "legal and actual equality of rights and obligations" as one of their aims. Primarily, however, the memorandum described gaining full national sovereignty and creating democracy as the overarching goals of the activists.[58]

In 1979, one of ROPCiO's main activists, Leszek Moczulski, even founded a political party, the Confederation for an Independent Poland. Its programmatic declaration described "inalienable human and civil rights" as well as "mutual tolerance and respect for other people's rights" as the foundation for the democratic system the party wanted to build. However, the same statement also said that "the aspirations of individual people and entire groups" were fulfilled within the "historically formed national community uniting past, present, and future generations of Poles." The new party's overarching aim, therefore, was to strive for full Polish sovereignty.[59]

---

[57] "Memoriał '59-ciu'," 235–236. For the genesis of the text see Jan Skórzyński, "'List 59' i narodziny opozycji demokratycznej w Polsce," *Zeszyty Historyczne* 163 (2008).
[58] "Deklaracja programowa 'U Progu'," in Waligóra, ed., *Dokumenty uczestników*, 407–408.
[59] "Deklaracja ideowa Konfederacji Polski Niepodległej," in Hemmerling and Nadolski, eds., *Opozycja demokratyczna*, 632–634.

The activism of KOR, too, reflected the human rights vernacular of Polish dissent. When the original committee was dissolved to be replaced by a new organization, its members decided against calling it Committee for the Defense of Human and Civil Rights, choosing the name Committee for Social Self-Defense "KOR" (KSS KOR) instead.[60] Tellingly, one of the arguments for this name was that the new committee was to be more than an institution documenting the violation of existing rights: "we are also a committee that fights for the change of legislation wherever it contradicts the human rights pacts."[61]

Two years later, the Committee published a statement which took the vernacularization of human rights further, combining it with a project for democracy and social justice. The first of them, an "Appeal to Society," did not begin by listing how the individual rights of specific people were violated but with an analysis of Polish society, depicting it as characterized by a complete lack of the rule of law, by material problems, and by profound social injustices. To solve these problems, the appeal insisted, Poles needed to adopt an approach combining human rights work with political aims. They should demand that the government respect freedom of opinion, expression, and association, as guaranteed in the International Covenant on Civil and Political Rights, in order to enable society to defend itself and give it a say in how the economy was organized.[62]

The founding documents of the free trade union committees combined human rights even more clearly with struggles for justice and social agency. A appeal, "To All Working People in Poland and Trade Unions Throughout the World," published in 1978, duly invoked the authoritative texts of human rights, calling the unrest of 1976 the beginning of a "new period in the struggle for material and human rights," guaranteed by the Polish constitution, the UN human rights pacts, and the conventions of the UN's International Labor Organization. It also ended by asking Amnesty International for support. Much like the previously cited appeal, however, human rights was meant to pave the way for collective agency. The appeal, after all, announced that workers and intellectuals had joined forces to fight for free trade unions.[63]

Eighteen months later, the committees published the "Charter of Workers' Rights" which may have been the clearest example of how

---

[60] On the choice for a name see Friszke, *Czas*, 250–251.
[61] "Meldunek operacyjny dotyczący spotkania działaczy KOR w dniu 17 września 1977 r.," 299.
[62] "Appeal to Society," in Lipski, *KOR*, 474–482.
[63] "To: All Working People in Poland and Trade Unions Throughout the World," in Lipski, *KOR*, 472–473. On the committees, see Biernacki, "Początki."

58   Poland's Solidarity Movement & the Politics of Rights

human rights activism could be used as the launching pad for a project of self-organization.[64] The Charter's text did begin with rights talk, noting how working people in Poland had been deprived of several fundamental rights such as the right to have a say in the issues that concern them; the right to safe and meaningful work, to hourly pay, and to rest; as well as the workers' right to defend themselves, that is, the right to strike. An appendix to the Charter extensively cited two UN documents, the conventions of the ILO and the International Covenant on Economic, Social, and Cultural Rights, to demonstrate that the committee's work was legal. The texts' main thrust, however, was a call upon Polish workers to organize. Whether or not the situation of Polish labor could be improved, the Charter's authors insisted, depended on whether the workers were willing to make a stand, "to shake off the feeling of powerlessness, to stop passively accepting the restriction of one's rights and the deterioration of one's living conditions" by holding strikes, publicly speaking up against injustices, and by creating independent trade unions.[65]

In 1980, as shown above, this activism had contributed to the creation of Solidarity, an event, as is now abundantly clear, which did not break with dissident practices but evolved out of an approach to human rights activism which had never been about a retreat from politics in favor of an abstract moralism but about the building of a social community. Western observers often noted the excitement of the trade union activists as they practiced democracy for the first time. "Self-Government" became a central term of Solidarity's lexicon denoting not only workers' self-management, but also the turning of citizens and social groups into agents of their own history. The union's program of September 1981 described Solidarity as a "Self-Governing Republic," a notion particularly favored by many veterans of KOR.[66]

The "dignity of the human person" was front and center in the events of 1980–1981. The "sense of human dignity, the consciousness of the rights to which man is entitled both in the civic sphere and the sphere of labor," was the source of Solidarity's strength, the editorial of the first issue of the *Solidarity Weekly*, penned by its editor-in-chief Tadeusz

---

[64] "Karta Praw Robotniczych," in Hemmerling and Nadolski, eds., *Opozycja demokratyczna*, 602–609.

[65] "Karta Praw Robotniczych," 605.

[66] "Solidarity's Program," in "The First Solidarity Congress," *World Affairs* 145 (1982), 1, 43–45. For a republican interpretation of Solidarity's ethos see Elżbieta Ciżewska, *Filozofia publiczna Solidarności: Solidarność 1980-1981 z perspektywy republikańskiej tradycji politycznej* (Warszawa: Narodowe Centrum Kultury, 2010). For additional important interpretations of Solidarity's style of governing see Sergiusz Kowalski, *Krytyka solidarnościowego rozumu: Studium z socjologii myślenia potocznego* (Warszawa: PEN, 1990); Ost, *Solidarity*.

Mazowiecki, said.[67] The Helsinki Accords or the Human Rights Covenants were invoked, and a Committee to Defend Prisoners of Conscience was formed to control the release of political prisoners, a major item in the Gdańsk agreement.[68] The occupied worksites appeared to many as places where the consequences of "sovietization" had been shrugged off and the Polish language had taken on its "true" meaning again. "We are a movement for truth," a Solidarity activist stated. "We can be described this way."[69]

Solidarity, to be sure, was not simply 1970s dissent activism writ large. As a movement with millions of members took shape, ideas and sentiments began to percolate which were at odds with the Warsaw intellectuals' learned essays. The intellectuals' religious sensibilities had always been somewhat abstract and philosophical. Solidarity's symbolism and culture were unabashedly Catholic: The gates of the Lenin shipyards were decorated with crucifixes, icons of Mary, and pictures of the pope; Masses were a regular part of occupation strikes as well as of the Solidarity congress of 1981.[70] While the Catholic hierarchy's stance on the strikes of 1980 was far from unequivocal, priests often supported the workers energetically, joining them on the occupied worksites to hear confession and say Mass, serving as chaplains for Solidarity's regional branches, or organizing pilgrimages for workers. Even more so than in the 1970s, human rights were understood in a deeplypersonalist way whose religious connotations were abundantly clear: In an influential sermon, the Dominican Fr. Józef Tischner interpreted "solidarity" in terms of the Epistle to the Galatians: "Bear ye one another's burdens, and so fulfil the law of Christ" (Gal. 6,2). Human dignity, in this view, was not primarily guaranteed by international conventions; its place was a social community whose members realized themselves by giving themselves to others, a community that was grounded in a transcendent order ("the law of Christ").[71]

---

[67] Tadeusz Mazowiecki, "Początek rozmów," *Tygodnik Solidarność*, Apr. 3, 1981.

[68] "Uchwała," *Biuletyn Gdańskiego Komitetu Obrony Więzionych za Przekonania* 1, Apr. 25, 1981, 1.

[69] Quoted in Roman Laba, *The Roots of Solidarity: A Political Sociology of Poland's Working-Class Democratization* (Princeton, NJ: Princeton University Press, 1991), 132.

[70] For what is still the best analysis of this aspect, see Kubik, *Power*, 183–238.

[71] Józef Tischner, "Solidarność sumień: Kazanie wygłoszone na Wawelu dn. 19 X 1980 r.," *Tygodnik Powszechny*, Oct. 16, 1980; Józef Tischner, *The Spirit of Solidarity* (San Francisco, London: Harper & Row, 1984), 5. For his homilies during the Solidarity congress in 1981 see "Polska praca jest chora: Homilia ks. Józefa Tischnera," *Tygodnik Solidarność*, Sep. 18, 1981; "Czas zakorzenienia: Homilia ks. Józefa Tischnera," *Tygodnik Solidarność*, Oct. 9, 1981; "Więcej światła: Homilia ks. Józefa Tischnera," *Tygodnik Solidarność*, Oct. 23, 1981. See also Tomasz Czeran, "'Czas nowych ludzi': Józef Tischner i idea solidarności," in Wojciech Polak, ed., *Czas przełomu: Solidarność 1980-1981* (Gdańsk: ECS, 2010), 204–214.

60   Poland's Solidarity Movement & the Politics of Rights

As human rights were further vernacularized, the personalist pendulum swung decisively toward more collectivist and even nationalist views. In its program, Solidarity called itself a "movement for the moral rebirth of the people" based on Christian values and national traditions. To be sure, that same document also described Solidarity as uniting "people adhering to various ideologies, with various political and religious convictions, irrespective of their nationality." People with a Communist past and Jewish background remained influential in the movement, while influential labor leaders held leftist and secular views.[72] Diversity, however, was no aim in itself, as Tomek Grabowski observes: "The desired 'good' society was to be functionally divided into harmoniously cooperating parts, not into conflicting interest groups with their particular, and inherently incompatible, claims."[73] Human rights were meant to enable people to join the collective search for the common good of the Polish nation – a term that left room for the liberal views of many intellectuals and labor activists, but which a significant segment of Solidarity's members – both intellectuals and workers – understood in an ethnic sense.

The work of Solidarity, then, went beyond 1970s Polish dissent. It was also a far cry from the limited approach of Soviet dissidents or the work of Amnesty International. Yet none of this means that Solidarity or Polish dissent do not belong in the history of human rights. What the Polish experience shows, rather, is that human rights activism did not necessarily lead to a moralist retreat from politics but that human rights language could be vernacularized in a number of ways. Many of the Polish activists understood human beings as "persons" – as inherently social beings endowed by God with an inalienable dignity. Moreover, they believed that the power of totalitarianism rested on its ability to destroy the social community which a person needed to flourish by banishing truth from public speech. For them, therefore, it was only natural that the struggle for the rights of the "human person" was simultaneously a struggle for Polish independence, for a central place of Catholicism in national life, and/or for a more just society. In fact, the very adaptability of rights talk to these causes may have been a major source of its appeal for it endowed the struggle for these causes with an immense moral force. To Polish activists, human rights appeared to be the expression of an objective, transcendent truth about the inviolable dignity of human beings that, in

---

[72] "Solidarity's Program," 26.
[73] Tomek Grabowski, "The Party That Never Was: The Rise and Fall of the Solidarity Citizens' Committees in Poland," *East European Politics and Societies* 10 (March 1996), 2, 233.

turn, could provide the foundation on which to resist totalitarianism's assault on truth. What made human rights appealing, in other words, was how their moral absolutism could be adapted to a variety of causes.

V

How crucial are these specific Polish views on human dignity and totalitarianism for the dissident discourse throughout the Soviet bloc? Though the Catholic-Marxist convergence of the 1970s was a Polish specificity, collective individualism was not. Dissidents throughout the Soviet bloc shared the view that totalitarianism was based on its ability to deform language and that the struggle for human rights did not mean the defense of a private sphere, but the reclaiming of the public space. Above, I have discussed the importance of Aleksandr Solzhenitsyn's "Live not by Lies" for the emergence of this view of state socialist societies. The most important and elaborate discussion of this idea, however, was Václav Havel's "The Power of the Powerless," an essay the idea for which was born over the rum, salami, and cheese Havel had brought to a clandestine meeting between Polish and Czechoslovak dissidents in 1978, which was simultaneously published in Polish and Czechoslovak samizdat.[74]

Famously, Havel used the figure of an allegoric greengrocer to explain how the post-totalitarian system enslaved its citizens. Significantly, all that the system required of the greengrocer was an outward expression of loyalty – placing an ideological slogan he did not believe in into his shop window. Havel's analysis of post-totalitarianism was thus different from George Orwell's dystopian vision in *1984* where the gaze of "big brother" penetrated every aspect of his subjects' life and ultimately even the very mind of the novel's main protagonist. Havel's greengrocer, in contrast, had the option of retreating into the relative safety of his private life. All he had to do was pay the prize of playing the system's game.

Given this analysis, resisting totalitarianism and living a life in truth was certainly a choice everyone had to make individually, but it could not remain a merely private act. Only by refusing to put phony ideological slogans into his shop display, that is, only by *publicly* manifesting his dissent from the system's ideology, would the greengrocer's choice of a life in truth have an effect. For only thus would he "shatter[...] the world of appearances, the fundamental pillar of the system ... show[ing]

---

[74] Václav Havel, "Siła bezsilnych," *Krytyka* 5(1979); Václav Havel, *Moc bezmocných* (Praha: Edice Ptelice [samizdat], 1979); Havel, "Power"; on the text's genesis in the meetings of 1978 and its importance for inspiring Solidarity, see Zbigniew Bujak et al., "Jak się zaczęło?," *Krytyka* 8(1981), 23–24.

everyone that it is possible to live within the truth." The aim of the life in truth was to reclaim the public space from a system that plastered it with phony ideological slogans.[75]

In Poland and Czechoslovakia, therefore, human rights and the struggle for spaces of citizenship were one and the same thing. Explaining Polish dissident strategy in 1976 at a conference in Paris to an audience of Soviet and East European emigres as well as Western journalists and intellectuals, Michnik argued that, given Soviet hegemony and the failure of reform Communism, the only feasible alternative for the "East European dissidents" was "an unceasing struggle for reform and evolution that seeks an expansion of civil liberties and human rights ..." Yet the approach Michnik went on to sketch focused on social self-organization. From these starting points of dissident activity, he believed, larger social groups, especially Catholics and workers, could join forces, begin articulating political programs and demands, and in this way create an independent society in a public space hitherto dominated by the regime.[76]

In a similar vein, the Charter 77, the founding document of Czechoslovak dissent, drafted only months after Michnik's essay, argued that the observance of international human rights treaties was not the responsibility of the state authorities alone:

Each and every one of us has a share of responsibility for the general situation and thus, too, for the observance of the [human rights] pacts that have been enacted and are binding not only for the government but for all citizens. The feeling of co-responsibility, faith in the idea of civic involvement and the will to exercise it and the common need to seek new and more effective means for its expression led us to the idea of setting up CHARTER 77 ...[77]

Tellingly, freedom of expression, of information, of the media, of religious exercise, and of association –rights guaranteeing communication among citizens and collective agency –featured prominently among the human rights whose violations the Charter enumerated.[78] A year later, Havel's "Power of the Powerless" was published in Polish samizdat alongside the "Parallel Polis" by the Czech Catholic dissident Václav Benda, an essay which made a point very similar to Michnik's "New

---

[75] Havel, "Power," 39–40.

[76] Adam Michnik, "A New Evolutionism," in his *Letters From Prison and Other Essays* (Berkeley, CA: University of California Press, 1985), 147.

[77] Declaration of Charter 77, dated Jan. 1, 1977, English translation confiscated by the Czechoslovak authorities, probably prepared for western correspondents, dated Jan. 1, 1977, available at www.libpro.cz/charta/docs/declaration_of_charter_77.pdf (accessed March 2015).

[78] Ibid.

Evolutionism" – dissent and the struggle for human rights was a struggle for democracy fought through social self-organization.[79]

During one of the Polish-Czechoslovak meetings of 1978, the participants adopted a declaration commemorating the tenth anniversary of the Prague spring, which encapsulated how they saw human rights alongside and in conjunction with a set of aims whose linchpin was human dignity:

On the tenth anniversary of the events of 1968 – united in the defense of truth, human and civil rights, democracy, social justice, and national independence – we declare our common will to remain faithful to these ideals and to act in their spirit. The meaning of the life of individuals and nations flows from inalienable human dignity – this idea is the source of all our aspirations and actions. Therefore, we feel a deep solidarity with our many friends around the world who share these ideals.[80]

In these writings, to be sure, democracy was understood in a deliberately abstract way. There was no larger utopian vision to it and its agent would not be a revolutionary party. "In searching for truth, or, to quote Leszek Kołakowski, 'by living in dignity'," Michnik said, "opposition intellectuals are striving not so much for a better tomorrow as for a better today. Every act of defiance helps us build the framework of democratic socialism, which should not be merely or primarily a legal institutional structure but a real, day-to-day community of free people."[81] Yet clearly, these texts show human rights to be compatible with a political project focused on social agency.

Notably, Central European dissidents used the terms "civil" and "human rights" largely as synonyms and in so doing they could invoke one of the major human rights documents of their time: the International Covenant on Civil and Political Rights which the UN had adopted in 1966 and which both Poland and Czechoslovakia ratified in 1976. Crucially, the Covenants first part consists of only one article which guarantees no individual right but the right of all peoples to self-determination.[82] The collective individualism of the dissidents may thus have been much more in line with the human rights discourses of the 1970s than the recent historiography of human rights suggests.

---

[79] Václav Benda, "Równoległa polis," *Krytyka* 5 (1979).
[80] "Nr 49: 1978 r., sierpień. Wspólne oświadczenie KOR I Karty 77 w X rocznicę inwazji państw Układu Warszawskiego na Czechosłowację," in Hemmerling and Nadolski, eds., *Opozycja demokratyczna*, 286–287.
[81] Michnik, "Evolutionism," 142, 148.
[82] *International Covenant on Civil and Political Rights*, available at www.ohchr.org/en/professionalinterest/pages/ccpr.aspx (last accessed January 2020).

64   Poland's Solidarity Movement & the Politics of Rights

★★★

In Poland and elsewhere in the Soviet bloc, this chapter has shown, human rights activism was no pragmatic strategy of striking broad bipartisan coalitions, but part of an almost existential moral commitment to truthfulness, to choosing what Kołakowski called a "live in dignity," to regaining control over the meaning of one's life and to reclaiming public speech from a system that had deformed it and rendered it meaningless. It thus had strongly religious connotations. In 1977, Michnik quoted a passage from a pastoral letter the Polish bishops had written in 1969: "If we want to preserve our dignity we must have enough courage to defend the truth."[83] In this appeal, he found the same view which Solzhenitsyn had expressed in his call to "Live not by Lies" and Kołakowski in his plea to "live in dignity" – the "anti-totalitarian view of the unity of human rights and human duties, since a life in truth and in search of the truth is both the right of man and his obligation."[84] Thus enriching the abstract concept of human rights with ideas they drew from a variety of sources – Soviet dissidence, Catholic social thought, the concept of totalitarianism – the Polish dissidents managed to infuse their dire situation with new meaning. If human dignity was absolute, their quest for individual autonomy was in itself worthwhile and every, even the most limited form in which they defended autonomy was a victory over the system's desire for total control. Against sovietization, Michnik wrote, "Authenticity is the defense. When authorities seek to control the entire culture, then every authentic gesture, every authentic movement, and every artistic or scholarly work conceived in authenticity is anti-totalitarian."[85]

The immediate context for the emergence of this discourse were national but its horizon was transnational. It emerged when nonconformist intellectuals in different parts of the Soviet bloc, connected with one another through the émigré centers, wove a set of ideas into an original interpretation of totalitarianism. What characterized this discourse most of all was not necessarily a political minimalism, but a moral absolutism—the quasi-religious belief in the absolute value of human dignity. In a time, in which truth itself seemed impossible, the defense of the right to freedom of expression through a samizdat publication was a victory over the totalitarian ambitions of the system.

Human rights were central to this discourse, but they were understood in a specific way: individual liberty was bound to normative commitments and a responsibility to shape collective life; freedom meant the

---

[83] "List na święto Chrystusa Króla," Oct. 1, 1969, in *Listy*, 576–579, at 577.
[84] Michnik, *Kościół*, 88. The translation is my own.   [85] Michnik, *Church*, 160.

Dissent and the Politics of Human Rights   65

freedom to participate in a community. The dissidents invoked human rights to protect themselves from a system whose domination was based on colonizing the public space with its empty rituals, on deforming public discourse and depriving its citizens of the ability to express their collective concerns. For all its moral rigidity and rejection of traditional politics, the "life in truth" was meant to be a public act, the first step toward wresting public discourse from the suffocating clutch of ideology and to create and empower citizens to follow their calling to "civic involvement" as the Charter 77 explained. Much as the rise of dissent was triggered by an age of ideological crisis, the human rights vernacular it developed was adaptable to a series of political concerns, democracy, and collective self-determination chief among them.

3 The Principle of Noninterference as Laid Down in the Helsinki Final Act
The Polish Crisis, the Cold War, and Human Rights

In histories of human rights, Soviet bloc dissent is usually seen as an essential actor in the "breakthrough" of human rights during the 1970s after which they became a permanent feature of international relations and Western political discourse. This narrative usually ascribes CSCE and its Final Act a central role for how dissent helped bring about the breakthrough of human rights. Obliging the Soviet bloc states to respect human rights and establishing periodical meetings to review its implementation, it is argued, the Final Act fundamentally transformed international politics, for it provided both a reference point for human rights activists and a forum where they could make their grievances known to the international community.[1]

At first sight, the international repercussions of Solidarity's rise and repression seem to confirm this view. From November 1980 to September 1983, a CSCE review conference was held in Madrid. Events in Poland overshadowed discussions there. During one of the conference's sessions, moreover, on February 9, 1982, ironically at the very time the Polish delegation was holding the proceeding's rotating chairmanship, Poland was turned into an international pariah. One by one, the foreign ministers of the NATO countries took to the stage, lambasting the imposition of martial law in Poland as a violation of the CSCE's Final Act, the UN Charter, and the Universal Declaration of Human Rights. A month before, both NATO and the European Community (EC) had decided that they would not grant Poland any additional credits until it suspended martial law, released all political prisoners, and resumed the social dialog with Solidarity and the Catholic Church.[2] Western politicians and commentators alike insisted that they

---

[1] Thomas, *Effect*; Snyder, *Activism*.
[2] For Poland's role and position in the CSCE process, see Wanda Jarząbek, "Hope and Reality: Poland and the Conference on Security and Cooperation in Europe, 1964-1989," *Cold War International History Project*, Working Paper # 56 (2008), Woodrow

The Principle of Noninterference as Laid Down   67

were not interfering in Poland's internal affairs. Warsaw's signing of the Helsinki Final Act, they claimed, had turned the violation of human rights into a concern of the international community.[3]

The cannonade of criticism the Poles had to endure on that day in Madrid might appear as a confirmation of how fundamentally international relations had changed since the 1970s when human rights had become a global language of protest. Yet the prehistory of that day suggests a very different story. The first response of both NATO and EC to the imposition of martial law had been to invoke not the CSCE Final Act's human rights provisions but its very principle of noninterference. Powerful European members of NATO insisted that the CSCE conference in Madrid had to go ahead regardless of repression in Poland. For US policy hawks, including President Ronald Reagan, on the other hand, the suppression of Solidarity confirmed the uselessness of a Helsinki process for which they had never had much use in the first place. For them, the logical conclusion of martial law in Poland was to pull out of the CSCE altogether. It was only the threat of the United States leaving the Madrid conference, and derailing the entire Helsinki process, which made the West Europeans suggest to invoke the Final Act to condemn martial law in Poland. The West's stance in Madrid was no show of unity, it was a compromise allowing the Americans to show resolve and the Europeans to salvage the Helsinki process.[4]

Wilson Center, Washington DC; Wanda Jarząbek, "A Growing Problem: The Polish People's Republic and the Problem of Human Rights in the Context of the CSCE Process, 1975-1983," in Brier, ed., *Protest*.

[3] Cable from USDel in Madrid to Secstate, "Secretary's Statement, CSCE, Madrid, February 9," dated, Feb. 9, 1982, US Department of State, Virtual Reading Room (hereafter: State Dep., Virtual Reading Room) http://foia.state.gov/searchapp/DOCUMENTS/foiadocs/311c.PDF (accessed Aug. 2014).

[4] On the row initiated by the Polish crisis, see Andrea Chiampan, "'Those European Chicken Littles': Reagan, NATO, and the Polish Crisis, 1981–2," *The International History Review* 37 (2014), 682-699; Gregory F. Domber, "Transatlantic Relations, Human Rights, and Power Politics," in Poul Villaume and Odd Arne Westad, eds., *Perforating the Iron Curtain: European Détente, Transatlantic Relations, and the Cold War, 1965-1985* (Copenhagen: Museum Tusculanum Press, 2010); Douglas Selvage, "The Politics of the Lesser Evil: The West, the Polish crisis, and the CSCE review conference in Madrid, 1981-1983," in Leopoldo Nuti, ed., *The Crisis of Detente in Europe: From Helsinki to Gorbachev, 1975-1985* (London: Routledge, 2009); Helene Sjursen, *The United States, Western Europe and the Polish Crisis: International Relations in the Second Cold War* (Houndmills: Palgrave, 2003). On transatlantic relations more broadly, see the contributions to Kiran Klaus Patel and Kenneth Weisbrode, *European Integration and the Atlantic Community in the 1980s* (New York: Cambridge University Press, 2013). For an account of the CSCE negotiations in Madrid, see Sarah B. Snyder, "The CSCE and the Atlantic Alliance: Forging a New Consensus in Madrid," *Journal of Transatlantic Studies* 8 (2010), 1.

The Western response to the Polish crisis, then, shows that the place of human rights in international politics remained precarious even after their seeming breakthrough in the 1970s. Moreover, the tougher stance which both the United States and West European governments adopted was to a significant extent the result of an unexpected public outcry over repression in Poland, especially in France and Italy. Yet in this field, too, a close analysis reveals not the aftereffect of a human rights breakthrough but controversy and conflict over human rights.

In civil societies and political parties, the Polish crisis had initiated a fierce dispute, spanning Western Europe and the United States and cutting across traditional ideological camps. The politicians, intellectuals, and social organizations speaking out for Solidarity, to be sure, were walking the walk and talking the talk of human rights, mimicking, as they did, the cultural and political practices popularized by Amnesty International and others. But as they did, they engaged in political and intellectual debates about what human rights actually were, how they related to democracy, socialism, or the Cold War, what political identities could be built upon them, and how they could replace ideological certainties that had been lost in the previous decade. These debates propelled solidarity with Solidarity in the West but often they fed into domestic and national discussions and conflicts that had little to do with events in Poland.

The events of February 9, 1982, as well as the larger Polish crisis of which they were a part, then, did not merely confirm how a human rights revolution had gotten underway in the previous decade, but require us to reassess the intellectual and political forces that had created it. This is the aim of Chapters 4 through 6. Exploring both why social groups did endorse the cause of Solidarity and why others did not I argue that the rise of human rights was embroiled in a broad transformation of the moral and conceptual landscape of West Europeans and Americans. At the center of that transformation was the crisis of the welfare state. Since 1945, it had come to embody Western promises of social progress and betterment to such an extent that its decline during the 1970s damaged the entire notional world that had sustained it – with its understandings of historical time and collective agency as the main casualties. As people looked past the state as an agent of social change, not nearly all of them discovered human rights as an ethical refuge from politics. Much like the Polish movement they admired, many of Solidarity's Western supporters saw human rights as a way of creating new communities and laying the foundation for a new form of politics.

Before delving into analyses of these various discourses, the present chapter is devoted to the immediate responses to martial law. It will show

The Principle of Noninterference as Laid Down   69

that human rights policies were not strongly anchored in Cold War international relations but saved by an almost accidental constellation of actors and interests. The chapter thus greatly complicates the view of how the Helsinki Accords related human rights to East–West diplomacy and puts it into the wider context of the political and intellectual history of the late twentieth century.

I

The Final Act of the CSCE, signed in Helsinki on August 1, 1975, was a milestone for the human rights breakthrough of the 1970s. Not only did it oblige its signatories to "respect human rights and fundamental freedoms," but it also infused these concerns into East–West détente and trade, two processes in which the Soviet Union was greatly interested. The meetings in which the signatories would come together to review the act's implementation, like the one in Madrid, thus created a forum where human rights violations in the Soviet bloc could be brought to the attention of the international community.[5] But just as the recent historiography has greatly complicated views of an inexorable rise of human rights so do we need to revisit simplistic stories of how the "Helsinki effect" brought human rights into Cold War international relations.

First, as we have already seen in the previous two chapters, contrary to a still widely held view, Soviet bloc dissent was not triggered by the publication of the Helsinki Final Act nor are the Polish and Czechoslovak dissidents, let alone Solidarity, aptly described as "Helsinki monitors."[6] The Moscow dissidents of the 1960s had turned to human rights in 1968, seven years before the signing of the Helsinki accords. Their example, along with other developments such as an emergent Catholic human rights discourse, provided the inspiration for

---

[5] For excellent work on the CSCE, see Snyder, *Activism*; Christian Peterson, *Globalizing Human Rights: Private Citizens, the Soviet Union, and the West* (New York: Routledge, 2011); Helmut Altrichter and Hermann Wentker, eds., *Der KSZE-Prozess: Vom Kalten Krieg zu einem neuen Europa 1975 bis 1990*, Zeitgeschichte im Gespräch (München: Oldenbourg, 2012); Wentker and Peter, eds., *KSZE*.

[6] This view especially in Thomas, *Effect*, 121–122. For the enduring influence of Thomas' work see the references to it in Jussi M. Hanhimäki, "Détente in Europe, 1962-1975," in Melvyn P. Leffler and Odd Arne Westad, eds., *The Cambridge History of the Cold War*, vol. II (Cambridge, MA: Cambridge University Press, 2010), 198–218, at 214; Olav Njølstad, "The collapse of superpower détente, 1975–1980," Matthew Evangelista, "Transnational Organizations and the Cold War," Rosemary Foot, "The Cold War and Human Rights," Melvyn P. Leffler and Odd Arne Westad, "Bibliographical Essay," all in vol. III of the *Cambridge History of the Cold War*, references to Thomas at 419, 456, 460–462, 562, 568.

70   Poland's Solidarity Movement & the Politics of Rights

independent intellectuals in Warsaw or Prague to become dissidents. If they established formal groups only after 1975, it was due primarily to domestic events – a crackdown against the musical underground in Prague and the labor unrests in Poland in 1976. A Polish Helsinki Commission was not founded until January 1980.[7] The Helsinki Agreement, to be sure, became a central text for the dissident community, but it was added to an existing body of texts that included the Universal Declaration of Human Rights and the 1966 International Covenants on Civil and Political Rights, the *Chronicle of Current Events* and *The Gulag Archipelago*, *Pacem in terris* and personalist philosophy, Hannah Arendt's *Origins of Totalitarianism* and George Orwell's *Nineteen Eighty-Four*.[8]

Second, the role of the CSCE review meetings as fora to expose human rights violations was significantly more complicated than is often believed. In 1977, to be sure, when the Polish Communist leadership discussed how to respond to KOR and ROPCiO, "Helsinki" loomed large and the CSCE review meeting beginning in Belgrade in 1977 was an important impetus for the amnesty of that year.[9] But when that review meeting took place, there was no joint Western approach, a fact the Polish Foreign Ministry seems to have realized rather quickly.[10] In fact, the American and Dutch approach of attacking the Soviet human rights record was deeply at odds with French and British foreign policy and even more so with Bonn's *Ostpolitik*.[11] Traveling to Poland in November 1977, Chancellor Helmut Schmidt made no secret of his views of Jimmy Carter's human rights approach. A Polish protocol of a confidential conversation quoted him as having said that the US president had

---

[7] "O powołaniu Komisji Helsińskiej w Polsce: Oświadczenie z dnia 17 stycznia 1980 r.," in *Dokumenty KOR*, 474–475.

[8] See Chapters 1 and 2.   [9] Brier, "Broadening."

[10] See, for instance, a memo from the Foreign Ministry for Gierek ahead of the opening of the CSCE meeting in Belgrade, which clearly documented the uneasiness of some Western states regarding Jimmy Carter's human rights campaign: Perspektywy spotkania Belgrad 77 i kierunki aktywności polskiej, not dated, AAN, PZPR, XIA/558.

[11] For a detailed study of the West German approach, see Matthias Peter, *Die Bundesrepublik im KSZE-Prozess 1975–1983: Die Umkehrung der Diplomatie* (München: Oldenbourg, 2015). On the human rights question as a source of tension in German–American relations see Klaus Wiegrefe, *Das Zerwürfnis: Helmut Schmidt, Jimmy Carter und die Krise der deutsch-amerikanischen Beziehungen* (Berlin: Propyläen, 2005), 123–154; for the former chancellor's own perspective see Helmut Schmidt, *Menschen und Mächte*, vol. II: Die Deutschen und ihre Nachbarn (Berlin: Siedler, 1990), 222–229. For French policies, see Veronika Heyde, "Nicht nur Entspannung und Menschenrechte: Die Entdeckung von Abrüstung und Rüstungskontrolle durch die französische KSZE-Politik," in Helmut Altrichter and Hermann Wentker, eds., *Der KSZE-Prozess: Vom Kalten Krieg zum neuen Europa 1975 bis 1990* (München: Oldenbourg, 2012).

The Principle of Noninterference as Laid Down 71

understood the "political mistakes connected with the dissidents and the defense of human rights."[12]

The Belgrade meeting ended in sharp disagreement and most participants viewed it as an example of how not to conduct the CSCE review process.[13] When the next conference opened in Madrid on November 11, 1980, the participating states vowed to avoid the mistakes of Belgrade. Largely, however, it took place against the backdrop of a rapid deterioration of superpower relations and of the events in Poland. The creation of Solidarity two months before had made world news, exerting a tremendous fascination on international observers and especially on Western labor activists. Solidarity's logo and the face of Lech Wałęsa became international symbols of nonviolent resistance, and trips by Polish delegations to France and Italy turned almost into state visits.[14]

But many Western observers were also worried about international repercussions at a time when superpower détente had all but collapsed. Following the Soviet invasion of Afghanistan, a Warsaw Pact intervention in Poland threatened to have unforeseeable consequences for international stability. The Polish crisis, as this period came to be known outside of Poland, hung like a cloud over deliberations in Madrid and dominated the foreign policy and security agenda of the Western alliance. Notably, though, explicit concerns that the Helsinki Final Act's human rights provisions might be violated played no discernible role in Western discussions. The act's principle that did feature prominently in debates was not no. VII, "respect for human rights and fundamental freedoms," but no. VI "non-intervention in internal affairs."

In December 1980, NATO had discussed possible sanctions against Warsaw should the Polish government itself use force against Solidarity.[15] Yet subsequent talks were dominated by the question of

---

[12] Informacja o wizycie Kanclerza Federalnego RFN - H. Schmidta w Polsce, w dniach 21–25 listopada 1977 r., dated Dec. 2, 1977, AAN, KC PZPR, XI/507.

[13] Peter, *Bundesrepublik*, 314–318.

[14] Generally on Western responses to the rise of Solidarity see Marcin Frybes, "Społeczne reakcje Zachodu na fenomen 'Solidarności' i rola emigracyjnych struktur związku 1980-1989," in Łukasz Kamiński and Grzegorz Waligór, eds., *NSZZ Solidarność 1980-1989*, vol. 2: Ruch społeczny (Warszawa: IPN, 2010); Patryk Pleskot, *Kłopotliwa Panna "S": Postawy polityczne Zachodu wobec Solidarności na tle stosunków z PRL 1980-1989* (Warszawa: IPN, 2013); Paweł Jaworski and Łukasz Kamiński, eds., *Świat wobec Solidarności 1980-1989* (Warszawa: IPN, 2014); for Western trade unions see Idesbald Goddeeris, ed., *Solidarity with Solidarity: Western European Trade Unions and the Polish Crisis, 1980-1982* (Lanham: Lexington, 2010). For the visit in Italy see Emilio Gabaglio, "Włoskie syndykaty a Solidarność,'" *Więź* 36 (May 1993), 5.

[15] Memorandum from G.G.H Walden for the Prime Minister, "Poland: Contingency Planning," dated Dec. 3, 1980, The National Archives, London (hereafter: TNA), Prime Minister's Office Records (hereafter: PREM), 19/559.

how to respond to a Soviet invasion. The alliance's overarching aim, NATO's Acting General Secretary wrote in March 1981, was to prevent external interference in Poland, describing this as violating "the principles of international law" especially "those contained in the UN Charter and the Helsinki Final Act." Primarily, this policy was meant to deter a Soviet invasion, an eventuality which was discussed exclusively as a fatal threat to détente and Western interests, not as a possible violation of human rights. Nonintervention, moreover, cut both ways. There should be "no intervention by any country," the Acting General Secretary's memo said, adding that the "Allies have no intention of intervening."[16] French and British representatives at NATO insisted on the "fundamental difference" between Solidarity's external repression as a result of a Soviet intervention and internal actions by the Polish government. The latter, they urged, required a measured response among others because condemning internal repression could "lay the West open to charges of interference in Polish internal affairs."[17]

When martial law was imposed, NATO's first statement, issued on December 14, 1981, did invoke the Helsinki Final Act, yet not to remind Warsaw of its human rights obligations, but to demand from all states involved – the Soviet Union and the West – a policy of strict noninterference.[18] A draft of the statement had been submitted by the West Germans, but its wording had been consulted with the United States, Britain, and France.[19] The German representative in the NATO council, moreover, demanded "a rapid but business-like conclusion" of the CSCE conference in Madrid, in spite of events in Poland, two days later even saying that "it would be a mistake to tie decisions to be taken

---

[16] Memorandum from the General Secretary to the Permanent Representatives, Studying Possible Measures on the Situation in Poland, dated Mar. 16, 1981, NATO Archives, Documents Related to Events in Poland (1980-1984), International Staff, available at www.nato.int/cps/en/natolive/81233.htm (accessed June 2016). Hereafter cited as NATO, Poland.

[17] Cable from UKDEL NATO to FCO, "Poland," dated Mar. 27, 1982, TNA, PREM 19/560. The British Foreign Secretary Lord Carrington drew that same distinction in internal debates. See Memorandum from Lord Carrington for the Prime Minister, "Contingency Planning about Poland," dated Mar. 9, 1981, TNA, PREM 19/560.

[18] Quoted in Leonard Downie, "NATO Officials Express 'Concern' Over Poland," *Washington Post*, Dec. 15, 1984.

[19] Summary record of a restricted meeting of the Council on December 14, 1981 on the declaration of martial law, dated Dec. 22 , 1981, West German position on 7, 16, French and British on 10 and 13 respectively, NATO, Poland, Private Records. On NATO Consultations of the statement see "Aufzeichnung des Ministerialdirektors Pfeffer," dated Dec. 13, 1981, AAPD, 1981/III, Dok. 366, 1968–1972, on 1969–1970.

The Principle of Noninterference as Laid Down   73

[in Madrid] with developments in Poland."[20] Again, Bonn merely expressed a West European consensus. On December 15, the foreign ministers of the European Community (EC) demanded a policy of strict nonintervention and a continuation of the CSCE meeting in Madrid.[21] Two days later, Willy Brandt, the towering moral figure of West German social democracy, issued a statement in his function as President of the Socialist International. Cleared beforehand with the French socialists, the statement reminded "all states concerned that they are bound by the principle of non-interference as laid down in the Helsinki-Final Act." It warned that "unwanted advice of strongly worded declarations will not help the people of Poland" and insisted that only "the restraint and the will for cooperation of those wanting peace constitutes effective assistance."[22]

Citing the Helsinki Final Act's noninterference clause, in sum, major West European players were willing to go ahead with the CSCE despite repression in Poland. To be sure, NATO had been invoking noninterference since the beginning of the Polish crisis to discourage a Soviet intervention in Poland. But given how much the CSCE is nowadays seen as a human rights document, it is striking that human rights aspects seemed to have played no role in the discussions of a Western alliance which continued to insist on noninterference even after Warsaw had, as Matthias Peter writes, "violated the Helsinki Final Act in every conceivable way."[23]

II

Within less than 10 days of the imposition of martial law, positions within NATO changed dramatically. Already on December 22, London had made a demarche to the Polish government on behalf of the EC whose

---

[20] Meeting of the Council on December 14, 1981, quote on 16; Summary record of a restricted meeting of the Council on December 16, 1981, on the situation in Poland, dated Jan. 7, 1982, quotation on 8, NATO, Poland, Private Records.

[21] "Europeans Take Low Profile on Poland," *Boston Globe*, Dec. 16, 1981. For a statement by the British government similarly demanding strict non-intervention see "Poland," dated Dec. 14, 1981, TNA, PREM 19/871.

[22] Socialist International Press Release No. 31/81, "Socialist International Statement on Poland," dated Dec. 17, 1981, quote on 8, Archiv der sozialen Demokratie (hereafter; AdsD), Willy-Brandt-Archiv (hereafter: WBA), A13, Mappe 72. For German–French consultations preceding it, see Bernd Rother, "Zwischen Solidarität und Friedenssicherung: Willy Brandt und Polen in den 1980er Jahren," in Friedhelm Boll and Krzysztof Ruchniewicz, eds., *"Nie mehr eine Politik über Polen hinweg": Willy Brandt und Polen* (Bonn: J.H.W. Dietz, 2010), 228.

[23] Peter, *Bundesrepublik*, 478, for the origins of NATO's policy of nonintervention see ibid., 401–414.

74 Poland's Solidarity Movement & the Politics of Rights

rotating presidency it held at the time. It denounced "the grave violations of the human and civil rights of the Polish people" and condemned repression in Poland as a "clear violation of the fundamental principles of [the Helsinki Final Act]." At a restricted meeting of the North Atlantic Council, Britain's permanent representative recommended that NATO embassies should be instructed to characterize martial law as "highly relevant to the Madrid conference" and a "violation of the Final Act of unprecedented magnitude." The French and the Italians agreed that the Madrid conference could not conduct business as usual. Rome even went so far as to say that, within the Helsinki process, events in Poland had ceased to be an internal affair.[24]

Brandt's office, meanwhile, was flooded with protest notes from the Socialist International's European and American members. Dutch and Italian socialists charged that the magnitude of events in Poland called for unambiguous condemnation.[25] France's ruling Socialist party even insisted on convening an emergency meeting of the Socialist International's presidium – a clear rebuke of Brandt's stance.[26] Held a couple of days later, the meeting pitted the French, Italian, and Portuguese socialists against the West German, British, Austrian, and Dutch representatives, with the French and Italians demanding to use Warsaw's foreign debt to pressure the Polish government into honoring human rights.[27]

The abruptness of this change is best illustrated by the fact that as late as December 22, on the day of the British demarche to Warsaw, NATO General Secretary Joseph Luns told US envoy Lawrence Eagleburger that there was little hope for a more forceful position within the alliance

---

[24] Summary Record of a Restricted Meeting of the Council held on Wednesday, December 23, 1981 at 10.15 am, dated Jan. 4, 1981, demarche cited on 3, NATO, Poland, Private Records.

[25] Hans-Eberhard Dingels, "Äußerungen der italienischen Parteiführer Craxi und Longo zur Erklärung des SI-Präsidenten," Vermerk, 22.12.1981, Cable from Max van den Berg and Maarten van Traa to Willy Brandt, Dec. 21, 1981, both in AdsD, WBA, A13, Mappe 100A.

[26] Telex from Bernt Carlsson to Willy Brandt, dated Dec. 18, 1981, AdsD, WBA, A13, Mappe 71.

[27] "Auch der Papst," *Der Spiegel*, January 4, 1982. The content of the discussion seems to have been deliberately leaked to the press. In a letter, Brandt's secretary at the Socialist Internationale, Bent Carlsson, noted how well the cited article reflected the actual discussion. Letter from Bernt Carlsson to Willy Brandt, dated Jan. 25, 1982, AdsD, WBA, A13, Mappe 68B, fol. 206. The Italian Socialists also used the forum of the European parliament to attack the SPD's stance on Poland. See Jiri Pelikan, "Considerations soumises à l'attention des membres à l'occasion de la discussion du groupe socialiste sur la situation en Pologne apres le 13 decembre 1981," AdsD, WBA, A10.2, Mappe 30; Vermerk von Andreas Zobel für W.B., dated Feb. 16, 1982, AdsD, WBA, A10.2, Mappe 30.

The Principle of Noninterference as Laid Down   75

toward Poland.[28] Two factors had brought these changes about – American policies and the public reaction to martial law, especially in Italy and France.

III

In assessing the position of the US government, it is important to note that Reagan initially had had little use for his predecessors' human rights policies. In autumn 1981, he had appointed Ernest Lefever to run the State Department's human rights bureau – a man who had publicly demanded to abolish this very bureau, a legacy of Carter's human rights policies. When Reagan failed to get Lefever through appointment hearings of a committee dominated by Republicans, it seems to have dawned on him that he could not simply do away with Carter's legacy.[29]

What Reagan did in response was to staff human rights positions almost exclusively with intellectuals and politicians belonging to the so-called "Jackson Democrats," a group of fierce Cold War hawks whose nickname derived from their close association with Senator Henry "Scoop" Jackson. During the 1970s, these intellectuals and activists had been one of the two groups who had turned "human rights" into a staple of American foreign policy discourse. Primarily, though, this championship for human rights was, as Barbara Keys aptly wrote, an attempt to "reclaim American virtue." Following the disgrace of Vietnam and Watergate, they came to see human rights as a means to reinforce the political differences between East and West and recreate confidence in America's essential "goodness."[30]

---

[28] Memorandum for the File, "Poland," dated Dec. 22, 1981, NATO, Poland, Private Records.

[29] Sarah Snyder, "The Defeat of Ernest Lefever's Nomination: Keeping Human Rights on the United States Foreign Policy Agenda," in Bevan Sewell and Scott Lucas, eds., *Challenging US Foreign Policy: America and the World in the Long Twentieth Century* (Basingstoke: Palgrave, 2013).

[30] Keys, *Virtue.* On the Jackson Democrats see Justin Vaïsse, *Neoconservatism: The Biography of a Movement* (Cambridge, MA: Harvard University Press, 2010), 81–148; for their role in the human rights breakthrough of the 1970s see Keys, *Virtue*, 103–126; Carl J. Bon Tempo, "From the Center-Right: Freedom House and Human Rights in the 1970s and 1980s," in Akira Iriye et al., eds., *The Human Rights Revolution: An International History* (Oxford, New York: Oxford University Press, 2012); Thomas J. W. Probert, "The Innovation of the Jackson–Vanik Amendment," in Brendan Simms and D. J. B. Trim, eds., *Humanitarian Intervention: A History* (Cambridge et al.: Cambridge University Press, 2011). By 1982, the following human rights related positions had been staffed with Jackson Democrats: the political scientist Jeane Kirkpatrick was US Ambassador at the UN in New York; Max Kampelman was the head of the American delegation at the CSCE in Madrid; Elliot Abrams was head of the

76   Poland's Solidarity Movement & the Politics of Rights

In the writings of the Jackson Democrats, we thus encounter a human rights discourse made of wholly different cloth than Amnesty International's culture of compassion and bipartisanship. In 1977, Daniel Patrick Moynihan, an intellectual darling of the Jackson Democrats, complained that the State Department treated human rights "as a special kind of international social work," while in his view, human rights were primarily a *political* issue. The gravest threat to human rights in the world, he wrote, was Soviet totalitarianism; the safest guarantees for human rights was – for all its flaws and mistakes – the political system of the United States. Human rights were thus political, in Moynihan's view, because they were part of the political struggle with Communism.[31]

A symposium on "Human Rights and American Foreign Policy," published four years later in *Commentary*, a major publication outlet of the Jackson Democrats, struck a tone very similar to that in Moynihan's article. Many people in America, Midge Decter complained, failed to see what human rights were – another way of stating American Cold War objectives. "If we mean [by rights] the possibility for ordinary people to think and lead their daily lives ... as they choose ... – in itself a dream still beyond the reach of billions of people – then ensuring the strength and success of the United States of America *is* a human-rights policy."[32]

State Department's human rights bureau; Michael Novak was US Ambassador at the United Nations Commission on Human Rights (UNCHR). In 1983, Carl Gershman became president of the National Endowment for Democracy. For Kirkpatrick, see Cathal J. Nolan, "Jeane Jordan Kirkpatrick," in Cathal J. Nolan, ed., *Notable U.S. Ambassadors Since 1775: A Biographical Dictionary* (Westport, CT: Greenwood Press, 1997). On Kampelman's role at the CSCE, see Snyder, "CSCE and the Atlantic Alliance." For his and Abrams' political views and role among the Jackson Democrats see Vaïsse, *Neoconservatism*, 87-89, passim on 121–127; on Abrams, see also the contemporaneous discussion in Judith Miller, "A Neoconservative for Human Rights Post," *New York Times*, Oct. 31, 1981. Novak was a Catholic theologian whom Kirkpatrick had asked "to go put forth our theory of human rights and democracy" in Geneva. See Michael Novak, *Writing from Left to Right: My Journey from Liberal to Conservative* (New York: Image, 2013), 213. In the 1980s, he made a name for himself by defending Reagan's defense policies against criticism from the Catholic bishops. Patrick Allitt, *Catholic Intellectuals and Conservative Politics in America, 1950-1985* (Ithaca, NY; London: Cornell University Press, 1993), 288–297. Gershman was executive director of Social Democrats, USA, a minuscule party to which many of the younger Jackson Democrats belonged. Vaïsse, *Neoconservatism*, 71–72, 91, 192; William King, "Neoconservatives and 'Trotskyism'," *American Communist History* 3 (2004), 2, 256–257; for his views on East–West relations, see Carl Gershman, "Left Illusions Promote Soviet Terror," *New America* 17 (Oct. 1980), 9.

[31] Daniel P. Moynihan, "The Politics of Human Rights," *Commentary* 64 (July 1977).

[32] William Barrett et al., "Human Rights and American Foreign Policy: A Symposium," *Commentary* 55 (Nov. 1981), 33; on Decter and her husband Norman Podhoretz, see Alan M. Wald, *The New York Intellectuals : The Rise and Decline of the Anti-Stalinist Left from the 1930s to the 1980s* (Chapel Hill, NC: University of North Carolina Press, 1987); on the Jackson Democrats' view of human rights, see also the views of the US

The Principle of Noninterference as Laid Down   77

While the ideas espoused by the Jackson Democrats provided ample reasons to condemn the suppression of Solidarity, it is central to note that they provided few grounds to believe that the dissidents' human rights activism stood a realistic chance of transforming the Cold War. Central to the approach of the Jackson Democrats was an analytical distinction which had been made most famously by Jeane Kirkpatrick, an intellectual standard bearer of the Jackson Democrats with a permanent seat in the NSC during Reagan's first term. In her article "Dictatorships and Double Standards," published in 1979, Kirkpatrick had drawn a distinction between right-wing autocracies, such as those in El Salvador and Guatemala, and the totalitarian regimes of the Soviet bloc. Whereas the former did "sometimes evolve into democracies," Kirkpatrick claimed, "the history of this century provides no grounds for expecting that radical totalitarian regimes will transform themselves." Whereas the former left traditional social structures intact and tolerated "limited contestation and participation," the latter destroyed them completely.[33]

From this perspective, then, Solidarity – an independent mass movement in a totalitarian society – should never have happened. At the height of the Polish crisis, many Jackson Democrats were thus highly skeptical of Solidarity's chances to succeed. Echoing Kirkpatrick's distinction, Bayard Rustin wrote in *Commentary*'s human rights symposium that "... while undemocratic allies of the United States have succeeded in democratizing, no similar examples exist in the Soviet bloc. And while Poland may well be a watershed, the gains made by Solidarity are anything but secure."[34] Norman Podhoretz, the editor of *Commentary* and a powerful voice among the Jackson Democrats, rejected the idea that Western economic leverage could be used for US human rights policies vis-à-vis Poland, calling this idea "a fantasy" flying in the face of how he believed totalitarian systems operated.[35]

Ambassador to the UN and her assistant Jeane J. Kirkpatrick, "Human Rights and the Foundations of Democracy," *World Affairs* 144 (1981), 3; Jeane J. Kirkpatrick, "Establishing a Viable Human Rights Policy," *World Affairs* 170 (2007), 2; Carl Gershman, "Human Rights in Chile," *World Affairs* 144 (1981), 3; Carl Gershman, "The New Totalitarianism: Soviet Oppression," *World Affairs* 144 (1981), 3; for a discussion, see Christopher Bright, "Neither Dictatorships nor Double Standards: The Reagan Administration's Approach to Human Rights," *World Affairs* 153 (Fall 1990), 2.

[33] Jeane J. Kirkpatrick, "Dictatorships and Double Standards," *Commentary* 68 (Nov. 1979), 37 and 44.

[34] Barrett et al., "Human Rights," 45, 62. Rustin was National Co-Chairman of Social Democrats, USA, a member of the Socialist International. He was among the first to strenuously criticize Brandt's statement on the Polish crisis. Cable from Bayard Rustin to Willy Brandt, dated Dec. 21, 1981, AdsD, WBA, A13, 100A.

[35] Tom Kahn and Norman Podhoretz, "How to Support Solidarnosc: A Debate," *Democratiya* 13 (Summer 2008), 241, 259.

When martial law came, many of these writers and policy makers demanded that the United States put repression in Poland into the international spotlight. In the National Security Council, Kirkpatrick asked for daily symbolic affirmations "about the loss of freedom in Poland," a letter to Brezhnev setting "this event in history," and even a possible suspension of the Helsinki Accords of 1975. Tellingly, though, these propositions were directed as much inward as outward. "One of our objectives is to prevent our own demoralization by inactivity," Kirkpatrick said. "It made me ill this morning to read a Post article on Afghanistan where the Afghans are still fighting Soviet tanks with ancient rifles."[36]

When the US Information Agency discussed "the U.S. position on the Polish crisis and identify ways of expressing that position internationally," Allen Weinstein, editor of the *Washington Quarterly*, urged the government to undertake "ruthless politics of symbolism and moral gestures [...] to prevent the Polish repression from becoming an accepted fact of global politics" and to reaffirm NATO as an alliance based on shared values. But here, too, such suggestions had as much to do with domestic debates as with foreign policy. In that same debate, Michael Novak argued that "creating a moral wave [over the Polish crisis] would not be an idle exercise because church and activist organizations are planning peace, disarmament, and El Salvador campaigns for next summer." Other participants of the debate drew up a list of suggestions ranging from soliciting a series of op-ed articles in major journals to convening an American-European summit on Newfoundland as the place where Franklin Roosevelt and Winston Churchill had signed the Atlantic Charta.[37]

But however bombastically the Jackson Democrats wanted to expose repression in Poland, there was also almost a common sense of relief in their comments when Solidarity was suppressed and thus an "anomaly" to their worldview had been removed. Walter Laqueur, an eminent neoconservative intellectual, wrote in March 1982 in *Commentary* that the Polish crisis' main lesson was that peaceful change was impossible in the Soviet bloc and that it was thus pointless to try to support it.[38] If

---

[36] Minutes, National Security Council Meeting, Dec. 21, 1981, Ronald Reagan Presidential Library (hereafter: RRPL), White House Staff Member and Office Files, Executive Secretariat, NSC: Meeting files (hereafter: Exec. Sec., NSC: Meeting files), NSC00033, at 12.

[37] Memorandum of Meeting, "U.S. Response to Polish Crisis," Dec. 22, 1981, National Security Archives (hereafter: NSA), Soviet Flashpoints: Poland 1980-82, box 26, quotations on 1 and 4–6.

[38] Walter Z. Laqueur, "What Poland Means," *Commentary* 73 (March 1982), 27, 30. For Laqueur's importance for the Jackson Democrats see John Ehrman, *The Rise of*

The Principle of Noninterference as Laid Down 79

martial law had taught anything, Charles Krauthammer reasoned in February 1982, it was that the belief in the power of social movements to change the conflict between East and West expressed an American "habit of failing to imagine the world as it is."[39]

However much the Jackson Democrats may have lionized the cause of the dissidents and Solidarity, then, it seems that they saw them primarily as witnesses to the totalitarian, and thus unchangeable character, of Communism, not as movements who stood a chance of changing the world of the Cold War. Crucially, many of them did not demand that the Reagan administration aggressively use the CSCE conference in Madrid to expose Polish human rights violations, but that the United States pulled out of the Helsinki process altogether.[40] For them, in other words, the Polish crisis had demonstrated the futility of trying to transform the Soviet bloc through a policy of supporting human rights.

It is important not to overstate the influence of the Jackson Democrats on a president who was as much an anti-Communist hardliner as an opponent of nuclear weapons and whose administration was notorious for the conflicts between its departments and agencies.[41] Significantly, though, those parts of Reagan's governments that dealt explicitly with human rights were staffed with people who saw them as little else than a reformulation of US Cold War objectives and who had much admiration for Soviet bloc dissidents but apparently little hope that their activism would make much of a political difference.

As a result, Jacksonite views were by and large adopted as official US human rights policy under Reagan. In a memo from November 1981, approved by Secretary of State Alexander Haig and leaked to the *New York Times*, the new head of the State Department's human rights bureau, Elliot Abrams, sketched a policy that would put human rights at the very center of American foreign policy.[42] This, the memo conceded, meant "trouble." The United States would have to insist that its

---

Neoconservatism: Intellectuals and Foreign Affairs, 1945-1994 (New Haven: Yale University Press, 1995), 50–57.

[39] Charles Krauthammer, "A Panglossian Warsaw," *The New Republic*, Feb. 10, 1982.

[40] Kirkpatrick in NSC minutes from Dec. 21, 1981; Letter from Midge Decter to Lane Kirkland, dated Jan. 4, 1982, AFL-CIO Unprocessed Records, International Affairs Department, Folder "Solidarność 1982 #2"; Norman Podhoretz, "The Neo-Conservative Anguish Over Reagan's Foreign Policy," *New York Times Magazine*, May 2, 1982.

[41] For a fine recent study on the internal conflicts and chaos in the early days of the Reagan administration, see James Graham Wilson, *The Triumph of Improvisation: Gorbachev's Adaptability, Reagan's Engagement, and the End of the Cold War* (Ithaca, NY: Cornell University Press, 2014).

[42] Miller, "Neoconservative."

80 Poland's Solidarity Movement & the Politics of Rights

Latin American allies improve their human rights record – a policy many Jackson Democrats had rejected as aiding the perceived allies of the Soviets in the region. At bottom, though, the memo articulated the Jackson Democrats' understanding of human rights. "Human rights" meant "political rights and civil liberties"; the memo even recommended "mov[ing] [gradually] away from 'human rights' as a term, and begin to speak of 'individual rights,' 'political rights' and 'civil liberties.'" As such, human rights conveyed what was "at issue in our conflict with the Soviet bloc." Human rights policies were meant to augment the necessary "military response to the Soviets" with an "ideological responses," a "battle of ideas" – a key idea of Jacksonite political thought. "We desire to demonstrate, by acting to defend liberty and identifying its enemies, that the difference between East and West is the crucial political distinction of our times."[43]

Reagan's clearest endorsement of Jacksonite ideas came in a speech he gave in June 1982 in London. The East–West conflict, he said drawing on a core idea of the Jackson Democrats, was a struggle whose "ultimate determinant ... will not be bombs and rockets, but a test of wills and ideas, a trial of spiritual resolve, the values we hold, the beliefs we cherish, the ideals to which we are dedicated."[44] The best way to both win this battle of ideas and promote human rights, he went on, was to aggressively promote the institutions of constitutional democracy. "We must be staunch in our conviction," Reagan insisted, "that freedom is not the sole prerogative of a lucky few, but the inalienable and universal right of all human beings. So states the United Nations Universal Declaration of Human Rights, which, among other things, guarantees free elections." The West's objective, Reagan went on, was "quite simple to state: to foster the infrastructure of democracy" – the system of political, legal, and civil institutions that sustained a democracy.[45]

In two statements in December 1982, one calling upon Americans to observe a Day of Prayer and Solidarity with the Polish People and the other on the occasion of Human Rights Day, Reagan also endorsed Kirkpatrick's distinction between totalitarian and authoritarian regimes. The statements were meant to reiterate the core idea of the Westminster speech of a "necessary link between human rights and constitutional

---

[43] "Excerpts from State Department Memo on Human Rights," *New York Times*, Nov. 5, 1981.

[44] Ronald Reagan, "Address to the Members of British Parliament, Westminster, June 8, 1982," *The Public Papers of President Ronald Wilson Reagan*, available at www.reagan.utexas.edu/archives/speeches/1982/60882a.htm (accessed April 2017).

[45] Reagan, "Address to British Parliament."

The Principle of Noninterference as Laid Down 81

democracy."[46] The State Department had insisted on this formulation to reinforce the message of Westminster that "democracy is the key to human rights." State explained the wider significance of this approach: The "concern for the long-term growth of democracy will take off some of the pressure to overreact to short-term human rights problems in El Salvador and Guatemala."[47]

Unsurprisingly, then, the Reagan administration's first response to martial law was not to hold Warsaw accountable for violating the Helsinki Final Act but to call upon the Western alliance to completely revise its relations with the Warsaw Pact.[48] Fixated on the likelihood of a Soviet invasion, Washington had initially been unsure as to how best to respond to events in Poland. Regaining its posture, the US administration quickly came to understand the Polish crisis as an opportunity to "assum[e] US leadership of the Western world in this very serious situation and explicitly stak[e] out the high moral ground for the United States and the Western world in supporting the democratic forces in Poland," as an internal memo put it.[49] This approach was very much in line with Reagan's personal convictions. He had been outraged by news of Solidarity's suppression and was exasperated by the timidity of whom he called "those 'chicken littles' in Europe."[50]

Over the following weeks and months, Reagan strongly endorsed Solidarity and lambasted the Polish government under General Wojciech Jaruzelski. Importantly, though, this approach had little to do with holding Warsaw accountable for violating the human rights provisions of the Helsinki Final Act and much more with Reagan's belief that the Soviets had consistently violated a CSCE process for which he had never had much use anyway. It made no difference, the White House argued, whether Solidarity had been suppressed by the Soviets or its own military. Jaruzelski was but a "Russian general in Polish uniform," as Secretary of Defense Caspar Weinberger put it in the National Security Council on December 21, 1981. Reagan asked whether the United States could afford "not to go all out? I'm talking about a total quarantine on

---

[46] Ronald Reagan, "Proclamation 5003 – Bill of Rights Day, Human Rights Day and Week, 1982, December 10, 1982," *The Public Papers of President Ronald Wilson Reagan.*

[47] Memorandum, L. Paul Bremer, III to Craig Fuller, "Bill of Rights Day/Human Rights Day Proclamation," Nov. 29, 1982, RRPL, White House Staff Member and Office Files, Anthony Dolan Files, Box 17, Human Rights in Poland – 12/10/1982 (3).

[48] For detailed and impressively documented study of Reagan's policies toward Poland, see Domber, *Revolution.*

[49] Memorandum from James W. Nance for Ronald Reagan, "Poland," dated Dec. 21, 1981, RRPL, Exec. Sec., NSC: Meeting files, NSC00033.

[50] Minutes, National Security Council Meeting, Dec. 22, 1981, RRPL, Exec. Sec., NSC: Meeting files, NSC00033.

the Soviet Union. No détente! We know – and the world knows – that they are behind this."[51] When the NSC discussed punitive measures against Moscow and Warsaw on the following day he preferred to "seek to isolate the USSR economically" and asked whether Washington should "declare Helsinki null and void."[52]

Haig advised against this, citing possible repercussions in NATO. Yet he toed the line of blaming Moscow for events in Poland and signaled to the allies that their reluctance might jeopardize the Helsinki process. Addressing the ambassadors of the EC-10 on December 28, he said he was "appalled" that some people believed Solidarity's alleged irrationality was to blame for the Polish crisis – the culprit, he said, was the Soviet Union.[53] Two days later at a meeting of the North Atlantic Council, he called upon the West Europeans to call an emergency session of the CSCE to discuss the Polish situation. The reasons were telling: Haig "had no illusion that the East would agree to this proposal," the minutes of the meeting stated. "But this would demonstrate that it was not possible to use the Helsinki process for its stated purposes." Calling for a session at the CSCE, in other words, was meant to demonstrate its uselessness.[54]

IV

Quickly, then, the West Europeans' approach of noninterference in Poland came up against Reagan's hardline stance, dictated by his and his advisors opposition to détente. At the same time, their position was also met with at times severe criticism from within their own societies. This section is devoted to discussing these social responses to Solidarity's repression in West Europe.

There were, it has to be noted, significant differences between the responses of West European societies to events in Poland. Among those West Europeans who were already deeply concerned about the collapse of superpower détente, the possible international repercussions of a Soviet invasion had created massive anxieties. This was especially true

---

[51] Minutes of NSC meeting from Dec. 21, 1981.

[52] Minutes of NSC meeting from Dec. 22, 1981.

[53] "Gesandter Dannebring, Washington, an Bundesminister Genscher," Dec. 28, 1981, AAPD, 1981, III, Nr. 390, 2061–2065, at 2062.

[54] Summary record of a restricted meeting of the Council on December 30, 1981, dated Jan. 18, 1982, on 6, NATO, Poland, Private Records. US embassies in NATO capitals were instructed to approach their host governments to support such an emergency meeting. Cable from Secstate to all NATO capitals, "CSCE: Emergency Meeting on Poland," dated Dec. 29, 1981, NSA, Soviet Flashpoints: Poland 1980–82, Box 26.

The Principle of Noninterference as Laid Down 83

for West Germany where a peace movement had emerged which had repeatedly managed to mobilize hundreds of thousands of protesters against the looming deployment of new nuclear missiles in Western Europe. Many of the activists in the movement were sympathetic to the plight of Solidarity and Polish emigres were invited to speak at the peace movement's meetings. West Germany, moreover, witnessed a massive outpouring of humanitarian aid for Polish society.[55] Yet overwhelmingly, this sympathy was politically toothless. Support for human rights in Eastern Europe, Polish exiles were told, threatened to trigger a political "landslide" in Central Europe, exacerbating an already tense international situation; others feared that by supporting Solidarity they would buy into American anti-Communism and jeopardize the peace movement's united front against the deployment of new nuclear missiles.[56]

In France, in stark contrast, Polish emigres could ride an almost flamboyant wave of support. On December 13, 1981, the morning that news of martial law broke, a demonstration of a few hundred protesters was held in front of the Polish embassy in Paris.[57] On the next day, the French capital witnessed a protest march of between 50,000 and 100,000 joined by representatives of all major political parties except the Communists, of all trade unions except the Communist-dominated one, and of social and political groups ranging from Gaullists to Trotskyites, from Catholics to anarchists. On the same day, trade unions, social groups of all stripes, and parties ranging from the extreme left to the far right organized meetings all over France bringing the total number of protesters close to 200,000.[58] Responses in Italy were less extravagant but here, too, a bipartisan coalition of political parties and social groups insisted that repression in Poland demanded a forceful Western response.

What is most striking about these social responses to Solidarity's repression is how the fault lines crisscrossed traditional camps and geographical boundaries. The Italian protests, spearheaded by the country's trade unions, included the powerful Italian Communist Party whose

---

[55] "Polen-Hilfe: Eine echte Volksbewegung," *Der Spiegel*, June 7, 1982.

[56] Heinrich Albertz, "Es gibt nichts Wichtigeres als den Frieden: Ein Interview," in Heinrich Böll et al., eds., *Verantwortlich für Polen?* (Reinbek bei Hamburg: Rowohlt, 1982). Memo from Jo Leinen for Petra Kelly "Polen und die Friedensbewegung," dated Jan. 30, 1982, AGG, PKA, 3450.

[57] *De Solidarność à l'entrée de la Pologne dans l'Union europénne: Un engagement citoyen* (Paris: Association Solidarité France-Pologne, 2008), 23–24.

[58] Bilan des manifestations qui se sont déroulées le 14 décembre 1981, not dated, and Les manifestations de soutien aux syndicalistes polonaises, Mar. 15, 1982, both in Archives du secretariat confédéral de la CFDT (hereafter: CFDT), Secteur International (hereafter: Sect. Int.), 8 H 1920.

84   Poland's Solidarity Movement & the Politics of Rights

chairman Enrico Berlinguer all but broke with Moscow after the Polish crisis, announcing that "the progressive force of the October Revolution had been exhausted."[59] Tellingly, however, Willy Brandt urged Berlinguer not to sever his ties with Moscow.[60] West European responses to martial in Poland, then, pitted Berlinguer and Reagan against Brandt and, at least initially, Margaret Thatcher. Many of those who spoke out against oppression in Poland, moreover, used the moral vernacular of human rights but did so in conjunction with larger social and political projects. The Jackson Democrats were one such group, others were trade unionists and the Italian Eurocommunists. Even some West German peace activists, especially from the Green party, led by their charismatic figurehead Petra Kelly, spoke out against human rights violations but did so within a quasi-utopian vision in which continent-wide social movements would dissolve the military blocks and build societies without violence.[61]

In fact, these larger social and political projects associated with human rights at times appeared to be more important to activists than actual events in Poland. Endorsing Solidarity, Reagan simultaneously claimed the Polish movement as his political ally. In his Westminster speech, he insisted that Poland was part of a family of democratic nations. In an artful sentence, Reagan combined this kinship metaphor with his understanding of human rights to produce an appeal for the West to be vigilant. "Poland's struggle to be Poland and to secure the basic rights we often take for granted demonstrates why we dare not take those rights for granted." In fighting for human rights, he implied, Solidarity did not fight for a specific political program or social system – it fought for Poland to be what it "really" was: a member of the Western family of free nations.[62] Solidarity, in Reagan's view, was a combatant of the Cold

---

[59] Jacques Lévesque, "Italian Communists versus the Soviet Union: The PCI Charts a New Foreign Policy," *Policy Papers in International Affairs*, Paper #34 (1987), Institute of International Studies, University of California, Berkeley.

[60] Problematyka polska na spotkaniu E. Berlinguera z W. Brandtem, dated 25 Jan. 1982, Archiwum Instytutu Pamięci Narodowej (hereafter: AIPN), BU 1585/3874/CD/2, 64–65.

[61] Gert Bastian et al., "Wo steht die Friedensbewegung? Erfahrungen, Probleme und nächste Aufgaben im Kampf gegen die atomare Bedrohung," *Blätter für deutsche und internationale Politik* 27 (July 1982), 7, 792–793; on Kelly and her party, see Saskia Richter, *Die Aktivistin: Das Leben der Petra Kelly* (München: DVA, 2010); Ruth A. Bevan, "Petra Kelly: The Other Green," *New Political Science* 23 (2001), 2; Stephen Milder, "Thinking Globally, Acting (Trans-)Locally: Petra Kelly and the Transnational Roots of West German Green Politics," *Central European History* 43 (2010), 02; Silke Mende, *"Nicht rechts, nicht links, sondern vorn": Eine Geschichte der Gründungsgrünen* (München: Oldenbourg, 2011).

[62] Reagan, "Address to the Members of British Parliament."

The Principle of Noninterference as Laid Down 85

War – a Commando unit, as it were, fighting the "war of ideas" behind enemy lines.

It was this view of events in Poland, which Reagan had sketched many times before the Westminster speech, that an activist of the West German Green party zeroed in on when he called upon his fellow activists to attend a pro-Solidarity rally. Attendance was important not only to show support for the Polish people, he wrote, but also to expose the American hypocrisy of displaying outrage over events in Poland while openly or covertly supporting military dictatorships elsewhere in the world.[63]

A few days later, a similar event to the demonstration in West Germany took place in the United States when such intellectual and artistic luminaries of the American Left as Gore Vidal, Susan Sontag, Pete Seeger, Allen Ginsberg, E. L. Doctorow, and Kurt Vonnegut joined El Salvadorian human rights activists and representatives of the left wing of the American labor movement for a solidarity event with Solidarity in the New York City Town Hall. The evening's aim was, its organizer said, "above all, to deny the cold warriors the support of a workers' mass movement in Poland, which they would be the first to crush in the US, just as their clients are doing in Turkey and El Salvador."[64] Some had even hoped that the "Evening for Solidarity" in New York might be a "harbinger, an intimation event, for the development of a left program in the US, distinct from the tumbrils of the Democratic Party lurching towards 1984."[65] What happened instead was that Susan Sontag told the audience that martial law should be an occasion for the American Left to examine its past allegiances with Communism, initiating a major row among New York intellectuals. In West Germany, Kelly's insistence on speaking out against repression in Poland almost led to a split in the peace movement.[66]

[63] Lukas Beckmann, "Polen-Solidaritätsaktion zum 30. Januar 1982/Eventuelle Parteineugründung 'Links von der SPD,'" Kreisrundbrief 3/82, dated Jan. 27, 1982, AGG, PKA, File 978.

[64] Ralph Schoenman, "Susan Sontag and the Left," Voice, Mar. 2, 1982.

[65] Alexander Cockburn and James Ridgeway, "The Poles, the Left, and the Tumbrils of '84," The Village Voice, Feb. 10–16, 1982.

[66] The bone of contention was a resolution criticizing Reagan ahead of his visit to Germany in June 1982. The Greens rejected it for failing to condemn repression in Poland and Afghanistan. See "Aufstehen für den Frieden – Widerstand verstärken! Keine neuen Atomraketen in Europa!," Flugblatt, AdsD, Arbeitsgemeinschaft Dienste für den Frieden (hereafter: AGDF), Ordner 12. On Kelly's role and the discussion on Poland, see also Volkmar Deile, ASF, Rundbrief an die Mitglieder der AEJ, an die Delegierten und Mitglieder in der MV der AEJ, an die Stadtjugendpfarrämter, September 7, 1982, AGDF, Ordner „Bundesweite Friedenswoche 1980–1984; "Polnische Ereignisse werfen Schatten auf die Friedensdiskussion," Evangelischer Pressedienst Zentralausgabe, Nr. 27 vom 9. Februar 1982, AGDF, Ordner 8.

As West European governments tried to shield East–West relations from the fall-out of the Polish crisis they saw themselves attacked by a rather odd coalition which included US Cold War hawks, Italian Communists, and West German peace activists. Yet this coalition did not emerge because a concern for human rights had subsumed or superseded other causes. To the contrary, they were enmeshed in overlapping political conflicts in which activists and politicians of various stripes sought to claim human rights as a source of symbolic power and moral authority.

V

Quickly, then, NATO's initial policy of noninterference toward Poland had come between the hammer of the Reagan administration's demand to revise the West's entire approach to détente and the anvil of public opinion, primarily in the United States, Italy, and France. Both led to the sudden change in NATO and the EC's stance toward Poland and the CSCE, from noninterference to human rights.

For the change in the British approach to Poland, the American position seems to have been most important. On December 19, 1981, Reagan sent a cable to Thatcher on the Polish situation. Describing a Soviet intervention and internal repression by the Polish government as essentially the same thing, he called events in Poland a possible "watershed in the political history of mankind – a challenge to tyranny from within" and demanded that the West live up to this occasion.[67] In a separate letter to the British Foreign Secretary Lord Carrington, Haig wrote that after months of interference the Soviet Union was "succeeding in bringing about repression and bloodshed by using their proxy – the Polish Army, Party, and Police."[68]

Both Thatcher and Carrington were notably surprised by the letters and seemed unsure what to make of them. Thatcher called Reagan's cable "so vague" she had not considered it worth discussing with Carrington when it came in. Noting that Reagan wanted to discuss measures against Poland, she exclaimed: "But it's simply an internal situation!" While she later considered a restriction of economic aid as a means of influencing Warsaw, Carrington remained opposed and quickly understood the gist of Reagan's approach, suggesting that the Americans were "moving to a situation in which they can take it out on the

---

[67] Cable from the White House to the Cabinet Office, London, dated Dec. 19, 1981, TNA, PREM 19/871.

[68] Letter from Alexander Haig to Lord Carrington, Dec. 19, 1981, TNA, PREM 19/871.

Russians," a policy Thatcher called "absurd."[69] Even at a time when a Soviet invasion had seemed the more likely outcome, there had been strong opposition in the British government to punitive measures against Moscow which both the Secretary of Trade and the Chancellor of the Exchequer rejected as ineffective and bad for the British economy.[70]

In this situation, London seems to have concluded that abandoning the approach of noninterference to Poland and focusing international criticism on Warsaw was less damaging than US sanctions against Moscow and a further deterioration in East–West relations. On December 22, Thatcher thanked Reagan for his letter, telling him that she had adjusted her government's rhetoric on Poland but notably failing to mention the Soviet Union.[71] On the same day, London made its demarche to Warsaw on behalf of the EC and stiffened its stance in the NATO Council.[72]

At around that time, Paris and Rome, too, started to take a hard line on Poland, but its representatives frankly admitted behind closed doors that they were acting under pressure from public opinion.[73] As ground shifted among NATO's main players, Bonn fell in line. Foreign Minister Hans-Dietrich Genscher suggested that the EC-10 use the UN and the Madrid conference to condemn Warsaw's policies.[74] Thus meeting some of Washington's demands, Bonn placated the socialist in Rome and Paris and managed to keep the Americans within the Helsinki framework.[75]

---

[69] Record of a Conversation between the Prime Minister and the Foreign and Commonwealth Secretary on on Sunday, Dec. 20, 1981 at 1045 hrs, TNA, PREM19/871.

[70] Memorandum from the Lord Chancellor for the Prime Minister, "Poland: Possible Economic Sanctions," dated Feb. 19, 1981, TNA, PREM 19/559; Memorandum from William John Biffen for Thatcher, "Poland: Possible Sanctions," dated Mar. 4, 1981, Letter from Michal Collon to Michael Alexander, dated Mar. 6, 1981, TNA, PREM 19/560.

[71] Letter from Thatcher to Reagan, dated Sep. 22, 1981, TNA, PREM 19/871.

[72] On British activities see also Memorandum from the FCO to Prime Minister's Office, "Poland," dated Dec. 24, 1981, TNA, PREM 19/871.

[73] In bilateral meetings with German politicians, the French, especially, admitted that they were primarily trying to assuage internal critics. See "Gespräch des Bundeskanzlers Schmidt mit Staatspräsident Mitterrand in Paris," Jan. 13, 1982, AAPD 1982, I, Nr. 20, 88–105 and Nr. 21, 97–105; "Gespräch des Bundeskanzlers Schmidt mit Staatspräsident Mitterrand in Paris," Feb. 24, 1982, AAPD, 1982, I, Nr. 63, 319–329, at 322. See also, "Aufzeichungen des Ministerialrats Fischer," Dec. 24 , 1981, AAPD 1981, III, Nr 385, 2046–2051, at 2047.

[74] "Runderlaß des Ministerialdirektors Pfeffer," dated Jan. 5, 1982, AAPD, 1982, I, Doc. 7, 27–29. On Bonn's role in the EC-10 meeting see NSC Meeting Minutes, "Poland," dated Jan. 5, 1982, RRPL, Exec. Sec., NSC: Meeting Files, NSC 00036.

[75] Cable from Amembassy Brussels to Secstate, "EC Political Cooperation," dated Jan. 15, 1982, NSA, Soviet Flashpoints: Poland 1980–82, box 27. See also Selvage, "Politics."

88   Poland's Solidarity Movement & the Politics of Rights

The Reagan administration agreed to return to Madrid, much to the chagrin of Decter and Podhoretz, who had wanted the United States to pull out of the Helsinki process. Taking the stage at the CSCE meeting of February 9, Haig gave a speech clearly reflecting the Jacksonite strategy of raising human rights to reinforce the ideological differences between East and West. He called the Helsinki Accords a "bill of rights" to whose standards the members of NATO "proudly" held themselves, contrasting this with a Soviet "pattern" of violating the agreement – invading Afghanistan, arresting human rights activists, limiting emigration, instigating and supporting oppression in Poland. Against this background, Haig left no doubt whose cultural property human rights were and who threatened them. "After a quarter century of iron curtain and Cold War, the Helsinki Final Act promised a new era" because it was based on the West's "vision of man as a creative and responsible individual."[76]

The Western show of unity at Madrid, however, failed to end the rift in the alliance over East–West relations. The debate after the Polish crisis shifted quickly from Poland to the Soviet Union. The Reagan administration demanded that the West Europeans pull out of the construction of a Soviet gas pipeline, a major economic project for both the Soviets and the involved West European countries. None of the latter, neither France nor Italy nor even Britain, followed suit, instead remarking bitterly that the United States asked them to make an economic sacrifice while Washington itself refused to apply the one sanction that would have truly hurt the USSR: reinstating a grain embargo which Carter had imposed in response to Afghanistan and whose lifting Reagan had promised as a presidential candidate to win the rural vote.[77]

★★★

In early 1982, Poland had been turned into an international pariah. The country's human rights record had never played much of a role at the CSCE. To the contrary, Poland's image as a comparatively liberal regime had turned it into a model interlocutor for Western supporters of détente. In February 1982, precisely when Warsaw held the chairmanship, it was at the center of the West's most massive "shaming" campaign yet. Witnessing these processes first-hand, the head of the Polish CSCE

---

[76] Cable from USDel in Madrid to Secstate, "Secretary's Statement, CSCE, Madrid, February 9," dated Feb. 9, 1982, State Dep., Virtual Reading Room.

[77] "Aufzeichnung der Ministerialdirektoren Fischer und Pfeffer," dated Dec. 29, 1981, AAPD, 1981, III, Doc. 391, 2066–2070, on 2069 and "Aufzeichnung des Ministerialdirektors Fischer," dated Dec. 30, 1981, AAPD, 1981, III, Doc. 398, 2102–2104, 2103.

The Principle of Noninterference as Laid Down 89

delegation in Madrid charged that they were the result of an orchestrated US campaign. He was wrong. None of this was the result of a coherent Western strategy, whether centered on the CSCE or anti-Communism. To the contrary, there had been a good chance in late 1981 that the human rights policies begun under Carter could have ended as a mere episode of Western Cold War foreign policy. For influential voices in the Reagan administration, the Polish crisis had not shown the necessity to support dissident movements but confirmed their longstanding belief that any attempt to transform a totalitarian society from within, however courageous and noble, was futile. Washington had not wanted to use the Madrid conference to lambast Warsaw for its human rights record – it had wanted to use the situation in Poland to get at the Soviet Union and possibly even end the CSCE. The first response of the West European members of NATO was to shield the CSCE process from the repercussions of the Polish crisis.

Solidarity was no natural ally of the West in the Cold War; its rise and suppression, rather, had undercut the common sense of Western approaches to the Cold War. Where proponents of détente believed the change in Communist societies would occur only gradually and anti-Communist hardliners believed change could not happen at all, a social mass movement had erupted. If Solidarity did not fit well into Western Cold War strategies neither did human rights. They had entered Cold War foreign policy a mere four years before the Polish crisis in a US human rights crusade which the major participants in the row over Poland – the United States and its main West European allies – had rejected. If the West did assume a unified position in Madrid, this was because it allowed the West Europeans to limit the damage that Washington's policies threatened to do to relations with the Soviet Union and the United States to show resolve against Communist repression. The western sanctions against Poland were neither a "Helsinki effect" nor the necessary result of a 1970s human rights revolution – they were the smallest common denominator of a Western alliance quarreling over how and where, if at all, to conduct a joint human rights policy.

This is not to say that developments during the 1970s were irrelevant. NATO's compromise was only possible because human rights had become an international source of authority. Events during the 1970s were also important for the massive outpouring of public support for Solidarity as Brandt had to learn when he came under criticism from his socialist "cousins" in France and Italy, and Reagan when he failed to get rid of human rights language. But the rift in the Socialist International also shows that it was not at all clear what a human rights policy meant or how human rights as a source of authority related to the political identities of those who were meant to conduct this policy. Debates over how to respond to Poland, then, had a wider political and intellectual context – they were intertwined with discourses in which social and political groups in the West were debating their own political projects and identities. These intellectual and political contexts will be the subject of the remainder of the following three chapters of this book.

4 The End of the Ideological Age
Human Rights and *Ostpolitik*

During the implementation of martial law, many activists of KOR and Solidarity were arrested and brought to so-called "internment facilities," detention camps not unlike those for P.O.W.s in wartime. Among the internees' few sources of information about the outside world were issues of the Communist press.[1] What Adam Michnik read there about West German reactions to martial law left him outraged. In an essay smuggled out of the detention camp, he attacked the editor of a West German newspaper "who seems to believe that only people living West of the Elbe deserve human rights, whereas the savages in the East have exclusive right to the knout and barbed wire as instruments that quite properly regulate their public life." In an "Open Letter to International Public Opinion" published in September 1982, he chided "the chancellors of Austria and West Germany" for "find[ing] so much forbearance for our generals."[2]

Some of the criticism that was heaped at West Germany at the time was misguided. On December 18, 1981, the *Bundestag* unanimously condemned martial law, the first political statement of this kind in the West.[3] Over the following months, the Federal Government and West German society provided millions of dollars in humanitarian support for Polish society.[4] As ground shifted among NATO's members, moreover,

---

[1] Karol Modzelewski, *Zajeździmy kobyłę historii: Wyznania poobijanego jeźdźca* (Warszawa: Iskry, 2013), 330.

[2] Adam Michnik, *Letters from Prison and Other Essays* (Berkeley, CA: University of California Press, 1985), 29; Adam Michnik, "An Open Letter to International Public Opinion," *Telos* 54 (Winter 1982–1983).

[3] Entschließungsantrag der Fraktionen der CDU/CSU, SPD und FDPzurErklärung der Bundesregierungvom 18. Dezember 1981, Dec. 18, 1981, Deutscher Bundestag, 9. Wahlperiode, Drucksache 9/1220.

[4] Friedhelm Boll, "Zwischen politischer Zurückhaltung und humanitärer Hilfe: Der Deutsche Gewerkschaftsbund und Solidarność 1980-1982," in Ursula Bitzegeio et al., eds., *Solidargemeinschaft und Erinnerungskultur im 20. Jahrhundert: Beiträge zu Gewerkschaften, Nationalsozialismus und Geschichtspolitik* (Bonn: Dietz, 2009); Friedhelm Boll and Małgorzata Świder, "The FRG: Humanitarian Support without Great Publicity," in Idesbald Goddeeris, ed., *Solidarity with Solidarity: Western European Trade Unions and the Polish Crisis, 1980-1982* (Lanham: Lexington, 2010).

92   Poland's Solidarity Movement & the Politics of Rights

Bonn had played a leading role in orchestrating the West's unified position in Madrid as well as in bringing the Polish situation before the forum of the U.N. Commission on Human Rights.[5]

Despite these expressions of solidarity, though, the Federal Government's tone toward Warsaw was usually conciliatory and its stance on Solidarity ambivalent. The Italian Communists all but broke with Moscow over Poland, and French president François Mitterrand, whose cabinet featured Communist ministers, emerged as one of Warsaw's loudest critics. Bonn urged restraint and continued cooperation with the Polish government. All but a handful of western capitals reduced diplomatic relations with Poland to the bare minimum; West Germany's ruling Social Democratic Party of Germany (*Sozialdemokratische Partei Deutschlands*, or SPD) sustained its comparatively close ties with the Polish Communist party, holding bilateral meetings throughout the 1980s.[6]

No one embodied this position more than Willy Brandt, West Germany's former chancellor, the SPD's chairman. Reconciliation with Poland had been at the center of his *Neue Ostpolitik*, Bonn's new approach to East–West relations that Brandt had designed together with his close aide Egon Bahr.[7] Under his leadership, the Federal Republic had played a central role in including the Basket III provisions on humanitarian questions, free movement, and human contacts into the Helsinki

---

[5] See previous chapter.

[6] Reflecting the cordiality of Polish–West German relations, Poland's Deputy Prime Minister MieczysławRakowski ended talks with an SPD politician, held on December 30, 1981 in Bonn, noting how good it was "to talk among friends." Aufzeichnungen über das Gespräch des stellvertretenden Parteivorsitzenden der SPD und Vorsitzenden des Arbeitskreises I der SPD-Bundestagsfraktion, Hans-Jürgen Wischniewski, mit dem stellvertretenden polnischen Ministerpräsidenten Rakowski am 30. Dezember 1981, um 16.30 Uhr, Bundeshaus, Bonn, not dated, AdsD, WBA, A11, Mappe 50. Only weeks after the imposition of martial law, the chairman of the SPD's parliamentary group, Herbert Wehner, the party's powerful *eminence grise*, even travelled to Poland to collect the Polish government's order of merit for his achievements in Polish-West German reconciliation. "Wehner Reisenach Polen," *Informationen der sozialdemokratischen Bundestagsfraktion*, 215/26 Feb. 1982, AdsD, Nachlass Walter Polkehn (hereafter: NL Polkehn), Mappe 221.On meetings between Polish and West German delegations, see BisherigeZusammenkünfte des "GesprächskreisesPolen" der SPD-Bundestagsfraktion, not dated, AdsD, NL Polkehn, Mappe 182; Letter from Walter Polkehn to GüntherVieser, dated May 24, 1982, SPDParteivorstand/InternationaleAbteilung (hereafter: SPD-PV/Intern. Abt.), Mappe 10955.

[7] Friedhelm Boll and Krzysztof Ruchniewicz, eds., *"Nie mehr eine Politik über Polen hinweg"*: *Willy Brandt und Polen* (Bonn: J.H.W. Dietz, 2010); on Brandt's foreign policy more broadly, see Bernd Rother, ed., *Willy Brandt's Außenpolitik* (Wiesbaden: Springer VS, 2014).For how Brandt and Bahr's ideas continued to inform the policy especially of the West German foreign ministry under Hans-Dietrich Genscher see Peter, *Bundesrepublik*, 410–415, 469–488; Agnes Bresselau von Bressensdorf, *Frieden durch Kommunikation: Das System Genscher und die Entspannungspolitik im Zweiten Kalten Krieg 1979-1982/83* (Berlin, Boston: de Gruyter, 2015), 256–265.

The End of the Ideological Age   93

Final Act.[8] After his resignation in 1974, however, when he conducted a kind of non-state diplomacy on behalf of the SPD and later the Socialist International, he was a critic of Jimmy Carter's CSCE policies and would often refuse to publicly support dissidents in the Soviet bloc.

In contemporary history, Brandt's policies have primarily been discussed within debates as to whose policies "won" the Cold War.[9] This chapter pursues a different aim. Deciphering the ideas and wider imaginaries that informed his actions, I argue, provides insights into the intellectual changes that powered the human rights revolution of the 1970s and 1980s. In his own view, Brandt *was* working toward the realization of human rights. Yet he understood this aim in a way still deeply indebted to the political and intellectual culture of the 1950s and 1960s – a culture revolving around a vision of competing political and social systems, antagonistic ways of organizing society, fundamentally different views of how long-term historical processes shaped the fate of nations. Enmeshed in this culture, Brandt believed that a successful human rights policy had to take these structural constraints and broad time horizons into account. The kind of activism Michnik stood for – calling upon the international community to intervene for the human rights of everyone, everywhere – seemed to Brandt not morally objectionable so much as simply implausible and unreasonable.

The social space where postwar thought was applied and thus acquired plausibility was the Western welfare state. No other project embodied its central promise more clearly: A policy guided by science and legitimated by constitutional democracy could overcome the social conflicts of industrial societies while leaving capitalism intact. So when the welfare state failed to deliver on its promise amid the economic travails of the 1970s, its crisis eroded the entire intellectual culture that had sustained it, a development which was nowhere more visible than in the predicament of Brandt's own social democracy.[10] The broad time horizon that

---

[8] Peter, *Bundesrepublik*, 99–101, 104–105; Kristina Spohr Readman, "National Interests and the Power of 'Language': West German Diplomacy and the Conference on Security and Cooperation in Europe, 1972-1975," *Journal of Strategic Studies* 29 (2006), 6, 1111–1115.

[9] See, for instance, Jeremi Suri, "Détente and Human Rights: American and West European Perspectives on International Change," *Cold War History* 8 (November 2008), 4.

[10] For this interpretation, see Habermas, "Obscurity," 1; for another contemporaneous text in the same vein, see Ralf Dahrendorf, "Die Leitsterne unser Politik erlöschen," *Zeit*, Aug. 26, 1977; on Habermas, see also Cord Anderes, "Neu gelesen: Auf der Suche nach dem roten Faden. Jürgen Habermas' Lesarten der europäischen Moderne in unübersichtlichen Zeiten," *Zeithistorische Forschungen/Studies in Contemporary History, Online edition* 7 (2010), 1. The most recent contribution to discussions about the 1970s, see Anselm Doering-Manteuffel, Lutz Raphael, and Thomas Schlemmer, eds.,

94   Poland's Solidarity Movement & the Politics of Rights

had delineated postwar social imaginaries shrunk and the collective actors that populated it dissolved. The last three decades of the twentieth century were, in Daniel Rodger's apt phrase, a great "age of fracture."[11]

One of the main casualties of this crisis was a specific understanding of historical time. The *Zeitgeist* of the postwar era had, as Jürgen Habermas wrote, merged historical consciousness with utopian thought. History was imagined as an ordered process whose direction could be deciphered by modern science. Historical consciousness, knowledge of the course, and direction of history thus opened up the future and became a source of utopian energies. By the time Habermas wrote this essay, in 1985, however, these utopian energies had evaporated. Deep pessimism was the order of the day, the future seemed "occupied with the merely negative," a "new obscurity" had taken hold of Western social thought.[12] The intellectual foundation of Brandt's policies, the optimism that science *can* decipher the laws of social development, crumbled.

Precisely this crisis opened a discursive space in which the human rights revolution of the 1970s and 1980s could occur. For as historical time was condensed and the collective actors populating it were broken down, human rights' absolute moral claim on the international community became plausible.[13] Michnik and Brandt were not divided by political aims – they inhabited different conceptual worlds. Mapping Brandt's world provides us with a surer grip of the modes of thought that had to give way for the human rights revolution of the 1970s and 1980s to occur.

I

Willy Brandt's defensive and conciliatory stance in 1981 left some observers wondering what had happened to the former refugee from Nazi Germany and staunch mayor of West Berlin who had stood next to John F. Kennedy during his famous visit in 1963. And, indeed, it was hard not to notice that Brandt had come a long way from when he first had sketched his *Neue Ostpolitik* in a speech given at Harvard University

---

Vorgeschichte der Gegenwart: Dimensionen des Strukturbruchs nach dem Boom (Goettingen: Vandenhoeck & Ruprecht, 2016). For the burgeoining literature in this fields, see Borstelmann, *The 1970s*; Doering-Manteuffel and Raphael, *Nach dem Boom: Perspektiven auf die Zeitgeschichte seit 1970*; Ferguson et al., eds., *Shock*; Müller, *Contesting Democracy*, 203–242; Therborn et al., "1970s."

[11] Rodgers, *Age*.   [12] Habermas, "Obscurity," 2.

[13] For a similar interpretation on the relation between the rise of human rights and changing notions of time which is based on the work of French historian François Hartog, see Stefan-Ludwig Hoffmann, "Human Rights and History," *Past & Present* 232 (2016), 1.

The End of the Ideological Age   95

in 1962. Brimming with confidence in the superiority of the Western system, Brandt had castigated Nikita Khrushchev's "peaceful coexistence" as an insincere attempt to continue old ideological battles. If the West wanted to prevail, West Berlin's mayor insisted, it could not shy away from criticizing these ideas openly.[14]

Crucially, human rights did feature in Brandt's speech. They, he insisted, had to be the basis for coexistence.[15] He even saw a "camp of freedom" whose membership cut across the East–West divide. "People within the Soviet orbit will become ever more vocal, more insistent in demanding human rights," he predicted, allowing the free world to open "a second front" in the struggle between East and West.[16]

Fifteen years later, when dissident groups had emerged in the Soviet bloc, Brandt seemed to be striking a very different tone. In an article on human rights in East–West relations, he praised Charter 77, misunderstanding it as a reform Communist movement in Aleksandr Dubček's vein, yet refused to support everything that was currently discussed "under the keyword 'dissidents.'" He also rejected the idea that the CSCE Final Act had created a kind of human rights court in Helsinki. Why, he asked, should the Helsinki Final Act – with all the compromises that had gone into its wording, *Formelkompromisse* – have a different effect than previous human rights treaties had had?[17] Talking to

---

[14] Willy Brandt, *The Ordeal of Coexistence* (Cambridge, MA: Harvard University Press, 1963); published in German as *Koexistenz: Zwang zum Wagnis* (Stuttgart: DVA, 1963). In addition to this text and the cited archival sources, my interpretation of Brandt's thought draws on his selected writings compiled in vols. 6 and 8–10 of the *Berliner Ausgabe*, ed. by Helga Grebing et al. (Bonn, 2005–2006). Hereafter cited as *Berliner Ausgabe*. My interpretation is also deeply indebted to the work of Gottfried Niedhart and Wolfgang Schmidt. See especially Gottfried Niedhart, "Revisionistische Elemente und die Initiierung friedlichen Wandels in der neuen Ostpolitik 1967-1974," *Geschichte und Gesellschaft* 28 (2002), 2; Gottfried Niedhart, "Deeskalation durch Kommunikation: Zur Ostpolitik der Bundesrepublik Deutschland in der Ära Brandt," in Corinna Hauswedell, ed., *Deeskalation von Gewaltkonflikten seit 1945* (Essen: Klartext, 2006); Gottfried Niedhart, "'The Transformation of the Other Side': Willy Brandt's Ostpolitik and the Liberal Peace Concept," in Frédéric Bozo et al., eds.,*Visions of the End of the Cold War in Europe, 145-1990* (Oxford, New York: Berghahn, 2013); Wolfgang Schmidt, "Die Wurzeln der Entspannung: Der konzeptionelle Ursprung der Ost- und Deutschlandpolitik Willy Brandts in den fünfziger Jahren," *Vierteljahrshefte für Zeitgeschichte* 51 (2003), 4. For a comprehensive analysis of Brandt's foreign policy see Rother, ed., *Brandts Außenpolitik*.
[15] Brandt, *Ordeal*, 41; Brandt, *Koexistenz*, 45.
[16] Brandt, *Ordeal*, 21; Brandt, *Koexistenz*, 26. The reference to a "camp of freedom" and a "second front" appears only in the German version of the text.
[17] "Nr 37: Artikel des Vorsitzenden der SPD, Brandt, für *Die Zeit*, 26. August 1977," in *Berliner Ausgabe*, vol. 9, 204–213, on 207, 209–210; for a similar position iterated 10 years later, see Willy Brandt, *Menschenrechte mißhandelt und mißbraucht* (Reibeck bei Hamburg: Rowohlt, 1987), 98.

96 Poland's Solidarity Movement & the Politics of Rights

the Soviet ambassador in West Germany in December 1980, he even called the Final Act a mistake, given how its *Formelkompromisse*had created illusions and false hopes.[18]

A year later, as darkness descended upon Poland, Brandt argued strenuously against punishing Warsaw for human rights violations. No, he responded to a journalist, it would not have helped if Chancellor Helmut Schmidt had interrupted his trip to the GDR and had pretended "that we could help those, who are in a difficult situation themselves after the events of Sunday [i.e., the Polish government after the imposition of martial law], with verbose declarations." Much as he criticized the internment of trade unionists, he insisted that the situation in Poland would not be improved by "scolding those in responsibility there." Martial law, he said, was a "new, very difficult attempt to prevent a break-up of the state and a further decline of the national economy."[19] He vigorously defended this position even after more and more Western politicians, including members of the Socialist International, had started condemning Warsaw's policies. In a news program on television, he criticized a Western "*Ersatz* heroism ... as if strong words and vacuous slogans here could help anyone in Poland."[20]

Brandt's statements, it has to be noted, went along with a silent diplomacy of intervening discreetly on behalf of individual prisoners. It also needs to be seen against the background of the international situation. As early as 1962, he had said that the West had to wrest the idea of "coexistence" from Soviet propaganda because "genuine coexistence is the only alternative to atomic war and universal suicide."[21] By the time of the Polish crisis, this concern for humanity's suicide had deepened. Using backchannels to Western political leaders, including Brandt, Moscow was doing its utmost to create the impression that, if necessary, it was ready and willing to act against "counterrevolution" in Poland.[22]

---

[18] "Nr. 61: Vermerküber das Gespräch des Vorsitzenden der SPD, Brandt, mitdemsowjetischenBotschafterSemjonow 11. Dezember 1980," in *Berliner Ausgabe*, vol. 9, 300–304, on 301.

[19] Brandt-Interview with Rainer Burchardt, *SPD-Presseerklärung* 755/15 Dec. 1981, 3–4.

[20] "Willy Brandt zu den lautgewordenen Vorwürfen gegenüber seinen zurückhaltenden Äußerungenzu den Vorgängen in Polen," BPA – Nachrichtenabt., Ref. II R 3, Rundf.-Ausw. Deutschland, ZDF/23.12.81/21.00/wei, AdsD, WBA, A13, Mappe100A, fol. 20–21.

[21] Brandt, *Ordeal*, 35.

[22] In confidential meetings, Hungarian party functionaries and even Fidel Castro told Brandt and other western socialists that the Polish crisis had become a problem for the entire Warsaw Pact, implicating that a Soviet invasion was inevitable. Vermerk von Dingels an Gen. Willy Brandt betr. Gespräche mit dem Abteilungsleiter für auswärtige Angelegenheiten und Mitglied des Zentralkomitees der ungarischen sozialistischen Arbeiterpartei, Dr. Janos Berecz, am 1. und 2. April 1981, dated April 6, 1981, AdsD,

The End of the Ideological Age   97

With superpower détente all but collapsed, a Soviet invasion of Poland would have had unforeseeable consequences.[23]

But the international tensions of the early 1980s cannot fully explain Brandt's stance. He did not argue that human rights policies needed to be suspended until a more favorable international situation had emerged. His statements, actions, and entire habitus, rather, embodied a complete refusal to engage in the kind of social and political practices that had come to be associated with human rights. The dissidents had discovered human rights as a set of absolute values. Through their experience, they had come to understand state socialism as a world in which no norm was safe from the state's arbitrary use of power, in which politics was impossible because a vacuous ideological language had eroded the very categories that made truthful public speech possible. Fidelity to ethical principles was a value in itself because it was the only antidote to a system embodying a collective lie. For the dissidents, powerful public gestures on behalf of political prisoners were not empty symbolic politics, they were what human rights was all about.[24]

By contrast, Brandt saw such ostentatious shows of support as vacuous gestures doing more harm than good. In December 1985, he visited Poland as part of an unofficial diplomacy to shore up support for disarmament initiatives. By that time, human rights issues completely dominated Poland's relations with the West and Western visitors would demonstratively meet Polish dissidents to show their support.[25] Ahead of the Brandt's trip, Lech Wałęsa had invited him to Gdańsk for a meeting of the two Nobel peace laureates. Concerned such a meeting might jeopardize his trip, Brandt declined and, save for a half-hearted meeting with Catholic intellectuals, avoided signs of open support for the Polish opposition. Instead, he courted Jaruzelski, at some point even

---

WBA, A11.4, Mappe 133; Veronika Isenberg, Aufzeichnung: Felipe Gonzalez überseinGesprächmit Fidel Castro, dated Mar. 27, 1981, AdsD, WBA, A11.4, Mappe 133. When in Bonn in November 1981, Leonid Brezhnev told Helmut Schmidt that any threat to the existence of a socialist Poland would be "an assault on the socialist community and the existence of the Soviet Union" which Moscow could not allow to happen. "Gespräch des Bundeskanzlers Schmidt mitdemGeneralsekretär des ZK der KPdSU, Breschnew, am 23.11.1981," in AAPD, 1981, III, Doc. 336, on 1818.

[23] For instance, Reagan told Schmidt during their first meeting that while the United States would not go to war over Poland, a Soviet invasion would mean the end of détente. "Ministerialdirektor von Staden, Bundeskanzleramt, z.Z. Washington, an BundesministerGenscher," dated May 22, 1981, AAPD, 1981, II, Doc. 151, 834–838, on 835.

[24] See Chapters 1 and 2 of this book above.   [25] See Chapter 10 of this book below.

98   Poland's Solidarity Movement & the Politics of Rights

comparing him to Charles de Gaulle.[26] This treatment contrasted sharply with the experience Jaruzelski had made just days before, during a trip to Paris where French protestors had likened the Polish leader to Chilean dictator General Pinochet.[27]

Brandt's public statements and texts were also saturated with calls for an unsentimental rationalism and for intellectual sobriety, for taking a hard look at social and global realities and basing one's politics on them – a stark contrast to Amnesty International that had turned emotions like empathy with suffering strangers into a new form of politics. In 1978, Brandt recalled how the crushing of the Prague Spring 10 years before had devastated him. But he also insisted that his policy of pressing ahead with détente regardless had been the right choice. Idealism alone could not change the power structure of the Soviet bloc. There was no "reasonable [vernünftige] alternative" to détente. What was discussed "by invoking human rights" at the time, he criticized, "ignored reality [gehtan derWirklichkeitvorbei]." The West had to stay course on détente "however difficult that may be emotionally."[28]

Ten years after this statement, Brandt published an extensive essay on his understanding of human rights. His main concern in writing it, Brandt explained, was his fear that human rights may be exploited for the East–West struggle and other ideological debates. Similar ideas also animated Amnesty International's attempt to place themselves above political and ideological divisions. But while Brandt shared with Amnesty this anxiety about the political exploitation of human rights, he drew very different conclusions from it. Where Amnesty chose the path of withdrawing from politics for the sake of an ethically pure humanitarianism, Brandt saw politics as a means to work realistically for human rights. His was a Weberian "ethics of responsibility," the view

---

[26] For an admirably even-handed account of the visit, see Bernd Rother, "Willy Brandts Besuch in Warschau im Dezember 1985," in Friedhelm Boll et al., eds.,*Versöhnung und Politik: Polnisch-deutsche Versöhnungsinitiativen der 1960er Jahre und ihre Bedeutung für die Entspannungspolitik* (Bonn: J.H.W. Dietz, 2008). For Brandt largely supporting Warsaw's position see also "Aus der Rede des Vorsitzenden der SPD, Brandt, vor der sozialdemokratischenBundestagsfraktion, 10 Dezember 1985," in *Berliner Ausgabe*, vol. 10, Doc. 30, 286–292.

[27] Klaus Lindenberg, "Vier-Augen-Gespräch Willy Brandt – General WojciechJaruzelski, Warschau, 7. Dezember 1985, imGebäude des ZK der PVAP, 9.35-11.25 Uhr," dated Dec. 17, 1985, on 10, AdsD, WBA, A19, Mappe 264, fol. 58–69. Published as document 28 in *Berliner Ausgabe*, vol. 10, 264–273. For the Polish version see "Informacja o rozmowach I Sekretarza KC PZPR tow. W. Jaruzelskiego z Przewodniczącym SPD W. Brandtem," tajne, KS/0195/1953/85 [not dated], AAN, KC PZPR, XI/437, 186–204.

[28] "Nr. 48: Beitrag des Vorsitzenden der SPD, Brandt, für den SPD-Pressedienst 15. August 1978," in *Berliner Ausgabe*, Bd. 9, 241–243, on 242–243.

The End of the Ideological Age 99

of the immorality of a politics which was primarily concerned with its own moral purity.

II

These differences in ethics and political outlook point toward fundamentally different ways of thinking about international politics. The realism that had such a prominent place in Brandt's writings was not only dictated by the perils of the Cold War but also out of the concepts and ideas he used to make sense of it. His thinking was still deeply indebted to a social imaginary of structural constraints resting on human agency and of "laws" that governed "ages" in the development of modern societies. Those who demanded to ostracize Poland for martial law, Brandt's close aide and co-architect of *Ostpolitik* Egon Bahr wrote in January 1982, were not merely acting imprudently – they acted against the very "law of the nuclear age."[29] Social structures, laws, and ages also delineated Brandt's thought on human rights. In his inaugural speech as president of the Socialist International, he demanded a threefold offensive – for détente, development, and human rights. The policies he suggested to promote human rights, however, were much more about fighting poverty and underdevelopment than about freedom of speech or free elections.[30]

Crucially, Brandt did not seem to have believed that human rights could be applied equally across the globe because they, too, had evolved in a long historical process and were dependent on certain structural conditions. When Jaruzelski brought up the human rights campaign against Poland in a one-on-one conversation in 1985, Brandt tried to change the subject saying that peace could not wait until the dispute over human rights and democracy was settled which, he said, would probably never happen. For the developing countries, this debate was irrelevant anyway; they would need time to orient themselves in the discussion on political and economic systems.[31] While this was partly an attempt to stay clear of a controversial subject, it did express a view Brandt had held for much of his political career. In a speech on international politics from 1958, he had asked: "But who gives us the right to believe that a system of government, which has emerged for 20% of humanity as a result of a long historical process of development, has now simply to be declared the only applicable model for the rest of humanity? The process toward the

---

[29] Egon Bahr, "Wie einfach, Freiheit für die Polen zu fordern," *Vorwärts*, January 21, 1982.
[30] "Nr. 11: Antrittsrede des Präsidenten der SI, Brandt, beimKongress der SI in Genf 26. November 1976," in *Berliner Ausgabe*, vol. 8, 161–177, on 172–176.
[31] Lindenberg, "Vier-Augen-Gespräch."

100 Poland's Solidarity Movement & the Politics of Rights

self-determination of the peoples is still very slow and long."[32] He reiterated that position almost 20 years later in his opening speech as President of the Socialist International and during a meeting in 1977 in solidarity with Chile.[33]

But if Brandt believed that the laws of historical development dictated a certain realism, he was also convinced that they provided insights into how to improve humanity's situation. What we encounter in Brandt's though, then, is precisely the fusion of historical consciousness and utopian thinking Habermas had defined as central to the postwar *Zeitgeist*, the idea that by understanding the laws that governed social development humanity would be able to shape its future. This thinking underpinned Brandt's approach to human rights in the East–West conflict.

III

At the height of the Polish crisis, the journalist Peter Bender published a book-length discussion of the achievements and future of *Ostpolitik*. Bender was a close friend of Egon Bahr, and Willy Brandt endorsed many of the book's conclusions.[34] Characteristically for the thought that informed *Ostpolitik*, the book prophesied the dawning of a new age – the post-ideological one. This may suggest an intellectual kinship with dissent. The dissidents, after all, had said that they were a "product of the failure of ideology."[35] But it seems that the dissidents and Bender were talking about very different ways in which ideology had become irrelevant. Calling his book *The End of the Age of Ideologies*, Bender argued that the importance of political ideas and values in East–West relations would give way to the powerful social forces of modernization. Developments in the East were not following "a socialist, but a natural path," he wrote.[36]

In the Soviet bloc, Bender and Brandt conceded, ideology was still invoked to legitimate party rule, but the policies of the Warsaw pact

---

[32] "Nr. 38: Aus dem Vortrag 'Betrachtungen zur internationalen Politik' des Regierenden Bürgermeisters von Berlin, Brandt, vor der Steuben-Schurz-Gesellschaft Berlin, Jan. 17, 1958," in *BerlingerAusgabe*, vol. 3, 233–237, on 234.

[33] "Antrittsrede des Präsidenten der SI," 168; "Nr. 16: Aus dem Manuskript der Rede des Präsidenten der SI, Brandt, bei der Chile-Konferenz in Rotterdam 29. August 1977," in *Berliner Ausgabe*, Bd. 8, 198–201, on 199.

[34] Peter Bender, *Das Ende des ideologischen Zeitalters: Die Europäisierung Europas* (Berlin: Severin und Siedler, 1981); for Brandt's review see his "Vier Stufen der Vision," *Der Spiegel*, June 1, 1981. See also Bernd Rother and Wolfgang Schmidt, "Einleitung: GemeinsameSicherheit, InternationaleBeziehungen und deutsche Frage 1982–1992," in *Berliner Ausgabe*, vol. 10, 22.

[35] Luxmoore and Babiuch, "Search," 79.   [36] Bender, *Ende*, 66, 68.

The End of the Ideological Age 101

countries were informed more by economic interests than ideological zeal. The average Communist politician, they held, was not an ideologue but a technocrat seeking to modernize his country and catch up with the West.[37] "Production" became more important than "dogma" in Soviet policies, as Brandt had said already in 1962, a shift he believed would expose the Communist world to the powerful liberalizing pressures of the social laws of modernization.[38] Underlying this prognosis was the view that the social and economic processes characteristic for modern industrial societies would become too complex to be managed by Communism's system rigid structures and citizens would demand a say in social life. The people of the Soviet bloc would be ever more vocally claiming their "human rights," Brandt had said in Harvard in 1962 because a "modern industrial society is incompatible with a regime of *total* oppression; such a society creates conditions which require, and also make room for, a certain amount of individual freedom. As an industrial society, the Soviet Union cannot evade these inherent pressures." Crucially, the German version of the speech referred not to "inherent pressures" of industrial societies but its "law."[39]

With a prudent policy, the architects of *Ostpolitik* argued, the West could foster and accelerate such changes in the East. Détente was a prerequisite for such a policy because an antagonistic international system and external pressures on the East were believed to strengthen hardliners in Communist countries, slowing down liberalization processes. Changes in the Soviet bloc, Bahr had said in his famous speech on "change through rapprochement," would be possible only in "homeopathic doses" to prevent a clampdown from Moscow.[40] Yet such change would be possible nonetheless by exposing the East to Western ideas,

---

[37] Ibid., 31–34.   [38] Brandt, *Ordeal*, 79; Brandt, *Koexistenz*, 84.
[39] Brandt, *Ordeal*, 21; Brandt, *Koexistenz*, 26. See also Willy Brandt, "The Means Short of War," *Foreign Affairs* 39 (Jan. 1961), 2, 206. For the importance of these ideas for the formulation of *Ostpolitik* see "Aufzeichnungen des Ministerialdirektors Bahr, z.Zt. New York" dated Sep. 21, 1969, AAPD, 1969, II, Doc. 296, 1047–1057, at 1051; "Gespräch des Bundeskanzlers Brandt mitPremierminister Heath," dated Apr. 6, 1981, AAPD, 1971, I, 593–599, on 596. These sources quoted in Niedhart, "Elemente," 246, 258–261; cf. Bender, *Ende*, 95–96. Karsten Voigt, who at the time emerged as the SPD's leading party expert on foreign policy, adopted these ideas in a series of articles on human rights and détente. Karsten D. Voigt, "Nur Veränderung löst Konflikte," *Vorwärts*, October 2, 1980; Karsten D. Voigt, "Sozialdemokratische Menschenrechtspolitik," *Die neue Gesellschaft/Frankfurter Hefte* 30 (August 1983); Karsten D. Voigt, "Motive und Ziele der ersten und zweiten Ostpolitik der SPD," *Kommune* 6(Sept. 6, 1985).
[40] Egon Bahr, "WandeldurchAnnäherung," speech given at the *Evangelische Akademie Tutzing*, 15 July 1963, available at www.fes.de/archiv/adsd_neu/inhalt/stichwort/tutzinger_rede.pdf (accessed May 2016).

102   Poland's Solidarity Movement & the Politics of Rights

fostering its economic development through international trade, and thus reinforcing the forces of modernization.

Having seen how state socialist economies collapsed under the weight of their inefficient and wasteful industries, Bender's and Brandt's optimism may retrospectively appear strangely out of place. Yet throughout the 1960s and 1970s, the ideas informing their writing and policies had been at the height of Western analyses of the Soviet bloc. In fact, the idea that Communism changed under the pressure of modernization was common sense among Western social scientists.[41]

Having sketched the conceptual world underpinning *Ostpolitik* we see that the Polish crisis did not expose a transformation of Brandt's thinking about human rights. To the contrary, consistent with ideas he and Bahr had been developing since the 1950s, he argued that the rise of Solidarity was a success of his policies. The modernization of state socialism and the exposure to Western arguments and ideas were bound to influence eastern societies, Bahr wrote in January 1982 to defend *Ostpolitik*. For now, these changes necessarily prompted resistance within the Communist regime. But as the East would fall further behind the West in its development, it would again be forced to intensify exchanges with the West, continuing the process of Communism's social erosion from within. "We have experienced that the pressure for social change – resulting from the development of modern industrial society – does not stop before eastern industrial societies; western industrial societies simply respond more flexibly and faster to it."[42]

That was why Brandt saw Jaruzelski, and not Solidarity, as his main partner in Polish–German relations, the General seemed like an interlocutor ideally suited to the aims of *Ostpolitik*. Even senior US analysts had initially characterized Jaruzelski as a patriotic officer torn between the necessity to please Moscow and prevent turmoil at home.[43] This view was reinforced after the imposition of martial law when Jaruzelski sent out signals that were unprecedented for a Communist leader. In speeches to Polish society as well as in messages to Western politicians, he insisted that he did not want to turn the clock back to the time before August 1980. Radicals in Solidarity had exploited the just aspirations and legitimate demands of the working class, leading Poland unto the path of civil war and turning it into a "powder keg in the heart of Europe," as

---

[41] Gert-Joachim Glaessner, *Die andere deutsche Republik: Gesellschaft und Politik in der DDR* (Opladen: Westdeutscher Verlag, 1989), 19–23.

[42] Bahr, "Wie einfach, Freiheit für die Polen zu fordern."

[43] Domber, *Revolution*, 23. See also the assessment of the British ambassador. Cable from UKE Warsaw to FCO, dated Feb. 19, 1981, TNA, PREM 19/559.

The End of the Ideological Age 103

Jaruzelski wrote in a letter to, among others, Ronald Reagan and Brandt. This threat, he claimed, had to be removed so that reforms could continue.[44]

The Polish Government went out of its way to convey this message to the West Europeans, summoning their ambassadors,[45] dispatching the cosmopolitan party liberal Mieczysław Rakowski to Bonn,[46] and even allowing him to give an extensive interview to the *Washington Post* and *Times* of London in which he underlined the need to reform the Polish system, even while placing the blame for martial law on a "bunch of anarchists" who had betrayed Solidarity.[47]

IV

Putting the responses to the Polish crisis into the context of the intellectual and cultural history of the 1970s and 1980s shows that discussions as to whether *Ostpolitik* and the Helsinki Final Act were conservative projects are really beside the point. The crucial aspect about them, rather, is that they were conceived in a period of postwar intellectual history which came to an end precisely at the time when the CSCE review process began. The moral visions and conceptual systems of the architects of the CSCE were thus fundamentally different from those of the people who would invoke the Final Act for their protection – the dissidents. One of the most important differences seems to have been different understandings of historical time.

For Brandt, steeped as he was in the social thought of the postwar era, human rights treaties *could not* provide guarantees for the immediate protection of individual liberties around the world. To him, pursuing

---

[44] Letter from Wojciech Jaruzelski to Ronald Reagan, Jan. 4, 1982, RRPL, WHORM: Subject File, CO126, ID# 048376; German translation of a letter from Jaruzelski to Willy Brandt, not dated, AdsD, SPD-PV/Intern. Abt., Mappe 11145. The quotations are from the English translation Reagan had received.

[45] Restricted North Atlantic Council meeting from Dec. 14, 1981., on 6, 10, 12; Letter from Hans-Dietrich Genscher to Willy Brandt, dated Dec. 16, 1981, AdsD, WBA, A13, Mappe100A; "Gespräch des Bundesministers Genscher mit dem polnischen GeschäftsträgerWojtkowski," dated Dec. 16, 1981, AAPD, III, 1981, Doc. 373, 1995–1998.

[46] Gespräch Wischniewski-Rakowski, AdsD; Notatka z pobytu w Republice Federalnej Niemiec w dniach 30-31 grudnia br., not dated, AAN, KC PZPR, LXXVI-610; Mieczysław F. Rakowski, *Dzienniki polityczne, 1981-1983* (Warszawa, 2004), 151–152; Cable from Amembassy Bonn to SecState, "Preliminary FRG account of Genscher-Rakowski meeting December 30," dated Dec. 30, 1981, National Security Archive (hereafter: NSA), Soviet Flashpoints (Originals) Poland 1980-82, Box 1.

[47] Mieczysław F. Rakowski, "'Even an Angel Can Become a Whore'," *Washington Post*, Feb. 21, 1982.

such a policy was morally objectionable because it was *unreasonable*. In his conceptual universe, human beings were embedded in wider social structures which evolved in long historical processes. The struggle for individual rights had to focus on the transformation of these structures, a process which would take time. Human rights were a promise to be fulfilled by fostering social change.

That was why Brandt was taken aback when dissidents and Western politicians turned the CSCE review meetings into human rights courts. In his view, the human rights provisions in Basket I were a promise to be fulfilled through the measures of Baskets II and III to foster economic and social exchanges between East and West. By helping the Soviet bloc countries to modernize their economies and by exposing them to Western ideas, these measures would reinforce the liberalizing pressures inherent in modern industrial society and thus lead to greater respect for individual freedoms in Eastern Europe. The ostentatious public shows of support for dissidents and the policy of linkage that that became the hallmark of human rights policies were counterproductive in this view for they would merely strengthen Communist hardliners. Making economic cooperation with the East conditional on Communist respect for human rights would deprive the modernization process of its "fuel." For Brandt, East–West trade was not a prize for Communist respect for individual rights, it was the means by which it was to be achieved.

The dissidents' understanding of human rights could not have been more different. Brandt's politics would not work in their situation, they had come to believe. The experience of arbitrariness, where even truthful public speech had become impossible, had sent them on a quest for moral absolutes. They found them in a quasi-religious understanding of human dignity and individual rights. For the dissidents, human rights were not a promise for the future but precisely a guarantee for the here-and-now. Democracy would not be the outcome of long-term processes of social change but, as Adam Michnik had written, would emerge out of the "real, day-to-day community of free people."[48] In the world of the Soviet bloc, politics could not be a way to achieve respect for human rights, but human rights were the foundation on which politics would be possible again. What Brandt saw as a naïve idealism, the dissidents saw as a realism dictated by the realities of their social world.

The dissidents, then, did not proclaim the "end of ideology" in order to set aside moral and political debate and focus on large-scale social transformation. They did not want to avoid ethical questions and moral

---

[48] Michnik, "Evolutionism," 142, 148.

choices, but were looking for an ethics which – in its simplicity, focused as it was on "mere humanity" – was self-evident and thus allowed only for stark moral choices. For the dissidents, Communist ideology's loss of revolutionary zeal and ossification did not open up possibilities for pragmatic cooperation between East and West – it entangled the citizens of the Soviet bloc in a web of lies and made them complicit in their own oppression. Only by bringing the system's lies to light, by choosing the "life in truth" could it be changed.

The views of Brandt and the dissidents could not but clash. For Brandt, the dissidents' moral absolutism appeared as an irresponsible denial of the realities of the Cold War and the development of industrials societies. Yet for all this realism, *Ostpolitik* also had a deliberately optimistic side to it. Drawing on the state of the art social sciences of their time, *Ostpolitik*'s architects argued that the antagonistic systems of the Cold War were governed by the same universal laws of development, laws which would gradually push Communism toward more liberal positions. The broad temporal horizons within which Brandt thought – with their different "ages" and "laws" of development – opened up a new future which politicians could shape. "Social democrats think in terms of processes," an article in the SPD's weekly *Vorwärts* read, defending the party's stance on Poland. "They take humans and their political systems as well as their systems of thought to be capable of changing; and because [Social Democrats] reject Communism, they – without being overly trusting – rely upon the Communists' ability to change for the better."[49]

Yet by the mid- to late 1970s, this optimism began to lose adherents rapidly. Partly, this was due to how the systemic deficiencies of state socialist societies became more and more obvious. But it was also due to the fact that the very optimism of the modernization paradigm began to evaporate. For many in the West, such as many peace activists, the decline of postwar thought's main paradigms initiated an era of what Habermas called a "new obscurity."[50] But the decline of postwar thought also opened up possibilities for new forms of politics. One of them was "democracy promotion." Unlike the development policies of the 1960s, it focused primarily on Western political institutions which were now seen as transferable to different societies and cultures. Underpinning this new policy was a conceptual change. "History," so crucial to Brandt's world view, disappeared as a force shaping human beings and their societies. In its place, human beings were now imagined as disembedded actors universally driven by rationality and self-interest.[51]

---

[49] Heinz Rapp, "Das Kriegsrecht in Polen und die Seele der SPD," *Vorwärts*, Feb. 4, 1982.
[50] Habermas, "Obscurity."   [51] Rodgers, *Age*.

The exhaustion of postwar thought's utopian energies also became a source of energy for the human rights movement. As history disappeared as the backdrop for politics, the claims of the dissidents became plausible. Brandt's posture, in contrast, based as it was on views which had been common sense during the 1950s and 1960s, appeared as a betrayal of Western values, an abandonment of the views he had espoused in his speech in Harvard. But this was an optical illusion. There was, in fact, a remarkable consistency in Brandt's views from his 1962 speech in Harvard to his one-on-one conversation with Jaruzelski in December 1985. What had changed since the early 1960s were the ideas and imaginations of time that his contemporaries used to interpret and understand his actions. *Ostpolitik* was neither conservative nor defeatist; it was merely old-fashioned.

5 Solidarity, Human Rights, and Anti-Totalitarianism in France

The imposition of martial law stranded some 500 members of Solidarity in the West who had left Poland on delegations to Western trade union meetings and were now unable to return home. Dispersed over the United States and Western Europe, many of them joined Polish émigré groups to establish support committees for Solidarity which formed the backbone for an impressive international campaign.[1] One of them was Seweryn Blumsztajn, a former student radical and founding member of KOR. He had been in Paris in December 1981 where he helped set up a committee to coordinate the international work on behalf of Solidarity. Its offices were in the headquarters of France's second-largest trade union, the *Confédération française democratique du travail*, or CFDT, which had also orchestrated the wave protests that swept through France in support of Solidarity on December 14, 1981.[2] Working with French trade unionists, Blumsztajn encountered people much like the militants he had met in the ranks of Solidarity. The bushy mustache of

---

[1] Marek Zieliński, Struktury emigracyjne b. NSZZ "Solidarność" (1981-1984)," Warszawa, MON, Szefostwo Wojskowej Służby Wewnętrznej, 1985, quote on 4, Hoover Institution Archives (hereafter: HIA), Poland: Służba Bezpieczeństwa/Subject File, Box 3, File 3 "Émigrés Centers." For an incomplete list of the committees see the invitation list for a conference held in France in August 1982: Collectif "Solidarité avec Solidarność," La list des invitées, not dated, Records of the Association Solidarité France-Pologne (hereafter: ASFP), Box "ASFP, BIL," File "Courier, informations." For the most extensive study of the committees and especially the central Coordinating Office in Brussels see Idesbald Goddeeris, "Ministerstwo Spraw Zagranicznych Solidarności. Zagraniczna Placówka Koordynacyjna NSZZ Solidarność, 1982-1989," published in two parts in *Pamięć i Sprawiedliwość* 5, 2 (2006), 315–347 and 6, 1 (2007), 309–334. For an abbreviated English version see Idesbald Goddeeris, "Lobbying Allies? The NSZZ Solidarność Coordinating Office Abroad, 1982–1989," *Journal of Cold War Studies* 13 (Summer 2011), 3.

[2] Compte rendu des réunions des 23 décembre et 4 janvier entre la CFDT et le "Comité de Coordination NSZZ Solidarność en France," not dated, CFDT, Sect. Int., 8 H 1920; "Nr 177: 1982 marzec 16, Warszawa – Informacja Departamentu V MSW na temat komitetów I biur informacyjnych Solidarności na Zachodzie, tajne," in Patryk Pleskot, ed., *Solidarność, "Zachód" i "Wężę": Służba Bezpieczeństwa wobec emigracyjnych struktur Solidarności 1981-1989* (Warszawa: IPN, 2011), 414–423, on 415–416.

108   Poland's Solidarity Movement & the Politics of Rights

Jacques Chérèque, the CFDT's secretary for international affairs, even rivaled Lech Wałęsa's. But Blumsztajn also met a man who – bald, bespectacled, always sporting a turtleneck jumper – must have seemed a little out of place among the labor activists, an intellectual and professor at the Collège de France whose field of specialization was not labor history or Soviet studies, but the "history of systems of thought." "With an exceptional devotion," Blumsztajn later remembered, "this man spent hours on end to help us with the most routine bureaucratic work ... I'm sure that he would have had something better to do."[3] The man's name was Michel Foucault.

Foucault was the chairman of a joint committee of French intellectuals and trade unionists created to shore up public support for the Polish trade union. For many of them, their work on behalf of Solidarity was the apogee of what Michael Scott Christofferson has called the "anti-totalitarian moment."[4] It had begun in 1974, the year in which Aleksandr Solzhenitsyn's *The Gulag Archipelago* triggered a fierce debate among French left-wing intellectuals on Communism and Marxism, revolutionary politics, and political ideology. In one of the more spectacular reversals of intellectual history the once dominant framework of the French Left – Marxism – collapsed completely, while human rights moved from the fringes of French leftwing thought to its very center. Support for Soviet and East European political prisoners became a major concern and the "dissident" a celebrated figure. An intellectual discourse emerged whose central metaphor was the "Gulag" and whose linchpin was "totalitarianism" – hitherto a concept only used by political renegades like Raymond Aron.[5] Next to the dissidents, French left-wing intellectuals are the clearest example of how the rise of human rights was an answer to the collapse of ideological schemes of revolutionary change.

Several historians have interpreted the anti-totalitarian moment as an exclusively negative phenomenon. It was all about shedding the

---

[3] Quote in Pierre Bourdieu, "Die Intellektuellen und die Macht," *Michel Foucault: Eine Geschichte der Wahrheit* (München: Raben, 1987), 103.

[4] Michael Scott Christofferson, *French Intellectuals Against the Left: The Antitotalitarian Moment of the 1970s* (New York, Oxford: Berghahn Books, 2004).

[5] For brief surveys of the anti-totalitarian moment see Tony Judt, *Postwar: A History of Europe Since 1945* (New York: Penguin, 2005), 559–566; Moyn, *Utopia*, 167–170. The two most extensive studies in English are Sunil Khilnani, *Arguing Revolution: The Intellectual Left in Postwar France* (New Haven: Yale University Press, 1993); Christofferson, *Intellectuals*; see also Robert Horvath, "'The Solzhenitsyn Effect': East European Dissidents and the Demise of the Revolutionary Privilege," *Human Rights Quarterly* 29 (November 2007). For the wider intellectual history of post-1968 France see Julian Bourg, *From Revolution to Ethics: May 1968 and Contemporary French Thought* (Montreal, et al.: Mc Gill-Queen's University Press, 2007).

revolutionary tradition of French political and intellectual life but did not replace it with anything new and creative. Kristin Ross, for instance, writes that by replacing the symbolic heroes of 1968, "the worker and the colonial militant," with the "dissident" the anti-totalitarian intellectuals "*reanchored* French attention to a Cold War narrative."[6] For Richard Wolin, the discussions of the 1970s were part of a revival of republican traditions, a rebirth of "the ethos of *droits de l'homme* – human rights."[7]

The problem with this view is that, in 1981, there was no human rights tradition the French Left could have returned to. The French Revolution's "rights of man and of the citizen" were an obvious historical point of reference, but as an international norm, as a norm that trumped the norm of sovereignty, human rights was still something comparatively new, and so was a political activism that put human rights at its center. The work of the CFDT and Foucault on behalf of Solidarity was no return to French traditions – its participants were still learning to speak the language of rights, mimicking the symbolic and social practices of dissidents and Amnesty International. But while their work was genuinely about helping Polish trade union activists, they deliberately used the language of human rights to articulate and discuss an issue much closer to home – the future of left-wing politics and democratic socialism in an age in which its principal vehicle, the state, had lost its allure.

The intellectual backdrop of French support for Solidarity was thus the same development against which Willy Brandt's *Ostpolitik* began to appear like a betrayal of Western values – the "new obscurity" triggered by the crisis of postwar social thought. The conclusions toward which many of Solidarity's French admirers gravitated, however, were strikingly similar to those some of the dissidents in Central Europe had drawn. Like the latter, many French intellectuals believed that totalitarianism was a system that had made politics impossible. As its antidote, human rights were understood as laying the foundation of a new form of politics. Much as in Central Europe, human rights activism was interpreted as a path to building communities and enabling forms of social self-organization.

I

For several days after the imposition of martial law, the Polish crisis completely dominated French public life. Television programs were

---

[6] Kristin Ross, *May 68 and its Afterlives* (Chicago, London: University of Chicago Press, 2002), 12, 158. Emphasis added.

[7] Richard Wolin, *The Frankfurt School Revisited and Other Essays on Politics and Society* (New York, NY ; London: Routledge, 2006), 176.

110   Poland's Solidarity Movement & the Politics of Rights

interrupted for breaking news from Poland and, well into 1982, most newspapers devoted several pages to the Polish crisis. Few media outlets hid their sympathies; where German politicians and peace activists – concerned about worsening East–West relations – invoked the Helsinki Agreement's passages on noninterference, French commentators invoked nothing short of an "obligation to interfere."[8] Where Blumsztajn's usage of the term "totalitarianism" raised eyebrows among German interlocutors, anti-totalitarianism was the order of the day in France.[9]

The intellectuals around Foucault and the trade unionists of the CFDT had led the charge in supporting Solidarity, founding the aforementioned joint committee and engaging in an array of activities. But their work was only the most visible among a whirlwind of similar initiatives. French newspapers published a series of open letters and appeals for support,[10] while Solidarity committees with Poland were founded by the French P.E.N. club, in *lycées*, among the faculty of universities and the staff of research institutions, by professional associations and editorial boards of journals.[11] Engaging in what a CFDT document called "Amnesty International style initiatives," these groups drew on the entire repertoire of human rights practices that had emerged over the previous decade.[12] They sent letters of protest to the Polish embassy and the authorities in Warsaw, compiled lists of political prisoners, and discussed ways of organizing legal aid for Polish activists on trial. Drawing on Amnesty's most well-known form of activism, members of professional organizations, researchers, or workers symbolically adopted one or more of their imprisoned Polish peers to raise awareness of their internment, protest on their behalf, and help their families.[13]

---

[8] Patrick Viveret, "Le devoir d'ingérence," *Le Matin*, Dec. 16, 1981.

[9] "La France et le totalitarisme," *Le Monde*, Jan. 12, 1982.

[10] "La liberté de tous se joue aujourd'hui en Pologne," *Le Monde*, Dec. 23, 1981.

[11] Circular letter from René Tavrnier, "Le P.E.N.: Solidarité avec des ecrivains étrangers," dated Apr. 1, 1982, ASFP, Box "BIL," letter from C.N.R.S. comitee to the director of IFiS PAN, dated Jan. 12, 1982, circular beginning with "Les slavistes soussignés ... ," dated Jan. 18, 1981, "Pologne: ne dites pas qu'il n'y a rien a faire," dated Dec. 19, 1981, "Appels et petitions des jurists" and "Appel du syndicat de la psychiatrie," clippings from *Libération*, Dec. 21, 1981, all documents in CFDT, Sect. Int., 8 H 2080; Circular letter by Jacques LeGoff, dated 25 Mai 1982, ASFP, Box "BIL."

[12] Memo from Michel Garicoix for the members of SJF, "A propos de la solidarité avec Solidarnosc," dated Dec. 21, 1981, on 2, CFDT, Sect. Int., 8 H 1920.

[13] Letter from Edmond Maire to the ambassador of Poland in France, dated Dec. 16, 1981, Commission executive CFDT, Procès-verbal de la reunion du 16 décembre 1981, dated Dec. 16, 1981, Commission executive CFDT, "Cellule Pologne," dated Jan. 15,

Solidarity, Human Rights, and Anti-Totalitarianism 111

These symbolic activities expressed a general rejection of the existing model of détente, especially in its *Ostpolitik* variety, and demanded that Communist governments be held accountable for the human rights norms of the CSCE.[14] Some of Solidarity's French sympathizers even sought to implement this linkage policy themselves. Until January 18, 1982, some 5,000 academics and scientists, including two Nobel Prize laureates and 64 members of the Collège de France, signed a manifesto declaring that martial law was not anymore "an internal Polish affair but violated [met en cause] the rights of peoples and human rights." Until the situation improved, the manifesto's signatories threatened, they would break off their contacts with East European institutions.[15]

Another important activity was what a CFDT document, in complete disregard of the actual media storm around Poland, called "breaking the wall of silence" – creating publicity for human rights violations through public relations work and symbolic gestures.[16] The CFDT marked the 13th of every month with an initiative devoted to the situation in Poland[17]

1982, all in CFDT, Sect. Int., 8 H 1920; "Compte rendu succinct de la reunion organisée par l'Association Solidarité France-Pologne," dated Jan. 11, 1982, "Exposition et vente publique de peintures et de sculptures au profit de Solidarnosc," dated Jan. 21, 1982, both in CFDT, Sect. Int., 8 H 1921; Réunion CFDT – intellectuels: 12.2.82, Comité des sociologues pour la Pologne, C.R, de la reunion du 7.1.1982, not dated, both in CFDT, Sect. Int., 8 H 2080. The adoption of political prisoners and their families was also a central concern of the *Association Solidarité France-Pologne*, an organization of Polish émigrés and French academics. See circular letter from Piotr Słonimski, dated Dec. 31, 1981, Appel pour la parrainage, not dated, and ASFP circular dated Sept. 15, 1982, ASFP, Box "BIL." On the ASFP, see Marek Kunicki-Goldfinger, "Stowarzyszenie Solidarité France–Pologne i jego pomoc dla Polski w latach osiemdziesiątych XX wieku," in Paweł Jaworski and Łukasz Kamiński, eds., *Świat wobec Solidarności 1980-1989* (Warszawa: IPN, 2014).

[14] Michel Foucault, "Notes sur ce qu'on lit et entend (même sujet)" and " Un premier pas de la colonization de l'Occident," in his *Dits et écrits*, vol. IV (Paris: Gallimard, 1994), IV, 211–212, 261–269, on 263–265 (hereafter: *Dits*); Réunion CFDT-intellectuels, on 3–4, memo from Paul Thibault "Liberté pour la Pologne et l'Europe de l'Est," not dated, both in CFDT, Sect. Int., 8 H 2080; "Information sur la dette polonaise," dated Jan. 21, 1981, and "Les dépendances de la France dans les relations économiques avec l'Europe de l'Est," dated Jan. 22, 1982, CFDT, Sect. Int., 8 H 1921.

[15] "Manifeste d 5000 scientifiques pour la Pologne," *Le Monde*, Jan. 18, 1982. For similar activities see "Colloque sur la recherché et la technologie," dated Jan. 15, 1982, "Solidarité ou spationaute: il faut choisir," not dated, letter from Patrice Berghain and Jean-François Troglic to Jean-Pierre Chevenèment, dated Mar. 26, 1982, letter from Raymond X. to Alexandre Bilous, dated 28 April 1982, "Pologne: ne dites pas," all in CFDT, Sect. Int., 8 H 2080.

[16] CFDT flyer titled "Ne laissez pas le silence s'installer en Pologne," dated 13 Mar. 1982, CFDT, Sect. Int., 8 H 2080.

[17] "Plusieurs initiatives de solidarité sont annoncées par la C.F.D.T. et des 'coordination' d'intellectuels," newspaper clipping dated Jan. 5, 1982, CFDT, Sect. Int., 8 H 2080; CFDT circular, "A propos du 13 mars: Une grande operation nationale," dated Feb. 24, 1982, CFDT, Sect. Int., 8 H 1921. See also Association Solidarité France-Pologne,

112 Poland's Solidarity Movement & the Politics of Rights

and produced thousands of Solidarity badges its members proudly wore on their sleeves and shirts. Two people who wore their badges with particular pride were Foucault and the singer Yves Montand whose sold-out concerts in Paris' Olympia music hall ended with a huge Solidarity banner descending onto the stage.[18] In October 1982, Foucault joined Montand's wife Simone Signoret and Bernard Kouchner, a co-founder of Doctors without Borders and outspoken French human rights activist, on a truck convoy that brought food and medical supplies to Poland. Upon their return, they gave a series of interviews to sustain French awareness for human rights violations in Poland.[19]

The CFDT also supported Polish émigré groups who had established an infrastructure of human rights advocacy focused on the Soviet bloc. Around the CSCE review conference in Madrid, a second international conference had sprung up, when human rights groups and East European exile organizations had set up shop to lobby the Western delegations. The émigré groups used these channels to make a human rights report, compiled in the Polish underground and smuggled to the West, available to the Western delegations in Madrid. Similar work was done to bring Solidarity's case before two UN bodies: the UN Commission on Human Rights (UNCHR) and the International Labor Organization (ILO).[20]

This massive outpouring of support for Solidarity forced the French government to significantly sharpen its tone toward Poland. On December 13, France's ministers for foreign affairs and trade respectively had both called martial law an "internal affair" about which Paris could do nothing. A statement issued by the Quai d'Orsay on the same day failed to name a culprit in the Polish drama, deploring merely "the chain of events which had led to the detention of the leaders of the Solidarity trade union movement."[21] Confronted with a barrage of

---

Avant projet, dated May 19, 1982 and Appel de l'Association Solidarité France-Pologne, dated Sep. 28, 1982, ASFP, Box "BIL."

[18] "Yves Montand trägt das Abzeichen der 'Solidarität,'" *Die Welt*, Jan. 15, 1982.

[19] David Macey, *The Lives of Michel Foucault: A Biography* (New York: Pantheon Books, 1993), 444–448. The interviews are reprinted in Michel Foucault, "Michel Foucault: 'Il n'y a pas de neutralité possible'," "En abandonnant les Polonais, nous renonçons à une part de nous-mêmes," "Michel Foucault: 'L'expérience morale et sociale des Polonais ne peut plus être efface," in *Dits*, vol. IV, 338–350.

[20] Goddeeris, "Allies," 110.

[21] Jean-François Sirinelli, *Intellectuels et passions françaises: Manifestes et pétitions au XXe siècle* (Paris: Fayard, 1990), 297–298. Cf. Marcelle Padovani, "P.S.: comment le ton a monté," *Le Nouvel Observateur*, Dec. 16, 1981 (special issue).

public criticism of this policy, especially from traditional allies of the ruling Socialists like the CFDT, Paris changed its approach to Poland. On December 16, Mitterrand convened a special cabinet meeting and issued a statement denouncing "the loss of public, collective, and individual liberty" in Poland."[22] Six days later, it was read out by actress Romy Schneider at the end of a gala evening in support of Solidarity in the Paris Opera, organized by the minister of culture and attended by 2,000 people, including the prime minister and ten cabinet members.[23]

It is questionable, though, whether these statements were backed up by a substantial change in policy. While the French officials criticized West Germany's conciliatory stance publicly, they readily conceded behind closed doors that their attitude toward Poland was very close to the German one.[24] Paris also took great care to protect its relations with Moscow from the fall-out of the Polish crisis. On February 22, 1982, the French government finalized French–Soviet negotiations on the gas pipeline that outraged the US government so much. "It would not do any good," Prime Minister Mauroy commented, "to add to the Polish drama an additional drama for the French who would not be provided with gas."[25] As in other West European capitals, attacking Poland seemed a lesser evil than jeopardizing East–West relations more broadly.

II

The powerful response of the French public to martial law had many reasons. A very important one was that France had a very active Polish diaspora community and French and Polish scholars had forged close ties during research trips and membership in international organizations.[26] However, the major actors in French support for Solidarity, the intellectuals around Foucault and the CFDT, had not been particularly active in these networks before 1980, and neither cast their work for Solidarity as a continuation of a long-standing Polish–French friendship. In fact, they did not cast their work for human rights as evolving out of any tradition but as a new form of activism that emulated the struggle of

---

[22] Transcript of statement by François Mitterrand, "Situation en Pologne," dated Dec. 16, 1981, CFDT, Sect. Int., 8 H 1920.
[23] Sirinelli, *Intellectuels*, 308–309; Diana Johnstone, "How the French Left Learned to Love the Bomb," *New Left Review* I/146 (July–August 1984), 20–21.
[24] See Chapter 3, Section V, above.   [25] Sjursen, *United States*, 77.
[26] Jean-Marie Domenach, "Rozmowa z Jean-Marie Domenachem," *Krytyka* 3 (1978). Paul Thibaud, "Mauvais neige," *Esprit* (Mar. 1982); for these contacts see also Kosicki, "L'avènement"; Marcin Frybes, "Solidarność-CFDT: L'expérience d'un dialogue Est-Ouest," *La Revue de la CFDT* 3 (September 1997), 10–11.

114   Poland's Solidarity Movement & the Politics of Rights

the dissidents. Thanks to their efforts, the philosopher Claude Lefort had written in 1980, "availing themselves of the Helsinki Agreements in order to demand respect for human rights, ... [t]hese rights no longer seem to be formal, intended to conceal a system of domination; they are now seen to embody a real struggle against oppression."[27]

The French campaign for Solidarity has thus to be seen within the anti-totalitarian moment, triggered by Solzhenitsyn's *Gulag Archipelago*, that so transformed French intellectual life during the 1970s. In *Interpreting the French Revolution* of 1978, François Furet provided an influential explanation of this process and its relation to Solzhenitsyn.[28] With the Bolshevik revolution, he argued, French intellectuals had lost their role as standard bearers of progressive politics, a process reinforced by the disgrace of the Vichy government during World War II. To compensate for this loss, French intellectuals had claimed a kinship between the French and the Russian revolution. By declaring "1917" as the legitimate heir of "1789," French intellectuals of the Left could remain true to their national traditions while still claiming a place at the center of historical progress. Many of them joined the Communist party or became "fellow travelers."[29]

All of this changed, Furet's interpretation continued, when Solzhenitsyn's *Gulag Archipelago* exposed the horrors of the Soviet labor camps as an essential part of the Soviet experience. With Solzhenitsyn "locating the issue of the Gulag at the very core of the revolutionary endeavor ... the Russian example was bound to turn around, like a boomerang, to strike its French 'origin,'" Furet concluded, smashing France's entire postwar left-wing discourse.[30] In the self-understanding of many anti-totalitarian intellectuals, Solzhenitsyn had initiated a

---

[27] Lefort, *Forms*, 240–241, 272.

[28] François Furet, *Interpreting the French Revolution* (Cambridge: Cambridge University Press, 1981); François Furet, *The Passing of an Illusion: The Idea of Communism in the Twentieth Century* (Chicago, IL: 1997). The original titles of the books are *Penser la Révolution française* and *Le Passé d'une illusion, essai sur l'idée communiste au XXe siècle*.

[29] Furet, *Interpreting*, 11–12. See also Khilnani, *Revolution*, 3–16, 125–128; Horvath, "Solzhenitsyn," 882–895. Jean-Paul Sartre, *The Communists and Peace, with an Answer to Claude Lefort*, trans. Irene Clephane (London: Hamilton, 1969). Probably the most well-known study of this aspect of French intellectual history is Tony Judt, *Past Imperfect: French Intellectuals, 1944-1956* (Berkeley, CA: University of California Press, 1992). He enumerates a number of additional reasons for French intellectuals' "will to ignorance" (158) of Soviet crimes. One is that the experience of political radicalism during the 1930s and of violence during the occupation fueled a Manichean view of politics. Another is the lack of a liberal tradition in French political thought; in France, Judt argues, rights did not protect the individual against the state, but were a claim on the individual by the political community.

[30] Furet, *Interpreting*, 11–12.

Solidarity, Human Rights, and Anti-Totalitarianism

painful cathartic process, a collective exorcism even.[31] He had torn away their ideological blinders, forcing them to confront the horrifying results of a project they had passionately supported.[32]

The most outspoken proponents of this understanding of the anti-totalitarian moment were a group of self-styled "new philosophers," former Maoist student radicals of May 1968. Misunderstanding Foucault's ideas about the ubiquity of power, they argued that Solzhenitsyn had revealed the totalitarian potential not merely of Marxism but the whole of modernity. In a string of national bestsellers, they sketched a deeply pessimistic view of a modern world of concentration camps and mass-slaughter. In this situation, Andre Glucksmann believed, philosophy's main question was not anymore Kant's "What can I hope for?" ("Que m'est-il permis d'espérer?"), but "What should we despair of?" ("De quoi faut-il désespérer?").[33]

In this conceptual world, a commitment to human rights could not be more than a last line of defense, keeping modernity's destructive powers at bay by saving one life at a time. The writings of the new philosophers are thus the clearest examples of how human rights emerged in the 1970s as a purely ethical and deliberately minimalist program of alleviating suffering rather than aiming for positive political change. Significantly, the two most prominent new philosophers, Glucksmann and Bernard-Henry Levy, would later become proponents of "humanitarian interventionism."[34]

Yet the new philosophers did not represent nearly all of the French anti-totalitarian discourse, despite the publicity and notoriety they gained. While Foucault published a glowing review of one of their books, Glucksmann's *The Master Thinkers*,[35] most intellectuals derided their

---

[31] Wolin, *Frankfurt School*, 187; Khilnani, *Revolution*, 121.

[32] Khilnani, *Revolution*, 134.

[33] Quoted in Michel Foucault, "La grande colère des faits (sur A. Glucksmann)" and "Pouvoirs et stratégies," in *Dits*, III, 277–281, on 277.

[34] Eleanor Davey, *Idealism Beyond Borders: The French Revolutionary Left and the Rise of Humanitarianism, 1954-1988* (Cambridge: Cambridge University Press, 2015).

[35] Michel Foucault, "La grande colère" and "Pouvoirs et stratégies," in *Dits*, III, 277–281, 418–428, quotations on 420. For Foucault's attitude toward the new philosophers and the role of his ideas in their writings see Macey, *Lives*, 381–388; Christofferson, *Intellectuals*, 198–201. The main works of Lévy and Glucksmann from this period are Andre Glucksmann, *La cuisinière et le mangeur d'hommes: Essai sur les rapports entre l'état, le marxisme et les camps de concentration* (Paris: Éditions du Seuil, 1975); Andre Glucksmann, *The Master Thinkers* (New York: Harper & Row, 1980); Bernard-Henri Lévy, *Barbarism with a Human Face*, trans. George Holoch (NY: Harper, 1979); Bernard-Henri Lévy, *Testament of God* (New York: Harper & Row, 1980). For a useful contemporaneous survey of their thought see Johannes Thomas, *Engel und Leviathan: Neue Philosophie in Frankreich als nachmarxistische Politik und Kulturkritik* (München: Olzog, 1979).

116   Poland's Solidarity Movement & the Politics of Rights

books, written as they were in a sometimes pompous, sometimes vulgar, always pretentious language. A much more influential reading of Solzhenitsyn and totalitarianism came from the aforementioned Lefort, an active member of the committee of intellectuals in support of Solidarity.[36] In a book-length interpretation of the *Gulag Archipelago* and a string of essays, Lefort developed an interpretation of human rights and totalitarianism which bore striking resemblance to the thought of East–Central European dissidents. Like the latter, Lefort understood totalitarianism as a system that had destroyed the foundation of politics. For him, totalitarianism's central aspect was its "image of the political body" as a homogeneous and unified society, the "People-as-One." The only social division which the totalitarian party accepted was the one between itself – as society's embodiment – and the inimical world outside of it.[37] Totalitarian parties destroyed the very stuff of politics – the competition of ideas, the clash of opinions, the articulation of interests, the spontaneity and indeterminacy of life in a diverse society. Totalitarianism was not too political, in Lefort's view, it was anti-political.[38]

Precisely by invoking human rights, Lefort argued, the dissidents' approach was profoundly political. The dissidents, to be sure, avoided

---

[36] Letter from Claude Lefort to Edmond Maire, dated Jan. 7, 1981 [sic!], CFDT, Sect. Int., 8 H 2080. For his importance see Christofferson, *Intellectuals*, 105; Dick Howard, "Claude Lefort: A Political Biography," in Martín Plot, ed., *Claude Lefort: Thinker of the Political* (Basingstoke: Palgrave Macmillan, 2013), 16–17; see also James D. Ingram, "The Politics of Claude Lefort's Political: Between Liberalism and Radical Democracy," *Thesis Eleven* 87 (Nov. 2006), 1, 38–39. In addition to shorter pieces which Lefort wrote on dissent, Solidarity, and the Polish crisis, my reading of his ideas draws on his book-length essay on Solzhenitsyn as well as on two collections of essays in political theory and analysis which Lefort wrote from the late 1970s to the late 1980s: Claude Lefort, *Un homme en trop: Réflexions sur "L'Archipel du Goulag"* (Paris: Éditions du Seuil, 1976); Lefort, *Forms*; Claude Lefort, *Democracy and Political Theory* (Cambridge: Polity, 1988). The three central essays for my interpretation from *Forms* are "Politics and Human Rights," "The Logic of Totalitarianism," and "The Image of the Body and Totalitarianism." All three had been republished in 1981 in *L'invention démocratique*, a volume whose publication Lefort deemed necessary given Mitterrand's election and events in Poland. I also relied heavily on an excellent secondary literature. For a systematic analysis of Claude Lefort's political thought see Bernard Flynn, *The Philosophy of Claude Lefort: Interpreting the Political* (Evanston, IL: Northwestern University Press, 2005). See also Raf Geenens, "Democracy, Human Rights and History: Reading Lefort," *European Journal of Political Theory* 7 (2008), 3; Martín Plot, ed., *Claude Lefort: Thinker of the Political* (Basingstoke: Palgrave-Macmillan, 2013), esp. the contributions by Dick Howard, Flynn, Samuel Moyn, and Jean L. Cohen ; Andreas Wagner, ed., *Am leeren Ort der Macht: Das Staats- und Politikverständnis Claude Leforts* (Baden-Baden: Nomos, 2013), esp. the contributions of Ersin Yildiz, Felix Trautmann, Stefan Militzer, and Oliver Marchart; Dick Howard, *The Specter of Democracy* (New York: Columbia University Press, 2002), chs. 6 and 8.

[37] Lefort, *Forms*, 297. ibid., 300.   [38] Ibid., 251.

Solidarity, Human Rights, and Anti-Totalitarianism 117

politics understood in a narrower sense, as the specific realm of society populated by parties and institutions. But by claiming a universal right to express a dissenting opinion, they had defied the totalitarian vision of the "People-as-One"[39] and posed a fundamental challenge to the very foundation of totalitarian rule – its image of the body politic.[40]

If the dissidents' struggle was political, Lefort's argument continued, so were human rights. They did not belong in the "sanctuary of morality," where the new philosophers placed them, but implied a specific vision of society[41] – democracy.[42] Where totalitarianism envisioned the political as an organic whole – the "People-as-One," embodied by the totalitarian party – democracy envisioned the political as a public space – a political stage where different opinions and ideas competed with each other.[43] Where legitimacy in totalitarianism derived from an ideology pretending to answer all questions, democracy knew only one form of legitimacy, *"the legitimacy of a debate as to what is legitimate and what is illegitimate* – a debate which is necessarily without any guarantor and without any end."[44] Human rights laid the foundation for democracy because they protected and engendered divisions and diversity – they enabled ways of life, forms of social activity, and practices of public discourse which remained outside of the orbit of power and were thus indeterminate.[45]

Clearly, then, Lefort's reading of human rights placed them at the center of a program of social change. His theory of human rights, moreover, both criticized Marx and took his views of human rights seriously.

---

[39] In 1976, Lefort gave a talk at a conference attended by East European émigrés in which he described the Hungarian revolution of 1956 as anti-totalitarian in this sense, that is, as shattering totalitarianism's vision of a society "delivered" from division. He later applied the same interpretation to Solidarity. Claude Lefort, "La première révolution antitotalitaire," in Pierre Kende and Krzysztof Pomian, eds., *1956: Varsovie-Budapest - La deuxième révolution d'Octobre* (Paris: Seuil, 1978), 94; Lefort, *Forms*, 309–310. In *Un homme en trop*, his reflections on *The Gulag Archipelago*, Lefort had underlined how Solzhenitsyn adopts a decisively political perspective on his time in the labor camps. Raf Geenens, "'When I Was Young and Politically Engaged...': Lefort on the Problem of Political Commitment," *Thesis Eleven* 87 (November 1, 2006 2006), 1, 20–22.

[40] Lefort seems to have introduced this distinction in an article published one year after his essay on human rights: "Permanence du théologico-politique?," *Le Temps de la Réflexion* 2 (1981), translated as "The Permanence of the Theologico-Political?," in his, *Democracy*, 213–255, at 216–217. But he certainly used this analytical distinction in the cited article. For instance, he wrote that what distinguished a struggle in the name of rights was that it did not "attack the state head on, but obliquely; by circumventing [the state], as it were, it touches the center from which [the state] draws the justification of its own right to demand the allegiance and obedience of all." Lefort, *Forms*, 254, 264–265. For an indepth discussion of Lefort's distinction between "politics" and "the political" see Ingram, "Politics"; see also Howard, "Claude Lefort," 18.

[41] Lefort, *Forms*, 243.   [42] Ibid., 259.   [43] Lefort, *Democracy*, 18.   [44] Ibid., 39.

[45] Lefort, *Forms*, 256–257.

118   Poland's Solidarity Movement & the Politics of Rights

On one hand, Lefort saw a totalitarian potential of Marx's thought. Marx, he believed, had misunderstood the diversity of modern social life – the conflict of opinions and interests, the division of labor – as a form of social alienation, an artificial separation of social classes and spheres that belonged together. His project of a society in which social divisions would be "abolished within the purity of the social, ... culminate[d] in the totalitarian fantasy ...," Lefort charged.[46]

On the other hand, however, Lefort's vernacularization of human rights remained indebted to his Marxist heritage, as especially Samuel Moyn has shown.[47] Marx, Lefort readily conceded, had been correct that human rights could be, and had been, exploited to justify social egoism. Where Marx had erred was in arguing that social egoism was inherent in human rights. The reality of totalitarianism, Lefort believed, had shown this clearly. Insisting that the "individuality [of human beings] must be dissolved in a good body politic, the Soviet people or the party," totalitarianism had isolated people from one another in the most radical way. It was not the institutionalization of human rights, but their abolishment that had led to radical alienation.[48]

As the antidote to totalitarianism, human rights were a means to build a social community. Where Marx had argued that the right to individual liberty would sanctify social isolation, Lefort argued that this right made new forms of social association possible. The individual freedom of opinion made no sense without others who would listen to one's opinion. In Lefort's hands, an individual political right thus became a social right because it established the right to communicate, "to step out of [one]self and to make contacts with others, through speech, writing, and thought." Its realization was profoundly political and social, it established a sphere of communication beyond the tutelage of power – freedom of opinion was "a freedom of relationships."[49]

Lefort's idea that human rights were meant to empower people to freely discuss and shape their collective affairs placed him within a wider current of French intellectual life whose origins lay in the 1960s and

---

[46] Lefort, *Democracy*, 33–34.
[47] Samuel Moyn, "The Politics of Individual Rights: Marcel Gauchet and Claude Lefort," in Raf Geenens and Helena Rosenblatt, eds., *French Liberalism from Montesqieu to the Present Day* (New York: Cambridge University Press, 2012).
[48] Lefort, *Forms*, 245–246. For broadly similar interpretations of Lefort's understanding of human rights see Jean L. Cohen, "Rethinking the Politics of Human Rights with and beyond Lefort," in Martín Plot, ed., *Claude Lefort: Thinker of the Political* (Basingstoke: Palgrave Macmillan, 2013); Howard, *Specter*, ch. 6; Stefan Militzer, "Meinungsfreiheit und politischer Widerstand: Claude Leforts Menschenrechtskonzeption als Beitrag zu einer Ontologie der Demokratie," in Wagner, ed., *Ort*; Moyn, "Politics."
[49] Lefort, *Forms*, 248–251, 257–258, quotations on 250, 257.

Solidarity, Human Rights, and Anti-Totalitarianism 119

which was at least as important for the anti-totalitarian moment as the revelations of Solzhenitsyn. What propelled this current was not so much the question of revolutionary violence as the role of the state in effecting social progress. During the 1960s, a French left-wing discourse had emerged which was still saturated with a Marxist terminology, but which increasingly combined revolutionary politics with a quest for individual autonomy and self-fulfillment. Strongly anti-authoritarian, the participants of this discourse grew sharply critical of the French state, traditionally the vehicle for leftist politics in France. Its ever-extending bureaucracy and authoritarian institutions, they feared, threatened individual liberation; practices of grass-roots democracy, such as workers' councils, emerged as possible alternatives.[50]

These developments culminated in the revolt of May 1968, onto which the nonorthodox Left projected its ideas of anti-authoritarianism, spontaneity, and grass-roots democracy.[51] At least in the short term, however, May 1968 produced few tangible results. More than that, the very state-centered ideology the students so despised dominated the political parties of the Left – the Socialists, revitalized under Mitterrand, and the pro-Soviet Communist party. In 1972, the two parties even struck an electoral alliance. The ideas projected on 1968, it seemed, had been defeated.[52]

This conflict among different factions on the French Left was the main background for the debate around the *Gulag Archipelago*, a book that revealed little that had not yet been known about Soviet atrocities. When the French Communists attacked Solzhenitsyn, the nonorthodox Left could portray him as a victim of both Soviet and French Communism. When the French Communists broadened their attack to include the nonorthodox Left,[53] the latter could claim the mantle of dissent for itself. The nonorthodox Left read the *Gulag Archipelago* as a general theory of totalitarianism, a vision of what would happen to France if

---

[50] Frank Georgi, "Jeux d'ombres: Mai, le mouvement social et l'autogestion (1968-2007)," *Vingtième Siècle* 98 (2008); Frank Georgi, "Le monde change, changeons notre syndicalisme: La crise vue par la CFDT (1973-1988)," *Vingtième Siècle* 84 (2004); Bernard E. Brown, *Socialism of a Different Kind: Reshaping the Left in France* (Westport, London: Greenwood Press, 1982), ch. 3-5, on Maire as "the most forceful and enthusiastic" supporter of autogestion see ibid., 45–49.
[51] For an account characterizing May 1968 as a quest for a new form of revolutionary politics see Ross, *May 68*, ch. 2.
[52] On socialism under Mitterrand see Brown, *Socialism*; Julius Weis Friend, *The Long Presidency: France in the Mitterrand Years, 1981-1995* (Boulder, CO: Westview Press, 1998), 6–22; for the discrepancy between the Socialists' more traditional views and the new Left in France see Hélène Hatzfeld, "Une révolution culturelle du parti socialiste dans les années 1970?," *Vingtième Siècle* 96 (2007), 77–90.
[53] Christofferson, *Intellectuals*, 92–96.

120   Poland's Solidarity Movement & the Politics of Rights

the state-centered ideas of the Communists and Socialists won out – an argument powerfully underscored by the figure of Solzhenitsyn, a victim of both Soviet violence and attempts by the French Communists to silence him.[54]

If Solzhenitsyn's role was largely negative, as a witness to the totalitarian potential of French etatism, the Polish opposition seems to have provided a more positive example. Adam Michnik's essay "A New Evolutionism" of 1976 was based on a talk he had given in Paris at an East European émigré conference. To an audience that included Lefort and other non-Communist Left-wing intellectuals, he described the struggle for "an expansion of civil liberties and human rights" in Poland primarily as a struggle for society's self-organization.[55] This approach anticipated Lefort's post-Marxist reading of human rights and it resonated strongly with a central idea of the heirs of May 1968 – *autogestion*.

Autogestion is the French translation of the Serbo-Croatian expression for workers' self-management in Yugoslavia but it came to denote a broader understanding of society's democratic self-organization. Its main theoretician was Pierre Rosanvallon – an intellectual closely associated with the CFDT and a later student of Lefort. He defined *autogestion* as "the *collective* exercise of decision, the possibility of direct intervention by each in the problems that concern him or her … the living practice of a true democracy." Like Lefort, Rosanvallon saw civil society as the social sphere where this form of politics was to be implemented. Human rights were meant to shield its independence. Again, the guarantee of individual liberties was meant to enable new forms of social association.[56]

Lefort too had argued that civil society was to be the locus of democracy. Demanding the recognition of new rights, the citizens did not address their claims primarily at the state, but at each other. Lefort

---

[54] Khilnani, *Revolution*, 146–147.

[55] Adam Michnik, "Une stratégie pour l'opposition polonaise," *Esprit* 1 (Jan. 1977); quotation from Michnik, *Prison*, 142.

[56] Pierre Rosanvallon, *L'âge de l'autogestion* (Paris: Éditions du Seuil, 1976), 42–45; see also the classic treatise on this concept in Pierre Rosanvallon and Patrick Viveret, *Pour une nouvelle culture politique* (Paris: Éditions du Seuil, 1977). Interestingly, Rosanvallon rejected Marxism, because it was too individualistic, likening it to what he called "utopian liberalism." Both were aimed, Rosanvallon wrote, at "the extinction of politics and the critique of the rights of man." See his "Marx and Civil Society," in *Democracy, Past and Future*, 160–186, quotation on 161. On Rosanvallon see Andrew Jainchill and Samuel Moyn, "French Democracy between Totalitarianism and Solidarity: Pierre Rosanvallon and Revisionist Historiography," *The Journal of Modern History* 76 (2004), 1; Samuel Moyn, "Introduction: Antitotalitarianism and After," in Pierre Rosanvallon *Democracy Past and Future: Selected Essays* (New York: Columbia University Press, 2007).

Solidarity, Human Rights, and Anti-Totalitarianism   121

located this struggle "at the heart of civil society, in the name of an indefinite need for mutual recognition of liberties, a mutual protection of the ability to exercise them."[57] For Lefort, then, conquering government was not necessary to change society – the defense of existing rights and the demand for new ones constantly challenged and shifted the boundaries of the political.

This understanding of human rights as being about diversity and social self-organization renders even Foucault's human rights activism more consistent with his philosophy than it appears.[58] Every society, Foucault argued, had its own "politics of truth" – the rules and practices, linguistic conventions, and systems of knowledge that defined truth. To deny this connection, to take one's philosophical system as "objectively true," to provide an overarching theory for society's liberation from power, could have totalitarian consequences – such a "dominant thought" merely concealed its own new "politics of truth." Rather than replacing one hegemonic politics of truth with another, the task of the political intellectual was to unmask them, to show that it was always "possible to constitute a new politics of truth," and give a voice to those who were excluded, imprisoned, or even tortured and murdered under an existing hegemony of truth.[59]

For Foucault, the struggle for human rights was thus not necessarily a struggle for their international codification. Foucault, in fact, was skeptical about an international institutionalization of human rights. It would be good if governments based their policies on human rights, Foucault acknowledged, but he rejected any rigid framework of international law. "One has to be careful," he warned "not to reintroduce a new dominant thought under the pretext of presenting a theory or politics of human rights. Leninism, after all, had presented itself as a politics of human rights...." The power of human rights was that they had engendered a "certain moralization of politics and a politicization of life [existence] which is based not anymore on an obligatory reference to an ideology or membership in a political party but which is based on a more direct contact of people with the events and with their own life choices [choix d'existence]."[60]

This discourse also explains why secular French intellectuals were so enthusiastic about Solidarity despite the fact that it was such a strongly

---

[57] Lefort, *Forms*, 266, 262; see also Claude Lefort, *L'invention démocratique: Les limites de la domination totalitaire* (Paris: Fayard, 1981), 27–30.

[58] Cf. Wolin, *Frankfurt School*, 176–181; Bourg, *Revolution*, 325–328.

[59] Michel Foucault, "La function politique de intellectuel," in *Dits*, III, 109–114, on 114.

[60] Foucault, "L'experience," 344, 349. For a discussion of Foucault's views on human rights that reveals similarities to Lefort's understanding of rights as generating democracy see Ben Golder, "Foucault and the Unfinished Human of Rights," *Law, Culture and the Humanities* 6 (2010), 3.

122   Poland's Solidarity Movement & the Politics of Rights

Catholic movement. It seems that they did not admire the Polish trade union primarily for what it was, but for what it did – oppose totalitarianism in the name of social self-organization. In December 1981, in a discussion with Foucault and Lefort, Rosanvallon interpreted Solidarity in this sense in *autogestionnaire* terms. What set the Polish movement apart from the Prague Spring or the resistance in Chile, he said, was that it had acknowledged the existence of the party state, in order to carve out a space for civil society. By avoiding "politics" – where the alternative would have been reform or revolution – Solidarity had initiated a struggle for a new way of envisioning "the political" – one in which society had an autonomous existence from the state.[61]

Lefort's interpretation was similar. By forcing the party to make concession after concession, by forcing it to negotiate with the working class, Solidarity had forced it to publicly abandon the totalitarian image of society, it had pushed it off "the symbolic position of the incarnating power."[62] Asserting "the independence of civil society,"[63] the Polish workers and intellectuals had introduced a new right into Polish society: the right to make demands – they had opened up "an unlimited capacity to take initiatives" and had established a democratic principle: the ability to contest power.[64]

In France, in sum, the Left's embrace of human rights was clearly caused by the collapse of Marxism. Yet the French answer to this crisis was not universally a celebration of individualism and retreat to a morally pure, strictly humanitarian activism. Solidarity's supporters, which included some of France's leading intellectuals of the time, understood human rights as a way of laying the foundation for a new form of politics, as a path toward building communities of engaged citizens who would have a direct influence on their common affairs.

III

Understanding the struggle for human rights as one for social self-organization, Solidarity's supporters used the practices of Amnesty International and other groups for a campaign which was self-consciously about solidarity with Polish activists. Solidarity's French supporters openly identified with the Polish movement in ways similar to how student radicals of the 1960s had identified with anti-colonial revolutionaries. The committee Foucault presided over imitated how

[61] Michel Foucault, Claude Lefort, and Pierre Rosanvallon, "Convergences," *Syndicalisme Hebdo*, Dec. 31, 1981.
[62] Lefort, *Forms*, 309–310.   [63] Ibid., 313.   [64] Ibid., 309–311.

Polish workers and intellectuals had worked together to create Solidarity. In joining forces, a manifesto of the intellectuals and the CFDT explained, French intellectuals and labor activists were "faithful to the spirit of Solidarność in which [the Polish] trade unionists and intellectuals have worked and struggled together to free themselves from the totalitarian yoke [emprise] ... The struggle of the Poles," the manifesto concluded, "is our struggle."[65]

Just as had been the case with Solzhenitsyn, the most important context for this activism was not international, but domestic. In fact, Foucault and almost everyone else involved would readily concede that their support for Solidarity was not only about championing a distant cause or making a point about East–West relations, but also, as Foucault said, about "constituting a new form of political activity in France."[66] In May 1981, a Socialist government had come to power, which remained indebted to the etatist ideas despised by the anti-totalitarian Left. And while the Socialists won an absolute majority in the *Assemblée Nationale,* they formed a coalition government with the Communists. Its program of 1981 was thoroughly statist complete with a promised "rupture with capitalism" and a nationalization of key industries.[67]

When this government responded only cautiously to martial law in Poland, the anti-totalitarian intellectuals initiated another debate about the totalitarian potential of the orthodox Left's focus on the state. *Solidarité avec Solidarité* was as much about the future and direction of French socialism as it was about the Cold War. "I was struck, last December," Foucault said in October 1982, "when some insisted that now is not the moment to raise the problem of [the division of] Europe because there's a socialist experience in France in which the Communists take part and which is in danger of being compromised." Foucault believed these people had it the wrong way around: "...to the contrary, it is because we have a socialist experience that we have to raise this problem."[68]

Significantly, the anti-totalitarian intellectuals directed their wrath after December 13, not only at Jaruzelski or Brezhnev but primarily at the inactivity of the French government. In comments, speeches, and editorials, the symbolic date of May 10, 1981, the day of Mitterrand's electoral victory, was mentioned just as often as December 13, 1981. In a special issue of the *Nouvel Observateur,* a major outlet for anti-totalitarian thinkers, on martial law in Poland, for instance, the magazine's editor in chief Jean Daniel noted the surprise of French politicians about the

---

[65] "Appel commun."   [66] Foucault, "Un premier pas," 267.
[67] Friend, *Presidency,* 20–22; Brown, *Socialism,* 49–54, 68–72; Howard, *Specter,* 150–160.
[68] Foucault, "L'expérience," 347–348.

breadth of solidarity with Poland. This massive manifestation of anti-totalitarian sentiment, he noted, was due in no small part to the work of "those marginal movements, those libertarian [libertaires] personalities, those dissidents from the countries of the East, those heirs of May 68, in short, all those French intellectuals who may not always have known how to stay tuned to French popular sentiment but who, one sees this well today, gave the victory of 10 May its true meaning and its true content of international solidarity."[69]

In a letter to the CFDT from April 1982, the sociologist Alain Touraine, a main proponent of *autogestion* and author of a sociological monograph on Solidarity, wrote how interested he was in participating in the discussions between the CFDT and the intellectuals. For a long time, he wrote, he had been convinced about the necessity of such a cooperation "not only to organize aid for Solidarity but also and most of all to reflect on the French situation." The Socialist Party was currently seeking to concentrate political, economic, and ideological power in the hands of the state. "This can lead to totalitarianism; in contemporary France, this leads to the imposition of a paralyzing politico-ideological discourse on social practices."[70]

Many French commentators saw Solidarity as a template to counter such threats. The response of the French government to martial law, Cornelius Castoriadis criticized, exposed a poverty of innovative ideas in France. The nationalization of key industries was certainly not one of them. What to do? "The Polish movement itself has shown us the way: The source of political invention can be nothing else but the creativity of thousands of people joining together in a movement."[71] In an interview with *Libération*, Pierre Bourdieu, too, said that "The power of conceiving society and changing it cannot be delegated, above all not to a state that arrogates itself the right to effect the happiness of its citizens without their involvement, or even despite them.... That is something that the Polish movement brought home: the bankruptcy of a system in which movement is supposed to take place from above."[72]

---

[69] Jean Daniel, "Pour qui sonne le glas?," *Le Nouvel Observateur*, Dec. 16, 1981 (special issue); see also Serge July, "Les rendez-vous polonais," *Libération*, Dec. 23, 1981.

[70] Letter from Alain Touraine to Edmond Maire, dated Apr. 22, 1982, CFDT, Sect. Int., 8 H 2080. On Touraine as a proponent of autogestion see Brown, *Socialism*, 58–63. In his letter to the CFDT, Touraine explained that he had been in the Middle East at the time. This could explain why he does not seem to have participated in the protests of 1981–1982 though he was the main French analyst of Solidarity.

[71] Cornelius Castoriadis, "Illusions ne pas garder," *Libération*, Dec. 21, 1981.

[72] Pierre Bourdieu, *Political Interventions: Social Science and Political Action*, ed. Franck Poupeau and Thierry Discepolo (London, New York: Verso, 2008), 128–129.

Solidarity, Human Rights, and Anti-Totalitarianism 125

The CFDT – the epicenter of *solidarité avec Solidarité* – placed their work in the same deliberately political context. In 1982, the historians Hervé Hatmon and Patrick Rotman published a history of the CFDT. Titled *La deuxième gauche – The Second Left,* the book portrayed the CFDT as an innovative voice on the French Left, one that remained committed to socialist politics, but was untainted by the totalitarian temptation. Though Poland's Solidarity did not feature in the book at all, it began with the demonstrations of 13 and December 14, 1981 in Paris. They had revealed the CFDT's very identity, as a review of the book in the CFDT's weekly argued: the "ancient anti-totalitarian reflex which is the organization's very essence." "In a specific context," the weekly went on, "Wałęsa and his ten million comrades illustrate the CFDT's vision of social change."[73]

At least for the CFDT and its intellectual allies, then, human rights activism was bound up with French politics: the demonstrations and the proud displaying of Solidarity badges, the press conferences and resolutions, the documentation of repression and the humanitarian aid, the discussions on totalitarianism and international politics – in and around these activities a collective identity of the French workers and intellectuals was constructed, and it was sharpened and reinforced by setting it off from the rest of the French Left. No CFDT comment on the response to martial law failed to mention the absence of the Communists from the demonstrations of December 13 and 14 and the cautious response of the Socialists.[74]

The main lesson of the Polish coup, CFDT president Edmond Maire wrote in an essay titled "What Kind of Socialism?," is that "anti-totalitarianism, the struggle for individual and collective human rights, is an essential task without which emancipation will not make any progress." Yet opposing Communism is not enough, he went on. "No, socialism is not dead. But it remains to be created, translated into social reality, into our reality." The vehicle for this aim was "*socialisme autogestionnaire*" – rooted in May 68 and directed against both Communist totalitarianism and "the

---

[73] Hervé Hamon and Patrick Rotman, *La deuxième gauche: Histoire politique et intellectuelle de la CFDT*, 2nd ed. (Paris: Ramsay, 1984), 11–12; "'Si la CFDT réussit sa propre révolution culturelle, si elle parvient à grandir en préservant son identité...','" *Syndicalisme Hebdo*, Oct. 28, 1982.

[74] Hamon and Rotman, *La deuxieme gauche*, 11. See also CFDT circular, "Communications aux unions régionales et fédératons," dated Dec. 15, 1981, CFDT, Secteur International, File 8 H 1920. Another document observed a pro-Solidarity "entente cordiale" rejected only by the Communists. CFDT circular, "Les manifestations de soutien aux syndicalistes polonais," Dec. 15, 1981, CFDT, Secteur International, File 8 H 1920. For a very early example of the symbolic uses of Poland in French trade union politics see CFDT circular, "Le PCT, la CGT et les greves polonaises," dated Sep. 2, 1980, CFDT, Fond Edmond Maire, 15 P 120.

development of the Western capitalist societies in crisis." The aim was nothing less than "charting the path and laying firm and secure foundations for the construction of socialism. The experience of Solidarity has provided them." Demonstrating how, even in a totalitarian society, a social mass movement could emerge from the ordinary lives of workers, Solidarity had demonstrated that socialism meant neither the nationalization of the economy nor a political victory for a socialist party. What was needed in France, therefore, was a "diffusion of power through all of society, progress in terms of the autonomy of the person and the self-determination of collectivities." "The example of Solidarność," Maire concluded "has confirmed our will to construct *socialisme autogestionnaire.*"[75]

★★★

Seweryn Blumsztajn remembers his work with the CFDT very fondly. The French trade unionists, he believes, were among the very few in the West who understood Solidarity.[76] Whether that is true is at least doubtful, given how strongly the French campaign was influenced by domestic debates. What is beyond doubt is that this campaign shows once again that the human rights revolution of the 1970s did not lead to the dominance of one interpretation of human rights. *Solidarité avec Solidarité*, rather, was an attempt to experiment with this language, to test its possibilities and limits, to discuss which political and social project could be built around it, how long-existing concerns – about social self-organization and even democratic socialism – could be articulated with it.

The Second Left's turn to human rights, then, was no retreat from politics into a sphere of pure ethics. As much as it was a response to the collapse of Marxist discourses, human rights were to enable a democratic politics in which goals, methods, and visions of social change could be continuously discussed, revised, and challenged. In France, human rights could be just as much part of an effort to redeem a socialist project as they could be a purely ethical alternative to all kinds of politics.

---

[75] Edmond Maire, "Quel socialisme?," *Syndicalisme Hebdo*, Feb. 25, 1982; for a similar statement by the national secretary see Pierre Hureau, "Solidarité avec Solidarność," *CFDT magazine* 57 (Jan. 1982); see also Andrzej Chwalba and Frank Georgi, "France: Exceptional Solidarity?," in Idesbald Goddeeris, ed., *Solidarity with Solidarity: Western European Trade Unions and the Polish Crisis, 1980-1982* (Lanham: Lexington, 2010), 209–214; Frybes, "Solidarność-CFDT," 20–25.

[76] Maire, "Quel socialisme?"

6 The "Bedrock of Human Rights"
US Labor, Neoconservatism, and Human Rights

In concluding the discussion of Western responses to the imposition of martial law in Poland, this chapter focuses on the human rights discourse of an American organization: the American Federation of Labor and Congress of Industrial Organizations, or AFL-CIO, the United States' largest trade union. Alongside the CFDT, the AFL-CIO was probably Solidarity's most active supporter in the West. This work on behalf of the Polish union evolved organically out of the US trade union's uncompromising Cold War stance. Notably, many of its leaders were Jackson Democrats. But for the same reason, the rise of Solidarity was an event equally exhilarating and puzzling for them. On the one hand, the creation of an anti-Soviet trade union resonated strongly with their views about labor's role in the struggle with Communism. But, on the other, the Polish events of 1980–1981 undercut their Jacksonite views of how the societies of the Soviet bloc operated. In a totalitarian state, they believed, change from within was impossible. In January 1981, the AFL-CIO had thus dispatched Tom Kahn to Rome to secretly meet members of a Solidarity delegation there. The reason was that Solidarity had asked Washington to provide economic assistance to Poland, a member of the Warsaw Pact – something Kahn whom an admirer called a "gallant Cold Warrior"[1] abhorred of. Kahn's main mission was to make sure that Western support was really what Solidarity wanted.[2]

When Solidarity was suppressed, many Jackson Democrats felt that their stark views of totalitarian societies had been confirmed. "If peaceful, gradual change in the Soviet empire were possible," Walter Laqueur reasoned, "it would certainly be in the interests of the West to assist in the process." Yet for him, Poland's "main lesson" was that change in

---

[1] Eric Chenoweth, "The Gallant Warrior: In Memoriam Tom Kahn," *Uncaptive Minds* 5 (Summer 1992), 2.
[2] Karol Modzelewski, "Włoski łącznik," *Wolność i Solidarność* 4 (2012), 154–159.

Eastern Europe occurred only from above and "through violent spasms."[3] The leadership of the AFL-CIO, in contrast, changed its views on totalitarian societies. Throughout the 1980s, it led a sustained effort to keep Solidarity's repression in the public eye and, crucially, to funnel money into Poland. Laqueur was wrong to dismiss Solidarity's gains, a leading figure in this campaign wrote. Change from within a totalitarian society seemed possible after all.[4]

Given how many resources the AFL-CIO poured into supporting the Polish union, its leadership's change of mind was certainly genuine but it is also puzzling, given Solidarity's swift repression and dim perspectives of success. As was the case with Willy Brandt and France's Second Left, an explanation for US labor's support for Solidarity has at least as much to do with intellectual changes and political battles at home as with the situation of human rights abroad. And, as was the case with Brandt and France's anti-totalitarian Left, those were battles fought over the role of the state in effecting social change.

Since its beginning, the Cold War had structured US domestic debates almost as much as discussions on foreign policy, not least in the case of human rights. In the 1970s, the Jackson Democrats had started to use the language of universal rights to reinforce the ideological differences between East and West, to "reclaim American virtue," in Barbara Keys's apt formulation.[5] They welcomed the election of Ronald Reagan, an anti-Communist hardliner who made the "shining city on a hill" a central trope of his rhetoric, and many of them started to work in his administration. Yet Reagan's election was only a victory of sorts for the Jackson Democrats. For the new president did not reclaim American virtue so much as redefine it. In his rhetoric, the West's struggle with Communism was not one between two social systems or structures, but a struggle against any system or structure which he believed unnecessarily stifled the creativity of individual human beings. "Totalitarianism" ceased to denote the terrifying other abroad and came to denote only the most extreme form of the general threat of the modern state to silently encroach on the lives of individuals. Even as he revived the ideological Cold War, Reagan went on to reshape the social imagery underpinning it – a change few organizations felt more painfully than the AFL-CIO when he curbed the power of organized labor.

Against this background, Solidarity fascinated the AFL-CIO not primarily as an anti-Communist movement, but as a trade union.

---

[3] Laqueur, "What Poland Means," 30.
[4] Eric Chenoweth, letter to the editor, *Commentary* 73 (June 1982), 11–12.
[5] Keys, *Virtue.*

The "Bedrock of Human Rights" 129

As Reagan dismantled the welfare state and reduced the influence of trade unions, the AFL-CIO invoked Solidarity to argue that it was not human rights as such that expressed the difference between East and West, but a particular human right – freedom of association. In the United States, we will see, Solidarity became a contested icon in a political and intellectual struggle initiated not by different foreign policy aims – in this field, the AFL-CIO agreed with Reagan – but by a reconfiguration of the normative and conceptual world of US politics.

I

In many ways, the AFL-CIO shared the Reagan administration's approach to human rights. There was, in fact, a significant degree of ideological and institutional overlap between the Jackson Democrats and the leadership of the AFL-CIO. Senator Henry Jackson was one of the union's closest allies in Congress. The AFL-CIO's longtime president George Meany, on the other hand, shared Jackson's uncompromising anti-Communism, priding himself with never having supported détente in any way. He had even pulled the AFL-CIO out of the International Confederation of Free Trade Unions (ICFTU), an alliance he had helped create, because of the other members' support for détente.[6] Both he and his successor in 1980, Lane Kirkland, were members of the Coalition for a Democratic Majority, or CDM, the main organization of the Jackson Democrats.[7]

Notably, this cooperation extended to the field of human rights work. Meany's and later Kirkland's assistant for international affairs, Tom Kahn, put the AFL-CIO at the center of the Jackson Democrat's campaign for Soviet dissidents. It hosted many of the events which the Jackson Democrats organized for them such as a welcoming ceremony for Aleksandr Solzhenitsyn when he came to the United States in 1975, a "Human Rights Dinner" in 1978 to support a campaign to have the Soviet Helsinki monitors win the Nobel Peace Prize, and a national speaker tour for Vladimir Bukovsky.[8]

---

[6] Arch Puddington, *Lane Kirkland: Champion of American Labor* (Hoboken, NJ: John Wiley & Sons, 2005), 218–219.

[7] Vaïsse, *Neoconservatism*, 141–145.

[8] Rachelle Horowitz, "Tom Kahn and the Fight for Democracy: A Political Portrait and Personal Recollection," *Democratiya* 11 (Winter 2007), 233–234; Vaïsse, *Neoconservatism*, 141–145. For the human rights events, see "Original invitation to a 'Human Rights Dinner' organized by the Coalition for a Democratic Majority at the Waldorf Astoria hotel (New York city) on 30 September 1978," available at http://neoconservatism.vaisse .net/doku.php?id=dinners_and_ceremonies (accessed July 2015); Alexander Solzhenitsyn, ""We Beg You to Interfere," *Washington Post*, July 6, 1975.

130   Poland's Solidarity Movement & the Politics of Rights

The rise of Solidarity, however, brought about a divergence between the AFL-CIO and the majority of the Jackson Democrats. Whereas the latter were skeptical about the prospects of Solidarity, Kahn and Kirkland made sure that the AFL-CIO supported the Polish movement vigorously. Overriding concerns from the Carter White House, it gave publicity to the cause of Poland's workers and raised over $300,000 to purchase necessary equipment for Solidarity.[9] In early 1981, after Kahn's trip to Rome, the AFL-CIO even supported legislation to provide economic assistance to Warsaw, a move that ran counter to everything the AFL-CIO had hitherto advocated in East–West relations.[10]

In a public discussion among the Jackson Democrats, Norman Podhoretz attacked this decision as based on "a fantasy ... no communist system can tolerate what Solidarity represents ...." Any economic help would merely help the Soviets. Rather than "dampening" the Polish conflict, the West should let it take its course and otherwise strengthen US defense policy and focus on the Cold War in the Third World. Kahn would have none of it. "[W]hat has occurred in Poland is historically unique," he argued. An independent power center had been established in a Communist country, a chance had emerged to work toward "the transformation of the Soviet system, however long it takes; to its dismantling by non-nuclear means."[11]

The AFL-CIO stuck to this course even after the imposition of martial law. At a spontaneous meeting held on December 13, 1981 at AFL-CIO headquarters in Washington, George Higgins – a Catholic priest and longtime labor activist – led the gathering in reciting the Lord's Prayer for "the safety of our Polish brothers and sisters and for the restoration of human rights in that country." In his address, Higgins described Solidarity as "the most significant social movement of this century, perhaps the most significant social movement since the industrial revolution. It has caught the attention of the entire world as nothing, I think, in my lifetime has, and it will not be put down."[12]

---

[9] Chenoweth, "Gallant Warrior," 12–13.

[10] "Dotyczy: działalności amerykańskich związków zawodowych AFL-CIO oraz kanałów wywierania wpływu na wydarzenia w Polsce," *Wolność i Solidarność* 4 (2012), 154–159. In his recent comment on the document, Modzelewski is unaware of the congressional discussions on Poland. He thus misinterprets Kahn's question as an anticipation of Reagan's sanctions of 1981 and – prematurely, in my eyes – disregards the document as a fabrication. Modzelewski, "Włoski łącznik."

[11] Kahn and Podhoretz, "Support," 235–237, 241, 259.

[12] Transcript of remarks in support of Poland's Solidarity Labor Federation at a rally held Monday, December 14, 1981, in the lobby of the AFL-CIO headquarters building in Washington, D.C., undated press release, George Meany Memorial AFL-CIO Archives (hereafter: GMMA), Information Department Records, RG20–003, Series 2, File 47/6, 1.

The "Bedrock of Human Rights" 131

Much like French trade unionists and intellectuals, the AFL-CIO drew on the social and political practices of human rights activism in its support for Solidarity. In December 1981, US labor activists and Polish exiles founded the Committee in Support for Solidarity, or CSS. Financed by the AFL-CIO, it conducted Amnesty International–style work for political prisoners, compiling lists of them, lobbying NGOs to adopt them, and compiling dossiers of prominent Solidarity activists in prison. It was also involved in translating and publishing human rights reports for the CSCE meeting in Madrid and other international organizations.[13] When Congress' Helsinki Commission held hearings to discuss the Polish events both Kahn and members of the CSS testified there.[14]

The AFL-CIO, meanwhile, engaged in manifold activities to keep Poland in the public eye. For weeks, vigils were held in front of the Polish embassy or local consulates while meetings organized on symbolic dates like the thirteenth of every month to create publicity for Solidarity's plight. Ads were placed in newspapers and, on the initiative of the AFL-CIO, a minute of silence for the Polish people was observed at the 1982 Super Bowl. The AFL-CIO headquarters displayed a seven-story Polish flag, and the International Union of Electrical, Radio, and Machine Workers – located vis-à-vis the Soviet embassy in Washington – displayed a pro-Solidarity banner. The AFL-CIO produced badges and bumpers stickers and started a nationwide petition campaign that collected more than 100,000 signatures in seven months.[15]

---

[13] For an overview see Annual Report: Committee in Support of Solidarity, 1983, Committee in Support of Solidarity records (hereafter CSS records), Box CSS 2 (Records of Activities), File "CSS Annual Reports 1983-1986." On the CSS, see also Domber, *Revolution*, passim.

[14] Tom Kahn, "World Peace is Linked to Solidarity's Fate," *Free Trade Union News* 37 (Jan. 1982), 1. Committee in Support of Solidarity, Press Advisory, Jan. 24, 1982, CSS records, Box "CSS 4 (Originals, General.Special, Calendars)," Folder "CSS Activities 1982: Congressional Testimony (CSCE: Dec–Feb)."

[15] "Solidarity with Solidarność," *Free Trade Union News* 37 (Jan. 1982), 1. For additional activities by the AFL-CIO and related groups see the untitled press release listing planned AFL-CIO activities in support for Solidarity for December, dated Dec. 15, 1981, GMMA, RG20–003, Series 2, File 47/6; letter from Eric Chenoweth to Tom Kahn, dated Nov. 30, 1982; letter from Bruce F. Vento to Ronald Reagan, dated Oct. 13, 1982, both in AFL-CIO Unprocessed Records, International Affairs Department, Folder "Solidarność 1982 #1"; Summary of T.V. news program, "U.S. Longshoremen Protest Polish Labor Union Suppression," dated Dec. 23, 1981, memorandum from Tom Kahn to Don Slaiman, dated Jan. 21, 1982, letter from Edward F. Toohey to Tom Kahn, dated Mar. 23, 1982, memorandum from Jim Baker to Don Slaiman, dated May 19, 1982; "Report on Polish Solidarity Conference March 6th and 7th," not dated; Randy Furst, "Newsmakers/ Solidarity Supporters,"

132   Poland's Solidarity Movement & the Politics of Rights

On August 31, 1982, the second anniversary of the Gdańsk strikes, the AFL-CIO unveiled a 24-foot sign above the entrance of the union's headquarters, symbolizing American labor's top priorities: the number of Americans without jobs and the days that Solidarity had been held in captivity – the numbers were adjusted weekly.[16] On the first anniversary of martial law, the AFL-CIO and the Polish American Congress organized a rally in Washington, DC, attended by around 1,000 people including Vice President George H. W. Bush, Senators Edward Kennedy and Bob Dole, and other luminaries of US political life.[17]

US labor also heavily lobbied Congress and the Reagan administration to become active for Solidarity. The White House was flooded with letters and petitions by East and South European diaspora groups, Catholic and Jewish organizations, as well as trade unions and human rights organizations demanding US support for civil liberties in Poland.[18] The AFL-CIO even threatened to impose sanctions by itself by having its members refuse to load ships with goods for the Soviet Union or to organize work stoppages to pressure the White House into acting toward Poland – a threat that some in the Reagan administration seem to have taken seriously.[19]

<hr />

clipping from *The Minneapolis Star*, Mar. 4, 1982; Program of the Polish Solidarity Symposium 6 March 1982, all in AFL-CIO Unprocessed Records, International Affairs Department, Folder "Solidarność 1982 #2."

[16] Untitled news release, Jun. 14, 1982, GMMA, RG20–003, Series 2, File 49.2.

[17] "Report on AFL-CIO Sponsored Events to Mark the First Year of Solidarność's Suppression in Poland," not dated, circular from Lane Kirkland to AFL-CIO affiliates, dated Nov. 24, 1982, both in AFL-CIO Unprocessed Records, International Affairs Department, Folder "December 12 – Polish Demonstration"; letter from Eric Chenoweth to Tom Kahn, Nov. 30, 1982, AFL-CIO Unprocessed Records, International Affairs Department, Folder "Solidarność 1982 #1."

[18] Among the many letters in RRPL, WHORM: Subject File, CO126, Box 1 see Robert W. Zweiman to Ronald Reagan, Dec. 18, 1981, RRPL, WHORM: Subject File, CO-126, ID#53492; Jack Kemp to Kenneth Duberstein, Mar. 23, 1982, RRPL, WHORM: Subject File, CO126, ID#068257.

[19] In the NSC meeting of Dec. 21, 1981, Reagan himself mentioned pressures from labor. Minutes, National Security Council Meeting, Dec. 21, 1981, RRPL, Exec. Sec., NSC: Meeting files, NSC00033, 5. On labor pressures see also: Memorandum from Allen J. Lenz for James W. Nance, "Decisions on Poland from the December 22 NSC Meeting," Dec. 22, 1981, RRPL, Exec. Sec., NSC: Meeting Files, NSC00033; memorandum from Jack Burgess for Elizabeth Dole via Red Cavaney, "Presidential Identification with Poland," Jan. 13, 1982, RRPL, White House Staff Member and Office Files, Robert F. Bonitati Files, Box 6846, Folder "Polish Union-Solidarity." State had decided on December 17, 1981 to regularly brief NGOs and private sector organizations on US Polish policies. See memorandum from Michael Wheeler for Nancy Berg Dyke, et al., "National Security Council Meeting – Poland (c)," dated Feb. 2, 1982, Kirkland's threat mentioned on 6, RRPL, Exec. Sec., NSC: Meeting Files, NSC00039. For additional evidence on NGO and public opinion impact see cable from Secstate to Amembassy, Warsaw, "Department Briefing for AFL-CIO Executive Staff,"

The "Bedrock of Human Rights"   133

Even after the smoke of the Polish crisis had cleared and Solidarity's situation appeared increasingly hopeless, the AFL-CIO remained one of the strongest advocates for supporting the Polish movement and sustaining external pressures on Warsaw. It also made sure that the National Endowment for Democracy (NED), the vehicle for Reagan's human rights policy of democracy promotion, would provide funds for Solidarity. Kirkland had been a longtime advocate for such a foundation and the AFL-CIO's Free Trade Union Institute, led by Kahn, was one of the main institutions through which its funds were distributed. The vast majority of NED funds for Solidarity were transferred through the AFL-CIO.[20]

The Polish crisis, in sum, led to a divergence among US anti-Communist advocates of human rights. While most of them believed that the best human rights policy was to pressure the Soviet Union militarily and rhetorically while promoting democracy in authoritarian regimes, the AFL-CIO supported the dissident tactic of transforming totalitarianism from within.

In its efforts, US labor was far from alone. The AFL-CIO cooperated closely with East European ethnic constituencies in American society, Polish Americans most of all. The Polish American Congress had been out front in collecting humanitarian aid, publicizing the situation in Poland, and condemning human rights violations there. Polish Americans in the Catholic Church also provided important networks connecting US activists both to Poland and the Vatican.[21] However important, though, this background cannot explain why, unlike their fellow anti-Communist hardliners, Kahn and Kirkland did not see Solidarity's struggle as a lost cause, an anomaly in an unchangeable system of totalitarianism, but to the contrary as "[p]erhaps the central event in our lifetime."[22] Neither had particular affinities to Poland, neither was Catholic nor even only religious. Their fascination with the Polish movement had much more to do with how it could be fed into

---

Dec. 16, 1981, NSA, Soviet Flashpoints: Poland 1980–1982, Box 1; memorandum from James Nance for Ronald Reagan, "Your Meeting with Lane Kirkland," dated Dec. 17, 1981, RRPL, White House Staff Member and Office Files, Paula Dobriansky Files (hereafter: Dobriansky Files), Box OA 90892, Folder "Poland: Memoranda 1981-1983"; memorandum from Alexander Haig for Ronald Reagan, "Influencing European Attitudes on Poland," dated Dec. 26, 1981, NSA, Soviet Flashpoints: Poland 1980–1982, Box 26; memorandum from H. Allen Holmes for Alexander Haig, "Your Meeting in Chicago with Lane Kirkland," dated Jan. 29, 1982, NSA, Soviet Flashpoints: Poland 1980–1982, Box 3.

[20] Domber, *Revolution*, 114–118.

[21] See the documents in RRPL, WHORM: Subject File, CO-126, ID#138209.

[22] Kahn quoted in Chenoweth, "Gallant Warrior," 12.

134   Poland's Solidarity Movement & the Politics of Rights

intellectual and political struggles at home. Once more the transformation of postwar policies and paradigms emerges as the central background for international human rights policies.

II

Accounts of the Reagan presidency often underline how, after a decade of détente, his speeches reinforced a vision of the Cold War as a struggle between good and evil. The Jackson Democrats thus found much they could like in the rhetoric of the new president. But many of them were still reluctant to work for him. The reason was that, at least in their own view, their anti-Communism was not conservative, but liberal. A look at the life stories of some of the AFL-CIO militants working for Solidarity helps to bring out this aspect.

A particularly illuminating case in this respect is the career of Tom Kahn who had played a central role in orchestrating Jacksonite support for Soviet dissidents, whom the AFL-CIO unionists had sent to Rome in 1981, and who organized AFL-CIO's campaign for Solidarity.[23] Studying at Brooklyn College in the 1950s, Kahn became a follower of Max Shachtman. Over the course of his life, Shachtman undertook a dazzling political itinerary which took him from presiding over the founding congress of the Fourth International in 1938 to endorsing Richard Nixon in the early 1970s, all while insisting he stayed true to his Marxist roots. When Kahn met Shachtman, he was leading one of Trotskyism's many heretic sects, preaching the viability of a democratic socialist alternative to both capitalism and Stalinism. Increasingly, however, his views evolved to a "fervently anti-communist version of social democracy."[24] To him, the USSR was the gravest menace to the international workers' movement, a "new barbarism" even. The main lesson of the Stalinist "enslavement" of the working class was that the struggles for socialism and for political democracy were one and the same thing, an idea Shachtman impressed upon a young Tom Kahn in 1956 in a speech on the Soviet invasion of Hungary.[25]

---

[23] The following account draws for basic facts on Horowitz, "Tom Kahn"; Chenoweth, "Gallant Warrior."

[24] King, "Neoconservatives and 'Trotskyism'," 255.

[25] Tom Kahn, "Max Shachtman: His Ideas and His Movement," *Democratiya* 11 (Winter 2007), 253–254; for Shachtman's views and political milieu, see Wald, *Intellectuals*, 172–192; for the role he and his followers played among the Jackson Democrats, see Vaïsse, *Neoconservatism*, 24–27, 71–73, 91, 284; King, "Neoconservatives and 'Trotskyism'," 256–259.

The "Bedrock of Human Rights" 135

As his views evolved, Shachtman came to see the political system of the United States as the ideal framework to achieve socialism. He thus urged his followers to join the Democratic Party and most importantly the American trade union movement. Following this call, Kahn became active in the civil rights movement, working as an assistant to Bayard Rustin, himself a Shachtmanite. A formative development for him and other Shachtmanites, and their final reconciliation with the US system, came with the rise of the New Left. Rejecting traditional labor activism, critical of representative democracy and of anti-Communism, the New Left seemed to the Shachtmanites to misunderstand the core issues of the socialist movement: the struggle with the Soviet Union and the fight for political democracy.

During the 1970s, many Shachtmanites found political refuge in Senator Jackson's staff and the CDM. It was through these contacts that Kahn came into contact with the AFL-CIO. Like Kahn, many of the younger Jackson Democrats such as the NED's longtime president Carl Gershman had been members of organizations like the Young People's Socialist League, the League for Industrial Democracy, and Social Democrats USA all of which subscribed to Shachtman's view of a necessary link between anti-Communism and democratic socialism.[26]

The ideological framework of the more senior Jackson Democrats was what John Ehrman calls the "liberalism of the vital center," a reference to the intellectual manifesto of Cold War liberalism, Arthur M. Schlesinger's book of 1949 *The Vital Center*.[27] As an ideology, Schlesinger had argued, Communism posed the gravest threat not to American society as a whole, where its influence had always been negligible, but to the American Left, hijacking and undermining its goals of liberal reform and social progress. Precisely *as* liberals, Schlesinger concluded, the democratic Left in America needed to be anti-Communist as well. But the Left was not only particularly threatened by Communism, it also had an important role to play in combatting it. For restoring what Schlesinger called the "liberal nerve," regrouping and reinvigorating the democratic Left, was the best antidote to Communism and its false promises.[28]

The AFL-CIO's Kirkland was the quintessential "vital center liberal." Communism was uniquely dangerous to workers, he believed, precisely

---

[26] Gershman, "Illusions."   [27] Ehrman, *Rise*, 15.
[28] Arthur M. Schlesinger Jr., *The Vital Center: The Politics of Freedom* (Cambridge, MA: Riverside Press, 1949), 92–188; cf. Vaïsse, *Neoconservatism*, 27–30; Jennifer Delton, "Rethinking Post-World War II Anticommunism," *The Journal of The Historical Society* 10 (2010), 1; for the transatlantic roots of the Cold War liberal consensus see Angster, "'Safe'"; Nehring, "Westernization."

136   Poland's Solidarity Movement & the Politics of Rights

because it worked through the labor movement; all dictatorship repressed unions, but only the Communists tried to take hold of the workers themselves. For him, anti-Communism was not something to which labor activism had to be subordinated; they were merely two dimensions of the same struggle. In the 1960s, he had been a great admirer of Lyndon B. Johnson whose "Great Society Program" of massive welfare spending and war in Vietnam he consistently backed.[29] Senator Henry Jackson himself shared this ideological outlook. As hawkish as he was in terms of foreign policy, in his views on domestic policies he was, as a contemporary of his remembered, "the closest one in the Congress ... to a European Social Democrat."[30]

The political lexicon and conceptual world of the Jackson Democrats, in other words, had much more in common with that of Willy Brandt than Ronald Reagan. Theirs were still very much what Daniel Rodgers calls the "words of the Cold War" – a discourse revolving around how the structures of culture and society weighed down on individuals, constraining their choices, channeling their actions, defining their identities – an emphasis reinforced by an understanding of the Cold War as a struggle between two *systems*. For much of the postwar period, "freedom" – the central term of US Cold War culture – had been understood as something "inescapably social and public," as Daniel Rodgers observes. But as in Western Europe, this discourse went into steep decline during the 1970s. In political discourse and intellectual inquiry alike, a new metaphor for social entities of all kinds emerged, replacing older concerns with social and economic structure: the metaphor of the market, the vision of a social order emerging spontaneously from the interaction of rational individuals pursuing their interests and preferences. In this new vision, liberty was not socially circumscribed – it could only be artificially stifled by state structures. Once freed from these constraints, liberty would unleash an unlimited human potential for creativity and progress.[31]

One of the main agents of these changes was Reagan, much as he initially revived the rhetoric of the Cold War. In fact, a prime example for his revision of postwar political discourse was the speech he gave in London in June 1982 which he gave in the context of the Polish crisis

---

[29] Puddington, *Kirkland*, 68.   [30] Vaïsse, *Neoconservatism*, 111–114, quotation at 114.
[31] Rodgers, *Age*, 3 and 15–40. This fragmentation of the social imaginary was also the context for how Reagan defined human rights. See Carl J. Bon Tempo, "Antikommunistische Menschenrechte: Die Republikanische Partei und die Menschenrechtspolitik in den späten 1970er Jahren," in Jan Eckel and Samuel Moyn, eds., *Moral für die Welt? Menschenrechtspolitik in den 1970er Jahren* (Göttingen: Vandenhoeck & Ruprecht, 2012).

The "Bedrock of Human Rights"   137

and which turned Jacksonite democracy promotion into the centerpiece of US human rights policy. One of the address' central themes was the idea that the struggle with totalitarianism was merely the most extreme form of a wider struggle with the destructive tendencies of the modern state. Humanity faced a fundamental threat, Reagan warned, one that was on par with the danger of the thermonuclear destruction of "civilization as we know it" – the "threat posed to human freedom by the enormous power of the modern state. History," he went on, "teaches the dangers of government that overreaches – political control taking precedence over free economic growth, secret police, mindless bureaucracy, all combining to stifle individual excellence and personal freedom."[32]

Revealingly, the speech portrayed France's new philosophers and their apocalyptic vision of a hopeless world of concentration camps and mass slaughter as sharing concerns with the emergent proponents of the free market.

> The hard evidence of totalitarian rule has caused in mankind an uprising of the intellect and will. Whether it is the growth of the new schools of economics in America or England or the appearance of the so-called new philosophers in France, there is one unifying thread running through the intellectual work of these groups – rejection of the arbitrary power of the state, the refusal to subordinate the rights of the individual to the superstate, the realization that collectivism stifles all the best human impulses.

Reagan, to be sure, acknowledged "that among us here and throughout Europe there is legitimate disagreement over the extent to which the public sector should play a role in a nation's economy and life." But it was remarkable that the public sector's role in the economy was mentioned at all in a speech on foreign policy.

Like all such speeches, the Westminster address went through a series of drafts and revisions and, as was Reagan's habit, the President was heavily involved in this process, annotating and rewriting drafts.[33] Reading one of these drafts, a White House aide noted that the speech read in large parts like a "lectur[e] on the dangers of big government, not totalitarianism."[34] The speech's original version, written by Anthony Dolan, a self-described true "Reaganite," had defined the "dangers of government that overreaches" as "rampant inflation, stringent taxation,

---

[32] Reagan, "Westminster Address."
[33] For a detailed analysis of the writing process and content of the speech see Robert C. Rowland and John M. Jones, *Reagan at Westminster: Foreshadowing the End of the Cold War* (College Station, TX: A&M University Press, 2010).
[34] Ibid., 47.

138 Poland's Solidarity Movement & the Politics of Rights

mindless bureaucracy – all combining to stifle individual excellence and personal freedom." If anything, Reagan had further strengthened this line of thought in his revisions of Dolan's draft. The latter had written how the "abuse of government has always posed the most serious and enduring threat to the freedom of man"; Reagan replaced "abuse of government" with the "silent encroachment by government" – a term he had been using since the 1950s to warn of the corrupting influence of social welfare programs.[35]

Given how profoundly this domestic vision differed from that of many Jackson Democrats, they were initially reluctant to work on Reagan's staff. Jeane Kirkpatrick, the author of "Dictatorships and Double Standards," reportedly wanted to call off a meeting with Reagan at the last second, exclaiming that she could not meet him because she was "an A.F.L.-C.I.O. Democrat."[36] As anti-Communism moved to the center of the Jackson Democrats' concerns, at times to the point where it became an obsession, many of them eventually all but abandoned their political roots in Cold War liberalism, let alone democratic socialism. While mostly motivated by security policy, this "Democratic defection" also produced converts to the emergent market paradigm.[37] Even some of the Shachmanites, like Abrams or Gershman, became Republicans, with some of them wondering how much their fascination with Trotsky's former aide had ever had to do with revolutionary ideology and how much with anti-Communism.[38]

Yet for Kirkland and Kahn defection was not an option. A mere two months after Reagan's inauguration, Kirkland organized "Solidarity

---

[35] Speech draft, "Address to Parliament," (Dolan), dated May 19, 1982, 3:15 p.m., quote on 3, RRPL, White House Staff Member and Office Files, Office of Speechwriting: Research Office, Box 46, [06/08/1982] Westminster – Drafts; Speech draft, "Address to Parliament," (Dolan), May 19, 1982, 3:15 p.m. with handwritten remarks by Ronald Reagan, quote on 6–7, RRPL, Office of Speechwriting: Research Office, Box 47, [06/08/ 1982] Westminster – Drafts. For the term "silent encroachment" see ibid., 28–29, 45.

[36] Richard V. Allen, "Jeane Kirkpatrick and the Great Democratic Defection," *New York Times*, Dec. 16, 2006.

[37] Vaïsse, *Neoconservatism*, 205–208. The most explicit example is Michael Novak. A former sympathizer with the New Left, he published *The Spirit of Democratic Capitalism* (New York: Simon & Schuster, 1982), a theological defense of the Western political and economic system, arguing that democracy and capitalism presuppose one another while both require a firm moral and cultural foundation provided by Christianity. Patrick Allitt, *The Conservatives: Ideas and Personalities Throughout American History* (New Haven: Yale University Press, 2009), 233–234. For accounts placing the Jackson Democrats into the historical context of the "conservative ascendancy" of the 1970s and 1980s see Donald T. Critchlow, *The Conservative Ascendancy: How the GOP Right Made Political History* (Cambridge, MA: Harvard University Press, 2007), 104–122; Allitt, *Conservatives*, 191–254.

[38] Andrew Moravcsik quoted in King, "Neoconservatives and 'Trotskyism'," 258–259.

The "Bedrock of Human Rights"   139

Day" – a massive rally in Washington, DC. Drawing on the imagery of events in Poland, it was meant to show the new man in the White House that he was in for a tough fight.[39] The pivotal confrontation came in September 1981 when PATCO, the union of US air traffic controllers and a member of the AFL-CIO, went on strike. Reagan responded by giving the air traffic controllers 24 hours to return to work; those who refused were fired. Though no cause for the decline of US trade union-ism, the President's toughness – or ruthlessness – and the demise of PATCO came to symbolize Reagan's support for a larger assault on the influence of organized labor in the US economy.[40]

Reagan's rhetoric and policies, in sum, did not resurrect the Cold War consensus so much as redefine it, breaking up the dominant social imaginary of economic structures, long historical processes, and socially embedded individuals and replacing it with a vision of dis-embedded individuals whose potential for initiative and creativity the state artifi-cially stifled. Against this background, the rise and suppression of Solidarity were not just distant events for the AFL-CIO but became a symbolic battlefield between two visions of the Cold War while human rights provided the symbolic power to claim legitimacy for one of them.

III

After the PATCO incident, relations between the AFL-CIO and the White House became so icy that Kirkland would not even give Reagan credit for his stance on Poland.[41] Tellingly, however, the AFL-CIO stopped short of drawing a parallel between the PATCO strike and the crackdown in Poland. In criticizing the President, Kirkland instead chose to "out-hawk" him and to characterize him as being more concerned with the interests of big business than the defense of human rights.

---

[39] Puddington, *Kirkland*, 128–130. Walter Galenson describes Reagan's inauguration as "the beginning of the most difficult period for organized labor since the early 1930s. The administration was tilted sharply toward employers, who took advantage of the opportunity to mount a powerful attack against the unions. The concept of a 'union-free environment' gained currency. The unions were on the defensive in the legislature." *The American Labor Movement, 1955-1995* (Westport, CT: Greenwood Press, 1996), 53; see also Rick Fantasia and Kim Voss, *Hard Work: Remaking the American Labor Movement* (Berkeley, CA: University of California Press, 2004), 64–65.

[40] Joseph Anthony McCartin, *Collision Course: Ronald Reagan, the Air Traffic Controllers, and the Strike that Changed America* (New York: Oxford University Press, 2012); Puddington, *Kirkland*, 122–128.

[41] "An Interview with Lane Kirkland conducted for the Labor Diplomacy Oral History Project by John F. Shea and Don R. Krienzle," Nov. 13, 1996, quote on 10, GMMA, RG95–007, Series 7, File 4/18.

140   Poland's Solidarity Movement & the Politics of Rights

The core issue was Poland's international debt. When the White House discussed how to respond to martial law, some of Reagan's advisors, including Kirkpatrick and Secretary of Defense Caspar Weinberger, had proposed to declare Poland in default of repaying its foreign debt, that is, to force Warsaw to declare bankruptcy. Many people objected, mostly out of fear that this could collapse the Polish economy altogether with unforeseeable consequences in a volatile international situation. Another objection, however, had to do with Western economic interests. If Poland had declared bankruptcy the money of Western lenders would have been lost – a prospect that was particularly threatening for West German banks but could have had crippling effects on the American financial economy as well. Eventually, Reagan decided against declaring Poland in default, forcing him to pay out several hundred millions of dollars to US banks over the course of 1982 to cover Warsaw's past due payments.[42]

The reasons for Reagan's decisions were complex; among others, his advisors had argued that by forcing default, the West would have deprived itself of the only leverage it had over the situation in Poland. But for Kirkland the failure to use the most potent measure against Warsaw showed Reagan's complicity with the immoral policy of US business. American and West European banks had already come under public criticism during the Polish crisis when some of their top managers seemed overly concerned about stability in Poland. Some openly advocated giving Jaruzelski the benefit of the doubt and the *Washington Post* even quoted Citibank's Thomas Theobald as having said: "Who knows which system works best? All we ask is can they pay the bills?"[43]

It was this attitude Kirkland zeroed in on in a string of public statements, criticizing it as "a pseudo-pragmatism that perverts, even as it seems to draw upon, the American tradition."[44] Quoting Theobald in a speech on December 28, 1981, Kirkland said: "Once again, the American corporate and financial community exposes itself as the soft underbelly of freedom."[45] Half a year later, he criticized the "financial and commercial elites" in even harsher words: "No cry from the Gulag,"

---

[42] Gregory F. Domber, "Supporting the Revolution: America, Democracy, and the End of the Cold War in Poland, 1981-1989" (PhD thesis, George Washington University, 2007). For the possible impact of the measure see "Gesandter Dannenbring, Washington, an das Auswärtige Amt," dated Jan. 8, 1982, AAPD, 1982, I, Doc. 14, 56–60.

[43] Puddington, *Kirkland*, 233.

[44] Lane Kirkland, "Why Not Economic War?" *The Washington Post*, Feb. 24, 1982.

[45] "Text of an address by AFL-CIO President Lane Kirkland to the Industrial Relations Research Association," AFL-CIO press release, Dec. 26, 1981, GMMA, RG20–003, Series 2, File 47.6.

The "Bedrock of Human Rights" 141

he said "no shriek of pain from the dungeon, not even a businessman's arrest by secret police or an act of terrorism against their own colleagues stays their service of tyrants or outweighs a ruble on their scale of values." It was high time, Kirkland continued, that Americans stopped confusing the goals of these elites with US national interest. "A fifth column of capital will dwell in our midst as long as we have a privileged class that not only derogates our values but helps to feed, finance and arm our adversaries, just as the entrenched advocates of unvexed commerce helped to speed a Tory leader to Munich years ago."[46]

It was an "illusion," Kirkland said in January 1983 in a programmatic speech on foreign policy, to believe that the big issues and major changes in the world emerge from ministries or "multinational corporations ... They emerge from the streets." Poland was the best example of this. Therefore, "the promotion of human rights should be a central component of American foreign policy." The great obstacle to such a policy was, in Kirkland's view, an immoral business class, "the profiteers in East-West trade ... folks for whom the highest objective of American foreign policy should be not the defense of freedom but the rehabilitation, in [the] words [of the President of the US Chamber of Commerce], of 'our already poor international reputation for commercial reliability.'"[47]

Given this political context, the AFL-CIO campaign for Solidarity focused not on human rights in general but on a specific right – freedom of association. In August 1982, the AFL-CIO organized a rally at its headquarters in Washington, DC, to commemorate the second anniversary of the strikes in Gdańsk. The union's main speaker argued that the experience of Solidarity bore a lesson for "the entire world": "the unbreakable connection between trade union rights and human rights generally." What Poland had demonstrated, he went on, was that "the destruction of freedom of association results in the destruction of all other rights and freedoms."[48]

Another speaker drew the audience's attention to an advertisement the AFL-CIO had placed in the *New York Times* in which the AFL-CIO "drew together the lines of the American trade union movement, Solidarność in Poland, and the efforts of black workers in South Africa

---

[46] Lane Kirkland, "A Foreign Policy With a Purpose," *AFL-CIO American Federationist* (April–June 1982), 13.

[47] Lane Kirkland, "Labor, Foreign Policy, and Defense," *Free Trade Union News* 38 (Jan. 1983), 1.

[48] J.C. Turner, "Commemorating the Second Anniversary of the Formation of Solidarnosc," Aug. 31, 1982, quote on 1, AFL-CIO Unprocessed Records, International Affairs Department, folder "Solidarnosc 1982 #1 file"; see also "Report on the AFL-CIO's August 31 Rally to Mark Solidarność's Second Anniversary," *ibid.*

142   Poland's Solidarity Movement & the Politics of Rights

to form a free trade union."[49] The centennial Labor Day, the advertisement announced, would be a good occasion for "all Americans" to reflect on the "fundamental human right" of all people to create social organizations and institutions in order to protect and advance their interests. Without freedom of association, "plain people are naked before the arbitrary power of the state, the employer, or other potentially hostile forces." While "obviously the bedrock principle of trade unionism," therefore, freedom of association "also shields and sustains the entire panoply of human rights that constitute a democratic society." The best example for this connection, the AFL-CIO explained, was Poland where the fight for freedom of association had brought greater liberties, while the "crushing of Solidarność – of the right of free association" had suppressed all other rights as well.[50]

As Reagan broadened the Cold War to entail the general struggle with the modern state, the AFL-CIO cast the struggle for human rights as one at whose center were social organizations, trade unions chief among them. Responding to the global crisis of trade unionism, the AFL-CIO returned to several international fora it had left in protest over détente: The International Confederation of Free Trade Unions or ICFTU, the UN's International Labor Organization, or the Trade Union Advisory Committee of the OECD.[51] Like the AFL-CIO, the ICFTU had been a staunch supporter of Solidarity. In a meeting on Poland in May 1982, the ICFTU board had "made it clear at the outset that it could never accept that human and trade union rights could be considered merely an 'internal affair of the State.'"[52]

Here, too, trade union rights appeared in a broader context: The preparatory materials for the federation's congress in Oslo in 1983, for instance, noted attacks made on trade union rights "in the name of totalitarian ideologies and inhuman economic theories." A report compiled for the conference on the violation of trade union rights, which also featured a section on Eastern Europe and Solidarity, noted how trade unions depended on human rights but also underlined the "indispensable role [of trade unions] as watchdogs for the defense and promotion of

---

[49] Murray Seeger, Solidarność Rally, Tuesday, Aug. 31, 1982, quote on 2, AFL-CIO Unprocessed Records, International Affairs Department, folder "Solidarnosc 1982 #1 file."
[50] "Freedom of Association," advertisement in *The New York Times* Aug. 30, 1982, A17.
[51] Kirkland, "Labor."
[52] Minutes of the ICFTU Executive Board meeting, Brussels, May 13–14, 1982, Agenda Item 12: Europe, (c): Poland, quote on 1, International Institute for Social History (hereafter: IISH), International Confederation of Free Trade Unions Records (hereafter: ICFTU), Folder 256, quotation at 1.

The "Bedrock of Human Rights" 143

political and civil rights and of democracy in general." Whereas the bulk of the report focused on dictatorships, it also contained a section relating that "the governments of some countries with a long democratic tradition refuse to recognize the important role that the trade union movement has to play in the national economy and society as a whole."[53]

While the defense of freedom of association refocused the attention of the ICFTU on Eastern Europe, it led the AFL-CIO to broaden its approach and go beyond the authoritarian–totalitarian distinction central to Kirkpatrick's worldview and even the Cold War itself. At the 1981 AFL-CIO convention Kirkland said: "On the vital issue of human rights, we have been offered, in the past year, the posing of a fine choice between lice who are totalitarian and lice who are authoritarian. We reject this choice."[54] The ad in the *New York Times* claimed that a fight similar to that of Solidarity was "underway today in South Africa." The key to ending Apartheid and initiating democratic changes, the text argued, were the efforts of black workers to build independent trade unions. Therefore, the second George Meany Human Rights Award, which had been bestowed upon Lech Wałęsa in 1981, would this year be given to two South African labor activists. "In Poland, South Africa, and everywhere else workers struggle for trade union rights," the ad concluded, "freedom of association is at stake. Democracy itself is at stake."[55]

Four years later, Kahn gave a speech, arguing to replace the double standards of Left and Right with a single human rights standard: freedom of association. All other individual rights, he argued "depend upon people being able to organize to defend themselves and to defend themselves against any power that would try to trample on those rights, whether that power be the State or private special interests."[56] Support for freedom of association should thus be the center of a proactive "human rights strategy – a strategy for expanding democracy in the world."[57] Any human rights policy, Kahn went on, would cause tensions

---

[53] "General Introduction: Three Themes for a Congress," quotation on 2 and Report for the 13th ICFTU World Congress, June 23–30, 1983, quotation on 8, 12 ,"Human Rights," IISH, ICFTU, Folder 457a.

[54] The AFL-CIO convention had adopted a resolution on foreign policy condemning both the "the denial of human rights by the leftist, totalitarian regime in Nicaragua" and the "rightist military dictatorship of Augusto Pinochet in Chile." "Solidarity Around the Globe," *The American Federationist* (Dec. 1981).

[55] "Freedom of Association."

[56] Tom Kahn, "Beyond the Double Standard: A Social Democratic View of the Authoritarianism Versus Totalitarianism Debate," *Democratiya* 12 (Spring 2009), 155, 157.

[57] Ibid., 155.

and therefore it had to be supplemented by a strong national defense. Ultimately, however, the latter was not enough if it was not "accompanied by a strategy for making changes in the world – for changing authoritarian regimes into democratic regimes, and ultimately for dismantling the Soviet system by non-nuclear means."[58]

Around the Polish crisis, then, we encounter a surprising transnational convergence of views on human rights. For all the often fundamental differences between dissidents, France's Second Left, and US right-wing trade unionists, they nevertheless shared a reading of human rights in which they were meant to create communities and enable a form of politics that could fill the void left by the welfare state. Basing human rights policy on freedom of association, Kahn argued, implied moving its focus away from "governments, as they are, interacting with each other on the geopolitical chess board" and focusing instead on "those people in various countries around the world who are on the front lines struggling for the expansion of human rights ..." – whether in South Africa, Poland, or Chile.[59]

★ ★ ★

The conflict between the AFL-CIO and the Reagan administration over the role of trade unions in the anti-Communist struggle is a final example for how contested and unspecified the content of human rights claims still was in the early 1980s. What the Polish government mistook for a tightly coordinated Western attack at the CSCE meeting in Madrid concealed a fierce politics of human rights – a struggle over what they meant and what kinds of politics they established.

Among the most striking features of the debates triggered by the Polish crisis is that they were as least as much discussions on domestic problems in the West as about the fate of dissidents in the East. When the forces of globalization drained the welfare state of its utopian energies, discrediting an entire conceptual world in the process, some West Europeans and Americans shifted their gaze beyond their own borders, empathizing with suffering strangers in an attempt to find a morally unambiguous cause to support. But that was not nearly all that human rights could mean. For leading intellectuals and activists in Western Europe and the United States, as for their peers in Central Europe, human rights were a means to turn human beings into citizens, to empower them to take the problems that confronted them into their own hands, to create communities and shape their collective lives. They were not thought of as a path

---

[58] Ibid., 159.   [59] Ibid., 160.

beyond politics but as a foundation for a new form of politics that was not centered on the state as its main actor.

If human rights were not anti-political, they certainly were embroiled in a specific kind of politics. Defining freedom of opinion or association as a human right or even the most fundamental human rights placed them beyond the grasp of day-to-day politics. It defined them as liberties which had not been granted to human beings but rightfully belonged to them simply because they were human beings. To use a distinction coined by Claude Lefort, human rights were not meant to be the subject of "politics," understood as a specialized sphere of social life populated by parties and parliaments, but established a specific vision of "the political," the imaginaries, concepts, and values that defined what could legitimately be the subject of political debate.[60] Human rights, in other words, emerged as a source of symbolic power, at a time when existing sources had run dry; they bestowed upon political actors the power to define what could be said and conceived in political life.

The three cases discussed in this part, of Willy Brandt, the French Second Left, and the AFL-CIO, demonstrate the surprising and contradictory ways in which the rise of human rights was related to the crisis of the state as a vehicle for progress. The conceptual changes triggered by this crisis opened a discursive space in which human rights could flourish. As "History" disappeared as the inescapable backdrop of politics, human rights' absolute claim to a specific freedom already in the here and now became plausible. But human rights were also related to the crisis of the welfare state in that they were used in various ways to fill the void left by it. In France, the Second Left used the example of the dissidents to push back the retrograde forces of French etatism and defend the independence of civil society. In the United States, two different visions of a politics beyond the state clashed – one envisioning the unfettered interaction of individuals and the other one centered on the need of people to organize and defend their rights.

The role of Solidarity in all of this was that of a vessel for the desires and ideas of its supporters. Events in Poland were a canvass unto which West Europeans and Americans could project their own struggles. Through its suffering, the Polish movement endowed the claims of its supporters with moral authority and discredited those who opposed them. Events in Eastern Europe did show that the denial of freedom of opinion and association established a totalitarian vision of the political. This is not to deny the sincerity of Western support for Solidarity. French

---

[60] Ingram, "Politics"; see also Howard, "Claude Lefort," 18.

intellectuals, the CFDT, and the AFL-CIO both invested massive resources in helping Polish activists that they could have used elsewhere. But it does seem that they supported Solidarity because they could portray the Polish movement in a way that reflected their own ideas and political desires.

But even though solidarity with Solidarity was driven by domestic concerns, it did have important international effects. Warsaw may have been wrong about the motivations of the Western leaders at the CSCE meeting but he was correct to expect problems arising from the Western position. The symbolic significance that Solidarity had gained as an icon of human rights would greatly complicate the life of Jaruzelski in the following years.

7   Letters from Prison
The Prisoner of Conscience and the Symbolic Politics of Human Rights

On July 13, 1984, Jacek Kuroń, Adam Michnik, Henryk Wujec, and Zbigniew Romaszewski, all founding members of the Committee to Defend the Workers, were brought before the Warsaw District Military Court. In a small, packed courtroom, they were to stand trial for their alleged attempts to overthrow the political system of the People's Republic. Seven members of Solidarity's board, meanwhile, were awaiting trial on similar charges. The Prosecutor's Office had been preparing for this moment since before the smoke of December 13, 1981, had settled. Putting the eleven prisoners on trial – the US State Department called them the "Solidarity Eleven" – was meant to expose how these "extremists," supported by Western "propaganda centers," had hijacked the just aspirations of the working class and led the country to the brink of civil war.[1] The trial, in other words, was meant to provide the rationale for the imposition of martial law. A long time in the making, it ended rather abruptly: After five days, proceedings were adjourned never to reopen again. On July 22, the Polish parliament passed a comprehensive amnesty law and about a month later the Solidarity Eleven were free.

The amnesty of 1984 was followed by a period of intensified repression; two of the Solidarity Eleven were rearrested within six months after their release. But it was a milestone nonetheless. For the second time after 1977, a combination of domestic and international pressures had forced the regime to free all political prisoners. Its attempt to justify martial law as an internal affair, a "lesser evil" necessary to prevent "a bunch of anarchists" from turning Poland into a "powder keg," had failed.[2] Much as Warsaw tried to pretend otherwise, Poland's human rights record had become a central aspect of its international relations.

---

[1] Notatka, dated Mar. 22, 1982, 2 and Uwagi do notatki Biura Śledczego MSW z dnia 22 Marca 1982 r., dated Mar. 23, 1982, on 2–3, for the beginning of the investigation in early 1982 see the untitled memorandum from H. Walczyński for H. Starszak, dated Jan. 16, 1982, all in AIPN, BU 0204/1417, t. 53, fol. 154–158, 161–165, 5–8.

[2] See Chapter 4, above.

148   Poland's Solidarity Movement & the Politics of Rights

Yet just as had been the case with the Western response to martial law, Western pressures on Poland to free its political prisoners were no foregone conclusion of a human rights revolution or Western Cold War strategies. To the contrary, as hundreds of Polish activists remained in prison, as the broader dissident movement in the Soviet bloc seemed to have been crushed, and as East–West tensions reached levels not seen since the Cuban missile crisis, many Western governments saw Solidarity as a noble, but lost cause, wondering at the same time whether Poland could be kept in isolation forever.

Western pressures on Poland and the subsequent amnesty of 1984, then, were the result of a tenacious campaign of Polish activists to keep Solidarity's repression in the public eye. As Polish activists sought to keep human rights violations in Poland on the international agenda, they had to shift their focus. In the late 1970s, they had interpreted human rights as the starting point for a project of gradually transforming a totalitarian society from within. During the 1980s, they were thrown back upon much more basic goals – being released from prison. In this situation, they turned toward a discourse that had made such basic and universal goods as freedom from incarceration and torture into the exclusive goals of a new form of social activism – the global culture of human rights shaped and popularized primarily by Amnesty International. The Polish campaign against martial, thus, provides a case study to analyze central features of 1980s global human rights culture. The following three chapters are devoted to exploring these aspects.

In this context, the present chapter is devoted to an analysis of the "prisoner of conscience" – a symbolic figure central to both the Polish activism of the first half of the 1980s and to how Amnesty International transformed the imagery of and activism for political prisoners. Abandoning notions of political solidarity with activists and their ideological aims it turned toward universal notions of compassion and empathy with a human being struggling to preserve their very humanity. Drawing on this symbolic figure, Polish political prisoners translated their plight into a language that was readily understandable for international audiences and, crucially, resonated with their concerns. In the process, they turned themselves into *icons* of international human rights culture.

In what follows, the term "icon" will be used in a specific way. In popular parlance, it is often used to denote a widely known image which somehow captures the *Zeitgeist* of an era or the essence of an event. Yet an actual icon, i.e., a sacred image of Byzantine spirituality, does not need to be widely known to be recognizable as an icon. The reason we recognize an image as a Byzantine icon is that it was painted according to strict

Letters from Prison 149

artistic conventions. Byzantine artists stuck to these conventions because of the belief that divinely created images of Christ, Mary, and the saints existed, and that the first icons were authentic copies of these *Ur*-images or archetypes. The iconographic conventions were meant to ensure that every new icon was an authentic depiction of the actual image of the sacred. Like in a photo, where the image is an imprint of the actual event on the film, or like the moon, which reflects the light of the sun, icons were seen as an imprint or a reflection of the sacred. Even if they were not the divine itself, they brought the beholder in contact with the transcendent world; they were manifestations of the sacred.[3]

It was in this sense that the Polish political prisoners became icons. "Painting" their plight according to the "conventions" of global human rights culture, they turned themselves into quasi-religious symbols reflecting, incarnating even, the most hallowed principles of the international community. But just as Orthodox Christians do not venerate the material image of the icon but the sacred light it is believed to reflect, so did international observers increasingly cease to see Solidarity for what it was – a trade union – and venerate it as an instantation of their own values – human rights. This "iconization" of Solidarity proved to be an ambiguous process. It increased the symbolic power and moral authority of the Polish movement but it also dissolved the story of its struggle for social self-organization and economic justice into a universalizing narrative. Solidarity's depiction as a human rights icon concealed the rich intellectual debates on human rights which Polish intellectuals and their Western interlocutors had had in the 1970s, their translation into a language of collective agency and radical democracy. In the discourse of the prisoner of conscience and the symbolism of the Nobel Prize ceremony, the Polish movement became an example for an abstract

---

[3] This understanding of the term "icon" is derived from Cornelia Brink, *Ikonen der Vernichtung: Öffentlicher Gebrauch von Fotografien aus nationalsozialistischen Konzentrationslagern nach 1945* (Berlin: Akademie, 1998), 234–238; Ansgar Paus, "The Secret Nostalgia of Mircea Eliade for Paradise: Observations on the Method of the 'History of Religions'," *Religion* 19 (1989), 2, 140–144; Margaret E. Kenna, "Icons in Theory and Practice: An Orthodox Christian Example," *History of Religions* 24 (1985), 4, 348–350; Patrick Maynard, "The Secular Icon: Photography and the Functions of Images," *The Journal of Aesthetics and Art Criticism* 42 (1983), 2, 164. In adopting this understanding, I do not mean to come to a general definition of the term "icon." My point, simply, is that it provides a very precise way of grasping analytically how and why certain movements or people became human rights icons. For other definitions see, for instance, Lydia Haustein, *Global Icons: Globale Bildinszenierung und kulturelle Identität* (Göttingen: Wallstein, 2008), 25–30; Gerhard Paul, "Das Jahrhundert der Bilder: Die visuelle Geschichte und der Bildkanon des kulturellen Gedächtnisses," in Gerhard Paul, ed., *Das Jahrhundert der Bilder: 1949 bis heute* (Göttingen: Vandenhoeck & Ruprecht, 2008), 29–30.

150   Poland's Solidarity Movement & the Politics of Rights

human progress unconnected to any specific political or social aim. Turned into an icon of human rights, Solidarity was drained of its political content.

The discourse of the prisoner of conscience, then, encapsulates the very human rights vernacular which is too quickly seen as synonymous with human rights as such – a discourse replacing previous concerns with political solidarity and collective self-determination with notions of pity and empathy with individual suffering. But as the following chapters explore this discourse, it will demonstrate that global human rights culture concealed its politics more than it did away with it. Turned into a universal symbol, Solidarity became valuable for Western activists and politicians not because it pointed beyond politics but because it could be re-politicized and its symbolic power used in political struggles. If anything, iconization made Solidarity even more susceptible to competing political interpretations than before. In the early 1980s, US politicians tried to turn repression in Poland into a symbolic counterweight to one of the most powerful and, at least from a neoconservative perspective, problematic icons of 1980s human rights culture – Chile.

Human rights, then, were enmeshed in a global "political economy of symbolic power," a competition for power and influence whose main stakes were not material resources but what Pierre Bourdieu called "the power of preserving or transforming the social world by preserving or transforming the categories" in which this world is talked about and perceived.[4] Solidarity became a contested icon of human rights.

The remainder of this part of the book is structured as follows. The present chapter analyzes the discourse of the "prisoner of conscience" and how it was used by Polish activists to exert international pressure on Poland. The subsequent two chapters deepen the discussion of human rights culture by exploring the symbolism of the 1983 Nobel Peace Prize for Lech Wałęsa as well as discussions on the human rights situation in Poland at the UN.

I

Imposing martial law, the Polish authorities had arrested the vast majority of Solidarity's leadership and destroyed its infrastructure. A handful of labor leaders, however, had escaped detention and set up a provisional

---

[4] Bourdieu, *Language*, 235; on Bourdieu's sociology of symbolic power see also David Swartz, "Bridging the Study of Culture and Religion: Pierre Bourdieu's Political Economy of Symbolic Power," *Sociology of Religion* 57 (Spring 1996), 1; Swartz, *Symbolic Power*.

steering committee. Its members opted for the strategy of a "long march," effectively adapting the 1970s dissident strategy to the conditions of conspiracy. Through aid for political prisoners and victims of repression, through independent publishing, education, protest, and even independent economic initiatives an "underground society" was supposed to be organized. Its minimal aim was to achieve Solidarity's re-legalization as an independent trade union.[5] In some form at least, this underground society did in fact take shape. The first underground publications started to appear mere days after martial law had been imposed. Solidarity cells were founded in factories, with citywide structures set up between them. A resistance network of younger activists, the Social Defense Committees (Komitety Obrony Społecznej, KOS), emerged in Warsaw and other cities.[6]

These efforts were supported by a transnational network of human rights activists, trade unionists, and East European émigré groups which provided a steady flow of material support for the Polish underground and helped Solidarity keep its case on the international agenda. Partly as a result of these efforts, Poland's human rights record was discussed at the UN's Commission on Human Rights (UNCHR) and International Labor Organization (ILO), as well as in the final stages of the CSCE review meeting in Madrid. The latter's concluding document dealt with human rights in 10 out of 19 provisions. The signatories pledged to guarantee religious liberty and "effectively ensure [the citizen's'] right" to "know and act upon his right," an allusion to Helsinki monitor groups, and to convene a conference on human rights and human contacts in Ottawa in 1985. Most importantly for Poland, the text alluded to the East–West clash following martial law and called upon the signatories to guarantee the right to form independent trade unions.[7]

---

[5] For in-depth studies see the contributions to Andrzej Friszke, ed., *Solidarność podziemna 1981-1989* (Warszawa: ISP PAN/Stowarzyszenie "Archiwum Solidarności," 2006).
[6] Tadeusz Ruzikowski, *Stan wojenny w Warszawie i województwie stołecznym 1981-1983* (Warszawa: IPN, 2009), 187–290; Antoni Dudek, "Wstęp," in Antoni Dudek, ed., *Stan wojenny w Polsce 1981-1983* (Warszawa: IPN, 2003), 22.
[7] *Concluding Document of the Madrid Meeting of Representatives of the Participating States of the Conference on Security and Cooperation in Europe, Held on the Basis of the Provisions of the Final Act Relating to the Follow-Up to the Conference,* Madrid 1983, 6–7, available at www .osce.org/mc/40871?download=true (accessed June 2016). For Poland and Polish émigré documentations at the conference see "Solidarity Report on 'Human and Civil Rights During the State of War,'" press statement by Max Kampelman, March 25, 1983, IDEE, CSS records, box "CSS 2 (Records of Activities)," folder "CSS Annual Reports 1983-1986: Responses to CSS HRights Rep;" Max Kampelman, "The Madrid CSCE Follow-up Meeting: An Assessment," attachement to memorandum, Charles Hill to William Clark, July 15, 1983, RRPL, WHORM: Subject File, IT005, ID#159477, 2, 4.

152   Poland's Solidarity Movement & the Politics of Rights

Impressive though the final document of the Madrid conference was, however, its impact was far from guaranteed. By the time it was adopted, the KGB had arrested most Soviet human rights activists, leading members of Charter 77 and several hundred Poles were already incarcerated, and Solidarity was outlawed. It was also unclear whether the West was determined to see the pledges made in Madrid through. As it became apparent that Warsaw would not return unto the reform path from before December 1981, Western diplomats started arguing that Poland could not be indefinitely kept under isolation. The Polish government played these sentiments by making piecemeal concessions to the West. Shortly after December 1981, an amnesty had been declared for everyone who signed a declaration of loyalty to the Polish state. In November, the regime released Lech Wałęsa and a month later the vast majority of detainees arrested in late 1981 and 1982 – including top Solidarity advisors like Tadeusz Mazowiecki and Bronisław Geremek. In June 1983, Warsaw agreed to a visit by John Paul II, thus fulfilling a major Western demand, and in July lifted martial law and released more prisoners.[8]

The Polish underground argued that all of this was mere window dressing. Martial law had not been lifted, Polish activists and emigres said, its emergency measures had simply been adopted as permanent laws, and the amnesty of 1983 was partial at best, leaving many activists in jail.[9] Yet even the United States was showing signs of softening its position. Following the papal visit, the State Department recommended signaling Washington's willingness that, upon a release of a significant number of prisoners, debt rescheduling talks could be held.[10]

As Western attention wandered off to other concerns and sources of financial aid dried up, Polish émigré centers in the West, the hubs of the underground's transnational support network, were hanging on by the skin of their teeth. In Paris, Seweryn Blumsztajn's Coordinating Committee could build on the continued support of the CFDT, while the CSS in New York was funded by the AFL-CIO. In Brussels, Solidarity had established an official international representation, staffed

---

[8] Sowa, *Historia*, 546–551.
[9] "W sprawie zniesienia stanu wojennego," Aug. 11, 1983, *Tygodnik Mazowsze*; "Declaration Concerning the Lifting of the State of War in Poland," *Solidarność News*, 4 (July 22, 1983); "A Gesture Devoid of Significant Political Meaning," *Committee in Support of Solidarity Reports*, 16 (July 22, 1983).
[10] Memorandu from Charles Hill for William Clark, "Poland," dated June 25, 1983, RRPL, Dobriansky Files, box OA 90892, file "Poland: Memoranda 1981-1983." On US and West European policies during this time see Domber, *Revolution*, 88–123; Pleskot, *Panna*, 402–414, 424–428, 435–445, 458–465.

Letters from Prison 153

by emigres, authorized by the union's underground leadership, and financially supported by major Western trade unions. But most other Solidarity committees in the West folded in 1983 or 1984 for lack of support.[11]

By 1983, then, the Polish underground proved exceptionally tenacious but its situation began to look increasingly bleak. International attention had largely shifted and Western resolve to pressure Warsaw on its human rights record weakened, while the underground was under sustained pressure from the Security Service and hundreds of activists remained in jail.

II

In January 1984, the underground paper *KOS* published an open letter by a group of inmates from a prison in Braniewo in Northeastern Poland. In addition to the Solidarity Eleven, the prisoners in Braniewo were among an unknown number of people, estimates ranged between 2 and 700, who had been detained for political activities but who had not been released either in December 1982 or August 1983. The main aim of their letter, the prisoners in Braniewo wrote, was to explain why they engaged in different forms of protest actions, hunger strikes chief among them. While partly a form of self-defense against harassment, the hunger strikes' main aim was much broader – to acquire the "Status of a Political Prisoner."[12]

The letter from Braniewo was not the first of its kind in 1980s Poland nor was *KOS* the only underground journal to write about the struggle for the status of political prisoners. By September 1983, inmates of at least four prisons were staging hunger strikes both to protest against inhumane treatment and to demand that they were acknowledged as "politicals."[13] Activists who had remained at large or had been released also published an appeal to the Ministry of Justice to acknowledge incarcerated activists as political prisoners.[14] Underground papers

---

[11] Goddeeris, "Ministerstwo."

[12] "List Otwarty więźniów politycznych z Braniewa do społeczeństwa," *KOS*, Jan. 30, 1984.

[13] See, for instance, "O status więźnia politycznego," *Tygodnik Mazowsze*, May 2, 1983; "List otwarty więźniów z Barczewa do Gen. Jaruzelskiego," *KOS*, May 7, 1984. For further descriptions of the conditions in the prisons see "Głodówka," *KOS*, July 5, 1983; "Zakład karny w Hrubeszowie czeka na Papieża," "Głowa w mur," "Prowokacja w Barczewie," and "Głodówka w Strzelinie," published in *Tygodnik Mazowsze*, on June 30, 1983, July 14, 1983, and Dec. 15, 1983 respectively.

[14] "Apel," *KOS*, May 11, 1983. See also Edward Kortal, "Prawo dla politycznych," *KARTA* 1 (1983); Antoni Macierewicz, "Gdybym o Nich zapomniał, Ty Boże zapomnij o mnie," *Wiadomości*, May 27, 1984.

154   Poland's Solidarity Movement & the Politics of Rights

featured regular columns titled "From behind prison bars" or simply "Political prisoners" which relayed information on political trials and portrayed particular prisoners.[15]

Framing their protest this way, the prisoners put their struggle into a broader historical and international context. Incarceration for political reasons is a phenomenon which is as old as prisons themselves. As Padraic Kenney has shown, however, the "political prisoner" is a specific type of activist – someone who understands the prison not as an obstacle to their politics, but as a stage and vehicle for it. In addition to modern prisons and states, the emergence of modern political parties and movements were an integral element in the making of the political prisoner as we know it. Before the rise of modern ideologies, prison or exile had been an effective means of ending the one-off efforts of nobility-led insurrections. Ideology, in contrast, politicized larger segments of society and, often through utopian visions of revolutionary transformation, gave their cause a permanence that connected imprisoned activists to their comrades still at liberty. Rebeling against prison conditions and demanding a special status for themselves, militants cast their incarceration as a continuation, indeed a central element, of their revolutionary struggle. They ceased to be, as Kenney puts it, "imprisoned politicals" and became "political prisoners."[16]

In the 1880s, Polish socialists had been among the first who came to understand themselves as political prisoners in this sense. A century later, however, their heirs engaged in a politics of incarceration that had been notably transformed, a change closely connected to the human rights revolution. Well into the 1960s, radical ideology had cast political

---

[15] One of the leading underground journals, *Tygodnik Mazowsze,* frequently featured such columns on political prisoners. See, for instance, "Barczewo" and "Braniewo," *Tygodnik Mazowsze,* Oct. 6, 1983. *KOS* had a column titled "From Behind Prison Bars" ("Zza krat"). See, for instance, *KOS* Jan. 15, 1983 or Feb. 27, 1983. See also "Wywiad ze skazanym F.W." and "Więźniowie polityczni," published in *Tygodnik Wojenny* on Feb. 24, 1983 and Oct. 13, 1983 respectively; "List otwarty Zofii Romaszewskiej." *KOS,* July 5, 1983; "Notatki stamtąd," *Karta* 1 (1983), 97–103. In October 1983, the members of the underground group KARTA began conducting interviews with former political prisoners which were published in 1988 in a samizdat book under the title *The Politicals (Polityczni* [Warszawa: Przedświt, 1988]).

[16] Padraic Kenney, "'I felt a kind of pleasure in seeing them treat us brutally': The Emergence of the Political Prisoner, 1865–1910," *Comparative Studies in Society and History* 54 (2012), 4. Kenney is practically alone among historians to systematically study political incarceration in this fashion. For a political science approach see Fran Lisa Buntman, *Robben Island and Prisoner Resistance to Apartheid* (Cambridge, UK; New York: Cambridge University Press, 2003). For a useful, if somewhat selective overview see Aryeh Neier, "Confining Dissent: The Political Prison," in Norval Morris and David J. Rothman, eds., *The Oxford History of the Prison: The Practice of Punishment in Western Society* (New York: Oxford University Press, 1995).

prisoners as martyrs for the goal of revolutionary transformation; their suffering, even if unjust, served a wider cause. This changed with the collapse of systematic ideological visions. Recast as "prisoners of conscience," they became a symbolic figure in their own right whose moral authority did not spring from their faithfulness to a revolutionary cause but from their unjust suffering in defense of their very humanity. Though the prison remained to be a vehicle for political activism, this activism worked by concealing its ideology and politics rather than putting them front and center.

The most visible expression of political incarceration's re-envisioning of political incarceration was the work of Amnesty International. During its early years, its activism consisted mainly in local chapters symbolically "adopting" political prisoners, sending them letters of support, and lobbying their governments to release them or at least guarantee a fair trial. Amnesty's evolution into a more fully fledged human rights organization, beginning with its 1973 campaigning against torture, grew out of an activism focused on political prisoners. In contrast to the activists Kenney describes, Amnesty's work was deliberately non- or even antipolitical; it did not support *political* prisoners, but prisoners of *conscience*, people who had been jailed solely because they had manifested a worldview dissenting from the state's ideology. In theory at least, the prisoners' political views were irrelevant as long as they did not advocate the use of violence.[17]

Amnesty's work was thus not driven by political solidarity, but by empathy, pity even, with a fellow human being, an appealing approach in a time of collapsing ideological certainties. Campaigning on behalf of prisoners of conscience was a "struggle against the most pointless human suffering" as one former activist put it – it focused on concrete individuals in situations where guilt and responsibility could easily be established and the lines between good and evil seemed clear cut.[18] Underneath, however, this new form of activism remained profoundly political. In fact, a good deal of its appeal may have lain in how different political groups could project their own views on the "prisoner of conscience."

---

[17] For an excellent analysis of Amnesty's history and culture see Hopgood, *Keepers*; see also Buchanan, "Truth"; Jan Eckel, "The International League for the Rights of Man, Amnesty International, and the Changing Fate of Human Rights Activism from the 1940s through the 1970s," *Humanity* 4 (Summer 2013), 2; for the evolution of Amnesty's central concept, the "prisoner of conscience," see Edy Kaufman, "Prisoners of Conscience: The Shaping of a New Human Rights Concept," *Human Rights Quarterly* 13 (1991), 3.

[18] Kaufman, "Prisoners," 342.

156   Poland's Solidarity Movement & the Politics of Rights

An example for these politics of the prisoner of conscience is Amnesty's development in the United States where it became a mass organization only in the 1970s. Overwhelmingly, the organization's growth during this time was driven by an influx of people with politically liberal views. For them, Amnesty's approach provided exactly the kind of idealism they were looking for as they sought to "reclaim American virtue" after Vietnam and Watergate.[19] At the same time, however, the concept of the prisoner of conscience drew on core institutions of the West – *habeas corpus*, freedom of belief, and a right to a fair trial. As such, it was also appealing to conservatives and anti-Communists. In 1975, the US ambassador to the UN, the Jackson Democrats' Daniel Patrick Moynihan, called for a worldwide amnesty for political prisoners, an obvious attempt to retaliate for the UN's infamous resolution on Zionism and to bring the political differences between East and West into sharp relief.[20]

Given the popularity of this activism for prisoners of conscience, human rights activism had, by the late 1970s, become almost synonymous with the struggle against political incarceration and related issues like torture. So dominant was the focus on these issues that they tended to overshadow much worse forms of human rights violations.[21] To the emergent human rights culture, therefore, the "prisoner of conscience" was what anthropologist Sherry B. Ortner calls a "summarizing symbol" – it was "summing up, expressing, representing ... in an emotionally powerful and relatively undifferentiated way" what human rights meant for many people at the time: a putting aside of ideology for the sake of innocent, and thus "pure," human suffering.[22]

The "prisoner of conscience," and the larger imagery it summarized, proved highly susceptible to human rights movements behind the iron

---

[19] Keys, *Virtue*. On the liberal background and motivations of those Americans who swelled the ranks of Amnesty see ibid., 89–101; for how political imprisonment, together with torture, became a focal concern and lowest common denominator for early US human rights efforts see ibid., 133–152. On the former aspect see also Jan Ecke's careful study in his, *Ambivalenz*, 389–423; for an account focused on the role of repression in Latin America see Kelly, "Sovereignty," 243–247, 275–293.

[20] For a somewhat hagiographic account, see Gil Troy, *Moynihan's Moment: America's Fight against Zionism as Racism* (Oxford, New York: Oxford University Press, 2013); see also Keys, *Virtue*, 218–219.

[21] Barbara Keys, "Anti-Torture Politics: Amnesty International, the Greek Junta, and the Origins of the Human Rights 'Boom' in the United States," in Akira Iriye et al., eds., *The Human Rights Revolution: An International History* (Oxford, New York: Oxford University Press, 2012); Bradley R. Simpson, "Denying the 'First Right:' The United States, Indonesia, and the Ranking of Human Rights by the Carter Administration, 1976-1980," *The International History Review* 31 (2009), 4.

[22] Sherry B. Ortner, "On Key Symbols," *American Anthropologist* 75 (1973), 5, 1340.

Letters from Prison 157

curtain. Imagining the "prisoner of conscience," Amnesty's early members had drawn heavily on a specific reading of Dietrich Bonhoeffer, the German Protestant pastor whom the Nazis had imprisoned and executed in 1945. Notably, Polish translations of Bonhoeffer's writings had also been a major inspiration for the Polish ex-Marxists' turn toward religion.[23] As a symbolic figure, moreover, the "prisoner of conscience" shared important traits with the "dissident." What distinguished both was not a specific ideology, but the courage to express a dissenting opinion and suffer the consequences. In Czechoslovakia, the "symbolic name Charter 77" was chosen, the documents' authors explained, to denote that this group had "come into being at the start of a year proclaimed as Political Prisoners' Year" – an initiative by Amnesty International.[24] In Poland, KOR and ROPCiO had been founded by people who had initially planned to set up a Polish chapter of Amnesty International, an organization Polish dissidents later cooperated with.[25] The fourth point of the twenty-one demands of the strikes in Gdańsk was to release all political prisoners, and in December 1980, in response to a series of politically motivated arrests, Solidarity established A Committee to Defend Prisoners of Conscience (*Komitet Obrony Więzionych za Przekonania*) with local chapters set up in most major cities, while the underground press of the 1980s used the term "prisoner of conscience" interchangeably with "political prisoner."[26]

Reminiscent of Amnesty's symbolic practices, Solidarity's underground leadership declared in 1983 that the 31 October of each year would be "Political Prisoner's Day," initiating month-long activities to create awareness for "the problem of political incarceration and the status of the prisoner of conscience."[27] Similarly, a network of younger activists, closely cooperating with Solidarity, declared 1984 to be Prisoners of Conscience Year.[28]

The Polish prison inmates and underground activists, in sum, were part of a global transformation of the politics of political incarceration, not least because Amnesty International had adopted the internees of

---

[23] Hopgood, *Keepers*, 62–65; Bonhoeffer, *Wybór pism*. [24] "Declaration of Charter 77."
[25] Miedema, *Movement*.
[26] "The Gdansk Agreement: Protocol of Agreement between the Government Commission and the Interfactory Strike Committee Concluded on August 31, 1980 at Gdansk Shipyards," *World Affairs* 145 (1982), 1, 14. On the Committee see List do Przewodniczącego Rady Państwa z informacją o powstaniu Komitetu Obrony Więzionych za Przekonania, dated Dec. 20, 1981, KARTA, "'Solidarność'— Narodziny Ruchu," A/10.5.
[27] "Appel pour les prisonniers," *Solidarność – Bulletin d'information*, 76 (Nov. 16, 1983), 3 (retrieved at the International Institute of Social History, Amsterdam [IISH]).
[28] "Oświadczenie," *KOS*, Jan. 30, 1984.

158   Poland's Solidarity Movement & the Politics of Rights

martial law wholesale as prisoners of conscience and Solidarity's Western supporters used some of Amnesty's methods, most importantly the "adoption" of political prisoners.[29]

III

What seems to have given the symbolic figure of the "prisoner of conscience" their symbolic power was their innocence. Amnesty International defended people whose sole crime was that their innermost beliefs – informing their conscience – contradicted an official ideology.[30] Echoing this concern, Polish political prisoners usually described their identity only in the broadest sense. "We have been sentenced," sixty-seven prisoners wrote, "for having defended fundamental liberties and human rights."[31] The Braniewo prisoners did not even invoke human rights or national identity. They did not want to be considered "representatives of the suffering nation," they wrote "We consider ourselves to be innocent people ... that is all we want to say about ourselves."[32]

The Polish prisoners' claim to innocence was powerfully underscored by the tactic they chose to achieve the status of a political prisoner: hunger strikes. In the West, the history of hunger strikes dated back to at least the early twentieth century. But their meaning too changed with the imagery of the prisoner of conscience. In a hunger strike, the protesters hoped to exert pressure by drawing on their opponents' sense of righteousness and compassion; rather than seeing fellow human beings suffer or even having their blood on their hands, the prison authorities would give in to their demands. In this sense, hunger strikes were a desperate measure, the ultimate weapon of the weak.[33] Moreover, by

---

[29] For Amnesty's position on Polish internees of martial law as prisoners of conscience see *Amnesty International Report 1983*, Jan. 1, 1983, 265. The organization was working for the release of some 300 prisoners. See also *Amnesty International Report 1982*, Oct. 1, 1982, 280–285, on 285. Amnesty also submitted Poland-related testimony to the UN Commission on Human Rights. See *Amnesty International Report 1984*, May 1, 1984, 11, see also ibid., 293–297. For Amnesty lobbying before 1981 on behalf of prisoners of conscience belonging to KOR, ROPCziO, and other groups see *Amnesty International Report 1981*, Oct. 1, 1981, 308–312.

[30] Cf. Hopgood, *Keepers*, 60.

[31] "Nous exigeons l'amnisti totale," *Solidarność – Bulletin d'Information*, 57 (Mar. 15, 1983), 3; cf. "Idee KOR-u są i pozostaną żywe," *KOS*, Dec. 4, 1983.

[32] "List Otwarty."

[33] First used in Russia in the 1870s, British suffragists were the first to use hunger strikes successfully in the early twentieth century; these protests also brought about the most widely used countermeasure: forced feeding. Hunger strikes were also often used by Irish Republicans. It seems, however, that it had been Gandhi's adoption of hunger

venturing their own most basic human rights, prisoners demonstrated their status as prisoners of conscience: Even in their desperate situations, their actions suggested, they would rather hurt themselves than hurt others. If the hunger strikes underscored the prisoners' innocence, it reinforced the government's guilt. The only way the authorities could respond to a hunger strike, short of letting the protestors die, was to violate the prisoners' dignity in a very profound way – by force feeding them and depriving them of control over their own bodies, the last liberty left to them.[34]

Hunger strikes also underscored the protestors' moral steadfastness, another central virtue of the "prisoner of conscience." Conscience is a complex philosophical concept which even Amnesty International – the organization that had put it at the center of their activism – delineated only very broadly. According to its statutes, prisoners of conscience were people who had been imprisoned "by reason of their political, religious or other conscientiously held beliefs."[35] The Polish underground's initiative to commemorate 1984 as Prisoners of Conscience Year contained a similarly vague understanding of conscience in which a Solidarity underground group described Polish prisoners of conscience as people "whose conscience had compelled them to be [politically] active even during martial law."[36] "Conscience," thus, seems to have referred to what Immanuel Kant has called "an internal court in man ... incorporated in his being" – the innermost beliefs of people before which they hold themselves responsible for their deeds and against whose authoritative "voice" they could act only by forfeiting their very humanity.[37]

Imprisoning people for their "consciously held beliefs" was thus an attack on that person's moral integrity and dignity. By refusing to recant their views and remaining faithful to the "voice" of their conscience, the prisoners were defending their very humanity. In this sense, Polish prisoners wrote that they did not "ask anyone for sympathy, for we have

---

strikes within the general concept of civil disobedience that turned it into a global practice of political resistance. See Kevin Grant, "British Suffragettes and the Russian Method of Hunger Strike," *Comparative Studies in Society and History* 53 (2011), 1; Jason Perlman, "Terence MacSwiney: The Triumph and Tragedy of the Hunger Strike," *New York History* 88 (2007), 3; Pramod Kumar Srivastava, "Resistance and repression in India: The Hunger Strike at the Andaman Cellular Jail in 1933," *Crime, Histoire & Sociétés/Crime, History & Societies* 7 (2003), 2.

[34] Murat Sevinç, "Hunger Strikes in Turkey," *Human Rights Quarterly* 30 (2008), 3, 658. For force-feeding in Polish prisons see "Więźniowie siedzą," *Wiadomości*, Mar. 18, 1984.
[35] *Amnesty International Report 1983*, 339.   [36] "Oświadczenie."
[37] Immanuel Kant, *The Metaphysics of Morals*, ed. Mary J. Gregor (Cambridge, New York: Cambridge University Press, 1996), 189; cf. William Lyons, "Conscience – An Essay in Moral Psychology," *Philosophy* 84 (2009), 4; Jiwei Ci, "Conscience, Sympathy, and the Foundation of Morality," *American Philosophical Quarterly* 28 (1991), 1.

160   Poland's Solidarity Movement & the Politics of Rights

consciously chosen to be in prison, rejecting the authorities' pardon."
They were in prison, in other words, because, before their own conscience, they could not sign the declaration of loyalty that would have set
them free. This faithfulness to their innermost conviction was the main
reason they wanted to be recognized as political prisoners, the protestors
explained. By merely relaxing the prison regime, but denying the status
of a political prisoner, they argued, the authorities wanted to submit the
political prisoners to the same procedures of re-socialization applied to
"ordinary" prisoners. "The aim of these activities is obvious," they went
on, "the authorities are trying to force the politicals to change their
convictions." That was why they struggled to be recognized as political
prisoners, in order to be "treated humanely, that is, in a way that respects
our dignity and convictions, taking natural human needs into
account."[38] These prisoners had consciously chosen to remain in prison
to defend their moral integrity – and the respect for this integrity was
what they wanted to secure by the recognition as "politicals."

An open letter by Ewa Kubasiewicz, the leader of protests in a
women's prison and one of Amnesty's Polish prisoners of conscience,
provides another example for how Polish prisoners understood their fate
not as part of an ideological struggle, but a defense of their human
dignity.[39] Kubasiewicz described her prison sentence as "above all an
attempt to destroy the personality of a human being, to break him
spiritually and physically." Yet General Jaruzelski, she went on, had not
recognized, nor even only mentioned, the status of a political prisoner.
He had "proposed something else – a pardon."

> Maybe only those can fully understand how shameful this proposition is who have
> been through a trial, through remand and prison. After having struggled with
> myself for a year not to succumb to feelings of hate, despite everything, despite all
> the evil, I am now made to understand that it is I – sentenced to 10 years in prison
> and for 5 years stripped of my civil rights, with a son who has received a 3-year
> sentence only because he is my son – who is supposed to ask for forgiveness and
> mercy, to repent.

In the light of these propositions and out of responsibility to those who
were working to set her free, she went on, she deemed it necessary to
make her position clear: "Release – Yes! At any price – No!"[40] Not unlike

---

[38] "List Otwarty."   [39] *Amnesty International Report 1984*, 294.
[40] "List Ewy," *KOS*, Jan. 15, 1983. Defending one's integrity by not giving in to hate was a
recurrent theme of Polish prisoners' statements. Cf., for instance, "List otwarty Ewy
Romaszewskiej," *KOS*, July 5, 1983 (the author of this open letter was another prisoner
of conscience adopted by Amnesty [*Amnesty International Report 1984*, 294]); "Więzienie
jest do wytrzymania: Wywiad z Andrzejem Słowikiem," *Tygodnik Mazowsze*,
Nov. 3, 1983.

Letters from Prison

the activists of the nineteenth century, then, imprisonment could be the result of a conscious choice; but its motivation was not ideological but the desire to defend one's dignity and humanity.

IV

The most elaborate translation of this discourse on political incarceration, conscience, and dignity into the Polish context can be found in the prison writings of Adam Michnik, a former student radical and activist of KOR. During the 4.5 years he spent in confinement between 1981 and 1986, Michnik became Poland's most prolific prison writer, reflecting on his own moral choices, adding his voice to debates on Solidarity's strategies, and directly appealing to world opinion to speak out against repression in Poland and the world. Independent of whether Michnik was actually aware of the concept of a "prisoner of conscience," especially essays written between March 1982 and December 1983 show how he used the human rights discourse around political incarceration to endow his situation with meaning.

Written as letters to a friend, most of these essays were very personal, almost intimate reflections on Michnik's own choices. In one of them, written in March 1982 and published abroad in Polish and French, he explained why he could not sign the loyalty declaration that would set him free.[41] Defending his dignity, he explained, was the last line of defense for a human being, humiliated and impotent "in the face of armed evil."[42] Signing the declaration "would be to negate yourself, to wipe out the meaning of your life ..."[43] Since the stakes of the debate was personal dignity, "you score a victory not when you win power but when you remain faithful to yourself."[44]

In Michnik's writings the central values of the "prisoner of conscience" – moral steadfastness in defense of one's dignity – were connected to Solidarity's struggle outside of prison. If the individual stake of the prisoner's struggle was moral integrity, its larger stake was hope – Solidarity's main gift to Polish society.[45] The authorities, Michnik explained, were everywhere displaying their power because they wanted to crush the hope Solidarity had raised in Poland. This "is precisely what the battle is being fought over: the policemen want to force out of us a declaration that we are giving up hope." Herein lay the sense of incarceration: "So by refusing to talk with the policeman, by refusing to collaborate, by rejecting the status of informant, and by choosing to be a political prisoner you are defending

---

[41] All quotations are from the English translations in Michnik, *Prison.*   [42] Ibid., 4.
[43] Ibid., 6.   [44] Ibid., 7.   [45] Ibid., 24.

hope.... You are casting your declaration of hope out of your prison cell into the world, like a sealed bottle into the ocean. If even one single person finds it, you will have scored a victory."[46]

Characteristically for the discourse of the prisoner of conscience, however, this hope remained remarkably indistinct. There was no larger political vision to Michnik's essay, and it drew strikingly little on Poland's rich tradition of political resistance. His vision, Michnik insisted, was not romantic; he was not a hero. He wanted to be alive for Poland, not die for it. He wrote how he had always taken pleasure in his "inner freedom," but also "in beautiful women, and in wine." Martial law had surprised him "in the company of a pretty woman, not while ... planning an assault on the Central Committee headquarters."[47] It was not heroism that Poland needed but normalcy. Yet this normalcy, Michnik concluded, was to be had only through moral steadfastness. Confronted with an opponent whose *raison d'etre* was to break people, signing the loyalty declarations was not a compromise, but "acts of collaboration, and [they] have been conceived as such."[48]

At bottom, then, the struggle which Michnik described was not a struggle between political systems; it was not even primarily a struggle for national liberation. It was a struggle to defend one's humanity, and in doing so, to create sources of hope. "But you do know," Michnik finished his essay, "as you stand alone, handcuffed, with your eyes filled with tear gas, in front of policemen who are shaking their guns at you – you can see it clearly in the dark and starless night, thanks to your favorite poet [Czesław Miłosz] – that the course of the avalanche depends on the stones over which it rolls. And you want to be the stone that will reverse the course of events."[49]

V

As Polish prisoners drew on the discourse of the prisoner of conscience, political incarceration also moved to the center of the Polish opposition's international activities. In January 1984, Charta 77, Solidarity's underground leadership, and other Polish oppositionists issued a joint appeal "to all people in the world who hold dear the freedom and dignity of man to join our efforts to free political prisoners in Poland and Czechoslovakia ..."[50] Two months later, Solidarity appealed to "world organizations and institutions which are not indifferent to the issue of the defense of human rights to exert pressure on the government of the

[46] Ibid., 9–10.   [47] Ibid., 11.   [48] Ibid., 13.   [49] Ibid., 14.
[50] *Solidarność News*, Mar. 15, 1984.

Letters from Prison   163

[People's Republic of Poland]" to regulate the status of those on hunger strike.[51]

Such appeals reached Western audiences in various ways. The Polish Helsinki Committee's report for the CSCE conference in Madrid, for instance, featured a section on political prisoners.[52] In October 1983, Literature Nobel Laureate Czesław Miłosz attended a conference in Paris, convened by President François Mitterrand, where he read an appeal by Lech Wałęsa to release all political prisoners.[53] Western newspapers occasionally reported on the efforts of political prisoners in Poland, while the émigré centers translated and reprinted many of their open letters in the news bulletins and reports they send out to supporters and policy makers.[54]

Michnik assumed a central role in these international efforts. His excellent international contacts had turned him into one of Solidarity's most recognizable voices, even though he was actually not among Solidarity's leadership.[55] He regularly contributed texts to West

---

[51] "Apel TKK w sprawie więźniów politycznych," *KOS*, Mar. 12, 1984.

[52] Bureau d'Information du Solidarność á l'étranger, "Conference sur la Sécuritée et la Cooperation en Europe," not dated, 3–4, CFDT, Sect. Int., 8 H 2077, File "Comité contre le procès de Varsovie"; "Solidarity Report on 'Human and Civil Rights During the State of War," press statement by Max Kampelman, March 25, 1983, IDEE, CSS records, box "CSS 2 (Records of Activities)," folder "CSS Annual Reports 1983-1986 Responses to CSS HRights Rep."

[53] *Solidarność News*, Oct. 31, 1983.

[54] For examples see "Faut-il demander la grâce?," "Lettres de prison," and "Activités dans les camps et les prisons" in *Bulletin d'information* 59 (Apr. 13, 1983), 7–13; "Appel pour les prisionniers," *Bulletin d'information* 76 (Nov. 16, 1983); Appeal by Solidarity's Brussels Office, "Appel aux organisations syndicales et aux gens de bonne volonté dans tous les pays démocratiques," dated April 26, 1984, CFDT, Sect. Int., 8 H 2077, Folder "Comité contre le procès de Varsovie"; "Political Prisoners Demand Amnesty" and "Letter from Fordon Women's Prison," *Committee in Support of Solidarity Reports* 13 (Apr. 5, 1983), 5–7; Letter from Eric Chenoweth and Irena Lasota to Lane Kirkland, July 23, 1984, AFL-CIO, Unprocessed Records, International Affairs Department, File "Polish Political Prisoners"; Letter from Eric Chenoweth to Tom Kahn, April 16, 1984, AFL-CIO, Unprocessed Records, International Affairs Department, Folder "Committee in Support of Solidarity." For examples of how information from the prisons reached Western audiences see Bradley Graham, "Freed Activist Details Prison Regimen Of Crowding, Broken Sleep, Bad Food," *Washington Post*, Aug. 1, 1983; "In polnischen Gefängnissen," *Frankfurter Allgemeine Zeitung*, Dec. 12, 1983; "Wieder mehr politische Gefangene in Polen," *Frankfurter Allgemeine Zeitung*, Mar. 28, 1984; "Prisoners on Hunger Strike," *Guardian*, Feb. 2, 1984; "Solidarity faster said to be near death," *Boston Globe*, Feb. 7, 1984; "For a Polish Hunger Striker, No Compromise," *New York Times*, Feb. 19, 1984; "Rights Abuse Attacked by UN Chief in Polish Speech," *Guardian*, Feb. 20, 1984. See also ETUC Press Release, "Pologne: La dignité humaine refusées aux grévistes de la faim de Solidarnosc," dated Feb. 22, 1984, CFDT, Sect. International, 8 H 2077, File ""Procès de syndicalistes de KOR, Varsovie, 1984."

[55] "Hausmitteilung," *Der Spiegel*, Jan. 16, 1984.

164   Poland's Solidarity Movement & the Politics of Rights

Germany's influential weekly *Der Spiegel* and was widely quoted as an authoritative source in Western reporting on Poland.[56]

Reporting in the *New York Times* demonstrates how he used the imagery of the prisoner of conscience to reach international audiences. On April 26, 1984, the *Times'* front page displayed a photograph from an event in New York to commemorate the fiftieth anniversary of the University in Exile, an institution set up in the 1930s to provide a home for European intellectuals persecuted by the Nazis. The keynote speech was given by a former refugee from Nazi Germany and the picture on the *Times'* front page showed former secretary of state Cyrus Vance as a guest of honor of the meeting. Yet both the text accompanying the picture as well as a later article focused on something else – the "drama" of a dissident's letter.[57]

As part of the celebration, the New School for Social Research had awarded Michnik an honorary doctoral degree, alongside human rights activists from Chile, South Africa, the United States, and the Soviet Union. In prison awaiting trial, Michnik was the only one who could not attend the meeting. Thus, Miłosz accepted the degree in his name, reading an open letter by Michnik. First published in the underground, the open letter was addressed to Gen. Czesław Kiszczak, the Polish Minister of the Interior. In an interview, Kiszczak had said that Michnik could avoid a prison sentence if he left Poland for the French Riviera. Michnik responded to this offer unequivocally. "[T]o offer a man imprisoned for two years to go to the French Riviera in exchange for moral suicide," the *Times* quoted the letter, "one must be a pig, and to believe I could accept such a deal, one has to assume every man is no more than a police informer."[58]

The event in New York represented the stark dichotomy at the heart of the "prisoner of conscience," between the prisoner's moral integrity and his guard's self-disgrace. The whole letter, in fact, revolved around the central notion of the imagery of political imprisonment: conscience. The major reason why Kiszczak wanted him to leave, Michnik charged, had nothing to do with politics; it concerned the General himself. Getting Michnik to choose comfort over integrity would allow Kiszczak to deny the truth about himself: "The truth that you are a vindicative, dishonorable swine; the truth that even if there ever was a spark of decency in your heart, you have long buried this feeling in the brutal and dirty power

---

[56] Michnik, *Prison*, 29, 36.

[57] William G. Blair, "Drama Marks 50 Years of University in Exile," *New York Times*, Apr. 26, 1984.

[58] Ibid.

Letters from Prison

struggle which you wage among yourselves." What Kiszczak wanted was "to drag" Michnik down to his level.[59] "Well," Michnik continued, "I am going to deny you that pleasure." Prison was no punishment to him – forfeiting his moral integrity would be. If Kiszczak wanted to understand this choice, "[I] would like to suggest that the first thing you need to know, General, is what it is to have a human conscience." There were things – lying, insulting, imprisoning – which, however expedient, were forbidden.

Who forbids them? General, you may be the mighty minister of internal affairs, you may have the backing of a power that extends from the Elbe to Vladivostok and of the entire police force of this country, you may have millions of informers and millions of zlotys with which to buy guns, water cannons, bugging devices, servile collaborators, informers, and journalists, but something invisible, a passerby in the darkness, will appear before you and say: *this you must not do.* That is conscience.[60]

Though Michnik may have expected his letter to be published abroad, it had not been written for the awards ceremony. Nevertheless, read at a meeting to celebrate a university of refugees from totalitarianism, it brought the full power of the human rights imaginary to bear, sweeping the attendants "like a tornado," as one of them said, and bringing them to their feet in applause.[61] For at the letter's center was the symbolic figure of the prisoner of conscience – of someone who suffered for the sole reason that he was faithful to the voice of his conscience and who, through his witness, gave meaning to a hopeless cause. The effect of the letter was reinforced by the fact that the other human activists honored with a degree – coming from the Soviet Union, Chile, South Africa, and the United States – represented all three parts of the Cold War world.

VI

At a time when Western attention to Poland was slacking, the figure of the prisoner of conscience allowed the Polish activists to translate their plight into a powerful symbolic language whose meaning international audiences could easily grasp. And in the process, they themselves became powerful symbols – icons – of human rights culture. Again, the *New York Times* provided a telling example. When Michnik was finally put on trial, the front page of the *Times* from July 14, 1984, featured a picture of him and Jacek Kuroń in the courtroom with a policeman sitting between them. Grimly looking into the camera, marked by a hunger strike to

---

[59] Michnik, *Prison*, 68.   [60] Ibid., 68–69.   [61] Blair, "Drama."

166   Poland's Solidarity Movement & the Politics of Rights

force the authorities to begin the trial, Michnik had become an icon of human rights.

This is not to say that Michnik's name or face were widely known. Only few readers of the *Times* would have recognized his face, probably not even his name. And yet a picture subtitled "Polish dissident trial begins," showing a gaunt, yet defiant man sitting next to a Soviet bloc style policeman was iconic in the original sense of the term "icon" outlined at the beginning of this chapter. The image of Michnik sitting in the dock with his gaunt body and defiant look was a powerful rendition of a central archetype of human rights culture – the prisoner of conscience, a human being made to suffer for the sole reason that his views dissented from those of the state. And through his suffering, as well as the moral steadfastness it proved, he not only symbolized central values of human rights culture – innocence and integrity – he manifested (incarnated) them in a very tangible way.

A further analogy between human rights culture and Byzantine iconography is that, in both cases, there were authorities which confirmed the authenticity of an icon. The role ecclesiastical authorities played in the case of Orthodox Christianity could be attributed to Amnesty International in the case of human rights. At the core of Amnesty's identity were very strict criteria of who was, and who was not, a prisoner of conscience; a good part of Amnesty's activism was to conduct meticulous research in order to establish whether a prisoner fulfilled these criteria. So strict were these rules that in 1964 Amnesty ceased to consider Nelson Mandela a prisoner of conscience because he insisted on the right of black South Africans to use violence in self-defense.[62]

Looking at whom Amnesty adopted as prisoners of conscience thus helps to further accentuate Michnik's iconic status. A particularly telling comparison in this respect is with a case in the UK. Only months before martial law was imposed on Poland, Irish Republican militants had staged a widely publicized hunger strike in a British high-security prison – the infamous H-Blocks.[63] These protests gathered massive international attention and they produced a symbolic hero – Bobby Sands, the leader of the protests who died in the hunger strike. Yet the values which Sands manifested were markedly different from those of the Polish prisoners. As a paramilitary organization, the imprisoned IRA members were very much heirs to nineteenth-century political prisoners. Their hunger strike

---

[62] Ann Marie Clark, *Diplomacy of Conscience: Amnesty International and Changing Human Rights Norms* (Princeton, Oxford: Princeton University Press, 2001), 14.

[63] Grant, "Suffragettes"; Perlman, "MacSwiney"; George Sweeney, "Irish Hunger Strikes and the Cult of Self-Sacrifice," *Journal of Contemporary History* 28 (1993), 3.

Letters from Prison

was meant to have "Special Category Status" reinstated, a prison regime allowing the IRA members to pose as prisoners of war, wearing uniform, conducting military drills, and organizing lectures in revolutionary theory. In this case, therefore, the hunger strikes were merely a continuation of the armed struggle by other means.

Though these protests drew vastly more attention than the protests in Poland, the IRA prisoners were denied iconic status by such authorities like Amnesty International and the *New York Times*. An editorial in the *Times* chided Margaret Thatcher for her cool response to the hunger strikes, but it also called Bobby Sands a "terrorist."[64] Amnesty International was deeply involved in negotiations to find a solution to the conflict over the IRA prisoners, and it criticized the official British response to the protests as violating human rights. But the organization also underlined that it did not endorse the prisoners' political demands, nor did it adopt them as prisoners of conscience. This contrasts with the coverage of Michnik's case in the *New York Times* or the fact the Amnesty International had considered all internees of martial law prisoners of conscience.

VII

What impact did this campaign for prisoners of conscience have on the amnesty of 1984 that led to the release of the Solidarity Eleven? After 1982, as noted above, Warsaw had largely defied Western pressures. Though making certain concessions – releasing most of the detainees, lifting martial law at least nominally, allowing John Paul II to come to Poland – Warsaw refused to release all political prisoners and re-legalize Solidarity, two of the three conditions NATO had set for a lifting of its sanctions. Given that in 1982 the sanctions had been only the Western alliance's smallest common denominator anyway, more and more West European capitals began considering re-engaging Warsaw diplomatically and economically. Even Reagan had to concede that a mere policy of insisting on the demands from 1982 would not get Washington closer to achieving its aims in Eastern Europe.

Yet given NATO's own insistence on the release of the detainees and the salience of the "prisoner of conscience" discourse, Washington and its Western allies had to acknowledge that a rapprochement with Warsaw would have to include a solution to the issue of political prisoners in

---

[64] "If Mrs. Thatcher were Anwar Sadat," *New York Times*, May 6, 1981; for a systematic analysis of the *Times'* coverage and the background of the protests see Aogán Mulcahy, "Claims-Making and the Construction of Legitimacy: Press Coverage of the 1981 Northern Irish Hunger Strike," *Social Problems* 42 (1995), 4.

Poland. The US government thus shifted from a policy of completely isolating Warsaw to a "step-by-step" approach in which improvements in bilateral relations would be tied to tangible improvements in Poland's human rights situation and especially the release of political detainees, the Solidarity Eleven chief among them.[65] With the exception of the Italians, the West Europeans were much less willing to link an improvement in Polish–Western relations to specific human rights conditions.[66] But for most of them, too, the issue of political prisoners was standing in the way of an improvement in relations with Poland, "chief among them, the fate reserved for the members of the KOR and other well-known opposition leaders," as the NATO representative of France relayed a report by his embassy in Warsaw.[67]

The question of political incarceration was also salient in Warsaw's international relations outside the Soviet bloc. In May 1984, the International Labor Organization found Warsaw guilty of having violated its conventions on freedom of association. Among others, the ILO report demanded an immediate end of all trials against trade union leaders and the release of everyone sentenced for trade union activism.[68] Solidarity's supporters from Western civil society, moreover, made sure that the fate of the Solidarity Eleven was the central issue of Poland's relations with the West. In Paris, the CFDT, anti-totalitarian intellectuals, and Polish

[65] Memorandum from George P. Shultz for the President, "Poland: Next Steps," dated Oct. 13, 1983 and Memorandum from Robert C. McFarlane for the President, "Sanctions on Poland," dated Nov. 1, 1983, both in RRPL, Dobriansky Files, box OA 90892, folder "Poland Memoranda 1981-1983."

[66] Memorandum from Paula Dobriansky for William Clark, "Poland Update," dated May 27, 1983, RRPL, Dobriansky Files, box OA 90892, folder "Poland Memoranda 1981-1983." The fate of the Solidarity Eleven, however, was a central issue in the West European's relations to Poland. See, for instance, "Gesandter Graf von Brühl, Warschau, an das Auswärtige Amt," dated Apr. 27, 1984, in AAPD, 1984, I, Dok. 119, 566.

[67] Memorandum from the Chair of the Political Committee to the Secretary General, "Réunion du comité politique du mardi 2 août 1983," dated Aug. 2, 1983, Memorandum from the Chair of the Political Committee for the Secretary General, "La situation en Pologne depuis la levée de l'état de guerre," dated Sep. 5, 1983, both in NATO, Poland, International Staff. On Italian support for Michnik, see "Świadectwa w sprawie Adama Michnika," Kultura 11/434 (Nov. 1983).

[68] "Kurzfassung des Berichtes des von der Internationalen Arbeitsorganisation (IAO) eingesetzten Untersuchungsausschusses zur Prüfung der Klage betreffend der Einhaltung des IAO-Übereinkommens über die Vereinigungsfreiheit und den Schutz des Vereinigungsrechtes (Nr. 87) und des IAO-Übereinkommens über das Vereinigungsrecht und das Recht zu Kollektivverhandlungen (Nr. 98) durch Polen," dated Nov. 15, 1984, AdsD, DGB-Archiv, Intern. Abt., DGAJ000654; for how western trade unionists brought up the issue of political prisoners and the Solidarity Eleven in the ILO's deliberations see Ministerstwo Spraw Zagranicznych, Notatka informacyjna, dated Feb. 6, 1984, on 3, AAN, KC PZPR, LXXVI-982.

Letters from Prison   169

émigrés joined forces to create the Committee against the Warsaw Trials. Invoking the Moscow trials of the 1930s, it drew heavily on the anti-totalitarian imagery of the 1970s and managed to collect close to 50,000 signatures against the trial of the Solidarity Eleven. Alongside international trade union federations and various human rights organizations, moreover, the CFDT tried to send international observers to the trial and lobbied the French government on behalf of the four defendants in Warsaw.[69] More vexing for Poland's Communist rulers, Western Communists joined these protests. In April 1984, the head of the Italian Communists' first delegation to Poland since 1981 expressed his concern about the fate of the Solidarity Eleven.[70] A month later, even former Austrian Chancellor Bruno Kreisky – a politician with an even more cordial view of Poland's Communist government than the SPD – had asked the Polish authorities to release the Solidarity Eleven from prison.[71]

In June 1984, when the Polish authorities set a date for the trial against the KOR members, the Committee against the Warsaw Trials was received by high-ranking French and Italian politicians, while Polish embassies were flooded with petitions to free the prisoners or allow Western observers to attend the trial.[72] The opening of the trial made it

---

[69] For the creation of the Committee see Letter from Jacques Chérèque to Michel Foucault, dated Jan. 13, 1983, CFDT, Sect. Int., 8 H 2077, File "Comité contre les procès de Varsovie"; for its harking back to the anti-totalitarian imagery of the 1970s see the committee's untitled circular, dated March 16, 1983 and the untitled statement for a press conference held on Mar. 24, 1983, see also Meeting Minutes, "Procès Pologne: Réunion du 21 octobre 1983," not dated, for trial observers see Letter from Pierre-Edouard Weil to Raymond Juin, dated July 6, 1984, Untitled ETUC Circular, dated Oct. 17, 1983, ETUC Press Release, "Pologne: Des observateurs syndicaux internationaux réfuses au procès contre Solidarnosc," dated July 13, 1984, all in CFDT, 8 H 2077, File "Procès de syndicalistes de KOR, Varsovie, 1984"; for ICFTU initiatives see the letters sent between DGB president Ernst Breit and Polish ambassdor Tadeusz Olechowski, dated July 4, 9, and 10, 1984, AdsD, DGB-Archiv, 5/DGAJ000292. For a request by the International Commission of Jurists: Letter from Niall McDermott to Jerzy Zawalonka, dated Nov. 10, 1982, AIPN, BU 514/1/CD/20, 251–252; for requests by the youth organization of the Norwegian workers party and the Swedish social democrats: "Poparcie udzielone przez niektóre skandynawskie związki młodzieżowe przebywającym w areszcie przywódcom KSS KOR," dated Jan. 3, 1984, Informacja dot. procesu działaczy KSS KOR, 3 Apr. 1984. AIPN, BU 0204/1417/CD/56.
[70] Wizyta delegacji WłPK w Polsce, dated April 9, 1984, AAN, KC PZPR, LXXVI-634.
[71] RFE transcript, "Kreisky pośredniczy w konflikcie o polskich więźniach," dated May 31, 1984, AIPN, BU 514/17/CD/1, 223.
[72] Szyfogram Nr 3170/III z Kolonii, dated Sept. 2, 1984, AAN, PZPR, LXXVI-983; Działania podejmowane na Zachodzie w związku z procesem działaczy KOR-u, załącznik do informacji dziennej z dnia 14.07.1984 r., AIPN, BU 0204/1417/CD/57, fol. 35–36. Protests and visa applications came, among others, from France: Letter from Pierre-Edouard Weil to the Polish ambassador in France, dated July 8, 1984, CFDT, Sect.

170   Poland's Solidarity Movement & the Politics of Rights

on the front pages of major Western newspapers like the *New York Times, Frankfurter Allgemeine Zeitung, Le Monde, Libération,* and *Le Matin.*[73]

While Western pressures were piling up to release Poland's political prisoners, important voices in the Communist leadership were adamant that the Solidarity Eleven had to be put on trial. Internal documents warned that freeing the very people, whom the propaganda had branded as the main culprits for the events of 1981, would be interpreted as a sign of weakness by society and could even lead to the demoralization and demobilization of the security apparatus. There was, after all, the precedent of the 1977 amnesty which had at least indirectly brought Warsaw into its predicament in 1984.[74]

Party hardliners were also concerned that an amnesty would undermine Poland's credibility within the socialist camp, a point powerfully underscored in April 1984. On a visit to Poland, Soviet Foreign Minister Andrei Gromyko and Defense Secretary Dmitry Ustinov told Jaruzelski that he needed to do more to regain full control of the country. When the two reported back to the Soviet Politburo, the new General Secretary Konstantin Chernenko appeared exasperated at the lack of progress in Jaruzelski's struggle with the "counterrevolution." The situation in Poland did not concern the Polish comrades alone, he insisted, but was a concern for the entire Warsaw Pact.[75] In May, he thus summoned the Polish leader to Moscow, ostensibly to bestow the Lenin order on him and sign a treaty of close Polish–Soviet leadership. In reality, his visit seems to have been part of a Soviet campaign to reinforce discipline in the Warsaw pact.[76] Chernenko thus told Jaruzelski in no uncertain terms what he expected him to "root out [wyplenienie z korzeniami]

Int., 8 H 2077, File "Procès de syndicalistes de KOR, Varsovie, 1984"; West Germany: Letter from Ernst Breit to Tadeusz Olechowski, dated July 10, 1984, 5/DGAJ000292, DGB-Archiv; Die Grünen Pressemitteilung Nr350/84, "Grüne protestieren gegen Verweigerung der Einreiseerlaubnis nach Polen," dated July 13, 1984, AGG, PKA 459; and Italy: Telegrams, dated July 17, 1984, AIPN, BU 514/1/CD/2, 7–8.

[73] Michael Kaufman, "Pole, Author of Letters from Jail, Is Awaiting Trial He Long Sought," *New York Times,* July 12, 1984. "Solidarité au banc des accusés" and "Le procés de quatre dirigeants du KOR," *Le Monde,* July 14, 1984; "Warschau rechnet mit den Geburtshelfern der 'Solidarität' ab," *Frankfurter Allgemeine Zeitung,* July 14, 1984.

[74] "Koncepcje polityczno-prawne zakończenia postępowań karnych przeciwko członkom kierownictwa antypaństwowego związku pn. 'KSS KOR' i ekstremistycznym działaczom b. 'Solidarości'," Feb. 1984, załącznik do protokołu z posiedzenia BP w dniu 10 lutego 1984, on 3, AAN, KC PZPR, 3045; Notatka dot. procesów sądowych w sprawach tzw. KSS KOR (J. Kuroń i inni)I ekstremalnych przywódców b. NSZZ Solidarność (A. Gwiazda i inni), Apr. 3, 1984, AIPN, BU 0204/1417, t. 55, fol. 123–127.

[75] Zasedanie Politburo KPSS, dated 26 April 1984, available at www.bukovsky-archives .net/pdfs/poland/pol84-8.pdf (accessed Jan. 2017).

[76] "Gesandter Huber, Moskau, and das Auswärtige Amt," dated Sep. 11, 1984, in AAPD, 1984, II, 1078–1082, at 1079–1080.

the anti-socialist elements" and reestablish Marxist-Leninist orthodoxy.[77] Despite these clear demands by the Soviet leadership, however, the Polish leadership released all political prisoners. In fact, by the time of Jaruzelski's trip to Moscow, he and Minister of the Interior General Kiszczak had long since started looking for ways to avoid the trials.[78]

Domestic and international pressures seem to have been equally responsible for the release of the prisoners. A politburo memo mentioned how attention to the Solidarity Eleven had increased among "different social groups and specific circles in the West." Especially the episcopate continued to pressure for an amnesty, while "in the West, the ... hostile campaign against Poland continues, with petitions sent from different countries to the authorities of the [People's Republic of Poland] and to public figures. Demands are being raised and unequivocal threats are made to sustain or even tighten the economic restrictions."[79] Given the sorry state of the Polish economy, the latter would have proved particularly painful for Poland.[80]

For some time in late 1983, there was a chance of a face-saving measure for the Polish leadership regarding the issue of the Solidarity Eleven. The latter were offered a pardon if they agreed to abstain from political activities for some time. This compromise was supported by the Polish Catholic bishops as well as the pope. Western governments had signaled Warsaw that such a solution would be sufficient for them to lift some of their sanctions. Ultimately, however, the prisoners refused, arguing in effect that such a move would be against their conscience. Adam Michnik was particularly adamant in this respect.[81]

The government thus had no choice but to release the prisoners. After the talks with the prisoners had failed, the Prosecutor's Office recommended solving the problem of the Solidarity Eleven by freeing them unconditionally, a move which the party hardliners and rank-and-file saw as an expression of political opportunism, if not outright capitulation.[82] To give at least a minimal show of the government's determination, the

---

[77] Notatka informacyjna z wizyty w ZSSR tow. W. Jaruzelskiego w dniach 4 i 5 maja 1984 r., dated May 8, 1984, AAN, KC PZPR, V/228, 63–72, at 69.
[78] Mieczysław F. Rakowski, *Dzienniki polityczne, 1981-1983* (Warszawa: Iskry, 2004), 612, entry dated Oct. 21, 1983.
[79] "Koncepcje polityczno-prawne zakończenia postępowań karnych," 3.
[80] Notatka informacyjna, dated May 8, 1984, AAN, KC PZPR, V/228, 69.
[81] Bronisław Geremek, "Doradcy i więźniowie." *Wolność i Solidarność* 4 (2012), 113–130; Modzelewski, *Zajeździmy*, 347–352; Romaszewski, *Autobiografia*, 306–312.
[82] Mieczysław F. Rakowski, *Dzienniki polityczne, 1984-1986* (Warszawa: Iskry, 2005), 107, entry dated July 19, 1984.

172 Poland's Solidarity Movement & the Politics of Rights

four KOR members would be put on trial, to allow the prosecution to state its case.[83]

When Adam Michnik, Jacek Kuroń, Zbigniew Romaszewski, and Henryk Wujec were brought into the courtroom on July 13, 1984, then, the storm of domestic and international outrage accompanying the trial was already unnecessary; the decision to free them had been taken. And as crucial as the domestic and international support was for the amnesty, the Solidarity Eleven owed their unconditional release to no one but themselves.

★ ★ ★

The emergent human rights culture allowed Polish activists to translate their struggle into a language that resonated strongly with international audiences and even to fashion themselves into "icons" – incarnations of the sacred core of human rights culture. This was, to be sure, a language that was eminently political; the prisoner's intimate struggle for his dignity was simultaneously a social struggle for hope and thus enmeshed with the Solidarity's cause. Yet the "prisoners of conscience" concealed their politics. It was this latter feature that made them even more susceptible to the politics of those who admired him, a fact that will become apparent in the next chapter which is devoted to a Polish activist who was an icon in both senses of that word, as a sacred symbol and as a widely recognizable image – Lech Wałęsa.

---

[83] Koncepcja zakończenia spraw przeciwko aresztowanym działaczom b. "KSS KOR" i ekstremicznemu kierownictwu b. NSZZ "Solidarność," dated May 22, 1984, AIPN, BU 0204/1417, t.56, fo. 88–92.

8 Lech Wałęsa, the Symbolism of the Nobel Peace Prize, and Global Human Rights Culture

On the morning of October 5, 1983, Deputy Prime Minister and Communist party liberal Mieczysław Rakowski rang up Wojciech Jaruzelski. The General greeted him asking sarcastically, "I suppose you want to share your happiness about the new Nobel Prize laureate?" Jaruzelski had just been informed that Wałęsa had been awarded the 1983 Nobel Peace Prize. Meeting the general later that day, Rakowski recognized that he was visibly concerned about the award. "There'll be an incredible fuss in the world," he noted in his diary.[1]

If the Solidarity movement had an icon in the sense of a widely recognizable image, it was without any doubt the face of the trade union's president with his characteristic mustache and unpronounceable last name, Lech Wałęsa. The Nobel Prize merely confirmed this. Countless pictures taken on the Gdańsk shipyard in the summer of 1980 had turned him into an international celebrity. No less than eight Western newspapers had declared Wałęsa man of the year, in either 1980 or 1981, and both the Sorbonne and Harvard were among several Western universities that awarded him honorary degrees.[2] When martial law was imposed, Western governments regularly inquired about Wałęsa's whereabouts and the posters, banners, or flyers at Western demonstrations for

---

[1] Rakowski, *Dzienniki polityczne, 1981-1983*, 605, entry dated Oct. 5, 1983.

[2] Lech Wałęsa, *Lech Wałęsa dla Harvardu*, Podziemnia Oficyna Rolnicza Solidarność, not dated, KARTA, AO, III/28.1K.26; Lech Wałęsa, "Why Solidarity Sparked New Consciousness," *Labor and Trades Union Press Service* VIII, 6 (July/August 1983), AFL-CIO Unprocessed Records, International Affairs Department, Folder "Walesa, Lech"; Voice of America transcript, "Sprawozdanie z uroczystości nadanie Lechowi Wałęsie doctorat honoris causa na paryskiej Sorbonie," dated Mar. 10, 1984, AIPN, BU 514/21, t. 13, fol. 25. In May 1982, Wałęsa was the first person to receive a doctorate honoris causa in absentia from the University of Notre Dame. A month later, he was awarded an honorary doctor of law from Nasson College in Maine. See Note to the Media from Richard W. Conklin, dated May 16, 1982, AFL-CIO Unprocessed Records, International Affairs Department, Folder "Walesa, Lech;" *Committee in Support of Solidarity Reports,* 3 (June 7, 1982), 16–17. For other honors see Program for the 136th commencement of the College of the Holy Cross, not dated, GMMA, RG95–007: Lane Kirkland Papers, 1863-1998, File 2/13 "Programs 1982."

174 Poland's Solidarity Movement & the Politics of Rights

Solidarity often displayed a stylized drawing of Wałęsa's face, akin to the famous image of Ernesto "Che" Guevara.[3]

But though Wałęsa's was already an international celebrity, Jaruzelski had good reasons to be concerned that the Nobel Prize further enhanced the labor leader's position. Someone becomes an icon not through public exposure alone, but by conforming to conventions of "sanctity." If there was (and is) an institution with an unrivaled power to bestow an aura of sanctity upon someone, this was the Nobel Committee. Despite its repeated mishaps and controversial decisions, the Nobel Prizes turned the winners into exemplars – archetypes, even – of wisdom, creativity, or courage.[4] With the Nobel Prize, the British *Guardian* noted ironically, "Lech Walesa [had] formally joined the ranks of the great and the good ..."[5]

With the Norwegian Committee's decision, then, Jaruzelski's attempts to brand Solidarity a band of anarchists had suffered a severe blow. The Nobel Prize and its symbolism cemented his position as an icon in both senses of the word – as a highly recognizable person and as a morally unassailable reflection of secular sanctity. Turning the Polish electrician into a secular saint of sorts, the Norwegian committee drew heavily on the global human rights culture. I will thus analyze the symbolism of the Nobel Prize ceremony to continue with charting human rights culture and dissecting its inner workings. In so doing, a central aspect of this culture will come to the fore. Much as it elevated its icons, human rights also depoliticized them, turning them from specific actors fighting for concrete goals to larger-than-life symbolic personae who primarily reflected the values of the human rights community.

I

Domestically, the Nobel Prize could not have come at a better time for Wałęsa whose position was increasingly precarious. Already by the time martial law was imposed, his authority had diminished significantly due

---

[3] For how Wałęsa's opinions and position featured in US debates see Memorandum from George Shultz for Ronald Reagan, "Poland: Next Steps," dated Jan. 11, 1984, Memorandum from Robert McFarlane for Ronald Reagan, "Poland: Next Steps," dated Jan. 16, 1984, both in RRPL, Dobriansky Files, box OA 90892, folder "Poland Memoranda 1984-1985 (1)." For examples of flyers and leaflets from France and the United States see AFL-CIO Unprocessed Records, Intern. Affairs Department, Folder "Solidarność 1982 #1"; Arch. Conf. CFDT, Sect. Int., 8 H 1920.

[4] No academic history of the Nobel Prize exists. For a very good popular book see Burton Feldman, *The Nobel Prize: A History of Genius, Controversy, and Prestige* (New York: Arcade Pub., 2000).

[5] Michal Simmons, "Walesa Joins the Nobel Band," *Guardian*, Oct. 6, 1983.

to his erratic and often authoritarian leadership style, as well as his willingness to strike compromises with the government. His behavior over the following months seems to have regained him some of his high standing with many Poles. Upon arresting him, the Polish leadership had tried to get Wałęsa to chair a government-sanctioned trade union purged of "radical elements." When he refused and attempts to get him to support the government or at least to publicly declare his defeat failed, the regime released him on November 14, 1982.[6]

Setting him free, the government had tried to impress upon Wałęsa that his public career had ended. "There is no more Solidarity and no more Chairman Wałęsa," the Minister of the Interior told Wałęsa shortly before his release, "there only is Mr. Wałęsa [obywatel Wałęsa]." The Polish Press Agency announced that the "former Chairman of the former trade union Solidarity is now a private person." Yet returning home, Wałęsa was greeted by a large crowd and on the next day, he held a press conference in his flat, telling reporters of the underground press and Western correspondents that he would return to public life.[7] Showing how little the authorities themselves believed in Wałęsa being merely "Mr. Wałęsa," the Information Department of the Central Committee compiled yearly reports of Wałęsa's public statements.[8]

Impressive as Wałęsa's popularity was, though, he began to look increasingly like a general without an army, an impression reinforced during the papal visit to Poland of 1983. At papal Masses, the crowds displayed Solidarity banners, while John Paull II demanded respect for human rights, insisted on the right of workers to organize, and spoke in a willfully ambiguous way about the need for "solidarity." But he never explicitly criticized the regime, nor did he specifically call for the re-legalization of Solidarity. The trip itself, moreover, allowed the regime to showcase its apparent "liberalism." The pope moreover, had insisted on a meeting with Wałęsa. At the last minute, the Polish government relented but the meeting took place only on the last day of the pontiff's trip in a remote mountain hut. Held after a long meeting with Wojciech Jaruzelski, the pope's behavior left Western observers guessing: Had John Paul II wanted to strengthen Wałęsa or ask him to resign for the greater good of social peace? Feeding speculation, the *Osservatore Romano* interpreted the

---

[6] Skórzyński, *Zadra*, 99–118.

[7] Cited in Antoni Dudek, *Reglementowana rewolucja: Rozpad dyktatury komunistycznej w Polsce 1988-1990* (Warszawa: Arcana, 2004), 57; Skórzyński, *Zadra*, 115–116.

[8] Wydział informacji KC PZPR, *Dokumentacja wypowiedzi Lech Wałęsy w 1982 r.*, not dated, AIPN, BU 0397/521. These reports were compiled until at least 1984.

176   Poland's Solidarity Movement & the Politics of Rights

meeting as an honorable ending to Wałęsa's public career. The Vatican denied this interpretation and the author of the piece, the paper's editor in chief, was promptly fired, but the damage had been done.[9]

The regime for its part attempted to discredit Wałęsa both in Poland and internationally as a dangerous radical whose apparent heroism cloaked a reckless pursuit of political and material interests. In late September 1983, Polish television showed a film recorded by a surveillance camera secretly installed in Wałęsa's place of internment. Most likely a fabrication, it depicted Wałęsa toward the end of his internment in a conversation with his brother in which he allegedly boasted about large sums of money he had hid in the United States.[10]

In late 1983, then, Wałęsa was in a precarious situation. Though still an international celebrity, many Western observers had been wondering for some time whether he was, as the *Christian Science Monitor* wrote, more a "romantic memor[y] than [man] of the future."[11] In this situation, the international attention created by the Nobel Prize and the award ceremony itself provided Wałęsa with a powerful opportunity to pose as the leader of Solidarity and counter the regime's attempts to discredit him.

II

A Nobel laureate gives two speeches: a short acceptance speech during the award ceremony and the longer Nobel lecture.[12] Afraid that the

---

[9] "Schock nach Glück," *Der Spiegel*, July 4, 1983; Henry Kamm, "What Pope Told Walesa: A Debate Develops," *New York Times*, June 29, 1983; "Pope tied to deal for Walesa 'gag,' Polish normalcy," *Chicago Tribune*, June 28, 1983; Skórzyński, *Zadra*, 133.

[10] Skórzyński, *Zadra*, 137–139.

[11] Joseph C. Harsch, "Fading of Walesa, Arafat: bad times for revolution," *The Christian Science Monitor*, July 1, 1983.

[12] This analysis draws on these two speeches as well as the *laudatio* for Wałęsa during the ceremony both of which are available at www.nobelprize.org/nobel_prizes/peace/laureates/1983/ (accessed May 2016). My interpretation and conclusions are based on a close reading of the texts, their contextualization in contemporary human rights discourses, and an additional survey of French, US, British, and West German news coverage of the Prize and the ceremony. The latter allowed to identify which parts of the speeches both the laureate and the committee wanted to emphasize particularly and how they were received. For the justification given for the Prize at the times of its announcement and Polish reactions see "Walesa Gets Nobel Prize For Peace," *Washington Post*, Oct. 6, 1983; Eric Bourne, "Walesa's moderation mobilized Poland– and earned a peace prize," *Christian Science Monitor*, Oct. 7, 1983; "Walesa wins Nobel Prize, says it's for the people," *Atlanta Constitution*, Oct. 6, 1983; "Walesa Gets Nobel Peace Prize," *Times of India*, Oct. 6, 1983; "1983 Nobel Prize goes to Walesa," *Chicago Tribune*, Oct. 6, 1983; "Lech Walesa Wins Nobel Peace Prize," *Los Angeles Times*, Oct. 6, 1983; "Lech Walesa Wins Nobel Peace Prize for Union Effort," *New York Times*, Oct. 6, 1983; "Les embarras des autorités de Varsovie," *Le Monde*, Oct. 7, 1983; Jan Krauze, "M. Walesa, prix Nobel de la paix," *Le Monde*, Oct. 6, 1983. For news coverage of the

Wałęsa, the Symbolism of the Nobel Peace Prize 177

authorities might bar him from returning home, Wałęsa send his wife and oldest son Bohdan to Oslo to collect the award in his stead and read out his acceptance speech. He also asked Bohdan Cywiński, a Catholic intellectual centrally involved in the 1970s dialogue with the post-Marxists, to deliver his Nobel lecture on the day after the awards ceremony.

Drafting his two addresses, Wałęsa's speechwriters managed to turn his very absence in Oslo into an advantaeg, using it to underscore his authority to speak for the Polish working class. "You are aware of the reasons why I could not come to your capital," Danuta Wałęsa read her husband's message, "On that solemn day my place is among those with whom I have grown up and to whom I belong – the workers of Gdańsk."[13] Both speeches, moreover, underlined that Wałęsa did not regard the prize as being for himself but for Solidarity and even for the entire Polish nation, a point he had also emphasized strongly in his first responses to the prize in which he had pledged to donate the prize money to a foundation, overseen jointly by the Catholic Church and the Polish authorities, to help Polish agriculture.[14]

The addresses also underscored Solidarity's commitment to non-violence, insisting that peace and human rights were two sides of the same coin, and left no doubt who was to blame for the situation in Poland, even as they let "the veil of silence" fall over the events of martial law. They invoked the memory of those who had been killed "in the struggle for the workers' and civic rights in my country" and drew attention to political prisoners, those "who paid for the defense of 'Solidarity' with the loss of freedom, who were sentenced to prison terms or are awaiting trial."[15]

---

ceremony, see Peter Osnos, "Danuta Walesa Accepts Nobel for Solidarity Head," *Washington Post*, Dec. 11, 1983; "Ovation Is Huge as Wife Accepts Walesa's Nobel," *Los Angeles Times*, Dec. 11, 1983; Dan Fisher, "Walesa Calls His Nobel Award a Victory for Solidarity Ideals," *Los Angeles Times*, Dec. 11, 1983; "Award is Accepted by Danuta Walesa," *New York Times*, Dec. 11, 1983; "Walesa Appeals in Nobel Lecture For Polish Talks," *New York Times*, Dec. 12, 1983; Ray Moseley, "Walesa's Nobel raises Oslo cheer," *Chicago Tribune*, Dec. 11, 1983; "Einer der Sprecher der Welt für die Sehnsucht nach Freiheit," *Frankfurter Allgemeine Zeitung*, Dec. 12, 1983; "'Dialog und nicht Gewalt weist den Weg.' Walesas Hoffnung: Menschenrechte und die Nation," *Frankfurter Allgemeine Zeitung*, Dec. 12, 1983.

[13] Lech Wałęsa, Nobel Acceptance Speech, Dec. 10, 1983, delivered by Danuta Wałęsa, available from www.nobelprize.org/nobel_prizes/peace/laureates/1983/walesa-acceptance .html (accessed Apr. 2017).

[14] See any of the newspaper texts on Wałęsa's response referenced in footnote 12. See also "Unser Platz ist in den Betrieben," *Frankfurter Allgemeine Zeitung*, Dec. 7, 1983.

[15] Lech Wałęsa, Nobel Lecture, Dec. 11, 1983, delivered by Bohdan Cywiński, available from www.nobelprize.org/nobel_prizes/peace/laureates/1983/walesa-lecture.html (accessed April 2017). At the time, the speech was partly or in whole reprinted in Peter Osnos,

178 Poland's Solidarity Movement & the Politics of Rights

Both the members of the Nobel Committee and most Western media supported Wałęsa's account of Poland's social conflicts, painting him in their speeches as a man of moderation and compromise who suffered under Warsaw's unjust und unmerited repression.[16] More important than these comments on Poland's specific situation, however, was how the ceremony suffused Wałęsa with the moral authority of human rights culture. During the awards ceremony, the Chairman of the Norwegian Nobel Committee, Egil Aarvik, began his speech with a quote from the "sacred text" of human rights culture – the Universal Declaration of Human Rights (UDHR): "[R]ecognition of the inherent dignity and of the equal and inalienable rights of all members of the human family is the foundation of freedom, justice, and peace in the world," he said.[17] This understanding of peace, Aarvik went on, lay at the heart of the Committee's decision to honor Wałęsa, as it had in the case of previous laureates Albert Lutuli, Martin Luther King, Jr., Andrei Sakharov, or Adolfo Pérez Esquivel. "The Committee believes that this year's prize winner can justly take his place among this gathering of campaigners of human rights."[18]

Through the Nobel, Wałęsa was symbolically inducted into a pantheon of unassailable symbolic figures. Where Adam Michnik was an icon in the sense that he reflected the sanctity of human rights, Wałęsa became an iconic "archetype," an original representation of "sanctity." In Aarvik's speech, the fundament of this pantheon was human dignity and the accompanying sense of "humanity's oneness": "Every brother being in chains is my shame," Aarvik said. "Every longing for freedom which is suppressed, every human right which is violated is a personal defeat for me ..." This understanding of "human oneness" expressed the "deepest and most wide-ranging meaning" of "Solidarity," Aarvik

---

"Walesa Urges Dialogue," *Washington Post*, Dec. 12, 1983; "Excerpts From Lech Walesa's Nobel Speech," *New York Times*, Dec. 11, 1983; "Text of Walesa Lecture Read at Nobel Ceremony," *New York Times*, Dec. 12, 1983.

[16] "The Nobel Peace Prize 1983 - Press Release". *Nobelprize.org*. Nobel Media AB 2014. Web. May 9, 2016. www.nobelprize.org/nobel_prizes/peace/laureates/1983/press.html (accessed May 2016). Erik-Michael Bader, "Unruhe stiften als Friedensarbeit," *Frankfurter Allgemeine Zeitung*, Oct. 8, 1983; "Ein Streitwort," *Frankfurter Allgemeine Zeitung*, Oct. 6, 1983; "Une consecration pour les Polonais," *Le Monde*, Oct. 7, 1983; "Walesa: a fighter for peace," *Chicago Tribune*, Oct. 6, 1983; Flora Lewis, "Nobel panel made a wise choice in Walesa," *Atlanta Constitution*, Oct. 12, 1983.

[17] Egil Aarvik, Lech Walesa Award Ceremony Speech, Dec. 10, 1983, available from www .nobelprize.org/nobel_prizes/peace/laureates/1983/presentation-speech.html (accessed Apr. 2017). Excerpts of the speech were published, among others, in "Walesa Hailed as 'Victor in the Eyes of the Ordinary Worker,'" *Washington Post*, Dec. 11, 1983. The news coverage referenced in footnote 12 also quoted the speech.

[18] Aarvik, Award Ceremony.

Wałęsa, the Symbolism of the Nobel Peace Prize   179

went on, again charging the Polish movement with the energy of human rights culture.[19]

With Wałęsa's persona suffused with a universal, quasi-religious energy, the Polish regime's response to the prize – a complaint sent to the Norwegian government and the apparent threat that Wałęsa might not return home from the awards ceremony – made Warsaw look at best petty and at worst willfully opposing the progress of peace. "In the world we live in it is shockingly clear that détente and the peaceful resolution of conflicts is more necessary than ever before," Aarvik said, clearly implying that it was the Polish leadership which obstructed these efforts.[20]

The Polish regime's attempts to brand Wałęsa a "private citizen," on the other hand, made it look delusional when Danuta Wałęsa received standing ovations in Oslo, while Western news cameras filmed her husband in Gdańsk as he listened to a transmission of the Nobel ceremony on Radio Free Europe.[21] "Mindless bureaucrats desire that [Wałęsa] becomes a 'forgotten figure,' falsely believing that this would make everything easier," the vice president of the Nobel Committee said during a banquet in a toast to Wałęsa. "Fortunately, this desire is in vain. ... Let us raise our glasses to the most unforgettable of all forgotten men, to the most present of those who are absent tonight."[22]

At a time, in sum, when Wałęsa seemed to represent a noble, but lost cause – a "romantic memory" more than a "man of the future," as the *Christian Science Monitor* had put it – he was thrust back on the world stage and inducted into a pantheon of the "archetypes" of human rights culture. "... is Lech Wałęsa really silent today?" Aarvik asked at the end of his speech "... Has his cause suffered defeat?" No, the Norwegian replied with an overtly biblical reference. "Once again the stone rejected by the builder has become a cornerstone; this time a cornerstone in the building of freedom and democracy which humanity, with varying degrees of success, is attempting to raise in our world."[23] A year after

---

[19] Aarvik, Award Ceremony.

[20] "Poles protest Walesa prize," *Chicago Tribune*, Oct. 13, 1983. Soviet newspapers had been completely silent about the Prize, instead repeating the charges of financial fraud against Wałęsa. "Soviet, Silent on Prize, Again Assails Walesa," *New York Times*, Oct. 9, 1983.

[21] "Walesa Follows Wife's Speech By Radio in a Gdansk Church," *Washington Post*, Dec. 11, 1983; Jörg Bremer, "Wie Lech Walesa den Tag von Oslo begeht," *Frankfurter Allgemeine Zeitung*, Dec. 12, 1983; Hella Pick, "Champagne and tears as Walesa tunes in to Oslo," *Guardian*, Dec. 12, 1983.

[22] The toast was proposed by Gidske Anderson. The quotations are my translations from a German translation in "Friedensnobelpreis 1983/Prix Nobel de la paix 1983," ICFTU brochure obtained at the library of the Friedrich-Ebert-Foundation, call no. A98–03074, 23–24.

[23] Aarvik, Award Ceremony.

180   Poland's Solidarity Movement & the Politics of Rights

the Nobel ceremony, when a Politburo member came up with another elaborate plan to discredit Wałęsa, Rakowski told him to let it go already. Even writing that Wałęsa "had raped five girls on one evening" would not hurt his image, he said, but rather provide him additional publicity.[24]

III

As Polish activists struggled to keep their movement's cause on the international agenda, they could draw on the powerful resource of an international human rights culture. Condensing values such as innocence, conscience, or nonviolence into appealing symbols like the "prisoner of conscience," it allowed them to translate their cause into an authoritative language and to turn some of their most well-known members like Adam Michnik and Lech Wałęsa into icons – quasi-sacred images of this culture. Yet precisely the deliberately unpolitical thrust of human rights culture contradicts much of what we have learned about human rights in the previous chapters. For Polish dissidents, human rights were supposed to be the starting point of a political project – the transformation of a totalitarian society through social self-organization. These specific aspects, as well as Solidarity's character as a trade union, had won the Polish movement sympathizers in the West. The imagery of the prisoner of conscience or the symbolism of the Nobel ceremony, on the other hand, concealed these politics of human rights behind the veil of a universalizing, seemingly nonpolitical narrative. Turned into icons, the Polish activists were dissociated from the specific project they had associated with human rights.

Here we encounter another parallel between Byzantine icons and human rights culture. Imagined as copies of prototypical icons of Christ or the saints, icons are, Ansgar Paus explains, "revelations of transcendence, which alone is venerated and taken from the images." The artists may have some liberties in how they arrange the iconographic conventions and motives, but these artistic liberties are not meant to inspire admiration of the image itself, let alone the artists, but to lead the beholder to the transcendent reality of the sacred.[25] Human rights icons, I will argue, had a similar function. The value of the movements or persons who became such human rights icons did not lie in their individual story – their culture and personality, their social background and worldviews, not even the reasons for their suffering nor the goals they fought for; their value, instead, lay in how their story brought the

---

[24] Dudek, *rewolucja*, 60.   [25] Paus, "Nostalgia," 144.

Wałęsa, the Symbolism of the Nobel Peace Prize   181

international community into communion with the "transcendent reality" of human rights.

Paradoxically, this aspect was particularly prominent in how the Nobel ceremony underlined the authenticity of Wałęsa's message. The speeches in his honor repeatedly mentioned that he was an electrician of humble upbringing, thus underscoring that his "voice" – a word Aarvik used three times in relation Wałęsa – was the authentic voice of the downtrodden in Eastern Europe. The voice heard in Oslo, however, was obviously not Wałęsa's. Though having a radiating charisma and wit, at times even expressing streaks of rhetorical genius, Wałęsa's was a simple, almost anti-intellectual language in which he would frequently say things that contradicted one another. He also had no patience for intellectual questions, even if they came from the highest authority. When a priest gave Wałęsa a copy of *Laborem exercens*, John Paul II's 1981 encyclical on human work, he responded: "Why should I read this? I agree with everything the pope says!"[26] The sophisticated speeches Danuta Wałesa and Bohdan Cywiński gave were obviously not Wałesa's voice.[27] Underlining the Poles' simple upbringing and lack of education, therefore, did not serve to familiarize audiences with who he was, but to underscore a sophisticated message that was not his.

Turned into an icon Wałęsa was separated from his personality and his social background. Mark Bradley has noted how this aspect of human rights culture tended to drain "the structural forces and local particulars that gave rise to [rights] violations" from such iconic cases.[28] Characteristically, Aarvik avoided all but the most general references to the Polish government. Given the heroic image he painted of the Solidarity president, he might have left some of his listeners wondering who, precisely, Wałęsa was struggling against. But an equally important aspect of iconization was how it dissociated the venerated activist from their political aims and social visions.

This impartiality was the core of the "prisoners of conscience" who were supported not for their views, but for their suffering. Aarvik applied this value to Wałęsa and through him to Solidarity. "Solidarity" acquired its "deepest and most wide-ranging meaning ... precisely [in] the concept

---

[26] Skórzyński, *Zadra*, 105.

[27] The speech was most probably written by Geremek and Mazowiecki. Manuscript of Lech Wałęsa's Nobel peace prize reception speech with annotations by Geremek, not dated, AIPN, 0222/1443/CD/5, 75–85; cf. Józef Tischner, Adam Michnik, and Jacek Żakowski, *Między Panem a Plebanem* (Kraków: Znak, 1995), 448.

[28] Mark Philip Bradley, "Approaching the Universal Declaration of Human Rights," in Akira Iriye et al., eds., *The Human Rights Revolution: An International History* (Oxford, New York: Oxford University Press, 2012), 337.

182 Poland's Solidarity Movement & the Politics of Rights

of being at one with humanity." It was "more than the expression of the unity of a group campaigning for special interest." Wałęsa had not "raised a revolutionary banner," Aarvik said. Solidarity, instead, had become ever more "conscious of [its] standing for humanity and human rights." The actual goals of the striking Polish workers of the summer of 1980 – the self-management of factories, for instance – were thus dissolved into a universalizing narrative, and Wałęsa's struggle acquired a meaning which was not political, but spiritual, transcendent even: Having made "humanity bigger and more inviolable," Aarvik said, Wałęsa had "won a victory which is not of this world, our political world, ... [but] abides in one person's belief, in his vision and in his courage to follow his call."[29]

The point, of course, is that Solidarity *was* a movement that had evolved out of a special interest – the material interests of Polish workers – and in opposition to a specific political system – Soviet-style Communism. And in the context of the latter, the call for independent trade unions *was* a "revolutionary banner." Solidarity's contribution to the progress of humanity and human rights, then, overshadowed its original goal: improving the situation of the Polish workers.

To accentuate this aspect further, it is instructive to compare Aarvik's speech with Wałęsa's Nobel Lecture. Where Aarvik's talk began and ended with human rights, thus embedding Solidarity's struggle in his universalizing approach, Wałęsa's speech mentioned human rights only in support of Solidarity's central goal – its re-legalization. Where Aarvik characterized Solidarity's struggle only in abstract terms, granting Wałęsa a victory "not of this, our political, world," Wałęsa's lecture quoted John Paul II to invoke a very specific form of oppression. The workers in Poland, the pontiff had insisted during 1983 in Poland, had a right to a dialogue with the government "because the working man is not a mere tool of production, but he is the subject which throughout the process of production takes precedence over the capital."[30] The pope thus – and through him Wałęsa – saw Solidarity as engaged in a struggle with a quite specific form of oppression – the economic exploitation of workers, their subordination to the demands of capital in the process of production. Yet these aspects all but vanished from Aarvik's universalizing account.

There's another telling difference in how Aarvik and Wałęsa's advisors crafted their speeches. In Wałęsa's lecture, his Prize and life were firmly embedded into the history of Poland and the Solidarity movement. The Nobel Prize, Cywiński said in Wałęsa's stead, "has been granted to me as

---

[29] Aarvik, Award Ceremony.   [30] Wałęsa, Nobel Lecture.

to one of many."[31] Aarvik turned this order around. Rather than depicting Wałęsa as a representation of Solidarity, he subsumed the Polish movement under the symbolic figure of Wałęsa. In his speech, it was not Solidarity that had carried and uplifted Wałęsa, but Wałęsa who had "raised a burning torch, a shining name, the name of Solidarity."[32] The Polish movement – with its practical goals, but also its internal conflicts – was collapsed into the symbolic persona of Wałęsa, turning Solidarity's economic struggle into a spiritual, otherworldly one.

There was, then, a tension in Aarvik's account: insisting on the authenticity of Wałęsa's voice, the Norwegian dissolved Solidarity's practical goals into a universal narrative. This tension underlies the power of human rights culture as expressed in the Nobel ceremony. Wałęsa's simple upbringing cleared him of charges that he was some kind of ideologue, but it also underscored human rights' universality – they were not an elaborate ideology that had to be justified by philosophers but evolved "naturally" out of the struggle for freedom. Not only had Wałęsa not raised "a revolutionary banner," in Aarvik's account, he had not even sought "support from the declarations of human rights emanating from the United Nations and the Helsinki agreement."[33] All he had wanted was to negotiate with his employers. It had been by demanding something as obvious, natural even, as the right to negotiate, that Wałęsa's campaign became part of the universal struggle for human rights. By thus depoliticizing Wałęsa, human rights appeared not as a political program so much as the "natural" emanation of something as basic as the ability to negotiate with one's employer.

IV

Much like a Byzantine icon what mattered about human rights icons was not the individuality of a case of repression, but how this case brought people in contact with the "sacred core" of human rights culture. To quote Aarvik one final time: "Lech Walesa's contribution is more than a domestic Polish concern; the solidarity for which he is spokesman is an expression of precisely the concept of being at one with humanity; therefore he belongs to us all."[34] This statement, to be sure, was an endorsement of Wałęsa that came at a crucial time – Wałęsa's fate mattered to the world. But Aarvik appropriated the Polish electrician also for a discourse where Wałęsa's actual life became important

---

[31] Wałęsa, Nobel Lecture.   [32] Aarvik, Award Ceremony.   [33] Ibid.   [34] Ibid.

184   Poland's Solidarity Movement & the Politics of Rights

primarily to underscore the righteousness of human rights, not the actual goals Wałęsa struggled for.

Yet even as Solidarity was detached from the material struggles that had given rise to it and stylized according to the conventions of human rights culture, the international support campaign for Solidarity paradoxically did not become less political. To the contrary, the Polish movement became an empty canvass for other actors' political visions that had increasingly little to do with the movement's original goals. A brochure by the International Confederation of Free Trade Unions illustrated this nicely. On its cover was a drawn portrait of Wałęsa in which all features of his face – except for the characteristic mustache – were lacking and "Nobel Peace Prize" was written onto it.[35] Predictably, Solidarity's supporters from international labor organizations were quick to claim the Noble Prize as an affirmation of the struggle for freedom of association.[36] Yet trade unionism was far from the only cause Solidarity could now be associated with.

In October 1983, shortly after Wałesa had been announced as the Nobel Prize winner, the Ethics and Public Policy Center – a think tank led by Ernest Lefever, Reagan's failed candidate for the State Department's human rights bureau (see Chapter 3) – had bestowed its annual award for integrity and courage upon Wałęsa.[37] Reagan sent a videotaped message in which he called Wałęsa "a freedom fighter," a term associated with the White House's aggressive Cold War policies, who "insists that the blessings of liberty belong not just to his fellow Poles, but to people everywhere." Reagan also strongly accentuated Wałęsa's faith. Primarily, however, he integrated the Polish worker into his imagery of the Cold War as a struggle with the power of the state. According to Reagan, the Polish labor leader "symbolizes ... the victory of personal ideals over collective tyranny," he was "*everyman* [emphasis in original] – everyman at his best."[38] While Wałęsa himself contributed

---

[35] "Friedensnobelpreis 1983/Prix Nobel de la paix 1983."

[36] For responses by the ICFTU, AFL-CIO, and CFDT see ibid., 6; "From Lech Walesa," *Free Trade Union News* 38 (Oct.–Dec. 1983), 10–12; "Edmond Maire: 'un titre qui nous honore tous,'" *Syndicalisme Hebdo*, Oct. 13, 1983.

[37] "Lech Walesa to be Honored," undated press release by the Ethics and Public Policy Center, CSS records, box "CSS 1 (Records of Activities 1981-1985)," folder "CSS: Fundraising/grants, Institute for Educational Affairs." The Polish Ministry of the Interior also took note of the event, mentioning in its daily digest of important information for Poland's political leaders. Załącznik do informacji dziennej z dnia 14.10.1983 r., "Informacja dot. reperkusji przyznania Nagrody Pokojowej Nobla L. Wałęsie," AIPN, BU 1585/4822, fol. 83–85.

[38] Speech script "Salute to Lech Walesa," Oct. 17, 1983, RRPL, Office of Speechwriting: Speech Drafts, box 115, folder "Taping Salute to Lech Walesa, Oct. 17, 1983."

only a brief message of gratitude to the evening, the keynote address was given by Jeane Kirkpatrick, leading Jacksonite intellectual and US ambassador at the UN. In a talk titled "We and They," she only touched upon Poland and Solidarity arguing instead that the West needed to overcome its self-doubts and demoralization to confront what she saw as a "discouragingly familiar" pattern of Soviet expansionism.[39]

Several hours after Kirkpatrick gave her speech, some 6,000 km east of New York, another woman spoke to a major political gathering on a foreign policy question and, again, Poland's Solidarity was a point of reference. In Bonn, Petra Kelly, the figurehead of the West German peace movement, addressed several hundred thousand people who were demonstrating against the imminent deployment of medium-range nuclear missiles. The demonstrations in Bonn and elsewhere, Kelly said, were part of an international movement that transcended the competing political systems of the Cold War. "We now have the opportunity to live the beginnings of a society without violence," she concluded. "... a Solidarność for peace, not only in Poland."[40]

★★★

The anti-political language of the Nobel ceremony and the symbolic figure of the prisoner of conscience concealed what I called above, using a Bourdieuan metaphor coined by David Swartz, a "political economy of symbolic power."[41] Detached from its original goals and suffused with the most sacred values of the international community, Solidarity became a vessel for the ideas of actors struggling for the symbolic power to transform or preserve international society by transforming or preserving the collective interpretations and meanings sustaining it. Wałęsa and Solidarity became *contested icons*, powerful symbols their sympathizers sought to claim for their own reading of human rights.

---

[39] "Center Honors Lech Walesa," *Ethics and Public Policy Center Newsletter* 6 (Dec. 1983), 35–41; Jeane J. Kirkpatrick, "We and They," in her, *Legitimacy and Force: Political and Moral Dimensions*, vol. I (New Brunswick, NJ: Transaction, 1988). See also "Lech Walesa and Peace," *Wall Street Journal*, Oct. 7, 1983.

[40] Petra Kelly, "Für eine Solidarność des Friedens," in Marie-Luise Recker, ed., *Politische Reden* (Frankfurt am Main: Deutscher Klassiker Verlag, 1990).

[41] Swartz, "Study."

9   General Pinochecki
Poland, Chile, and the Global Politics
of Human Rights Culture

After 1981, the situation in Poland reached one of the central human rights institutions of the time, the UN Commission on Human Rights (UNCHR) in Geneva. If there was one institution in 1980s world politics which showed that human rights culture concealed rather than abolished its politics, it was the UNCHR. Until the 1970s, it had been what three authors described as "one of the most complicated trash baskets ever devised."[1] Yet as newly independent countries joined the UN as a result of de-colonization, the UNCHR was transformed into an institution actually monitoring human rights compliance. But because membership did not require adherence to human rights standards, the monitoring was done by notoriously repressive countries like Latin American military regimes, the Soviet bloc states, and African dictatorships like Uganda. By the early 1980s, the Commission's proceedings had started to resemble what one former delegate described as "political warfare" – the rhetorical waging of bilateral conflicts and Cold War battles.[2] After the imposition of martial law, the situation in Poland became the subject of such a battle.

At stake in this conflict was the status of one of the most powerful human rights icons of the time – Chile. During the 1970s, no other issue had come to embody – incarnate – what human rights meant to people in the West than resistance to the military dictatorship of Augusto Pinochet. Chile had become an iconic archetype – an authentic depiction of human rights' sacred core. Around it, a coalition emerged whose membership cut across the frontlines of the Cold War when both Warsaw Pact states and West European members of NATO attacked Chilean repression at the UNCHR and elsewhere.

---

[1] Thomas G. Weiss, David P. Forsythe, and Roger A. Coate, *The United Nations and Changing World Politics*, 3rd ed. (Boulder, CO: Westview Press, 2001), 180.

[2] Patrick James Flood, *The Effectivenes of UN Human Rights Institutions* (Westport, CT: Praeger, 1998), 39–42.

General Pinochecki 187

For American conservatives, however, Chile symbolized the very errors of the Left's "humanitarian" understanding of human rights – the illusion of a vantage point beyond the struggle between liberty and Communist tyranny. For them, human rights did not point beyond the Cold War, they encapsulated what was at stake in it. Publicly shaming an anti-Communist strongman like Pinochet, many of them believed, would only encourage "Soviet expansionism." For them, therefore, the Polish crisis presented an opportunity. Turning Solidarity into an anti-Communist icon of human rights, they hoped, would provide a symbolic counterweight to Chile's central position. Repression in Poland allowed American conservatives to challenge Chile's position within the symbolic hierarchy of human rights. The meaning of events in Poland and Chile became the stakes in a political struggle to claim the authority and symbolic capital associated with human rights.

The discussions in Geneva thus demonstrate how human rights culture, by depoliticizing its iconic cases, opened them to a re-politicization for the purposes of powerful actors in the international system. Yet they also showed something else – the representatives of these iconic cases were not necessarily just the passive objects of other people's political struggles. For, as this chapter shall show, Polish and Chilean activists proved savvy "entrepreneurs" in the global economy of symbolic power. Striking a symbolic alliance – establishing a "joint venture" of symbolic capital – they undercut attempts to exploit their cause.

I

Poland had the questionable honor of being the first Communist country whose human rights record became the subject of the UNCHR's deliberations. In March 1982, following a massive US lobbying effort, five West European NATO states tabled a successful resolution which condemned the imposition of martial law and called upon the UN General Secretary to investigate the situation. In December, a commission was appointed to travel to Poland, much to Washington's delight and Warsaw's outrage.[3]

The adoption of the resolution showed just how politicized the work of the Commission was. At the time, human rights violations in Uruguay

---

[3] Cable from SecState to USMission Geneva, "U.S. Seeks to Have U.N. Rights Unit Discuss Poland," Feb. 2, 1982, NSA, Soviet Flashpoints (Originals) – Poland 1981–1982, Box 4; Cable from SecState to Amembassies Bonn, et al., "38th U.N. Human Rights Commission: Resolution on Poland," dated Feb. 27, 1982, NSA, Soviet Flashpoints: Poland 1980–1982, box 1.

188   Poland's Solidarity Movement & the Politics of Rights

had been subject of the Commission's discussions. Montevideo thus wanted to have its human rights record removed from the UNCHR's agenda. Moscow had promised the Uruguayans that they would support them on this if Montevideo promised to abstain in the vote on Poland. In response, Washington managed to secure Uruguayan support for the vote on Poland by supporting its initiative to be removed from the agenda, even though the Uruguayan government had shut down an opposition newspaper the day before the relevant vote.[4]

The American initiative at the UNCHR was an obvious attempt to subject Communist human rights violations to UN scrutiny. Unsurprisingly, the US envoy in Geneva was another Jackson Democrat – the Catholic theologian Michael Novak whom Kirkpatrick had asked "to go put forth our theory of human rights and democracy" in Geneva.[5] Primarily, this involved attacking the standards under which human rights cases were being brought before the UNCHR. The commission handled its cases either under a confidential procedure or under a general agenda item. There were only three countries whose human rights abuses were considered so severe that they merited an individual point on the Commission's agenda – South Africa, Israel, and Chile. While South Africa and Israel had been almost ritualistically condemned since the late 1960s, the addition of Chile marked an important development in international human rights procedures and activism for this was the first time a commission was appointed in a context unrelated to anti-colonialism or racism.[6] In fact, no instance of political repression, including the struggle with Apartheid, has done more to shape human rights policies and activism than the opposition to the Chilean military dictatorship.[7]

---

[4] Cable from Amembassy Montevideo to Secstate, "Uruguay Issue in UNHRC," dated Jan. 28, 1982, Cable from Amembassy Montevideo to Secstate, "GOU Shuts Down Leading Oppositionist Weekly," dated Mar. 5, 1982; Cable from Secstate to Amembassy Montevideo, "38th Human Rights Commission: Uruguay Situation under 1503 Procedures," both at State Dep., Virtual Reading Room.

[5] Novak, *Writing from Left to Right*, 213.

[6] Mark Ensalaco, *Chile under Pinochet: Recovering the Truth* (Philadelphia, PA: University of Pennsylvania Press, 2000), 164–168; Philip Alston, "The Commission on Human Rights," in Philip Alston, ed., *The United Nations and Human Rights: A Critical Appraisal* (Oxford: Clarendon Press, 1992), 129–131, 139–141, 142–144, 158–160; Flood, *Effectiveness*, 87–93; Mel James, "The Country Mechanisms of the United Nations Commission on Human Rights," in Yael Danieli et al., eds., *The Universal Declaration of Human Rights: Fifty Years and Beyond* (Amityville, NY: Baywood, 1999), 75–77; Weiss, Forsythe, and Coate, *United Nations*, 180–181.

[7] For two extensive discussions both of the situation in Chile and its international significance for human rights, see Kelly, "Sovereignty"; Eckel, *Ambivalenz*, 583–710; the international aspect of Chile is also discussed in Jan Eckel, "'Under the Magnifying Glass': The International Human Rights Campaign Against Chile in the Seventies," in

To a large extent, the international attention paid to repression in Chile was due not only to Augusto Pinochet's horrific policies and the tenacity and ingenuity of the Chilean resistance movement but also to a favorable international situation. Since the Nixon administration supported Pinochet, the Soviet bloc orchestrated a campaign against Pinochet that included international congresses and even symbolic trials. But the Chilean human rights struggle also appealed to the non-Communist Western Left, given Allende's views and the prominence of left-wing groups in the resistance. The same is true for US liberals in search for redemption for the nightmare of Vietnam. The forms of repression in Chile – political incarceration, torture, the "disappearing" of opposition activists – moreover, resonated with the anti-political imagery of human rights NGOs, Amnesty International chief among them. With many West European states condemning the coup of 1973, the UN witnessed of a broad international coalition against Pinochet cutting across the front lines of the Cold War.[8]

For US Republicans, neoconservatives, and Jackson Democrats, meanwhile, the Chile campaign represented everything that was wrong with human rights policies. Reagan reportedly admired Pinochet as an upright anti-Communist, and he pledged to improve relations with the South American country. In the summer of 1981, Jeane Kirkpatrick traveled to Santiago de Chile as Reagan's emissary, refusing to meet with human rights activists while announcing publicly that the two countries would pursue a normalization of their relations "in a pleasant way."[9]

This friendly approach to Chile changed somewhat with Elliot Abrams's appointment as head of the State Department's Human Rights Bureau and his pledge "to speak honestly about our friends' human rights violations ..."[10] Discovering the UNCHR as a forum to publicize the US commitment to human rights, American representatives did not deny Chilean human rights violations, even if they insisted that the situation had improved, but argued that singling out Santiago, while passing over Communist repression in silence, amounted to a "double standard."[11]

Stefan-Ludwig Hoffmann, ed., *Human Rights in the Twentieth Century* (Cambridge: Cambridge University Press, 2011); for an earlier, still useful account of events in Chile, see Ensalaco, *Chile*, 98–155, 164–168.

[8] On the American response, see Eckel, "'Glass'"; Keys, *Virtue*, 148–151, 168–172.

[9] Quoted in Morris Morley and Chris McGillion, "Soldiering on: The Reagan Administration and Redemocratisation in Chile, 1983–1986," *Bulletin of Latin American Research* 25 (2006), 1, 3; Ensalaco, *Chile*, 162–163.

[10] "Excerpts from State Department Memo on Human Rights."

[11] Kirkpatrick, "Human Rights," 196, 198–200.

190   Poland's Solidarity Movement & the Politics of Rights

Discussions on the situation in Poland and Chile thus became entangled in wider debates on the hierarchy of values at the UNCHR. For Washington's critics, "Chile" became a stand-in for what they saw as the "hypocrisy" of the American focus on "Poland." Receiving a delegation of US congressmen in March 1983, General Jaruzelski lambasted a US policy that punished Poland for its "so-called human rights violations," while remaining silent over bloodshed in Chile and elsewhere in Latin America.[12] Chile had also featured prominently in the West German peace movement's criticism of Reagan and the refusal of many activists to speak out for human rights in Eastern Europe.[13]

For Washington, on the other hand, the stance of other governments on "Poland" became a yardstick for their willingness to abandon human rights "double standards." That was why the US delegation at UNCHR attached such great importance to have the Commission pass a resolution condemning Warsaw and appointing a commission to investigate the country.[14] After the commission had been appointed, a US representative at the UN expressed his satisfaction to his Chilean colleague that "the argument concerning double-standards on UN human rights discussions seems to have taken root."[15]

II

"Chile" and "Poland," then, became the stakes in struggles of powerful actors at the UN and elsewhere. However, Polish and Chilean activists proved to be inventive actors in the "political economy of symbolic power" themselves. Ahead of the Nobel ceremony, Wałęsa had been asked to provide a list of the people he wanted to attend the ceremony. One of them was Rodolfo Seguel, a Chilean trade unionist. Wałęsa's inviting Seguel, which had happened upon the suggestion by Western trade unionists, certainly was an expression of solidarity and sympathy. But the Chilean's presence also helps further understand the politics of

[12] Zapis z rozmowy Towarzysza Premiera Ge. W. Jaruzelskiego z grupą kongresmanów amerykańskich w dn. 17. VIII. 1983 r., dated Aug. 20, 1983, KC PZPR, XIA 1403, fol. 29–57.
[13] Lukas Beckmann, "Amerikanische Polen-Show eine zum Himmel schreiende Heuchelei," press release, dated Jan. 29, 1982, AGG, PKA, 3480.
[14] Cable, Secstate to USMission USNATO, Jan. 23, 1982, State Dep., Virtual Reading Room. On the US position on Chile see Gershman, "Human Rights in Chile."
[15] Cable from the USMission UN New York to SecState, "37th UNGA: Chilean Human Rights Resolution," dated Dec. 23, 1982, State Dep., Virtual Reading Room; Cable from Amembassy Bonn to Secstate, "38th U.N. Human Rights Commission: Resolution on Poland (item 12)," dated Feb. 27, 1982, NSA, Soviet Flashpoints: Poland, 1980–1982, Box 1.

General Pinochecki 191

interpreting and claiming human rights icons and the way victims of human rights abuses were actively involved in these struggles.

Wałęsa's gesture toward Seguel had had a precedent. In August 1981, Wałęsa had issued a statement in support of four deported Chilean activists.[16] In November 1982, after the Polish authorities had outlawed Solidarity, Chile's leading independent trade unionist Manuel Bustos had attempted to hold a day of solidarity with the oppressed Polish workers that was broken up by the police.[17] Similar actions were undertaken by Polish and Chilean exile groups. After the imposition of martial law, the Chilean Committee to Defend Human and Trade Union Rights in West Germany issued a statement calling Polish Solidarity a "challenge to all those governments in the world that are based on repression and violence." Opposition to the Chilean dictatorship and support for Solidarity were part of the same effort – "the cause of the Polish people is ours as well."[18] In autumn 1982, Jerzy Milewski, the head of Solidarity's office in Brussels, and Bustos, who had just been expelled from Chile,[19] signed a joint statement in which they pledged to "maintain close links and cooperation." Solidarity, the statement went on, "must always be shown wherever human and trade union rights are violated by dictatorship and totalitarian regimes."[20] Statements of support with the Chilean cause were also issued by Solidarity's underground leadership,[21] while Adam Michnik sent a message from his prison cell to *Le Monde* adding his "voice to the friends of liberty in Chile" and expressing his "admiration and solidarity with the political prisoners of that country."[22]

Neither the Chilean nor Polish activists had the resources to actually cooperate in any meaningful way. The value of their cooperation, rather, evolved out of the needs of the "political economy of symbolic power."

---

[16] Cable from Amembassy Santiago to Secstate, "Reactions to Expulsions of Head of Human Rights Commission and 3 Others," Aug. 29, 1981, State Dep., Virtual Reading Room.

[17] Cable from Amembassy Santiago to Secstate, "Annual Labor Report – Chile 1982," Apr. 7, 1983, State Dep., Virtual Reading Room.

[18] Hugo Sanchez, "Solidarität," *Polen: "Euch den Winter, uns den Frühling,"* 126–127, brochure of *die tageszeitung*, AGG, PKA, 3480.

[19] Cable from Amembassy Santiago to SecState, "Coordinadora President Manuel Bustos Expelled from Chile," date Dec. 3, 1982, State Dep., Virtual Reading Room.

[20] Manuel Bustos, Jerzy Milewski, Joint Statement, December 1982, computer print-out, AIPN, BU 514/21, t. 38, fol. 24; see also Radio Free Europe transcript, "Związki zawodowe twarzą w twarz z generałami – dwugłos działaczy związkowych z Polski i Chile," dated Mar. 26, 1983, AIPN, BU 514/21/CD, t. 11, fol. 87–90; Jerzy Milewski, "Address to the XIII World Congress of the ICFTU delivered by Jerzy Milewski, director of the Coordinating Office Abroad of NSZZ 'Solidarność' – Oslo, June 27, 1983," BU 0222/1569, AIPN.

[21] "Solidarność z Chile," *KOS*, Nov. 6, 1983.

[22] "Adam Michnik et le Chili," *Le Monde*, July 29, 1983.

In fact, the only political resources of Polish and Chilean human rights activists were symbolic – all they could do was to draw on their status as international icons in order to compel other state and non-state actors to act on their behalf. Yet at least the Polish activists had experienced that their iconic status was nothing they could take for granted. They thus had to carefully consider where to "invest" their symbolic capital in order to sustain and increase it. The way Polish activists drew on the imagery of the "prisoner of conscience" can be seen as a very successful such investment, because it made Solidarity's cause appealing to a wide audience. To use such economic metaphors does not mean that the Polish prisoners were cynics who jumped upon an international human rights bandwagon. Rather, it is a way of saying that in the figure of the "prisoner of conscience" they encountered a set of ideas which allowed them both to give meaning to the harsh experience of incarceration and to make the point that this experience was a concern for the international community.

In considering where else to invest their symbolic capital, the émigrés had to think about possible "trade-offs" – investments in one issue or alliance could disqualify the émigrés from investing in another. Among Italian trade unionists, for instance, Solidarity had lost some support because Polish exiles there had refused to join a demonstration against Reagan. Moreover, the Poles also had to consider that they were competing with other movements over "shares" of a "market" of international attention.[23] The solidarity committees of Italian trade unions, for instance, featured not only exiles from Poland but from Chile or El Salvador as well, countries that would often receive more interest and sympathy than the East Europeans and crowd out the struggle for human rights in the Soviet bloc.[24]

At least some Polish activists seem to have been keenly aware of these trade-offs and the competition for international attention. In a series of messages, the head of Solidarity's office in Brussels, Jerzy Milewski, tried to impress upon the union's leadership the necessity to address related issues. Human rights violations in Poland, he wrote in May 1983, were not the only problem in the world and he hinted at competition between Solidarity and Chilean trade unionists. In order to win support at the ICFTU and UN, Solidarity should try to strike alliances with labor and human rights activists in other parts of the world, especially in South

---

[23] Krzysztof Pomian, "Referat Krzysztofa Pomiana rozszerzonego spotkania Biura Koordynacyjnego NSZZ 'Solidarność' Za Granicą w dniach 29–30 stycznia 1983 r. w Brukseli," not dated, KARTA, AO III/218.

[24] Danuta Nowakowsa, "Protokół ze spotkania przedstawicieli komitetów 'Solidarności' oraz grupy delegatów I KśZ.D. za granicą w Oslo w dniach 17–19 lipca 1982 roku," KARTA, AO III/218, File "Solidarność Z. do końca 1985."

Africa and Chile. To be sure, Milewski argued at length why opposing Apartheid was morally the right thing to do. Undeniably, however, there was also a strategic background to his message.[25]

Staying within an economic metaphor, the Polish–Chilean cooperation could be seen as a symbolic "joint venture," a throwing together of symbolic capital in order to avoid competition and create synergy effects. What "returns" could Solidarity have hoped to receive from "investing" its symbolic capital into supporting the Chileans? In an open letter published in November 1983, Solidarity sent "the fraternal Chilean nation" expressions of its "respect and solidarity for your struggle for fundamental human and civil rights." "We know well what it looks like when demonstrations are broken up and defenseless people are shot at. We know what overcrowded prisons mean and the kind of courage it takes to voice your democratic beliefs in such a situation."[26] This comparison expressed not only a – most likely – heartfelt belief, but also turned an often drawn comparison between Poland and Chile against its authors. By Latin American standards, Polish Communist leaders would often tell their Western interlocutors, repression in Poland was mild. Solidarity's statement turned this argument around. We know what you are going through, they told the Chileans, that is, our situation is like yours. Tellingly, Polish oppositionists and their international supporters often referred to the Polish military government as a "junta" and Adam Michnik called Jaruzelski in *Le Matin* a "red Pinochet."[27]

Characteristically, the statement of Solidarity's underground leadership ended with the same central idea of human rights culture that Aarvik would use a month later at the Nobel ceremony – the unity of humanity. "Your success," the Poles told the Chileans, "limits the amount of evil in the world and will, therefore, be the success of all people working for human rights." From this, the Poles derived a belief in Solidarity's own eventual success: "We share with you," they told the Chileans, "our faith and hope for a better tomorrow."[28] Again, then, the statement claimed for Solidarity the "sacred values" that "Chile" embodied as a human rights icon.

For Chileans, the value of the alliance with the Poles seems to have had to do with events in Chile in 1983. Despite its iconic international

---

[25] Letter from Jurek [Jerzy Milewski] to Adam [Bogdan Lis], dated Oct. 30, 1983 and letter from Jerzy Milewski to the TKK, dated May 7, 1983 and July 15, 1983, AIPN, BU 514/21, t. 19, fol. 169–192, relevant passages on fol. 172, 178–180, 183, 184–186.
[26] "Solidarność z Chile," *KOS*, Nov. 6, 1983.   [27] "Adam Michnik et le Chili."
[28] "Solidarność z Chile."

194   Poland's Solidarity Movement & the Politics of Rights

role, Chile had not witnessed a broad social resistance movement comparable to Solidarity. This seemed to change in the summer of 1983 when Chile was hit by a wave of social protest.[29] Trade unions were the driving force of these protests and Rodolfo Seguel, president of the Copper Workers' Union, emerged as their leader.[30] For international observers, the similarities between Poland and Chile were too obvious and tempting not to mention them – a general opposed by a young, energetic labor leader, a social movement driven by trade union protests and supported by the Catholic hierarchy. A Chilean Cardinal even pitched this idea of the basic similarities between Poland and Chile to the pope, trying to get him to speak out more forcefully against repression in Chile. Even appearances seemed similar: Seguel sported a mustache not unlike Wałęsa's, and Pinochet, like Jaruzelski, appeared in uniform and wearing sunglasses. For many Western journalists, Rodolfo Seguel was the "Lech Wałęsa of Chile."[31]

III

But the Chilean–Polish alliance was not only useful for activists from these two countries but for their Western trade union supporters as well. This was particularly true for the AFL-CIO and its attempt to turn freedom of association into a campaign underscoring its anti-Communist credentials while simultaneously confronting the Reagan administration's neoliberalism.

When it comes to the AFL-CIO's anti-Communism, it has to be noted that relations between independent Chilean trade unions and the largest American labor federations had been strained since the late 1970s, given the AFL-CIO's then-president George Meany's dogmatic Cold

---

[29] Ensalaco, *Chile*, 135–139.
[30] See Cables from Amembassy Santiago to Secstate, "Copperworkers Leader Seguel held for Trail on Slander Charges," dated Sep. 16, 1983, "Cooperworkers Leader Seguel to be Released from Jail," dated Sep. 20, 1983, "Court Rules Against Cooperworkers Leader Seguel," Mar. 15, 1984, "Fired Copperworkers Enter Third Week of Hunger Strike," dated May 22, 1984, "Hunger Strikers End Strike and Accept Codelco Offer," May 25, 1984, "Chronology of political liberalization," undated, all in State Dep., Virtual Reading Room.
[31] John Dinges, "In Chile, A New Course–With a New Lech Walesa," *Los Angeles Times*, Jun. 16, 1983; "Chilean Copper Miners Call Strike," *Atlanta Constitution*, June 16, 1983; "Miners Defy Chile Regime," *Chicago Tribune* (June 16, 1983); Jackson Diehl, "Protests Seen Revitalizing Opposition Forces in Chile," *Washington Post*, July 14, 1983. On attempts to convince the pope, see Cable from Amembassy Rome to Secstate, "Report of the Meeting with Ambassador Riesle, Chilean Ambassador to the Holy See," dated Dec. 5, 1984, State Dep., Virtual Reading Room.

Warriordom and support for US policies in Latin America.[32] Though no less an anti-Communist than Meany, his successor Lane Kirkland was very critical of the Chilean dictatorship and invited the ICFTU to hold a Chilean human rights conference at the AFL-CIO headquarters in Washington, DC. Though Kirkland's invitation was a significant step for the AFL-CIO toward a more balanced approach to human and trade union rights, it also had, as the State Department noted, a "hidden agenda": He wanted to make sure that the ICFTU did not support Communist groups in the Chilean labor movement.[33] In 1981, Chilean Communists – a comparatively influential group in the resistance against Pinochet – had refused to condemn the imposition of martial law in Poland to avoid angering their supporters from the Soviet bloc. By insisting during a trip to Chile that the AFL-CIO would only support those trade unions that supported Solidarity in Poland, Kirkland made it unmistakably clear that US trade union support was to be had only without Communist participation.[34]

In what ways did the Polish–Chilean connection relate to the AFL-CIO's struggle with Reagan's neoliberal policies? As Chile was engulfed in social protest, a State Department memo for Lawrence Eagleburger outlined US objectives in the region as, among others, "to encourage Chile's peaceful evolution toward stable democracy, with increased respect for individual and political rights" and to "help obviate a Poland-like intensification of repression." But the memo also evidenced the double-edgedness of human rights arguments, noting how Pinochet's "authoritarian practices and unpopularity with labor and political activists in the United States make closer ties politically costly in terms of the credibility of US objectives in Central America, Poland and

---

[32] Manuel Barrera and J. Samuel Valenzuela, "The Development of Labor Movement Opposition to the Military Regime," in Manuel Barrera and J. Samuel Valenzuela, eds., *Military Rule in Chile: Dictatorship and Oppositions* (Baltimore, MD: Johns Hopkins University Press, 1986), 251–253.

[33] Cable from Secstate to Amembassy Santiago, "Washington Conference on Labor Repression in Chile," Mar. 19, 1983, State Dep., Virtual Reading Room.

[34] Airgram from Amembassy Santiago to Secstate, "Annual Labor Report for Chile – 1983," dated Apr. 26, 1984, State Dep., Virtual Reading Room; on the Chilean Communists' response to martial law see J. Samuel Valenzuela and Arturo Valenzuela, "Party Oppositions under the Authoritarian Regime: ," in J. Samuel Valenzuela and Arturo Valenzuela, eds., *Military Rule in Chile: Dictatorship and Oppositions* (Baltimore, MD: Johns Hopkins University Press, 1986), 211–212; on the Chilean Communist party and its exile leadership in Moscow, see Ingrid Wehr, *Zwischen Pinochet und Perestroika: Die chilenischen Kommunisten und Sozialisten 1973-1994* (Freiburg i. Br.: Arnold-Bergstraesser-Inst., 1996), 32–35, 86–89, 105–133; Carmelo Furci, "The Chilean Communist Party (PCCh) and Its Third Underground Period, 1973–1980," *Bulletin of Latin American Research* 2 (1982), 1.

196   Poland's Solidarity Movement & the Politics of Rights

elsewhere."[35] This point appeared even clearer in a second memo on Chile, written over a year later. Neither Pinochet nor the Chilean opposition guaranteed to serve US interests, the text said.

While a civilian regime will better serve intangible [U.S.] interests in democracy and human rights, Pinochet has served tangible interests in the UN, OAS, on Israel, Puerto Rico, Grenada, etc. At the same time, we have lost considerable intangible international interests by being seen to carry Pinochet and by dissimilar responses to similar situations in Poland and Nicaragua.[36]

Interestingly, in describing US stakes in Chile, the first memo mentioned not only "specific economic and security interests," but also the country's "considerable symbolic significance" because of is "overthrow of a Marxist regime and *adoption of a model free market economic system.*"[37] This "model free market economic system" was what set the country apart from previous military dictatorships. For two contemporaneous political scientists, the "extreme neoliberal ideology of the Chilean regime" was "its most prominent feature." More "than simply an attempt to dress up deep-seated anti-Communism," they argued, the regime's "neoliberalism or ultraliberalism ... was an elaborate 'system of thought' with specific intellectual exponents."[38]

Chile's role as the spearhead of neoliberal economic policies seems to have been a reason why the AFL-CIO changed its position on Latin America. During the aforementioned conference on Chile in Washington, DC, Kirkland called the fight of the Chileans "a struggle in which all of us have a vital stake ... a struggle for basic trade union rights against those who contend that those rights must be subordinated in the interest of ideological crusades, or theories of economic organization, or special historical circumstances, or in the name of social tranquility." He went on to compare Chile and South Africa – two countries where anti-Communism was the rationale to suppress trade unions – to Poland. "How ironic that communism and anti-communism both seem to require the repression of workers and their freely chosen institutions." Yet in all these struggles more than trade union rights were at stake, Kirkland went on. Describing "freedom of association" as essential to the defense of all other human rights, he zeroed in on neoliberalism. Chile,

---

[35] Memorandum from Langhore A. Motley for Ambassador Eagleburger, "Political Turmoil in Chile: Possible Scenarios and US Options," dated Jul. 28, 1983, on 2–3, State Dep., Virtual Reading Room.

[36] Memorandum, "Chile: Political Overview," dated Nov. 23, 1984, on 2, State Dep., Virtual Reading Room.

[37] Motley, "Political Turmoil," 3, my emphasis; Memo, "Political Overview," 2.

[38] Valenzuela and Valenzuela, "Party Oppositions," 5–6.

General Pinochecki 197

he said, had become "a laboratory test of the Chicago School of Dismal Economics" with every idea "advocated by the Friedmanites of this world" applied to it; the result, he concluded, was "total economic disaster."[39]

IV

As Polish and Chilean activists aligned their causes, both Washington and Warsaw had to accept that battling "double standards" could cut both ways; much as Poland was turned into an East European Chile, Chile was now seen as a Latin American Poland. For his part, Jaruzelski had to learn that the comparisons with Chile did not put Poland into a more favorable light; they turned him into a Polish Pinochet. In December 1985, he managed to arrange a meeting with President Mitterrand in the Élysée Palace. Sparking public outrage, Jaruzelski had to enter the palace through a back door. Some 1,000 protestors demonstrating in front of the Polish embassy all wore dark sunglasses, as did the anchor of a prominent midday news program. A pair of sunglasses was also sent to the French president. "They might come in handy," the protestors joked, "when you receive Mr. Pinochet." When Jaruzelski wanted to rent a boat for a trip on the Seine, the owner of the company refused, saying in a public statement that "The boats which had the honor of inviting Lech Wałęsa, when he held a press conference on them during his visit to Paris [in 1981], strongly refuse to put themselves at the service of General Pinochecki."[40]

US officials, on the other hand, would be confronted in both confidential talks and in public debate with references to "Poland" as an argument for the United States to show consistency and pressure Chile – or other dictators allied with the United States – for its human rights record. When three US senators traveled to Chile in January 1982, human rights activist Maximo Pacheco expressed his hope to them "that the Senators would help strengthen human rights in Chile as in other countries, such as Poland or Cuba, where those rights were denied."[41] In his regular

[39] "Remarks of AFL-CIO President Lane Kirkland to International Trade Union Conference on Chile, March 14, 1983, AFL-CIO Building, Washington, D.C.," on 1 and "Transcript of AFL-CIO President Lane Kirkland's News Conference at the International Free Trade Union Conference on Human & Trade Union Rights in Chile on Tuesday, March 15, 1983 in Washington, D.C.," on 5, both in GMMA, RG20–003, Series 2, File 50.4.

[40] Konstanty Gebert, *Magia słów: Polityka francuska wobec Polski po 13 grudnia 1981 r.* (London: Aneks, 1991), 64.

[41] Cable from Amembassy Santiago to Secstate, "Visit to Santiago by Codel Baker," dated Jan. 12, 1982, State Dep., Virtual Reading Room.

column for the *New York Times*, "Abroad at Home," the famous liberal commentator Anthony Lewis quoted Michnik's statement in support of Chilean activists to criticize how the "US position on human rights has been damaged by the Reagan administration's habit of winking at brutalities committed by right-wing regimes" in Latin America. " ... how much better it would have been if the Reagan people had understood from the start what is clear to Adam Michnik in a Polish prison: freedom is indivisible."[42]

The State Department thus may have lauded the UNCHR resolution on Poland as "nonpolemical, addressing human rights concerns in a nonpolitical manner" and a template for a resolution on Chile, yet this success also made it much more difficult, if not impossible, to get the human rights record of allied countries out of the spotlight.[43] Argentina, for instance, though vitally interested in improving its relations with Washington, refused to support a resolution on Poland. To the government in Buenos Aires, the US embassy there reasoned, "the Polish case in the [UNCHR] is simply too much like the Argentine case two years ago."[44]

★★★

As time passed after the imposition of martial law, Polish oppositionists and emigres were facing an uphill battle – while hundreds of activists remained in prison, sources of international support began to run dry and the Western front against Poland began to fracture. In this context, we have seen, human rights culture enabled Polish activists to translate their demands into a language distant audiences could easily grasp. Drawing on the imagery of the prisoner of conscience, inducted through the Nobel into a pantheon of exemplary figures, striking symbolic alliances with distant causes in Latin America, the Polish activists fashioned themselves into an international icon. This exposed them to attempts to claim Solidarity in the struggles of a "political economy of symbolic power", but the Poles were never the passive bystanders of the struggles for the meanings of their cause. Quite the contrary, they proved savvy symbolic entrepreneurs, as "General Pinoszecki" had to learn.

In turning themselves into international icons, the Polish activists joined the argument – sometimes forcefully so – as to what had happened

---

[42] Anthony Lewis, "From a Polish Cell," *New York Times,* Aug. 11, 1983, A21.

[43] Cable from USMission USUN to Secstate, "Chile and the UNHRC," dated Jan. 21, 1983, State Dep., Virtual Reading Room.

[44] Memo, "Ambassador Ender's Trip to Argentina and Chile, March 6–10, 1982," not dated, State Dep., Virtual Reading Room.

in Poland and how the international community was to respond to it. Much as human rights discourse can be analyzed as a "political economy of symbolic power," then, the currency in this economy were meanings, meanings which were constantly open to interpretations and re-interpretations, much as anyone involved may have sought to control them. And the Polish and Chilean activists were actively, and often skillfully, engaged in these symbolic politics.

10   Human Rights and the End of the Cold War

In concluding this book, this chapter addresses the question as to what the human rights culture analyzed so far contributed to the central transformation of late twentieth century international politics – the end of the Cold War. This aspect had been at the center of the earliest works on the human rights in contemporary international history. The more recent historiography of human rights, by contrast, has focused less on the impact of human rights than on their origins. In what follows, I will synthesize these two strands, discussing what role human rights played in ending Communist rule in Poland and the rest of Eastern Europe.

Directly after 1989, under the impression of mass demonstrations in Leipzig or Prague, the dissidents were widely seen as the main heroes of the peaceful end of the Cold War.[1] In the years since, a consensus has emerged that the dissolution of the Soviet bloc was primarily the result of Mikhail Sergeyevich Gorbachev's rise to power. Historians disagree strongly over what caused the rise of Gorbachev and his reform policies – the General Secretary's personality and ideas, détente, Reagan's aggressive foreign policy – but they agree that the focus needs to be on these policies.[2] Looking at the consequences of Gorbachev's election

---

[1] Timothy Garton Ash, *The Magic Lantern: The Revolution of '89 Witnessed in Warsaw, Budapest, Berlin, and Prague* (New York: Random House, 1990).

[2] Still the most important works ascribing events largely to Gorbachev's initiative and control are Archie Brown, *The Gorbachev Factor* (Oxford, England; New York: Oxford University Press, 1996); Archie Brown, *Seven Years that Changed the World: Perestroika in Perspective* (Oxford, New York: Oxford University Press, 2007); Jacques Lévesque, *The Enigma of 1989: The USSR and the Liberation of Eastern Europe* (Los Angeles, CA: University of California Press, 1997). For a related argument that focuses on the evolution of Gorbachev's "new thinking," see Robert D. English, *Russia and the Idea of the West: Gorbachev, Intellectuals, and the End of the Cold War* (New York: Columbia University Press, 2000). Vladislav Zubok, on the other hand, also argues for Gorbachev's predominant role, but believes he increasingly lost control over the processes he had initiated. Vladislav M. Zubok, "Gorbachev and the End of the Cold War: Perspectives on History and Personality," *Cold War History* 2 (January 2002), 2; Vladislav Zubok, "Gorbachev and the Road to 1989," in Vladimir Tismaneanu and Bogdan Iacob, eds., *The End and the Beginning: The Revolution of 1989 and the*

from the perspective of a Polish émigré and a political prisoner, I argue in this chapter, will force us to rethink central aspects of this interpretation. Human rights were central to the dismantlement of Communism in Europe, even if their history defies simplistic views of a "Helsinki Effect."

My argument will proceed along two lines. First, most historians of the Cold War agree that at some point the revolutionary changes of 1989 in the satellites states assumed a momentum of their own, evolved in a direction unintended by Gorbachev, and crucially ricocheted back into the USSR.[3] The important question is thus what set these latter events in motion. In Poland, I argue, they were almost exclusively driven by domestic and Western pressures to respect human rights, not by what happened in Moscow, even if Gorbachev did, of course, set crucial external parameters for events in Central Europe.[4]

Second, however, I argue that the end of the Cold War is no vindication for earlier Western policies – whether détente or "peace through strength." Dissidents and human rights activism had initially defied all Western approaches to the Cold War, whether they advocated

Resurgence of History (Budapest, NY: Central European University Press, 2012). Mark Kramer, finally, argues that Gorbachev did not intend the dissolution of the Soviet bloc but that, once it began, he actively fostered fundamental changes in Eastern Europe. Mark Kramer, "The Demise of the Soviet Bloc," *The Journal of Modern History* 83 (2011), 4. Even the most influential study in the social and cultural history of the post-Stalinist era, Alexei Yurchak's *Everything Was Forever, Until It Was No More: The Last Soviet Generation* (Princeton, NJ: Princeton University Press, 2006) sees Gorbachev's policies as the watershed of late Soviet history. For a highly important, though unnecessarily polemical, discussion of the East European political elites as important factors in 1989 see Stephen Kotkin, *Uncivil Society: 1989 and the Implosion of the Communist Establishment* (New York: Modern Library, 2009).

The most sophisticated explanation focusing on Reagan's policies can be found in William C. Wohlforth, "Realism and the End of the Cold War," *International Security* 19 (1994), 3; Robert G. Patman, "Reagan, Gorbachev and the Emergence of 'New Political Thinking'," *Review of International Studies* 25 (1999), 4; Robert G. Patman, "Some Reflections on Archie Brown and the End of the Cold War," *Cold War History* 7 (August 2007), 3.

For works focusing on détente and the CSCE see Oliver Bange and Gottfried Niedhart, eds., *Helsinki 1975 and the Transformation of Europe* (New York: Berghahn Books, 2008); Wentker and Peter, eds., *KSZE*; Thomas, *Effect*; Snyder, *Activism*; Yuliya von Saal, *KSZE-Prozess und Perestroika in der Sowjetunion: Demokratisierung, Werteumbruch und Auflösung 1985–1991* (München: Oldenbourg, 2014).

[3] This is among the main points of Lévesque's *Enigma*; see also Zubok, "Gorbachev," 287–289; and even Brown, *Years*, 221, 228. Mark Kramer sees Gorbachev as playing a more proactive role in the revolutions of 1989. See his Kramer, "Demise." But it was also Kramer who carefully documented how the revolutions of 1989 ricocheted back into the USSR. See his, "The Collapse of East European Communism and the Repercussions within the Soviet Union," published in three parts in the *Journal of Cold War Studies* 5, 4 (Fall 2003), 178–256, 6, 4 (Fall 2004), 3–64, and 7, 1 (Fall 2005), 3–96.

[4] For an interpretation that ascribes little to almost no independent agency to events in Eastern Europe prior to 1989 see Brown, *Years*, 226–227.

202   Poland's Solidarity Movement & the Politics of Rights

rapprochement or confrontation. In fact, the very West European states who would pressure Warsaw most effectively in the mid-1980s were the ones who had previously been most critical of raising human rights concerns at the CSCE meetings of the late 1970s in Belgrade and had wanted to bring the Madrid meeting to a swift end despite events in Poland. The Western pressures that led to the Polish revolution of 1989 did not evolve organically out of previous policies. They were part of a broader transformation in which human rights increasingly moved to the center of international politics.

I

In Poland, the end of Communism was triggered in January 1989 when representatives of the Polish opposition and of the Communist party (Polska Zjednoczona Partia Robotnicza, or PZPR) met at a famous round table, made specifically for this occasion, to discuss reforms to the political and economic system of the People's Republic. The most important outcome of these talks were semi-free parliamentary elections held in June which eventually led to the election of Eastern Europe's first non-Communist Prime Minister since the end of the war and to the abdication of the Communist party.[5]

To discuss what human rights activism contributed to these changes, it is important to note what the round table talks were not. First, they were not part of a long-term Soviet or Polish project to reform socialism. Gorbachev, to be sure, supported socialist reform efforts in Poland,[6] agreed in principle to the round table talks,[7] and ruled out the use of

---

[5] The following account can draw on quite a number of Polish studies. See especially Paweł Machcewicz et al., eds., *Polska 1986-1989. Koniec systemu*, 3 vols. (Warszawa: 2002); Dudek, *rewolucja*; Jan Skórzyński, *Rewolucja Okrągłego Stołu* (Kraków: Znak, 2009); Paweł Kowal, *Koniec systemu władzy: Polityka ekipy gen. Wojciecha Jaruzelskiego w latach 1986-1989* (Warszawa: ISP PAN/IPN/Trio, 2011). For three collections of primary sources see Antoni Dudek, ed. *Zmierzch dyktatury: Polska lat 1986-1989 w świetle dokumentów*, 2 vols. (Warszawa: IPN, 2013); Antoni Dudek and Andrzej Friszke, eds. *Polska 1986-1989: Koniec systemu*, vol. 3, Dokumenty (Warszawa: Trio/ISP PAN, 2002); Stanisław Perzkowski [Andrzej Paczkowski], ed. *Tajne dokumenty Biura Politycznego i Sekretariatu KC: Ostatni rok władzy 1988-1989* (London: Aneks, 1994).

[6] Nr 17: "1988 kwiecień 6, Moskwa – Zapis rozmowy sekretarza generalnego KC KPZR Michaiła Gorbaczowa z premierem Zbigniewem Messnerem, tajne," in Dudek, ed., *Zmierzch*, vol. I, 183–189, at 187, 189.

[7] Doc. 28: "Record of Conversation between Mikhail Gorbachev and Józef Czyrek, 23 September 1988," in Svetlana Savranskaya, Thomas S. Blanton, and Vladislav Zubok, *Masterpieces of History: The Peaceful Soviet Withdrawal from Eastern Europe, 1989* (New York, Budapest: CEU Press, 2010), 292–305, on 296. For the Soviet leadership complaining about the speed of the Polish reforms see Nr 53: "1989 luty 13, Moskwa – Szyfrogram ambasadora PRL w Moskwie Włodzimierza Natorfa dotyczący reakcji radzieckich na rozpoczęcie obrad okrągłego stołu, tajne," in Dudek, ed., *Zmierzch*, vol. I, 390–392.

Human Rights and the End of the Cold War 203

force should the Polish reform project go awry.[8] But he did little to initiate change in Poland. The Polish leadership, in fact, did not deem it necessary to ask for Gorbachev's permission to talk to the opposition. They merely informed him about their plans to do so in a conversation in which the Soviet General Secretary implored his comrades to make sure they remained in control of the reform process.[9]

If Polish Communists were acting largely independently from Moscow, they did not seem to have had a clear idea what, exactly, they hoped to achieve.[10] The only point that they had been adamant about since the end of 1982 and until the summer of 1988 was that they would not begin talks with Wałęsa nor even only consider relegalizing Solidarity.[11] In January 1989, however, they did begin talks with the opposition which, moreover, had made its participation conditional on Solidarity's relegalization. The fact, thus, that the government did eventually begin talks with Wałęsa about relegalizing Solidarity at the round table was a major defeat for it.[12]

If the round table talks did not evolve out of a project of socialist reform, they were no successful revolution of the dissident and opposition movement either. To the contrary, the opposition was struggling with serious problems in the second half of the 1980s. An amnesty for political prisoners, adopted in 1986, had effectively ended large scale repression, but the government continued to use other means to harass and surveil the opposition. Opposition activity, moreover, remained incomparably larger than in other parts of the Soviet bloc, but was ebbing away.[13] Those who remained active dispersed into an archipelago of diverse and often feuding groups, while the majority of society – trying to make ends meet in a dire economic situation – looked upon their struggle with increasing indifference. The only social institution whose authority had increased during the 1980s was the Catholic Church, a fact illustrated by the pope's triumphant third pilgrimage to Poland in 1987. But while John Paul II's sympathies for Solidarity were unbroken, the Polish episcopate saw itself more as a broker between government and

[8] Nr 136: "1989 sierpień 28, Moskwa – Szyfrogram ambasadora PRL w Moskwie Włodzimierza Natorfa dotyczący rozmowy z wiceministrem spraw zagranicznych ZSRR Iwanem Aboimowem, tajne," in Dudek, ed., *Zmierzch*, vol. II, 243–245.
[9] "Conversation between Mikhail Gorbachev and Józef Czyrek."
[10] Dudek, *rewolucja*, 91–109; Kowal, *Koniec*, 34–42.
[11] Nr 27: "1988 lipiec 14, Warszawa – Zapis rozmowy sekretarza generalnego KC KPZR Michaiła Gorbaczowa z I sekretarzem KC PZPR gen. Wojciechem Jaruzelskim," in Dudek, ed., *Zmierzch*, 263–268, at 266.
[12] Dokument nr 6: "Protokół nr 46 z roboczego posiedzenia Sekretariatu KC PZPR w dniu 1 września 1988 r.," in Perzkowski, ed., *Tajne dokumenty 1988-1989*, 37–44, at 38, 43.
[13] Kenney, *Carnival*, 157–164, 175–177; Sowa, *Historia*, 576–577, 580.

opposition than positioning itself firmly on Solidarity's side.[14] If anything, in sum, the opposition had been losing social support when the government decided to open talks with them.[15]

Unsure how to proceed and lacking meaningful social support, both opposition and government were in dead ends. What tipped the scales in favor of the negotiations of 1989, was a wave of strikes that hit Poland in spring and summer 1988. Yet these strikes were no rebirth of Solidarity, but largely spontaneous eruptions of protest instigated and led by younger workers with few direct ties to the union. Wałęsa, however, still commanded significant authority among Polish workers. The Communist party thus agreed to talk to him about Solidarity's relegalization, if he used his authority to end the strikes which he did.

The negotiations between opposition and government at the round table seemed to provide both sides a way out of their dead ends. The Communist side hoped that they could increase their legitimacy and share some of the blame for Poland's economic woes if they managed to coopt the opposition. The latter, on the other hand, believed that the chance to rebuild Solidarity was worth the price of agreeing to this scheme. The events which unfolded afterward, culminating in the dissolution of the Communist party in January 1990, were unforeseen consequences of these calculations.

II

Human rights activism and policies had a threefold impact on the developments sketched above. First, it kept opposition activists out of prison and, through the iconic international status of Solidarity, helped to sustain the movement as a legitimate interlocutor of the Polish government.

At first, the amnesty of 1984 had been followed by a fresh wave of repression, in which, among others, Adam Michnik was arrested just over six months after he had been released. As mentioned above, however, the government implemented another amnesty in 1986 after which large-scale repression largely stopped. At the time, the opposition was already struggling with the aforementioned problems – a diversification of opposition activity and dwindling social support. It thus may seem plausible to correlate the 1986 amnesty with Gorbachev's rise to power a

---

[14] On the Church, see for instance, Przewidywane następstwa wizyty Jana Pawła II w Polsce, poufne, dated Jan. 1987, AAN, KC PZPR, XXXVII–25. See also Dudek, *rewolucja*, 79–90.

[15] Ibid., 118.

Human Rights and the End of the Cold War 205

year before. There is, however, no evidence for this hypothesis. To the contrary, what we do know about Soviet–Polish relations in 1985 and 1986 suggests that Gorbachev saw the opposition and Western support for human rights as elements of an anti-socialist campaign.[16] In a speech at a Polish Communist party congress in June 1986, he commended Poland's Communists for "defending the revolutionary achievements" and "repulsing the attack of the enemies of socialism."[17]

At the time of this speech, the Polish leadership was already discussing the new amnesty. Though it is highly unlikely that Gorbachev had actively urged the amnesty, it is possible that the Poles consulted him about it and that he gave his consent. Whatever he did, his consent was hardly necessary for the PZPR's decision. Two years before, after all, Chernenko had explicitly told Jaruzelski what he expected of him – to root out the opposition, contain the influence of the Church, and reinstate Marxism-Leninism as the country's leading ideology. Back home, Jaruzelski released all political prisoners and allowed the Church to implement the most massive building program in Europe at the time.[18] All that we know about Polish–Soviet relations and Polish domestic policies, in fact, suggests that, by the time of the amnesty of 1986, Soviet opinion had long since ceased to be a major influence on events along the banks of the Vistula. In 1977, as seen in Chapter 2, Warsaw had implemented an amnesty in spite of Brezhnev's expressed wish that the Polish comrades deal with the dissidents. After August 1980, Moscow had relentlessly pressured the PZPR to end the "counterrevolution" – initially, to no avail. Yet when push came to shove and Jaruzelski asked for Soviet military support, the Soviet Politburo told him flat out that he

---

[16] "Document No. 106: Speech by Gorbachev at the Warsaw Treaty Summit in Moscow, April 26, 1985," in Vojtech Mastny and Malcolm Byrne, eds., *A Cardboard Castle? An Inside History of the Warsaw Pact, 1955-1991* (Budapest: CEU Press, 2005), 507–510, at 507, 510; notes from the Gorbachev archive quoted in Kramer, "Demise," 792; Handwritten note from Wojciech Jaruzelski to Stefan Olszowksi, et al. with two untitled and undated Russian memos attached, dated June 20, 1985, AAN, KC PZPR, XIA/1412, fol. 85–87; Notatka nt. specjalnego, zamkniętego spotkania przywódców partii państw członkowskich Układu Warszawskiego, Sofia, 23 Październik 1985 roku, tajne specjalnego znaczenia, dated Oct. 26, 1985, AAN, KC PZPR, XIA/1482.

[17] Przemówienie Michaiła Gorbaczowa na X zjeździe PZPR, not dated, AAN, KC PZPR, I/405, quotes at 1–6. See also Rakowski, *Dzienniki, 1984-1986*, 407, entry from July 4, 1986.

[18] In a 1987 confidential discussion with SPD politician Hans-Jochen Vogel, Jaruzelski claimed that one thousand new churches had been built in recent years and that another thousand were under construction. Even if these numbers are two high, anyone visiting Poland can testify to the sheer number of parish churches built during the 1980s. Informacja o wizycie Przewodniczącego SPD Hansa Vogla i delegacji SPD w Polsce, 29.9.-1.10.1987 r., not dated, on 16–17, AAN, KC PZPR, LXXVI-477, fol. 170–191.

206   Poland's Solidarity Movement & the Politics of Rights

was on his own. It is thus not very surprising that Jaruzelski responded to Chernenko's rant of 1984 by releasing the political prisoners, and it is also not surprising that Soviet wishes seem to have played no visible role for the amnesty of 1986. Western concerns, in contrast, did.

At the end of 1985, Warsaw drew up a rather mixed balance sheet of its relations with the West. Polish–American relations had dropped to another low point. When Jaruzelski came to New York for a session of the UN General Assembly, American officials received him at the lowest possible diplomatic level. A month later, Reagan met the director of Solidarity's representation in the West in the Oval Office.[19] Western trade unions were equally unrelenting in their support for Solidarity.[20]

Relations to West European states were somewhat better but not without problems either. On the one hand, West European governments had begun re-engaging Warsaw diplomatically after the amnesty of 1984. In December 1985, and during a stopover on a trip back from India, Jaruzelski had even managed to arrange a meeting with French President François Mitterrand in the Élysée Palace.[21] Days later, Willy Brandt arrived in Warsaw for a visit commemorating the fifteenth anniversary of the Warsaw treaty between the Federal Republic and Poland.

Yet pleased though the Polish leadership was when Brandt left,[22] the former chancellor's visit failed to revitalize 1970s *Ostpolitik* with its focus on intergovernmental relations, its emphasis on easing tensions, and its cultivation of personal relationships between leaders of the two blocs.

---

[19] Ronald Reagan, "Statement Following a Meeting with Solidarity Movement Representative Jerzy Milewski on the Situation in Poland, October 21, 1985," RRPL, *The Public Papers of President Ronald W. Reagan*, available at www.reagan.utexas.edu/archives/speeches/1985/102185c.htm (accessed August 2015). For the purpose of the meeting see Memorandum from Robert F. McFarlane for Ronald Reagan, "Meeting with Jerzy Milewski (ma-Lev-ski), director of Solidarity office abroad," dated Oct. 19, 1985, RRPL, WHORM: Subject File, CO126, ID#342721.

[20] For the Italian Communists see Stan i ocena informacji o Polsce w wybranych organach prasowych zachdonioeuropejskich partii komunistycznych w 1984 roku, dated Dec. 12, 1984, AAN, KC PZPR, LXXVI–992; Notatka informacyjna z rozmów w CGIL, CISL, UIL, Feb. 20, 1985, AAN, KC PZPR, LXXVI–646. Even a Hungarian trade unionist had to justify himself for Solidarity's oppression. Szyfogram Nr 1877/I z Budapesztu, dated Feb. 2, 1985, AAN, KC PZPR, LXXVI–985. Alongside Chilean trade unions, Solidarity became a member of two Western international trade unions. "Polnische und chilenische Arbeitnehmer schließen sich dem IBFG an," *Freie Gewerkschaftswelt*, Dec. 17, 1986; Andrzej Chwalba, *Czasy "Solidarności": Francuscy związkowcy i NSZZ "Solidarność" 1980-1990* (Kraków: 1997), 199.

[21] Domber, *Revolution*, 142–148; Pleskot, *Panna*, 402–590.

[22] Informacja o wizycie Przewodniczącego Socjaldemokratycznej Partii Niemiec, Willy BRANDTA, not dated, AAN, KC PZPR, XI/437, fol. 165–185.

If anything, it demonstrated how obsolete it had become. For while West European politicians began traveling to Poland again, the "choreography" of their trips to Poland had changed markedly compared to the 1970s. Previously, West European politicians had avoided anything that could have antagonized their Polish hosts; now they ostentatiously visited symbolic sites of the opposition movement such as the grave of Jerzy Popiełuszko, a Catholic priest murdered by Poland's secret police, and they demanded to be allowed to meet representatives of the opposition.[23] Western embassies, meanwhile, had started consulting opposition figures on current developments and openly invited them to their receptions.[24]

The issue of political prisoners, moreover, remained a central element of Polish–West European relations, when West European visitors to Poland made it clear that the continuing incarceration of opposition activists was the main impediment to a more substantial improvement of bilateral relations. Jaruzelski was outraged by Western criticism of the Polish human rights record. In a rare interview for a German weekly, he insisted that there were no political prisoners in Poland, only people who had committed felonies out of "non-criminal motivations," people who could be understood as "terrorists" in a wider sense.[25] But these attempts to brand the political prisoners "non-criminals" or even terrorists failed miserably, not least because the prisoners again proved to be their own best advocates. The wife and mother of an incarcerated Solidarity leader, for instance, wrote a personal letter to Nancy

---

[23] Antoni Lewek, *New Sanctuary of Poles: The Grave of Martyr – Father Jerzy Popiełuszko* (Warszawa: Parafia św. Stanisława Kostki, 1986), 6–7; Michael Kaufman, "Ostracism of Poland: The West's Unity Unravels," *The New York Times*, Dec. 14, 1985; on the symbolic role of Popiełuszko's grave for Western visits see Patryk Pleskot, "Potępić, nie obrazić: Reakcje zachodniej dyplomacji na zabójstwo ks. Jerzego Popiełuszki," in Wojciech Polak et al., eds., *Kościół w obliczu totalitaryzmów* (Toruń: FINNA, 2010); Robert Brier, "Tod eines Priesters: Der Erinnerungskult um Jerzy Popiełuszko aus globalhistorischer Perspektive," in Julia Obertreis and Martin Aust, eds., *Osteuropäische Geschichte und Globalgeschichte* (Stuttgart: Franz Steiner Verlag, 2014).

[24] The Polish activists whom Western embassies consulted most frequently were Bronisław Geremek and Solidarity's former spokesman Janusz Onyszkiewicz. Between January 1985 and June 1986, each held over twenty meetings with representatives of Western embassies, on average more than one per month. Wykaz ustalonych spotkań przedstawicieli opozycji z dyplomatami państw kapitalistycznych w latach 1985–1986, not dated, AIPN, BU 1585/3998/CD, fol. 9–12.

[25] Wojciech Jaruzelski, "Die Chance nicht voll genutzt," interview conducted by Rolf Winter, Jochen Schildt, and Uwe Zimmer, *Stern* (Hamburg), Nr. 50, Dec. 5, 1985, 36–38, 173; see also Notatka z rozmowy Przewodniczącego Rady Państwa PRL tow. gen. armii Wojciech Jaruzelskiego z Prezydentem Francji Francis Mitterrand, Paryż 1985.12.04, tajne egz. nr 124, KS/0188/1902/85, AAN, KC PZPR, XI/437, fol. 152–164, on 157.

208 Poland's Solidarity Movement & the Politics of Rights

Reagan.[26] Michnik smuggled a long "Letter from the Gdańsk Prison" out of his cell, which was published, among others, in the *New York Review of Books*,[27] and both Italian prime minister Bettino Craxi and French president Mitterrand took a personal interest in freeing him.[28]

It also became increasingly difficult for the Polish authorities to argue that, for the sake of peace, questions of individual rights or political systems had to be put aside. In January 1986, the PZPR organized an international peace congress for intellectuals in Warsaw – an obvious attempt to use the peace topic to break Warsaw's international isolation.[29] By most accounts, the congress was a total failure. Western attention – to the extent that there was any – focused on political prisoners and the harassment of opposition activists.[30] Peace and human rights, the Polish leadership had to acknowledge, could not be separated as easily anymore as in the early 1980s.

This fusion of the issues of disarmament and human rights was largely an achievement of a younger generation of Polish opposition activists who proved to be just as canny in establishing symbolic joint ventures and using a problematic issue to their own advantage as their older peers.[31] At around 1985, these younger activists initiated a campaign that focused on their right to conscientious objection, a cause that both drew on the dissident tactic of legalism – Polish citizens theoretically had

[26] Memorandum from Jack L. Courtemanche for Nancy Reagan, "Letter in Regard to the Polish Solidarity Movement," dated June 13, 1986, RRPL, WHORM: Subject File, CO126, ID# 419210.

[27] Michnik, *Prison*, 76–100.

[28] Załącznik do informacji dziennej, dated Jan. 16, 1986, AIPN, BU 0248/134/CD/3, fol. .49. Craxi's personal interest was also mentioned in a memo discussing ways of dealing with an appeal by Michnik. See Notatka służbowa dot. Adama Michnika, Jan. 23, 1986, AIPN, BU 0248/134/CD/3, fol. 50–51.

[29] Sprawozdanie z pobytu delegacji PRL pod przewodnictwem Prezesa Rady Ministrów, Tow. W. Jaruzelskiego na 40-tej, jubileuszowej Sesji Zgromadzenia Ogólnego ONZ w Nowym Jorku (24–28 września 1985 r.), tajne, not dated, AAN, KC PZPR, XI/437, fol. 92–130, on fol. 97–98; Koncepcja organizacyjno-programowa Światowego Kongresu Intelektualistów – Warszawa 2–9.05.1985 r., Projekt nr 1, not dated, AIPN, BU 01419/332, t. 1, fol. 244–246.

[30] Informacja, tajne, dated Jan. 15, 1986, Wyciąg z informacji operacyjnej od TW ps 'BARTEK' z dnia 13.01.1986 r., dated Jan. 15, 1986, Załącznik do informacji dziennej z dnia 17.01.1986 r. dot. Kongresu Intelektualistów w Obronie Pokojowej Przyszłości Świata – Warszawa '86, Informacja, dated Jan. 22, 1986, all in AIPN, BU 01419/332, t. 4, fol. 3–4, 8, 26–31, 125–127; Ocena przebiegu Kongresu Intelektualistów w Obronie Pokojowej Przyszłości Świata (Warszawa 16–19.01.1986), poufne, dated Jan. 24, 1986, AIPN, BU 01419/332, t. 3, fol. 8–21.

[31] For the following see especially, Kenney, *Carnival*, 57–120; Kacper Szulecki, "Hijacked Ideas: Human Rights, Peace, and Environmentalism in Czechoslovak and Polish Dissident Discourses" *East European Politics & Societies* 25 (May 2011), 2; Kacper Szulecki, "'Freedom and Peace are Indivisible': On the Polish and Czechoslovak Input to the European Peace Movement 1985-89," in Brier, ed., *Protest*.

Human Rights and the End of the Cold War

a right to refuse military service – and strongly resonated with the views of two Western constituencies – the peace movements and Amnesty International which had been lobbying for a right to conscientious objection since the early 1970s.[32]

Going on hunger strike or even to jail to defend the right to refuse military service, these activists came to "incarnate" sacred values of the peace movement. They thus infused human rights concerns into the debate on peace, but they also tied peace to human rights. Another "symbolic joint venture" emerged: Supporting the Polish struggle for conscientious objection, Western peace activists helped the Polish activists counter claims that human rights activism threatened international peace, while the Polish activists helped the Westerners counter criticism that peace activism entailed a passive acceptance of Soviet dominance over Eastern Europe.[33] Support for human rights in Eastern Europe, to be sure, remained a controversial topic among Western peace activists, but human rights had nevertheless become an issue they had to confront in their activism.[34] On this basis, one of the most sustained networks for transnational exchanges between East and West emerged, as Western peace activists or Greens traveled to Poland to discuss questions of disarmament, nonviolence, and human rights. The peak of these interactions was the Nowa Huta human rights conference of 1988 mentioned in the Introduction above.[35]

In 1986, in sum, a substantial improvement of Poland's relations with the West Europeans seemed within reach, but only if Poland released its political prisoners. Poland's economic situation, meanwhile, went from

---

[32] Jacek Czaputowicz, interview with the author and Daniel Stahl, Warsaw, Sep. 23, 2014. Conscientious objection was a central topic of Amnesty's work in Western Europe and the organization lobbied for an international right to conscientious objection at the Council of Europe and the UN. See Martin Ennals, "Introduction by the Secretary-General," in *Amnesty International Report 1970/71*, 7–11, on 10. See also Stephanie Grant, "Introduction" and the chapters "Relations with Other Organizations" and "Europe," in *Amnesty International Report 1974/75*, 29–30, 36, 107–108, 113, 116. For the issue in the 1985 report see the entries "Cyprus," "France," "Greece," "Italy," and "Switzerland" in *Amnesty International Report 1984/85*, 260, 265, 269, 275, 286.

[33] Jonathan Schell, "Introduction," in Adam Michnik, *Letters From Prison and Other Essays* (Berkeley, CA: University of California Press, 1985), xvii–xviii, xxxv, xxxvii–xxxviii; Steven Becker, "Peace Activists Protest Trial of Solidarity Leaders," *Peace & Democracy News* (Summer-Fall 1985).

[34] Uli Fischer et al., "Was soll das Geholze," *Kommune* 4 (June 1986), 6.

[35] On these interactions see also Mary Kaldor's letter to Freedom and Peace in *Wolność i Pokój Kraków* (samizdat) 2 (June 1987), 9–11; Letter from Joanne Landy to Piotr Niemczyk, Jul. 25, 1987, Memorandum from Elisabeth Weber for the members of the "Arbeitsgemeinschaft Frieden und Internationales" (AFI), "Bericht über eine Reise nach Warschau und Krakau im April 1987," dated Apr. 20, 1987, both in AGG, PKA, 461.

210 Poland's Solidarity Movement & the Politics of Rights

bad to worse, while Warsaw remained heavily indebted to its Western creditors. The way out of this malaise, the PZPR concluded, led through increased exports, and Poland needed hard currency to make the necessary investments. The solution to Poland's problems lay in the West.[36]

These developments, not Gorbachev's rise to power, formed the background for the amnesty of 1986.[37] While the Catholic Church and US government made important contributions in this context, Gregory Domber has demonstrated that the European Community (EC) played the central role in getting Warsaw to release all political prisoners. In July 1986 the EC stated categorically that the West Europeans did not see "fundamental improvement in the spheres of national reconciliation and human rights" in Poland, given exceptions to an amnesty the Polish government had implemented. Delivering the demarche, the British ambassador explained that "[nothing] less than the release of all political prisoners, and no new arrests on political grounds, could be regarded as a significant step forward." The Polish side rejected the statement as "interference in internal affairs," a form of "blackmail" even.[38]

A week later, though, Jaruzelski warned the Politburo that keeping the high profile prisoners in jail might seriously complicate Poland's attempts to reestablish normal financial and economic relations with the West.[39] Another month later, the Ministry of Internal Affairs and the legal department of the Communist party conceded that a release of all political prisoners would create problems with the security apparatus, the party's rank-and-file, and the other Soviet bloc countries, but recommended this step nevertheless. First, it wrote, this would help the government gain social legitimacy and, second, it would contribute "to overcome[ing] the impasse in international relations." All Soviet bloc countries, the department complained, had benefitted economically from the recent improvements in East–West relations, only Poland was left in the cold because the West made normalization of mutual relations dependent on its evaluation of the country's domestic situation. "One of the publicly presented criteria for the western countries to evaluate our internal situation is the question of the so-called political prisoners."

---

[36] Domber, *Revolution*, 152–153.

[37] The following account draws heavily on Domber, *Revolution*, 152–155; Andrzej Paczkowski, "Boisko wielkich mocarstw: Polska 1980-1989. Widok od wewnątrz," *Polski Przegląd Dyplomatyczny* 2 (2002), 3. See also Dudek, *rewolucja*, 73–79.

[38] Domber, *Revolution*, 156.

[39] Notatka w sprawie implikacji naszej sytuacji wewnętrznej dla stosunków Polski z państwami Europy Zachodniej, dated Aug. 6, 1986, AAN, KC PZPR, V/314, fol. 81–92; ibid.

Releasing the leading activists would be a step to remedying this situation. A few days later, all political prisoners were set free.[40]

In the years following the amnesty of 1986, human rights activism sustained the status of the Polish opposition as international icons, even as their domestic support waned.[41] Warsaw's attempts to brand Wałęsa a private citizen or Michnik a dangerous troublemaker, a quasi-terrorist even, were powerfully undercut when Western politicians insisted on holding widely publicized meetings with them. When US deputy secretary of state John Whitehead came to Poland in January 1987 as Washington's first high-ranking emissary since martial law, he snubbed his furious Polish hosts when he said that meeting Wałęsa, a "world leader," was the major event of his time in Poland.[42] By this time, Western correspondents and diplomats were consulting opposition activists about the social and political situation in Poland on an almost daily basis.[43]

In 1987, the Polish Foreign Ministry stopped discouraging Western visitors from such meetings, hoping that they would make them understand that the opposition was "a fragile group, deprived of a wider social base, and unlikely to play the role desired by the West."[44] This expectation, though not unrealistic, was a profound misunderstanding of what the Polish dissidents' role for Western visitors was – they were *icons*, symbols whose power derived not from how they reflected the intricacies of Polish society, but the quasi-sacred values of human rights culture.

Two visits by American politicians made this fact particularly manifest. In May 1987, Senator Edward Kennedy came to Poland to honor Michnik, the Solidarity leader Zbigniew Bujak, and posthumously

[40] "Nr 1: Propozycje w sprawie rozszerzenia zakresu ustawy amnestyjnej z 17 lipca 1986 r. przesłane członkom i zastępcom członków Biura Politycznego oraz Sekretarzom KC na posiedzenie Biura Politycznego 9 września 1986 r.," in Dudek and Friszke, eds., *Polska 1986-1989*, vol. 3, 13–19, quotes at 15–17. See also Domber, *Revolution*, 157–158; Paczkowski, "Boisko," 194–195.

[41] For the Security Service's acknowledgement of this phenomenon see Nr 7: "Nie podpisana ekspertyza na temat sytuacji wewnętrznej w kraju i stosunku państw zachodnich do PRL z 28 sierpnia 1987 r.," in Dudek and Friszke, eds., *Polska 1986-1989*, vol. III, 37–43, at 41.

[42] "Deputy Secretary of State John C. Whitehead, Statement to the North Atlantic Council, Brussels, Friday – February 6, 1987," noted dated, on 9, NSA, End of Cold War Collection, Domber Poland-FOIAs.

[43] D. Godlewski, Meldunek uzupełniający 136 spraw operacyjnego rozpracowania WA 0 30545 – kryptonim "Taternik" – identyfikator 6930/85, dated Mar. 6, 1987, AIPN, BU 0248/44, t. 4, fol. 188–189; Domber, *Revolution*, 107–108; Paczkowski, "Boisko," 200.

[44] Document 1: "The Note of Ministry of Foreign Affairs on experiences so far with the model of visits by Western politicians," and Document 2: "1987, October 19 Excerpt from the protocol of the session of the Secretariat of the CC of the PUWP," in *Cold War History* 3, 3 (2003), 130–141, quote on 134.

212   Poland's Solidarity Movement & the Politics of Rights

Popiełuszko with the Robert F. Kennedy Human Rights Award.[45] The Senator's trip was part of an informal human rights diplomacy of raising awareness for repression and supporting sanctions against human rights violators like South Africa and Poland.[46] Kennedy's program in Poland drew heavily on the imagery of human rights culture, providing him with multiple occasions to bath in the Polish icons' light. Among others, he had himself photographed with Michnik, Bujak, and Wałęsa with all of them wearing caps by the Massachusetts chapter of the AFL-CIO.[47]

A few months later, Vice-President George Bush also came to Poland. Following a low-key program, he visited Popiełuszko's grave where, standing next to Wałęsa, he gave a rousing speech in support of Solidarity's aspirations.[48] The microphone Bush used had been installed by his campaign staff to make sure his voice could be heard on the films they shot during the meeting with Wałęsa. In the electoral campaign of 1988, footage from the meeting was used to underline Bush's credentials as an anti-Communist and defender of religious freedom.[49]

While the Polish activists thus became vessels for the values and messages of Western visitors, they continued using such meetings for their own purposes. Before Kennedy's visit, Janusz Onyszkiewicz, the unofficial spokesperson of Solidarity, negotiated intensely with the US embassy. The senator should make public, he insisted, that the main aim of his trip was to meet the opposition, while talks with officials were

---

[45] D. Godlewski, Meldunek uzupełniający 696 spraw operacyjnego rozpracowania WA 0 30545 – kryptonim "Taternik" – identyfikator 6930/85, tajne spec. znaczenia, dated Dec. 17, 1986, D. Godlewski, Meldunek uzupełniający 697 spraw operacyjnego rozpracowania WA 0 30545 – kryptonim "Taternik" – identyfikator 6930/85, tajne spec. znaczenia, dated Dec. 17, 1986, AIPN, BU 0248/44, t. 4, fol. 168–171.

[46] Burton Hersh, *Edward Kennedy: An Intimate Biography* (Berkeley, CA: Counterpoint, 2010), 503–504. For Kennedy's views on sanctions against Poland and South Africa see also Encrypted cable from the Polish Embassy in Washington to Czesław Kiszczak, dated ct. 23, 1986, AIPN, BU 0236/344/1/CD, fol. 124–125.

[47] Załącznik do informacji dziennej, dated May 25, 1987, AIPN, BU 01304/920; "Informacja," dated May 28, 1987, AIPN, BU 0248/134/4, fol. 106. Talking to the Polish foreign minister, Kennedy acknowledged that there was a fine line between interfering with a state's internal affairs and support for people's human rights, but insisted that the latter were a legitimate concern for the international community. Notatka informacyjna o wizycie w Polsce senatora Edwarda M. Kennedy, dated May 31, 1987, AIPN, BU 01304/920.

[48] For the Poles' preparations and later assessment of the trip, see "Plan działań Departamentu II zabezpieczających wizytę wiceprezydenta USA George'a Busha w Polsce," dated Sept. 1987, AIPN, BU 01304/892; "Protokół nr. 46 z posiedzenia Biura Politycznego KC PZPR wraz z załącznikami, 6. X. 1987 r.," on 158.

[49] David L. Hoffman, "Chanting Polish Crowds Provide Bush with Footage for '88 Campaign," *Washington Post*, Oct. 4, 1987.

Human Rights and the End of the Cold War 213

merely an appendix of these meetings.[50] At the awards ceremony, some Western correspondents complained that they were not allowed in. Onyszkiewicz, apparently, had "accredited" only the correspondents of the *New York Times* and *Washington Post* because they were known for their favorable reporting on the opposition.[51]

In December, Wałęsa flew to Paris where, alongside Andrei Sakharov and Salvador Allende's widow Hortensia Bussi, he attended a conference to commemorate the fiftieth anniversary of the Universal Declaration of Human Rights. Celebrated by the French media, Wałęsa was received by President Mitterrand in the Élysée Palace and West German Foreign Minister Genscher came to Paris to see him.[52]

Whatever support the Polish opposition enjoyed at home, in sum, their iconic international status meant that the Polish government had to recognize them as serious interlocutors. Keeping them out of prison and sustaining this international status was thus the first contribution human rights activism made to the beginning of the round table talks.

III

The second way in which Western human rights policies contributed to the events of 1989 was through material support. The Polish language programs of Radio Free Europe, the BBC, and other stations remained crucial for the internal communication of the opposition, a fact evidenced by the authorities' attempts to jam the programs.[53] Western financial support also proved crucial. The two most important sources were Western trade unions and the National Endowment for Democracy (NED). The NED had been set up by the Reagan administration in 1983 as part of its human rights policy to provide financial aid for pro-democratic forces. Though the lion share of its funds went to anti-Communist and pro-Western groups in Latin America, it did, according to Greg Domber's estimates, provide more than 5 million dollars to the

---

[50] D. Godlewski, Meldunek uzupełniający 696 spraw operacyjnego rozpracowania WA 0 30545 – kryptonim "Taternik" – identyfikator 6930/85, tajne spec. znaczenia, dated Dec. 17, 1986, D. Godlewski, Meldunek uzupełniający 697 spraw operacyjnego rozpracowania WA 0 30545 – kryptonim "Taternik" – identyfikator 6930/85, tajne spec. znaczenia, dated Dec. 17, 1986, AIPN, BU 0248/44, t. 4, fol. 168–171.

[51] Załącznik do informacji dziennej, dated May 26, 1987 AIPN, BU 0248/134/4, fol. 104–105.

[52] "Wałęsa w Paryżu," *Tygodnik Mazowsze,* Dec. 14, 1988.

[53] Zakres słyszalności zachodnich radiostacji na terytorium PRL, not dated, AAN, KC PZPR, XI/427.

214   Poland's Solidarity Movement & the Politics of Rights

Polish underground and its émigré centers between 1984 and 1989.[54] This money helped the émigrés keep Solidarity's cause on the international agenda, to financially support political prisoners and their families, to counter the financial fines that became the authorities' weapon of choice after 1986, and most of all sustained an independent public in Poland. Dozens of samizdat journals were published and an entire second book market – complete with market analyses of samizdat publishing houses – emerged. Publishing these journals both allowed discussing ideas and options that would play a role during and after 1989 and it gave oppositionists a cause that sustained their activism. Western money, Domber shows, also had a direct influence on the transition in Poland when the AFL-CIO made NED funds available to support striking workers in 1988.[55]

Third, Western governments not only supported the Polish opposition financially and politically but also nudged the Polish leadership toward beginning negotiations with it. Diplomatic relations with the West had been revived after 1984, but, as Jaruzelski complained to his East German comrade Erich Honecker in September 1987, "this does not give more bread." Poland's massive debt had not gone away, he said, and the West remained unwilling to provide new credits. "An economic war continues to be waged against Poland."[56] These external pressures played a direct role in the decision to begin the roundtable talks. When Jaruzelski had to convince a recalcitrant Central Committee to begin negotiating with Wałęsa he made three main arguments: First, the talks would prevent further social unrest and, second, a failure to begin talks would deprive the Communist party of any legitimacy. His third argument drew on "how profoundly the economy's ability to recover and develop depends on a normalization of our international financial and economic relations. Without that, comrades, without this Club of Paris [uniting Poland's western creditors], without these funds, without these different connections, credits, the rescheduling of at least some

---

[54] Domber, *Revolution*, 283–288. For documentation of the NED funds used by the Coordinating Office in Brussels, see the report, "Disbursements of the AFL-CIO Donation in 1986 as of December 31, 1986," dated Jan. 15, 1987, AFL-CIO Unprocessed Records, Free Trade Union Institute, "NED. FTUI - Poland – Correspondence."

[55] Domber, *Revolution*, 267–280; Romaszewski et al., *Autobiografia*, 335–341.

[56] Nr 8: "Zapis stenograficzny rozmowy Ericha Honeckera z Wojciechem Jaruzelskim 16 września 1987 r. (fragment)," in Dudek and Friszke, *Polska 1986-1989*, vol. III, 44–54, at 48. For an assessment of Poland's massive international financial problems during this period see Notatka w sprawie porozumienia zawartego z Klubem Paryskim dotyczącego odroczenia zobowiązań gwarantowanych przypadających pierwotnie do spłaty w 1981 roku, dated May 16, 1987, AAN, KC PZPR, XIA/1464.

Human Rights and the End of the Cold War   215

payments, we cannot make the economic wheel turn faster. That is simply impossible and maybe it even gets worse."[57]

★★★

Human rights activism, in conclusion, had made a significant contribution to the fall of Communism in Poland and thus to the end of the Cold War as well – it had helped keep Polish activists out of prison and provided them with the symbolic authority to become the government's interlocutors at the round table, it had helped mobilize funds to sustain opposition activity, and it had nudged the Polish government toward beginning talks with the opposition. In concluding this chapter, however, it is crucial to note that these findings defy the dominant approaches in Cold War history.

For one, the amnesty of 1986 was neither the result of a Gorbachev effect nor of American pressures – the West Europeans, not Washington, had played the main role in pressuring Warsaw to free its political prisoners. But it would be equally wrong to see the amnesty as a long term "Helsinki effect" or the accomplishment of a West European variety of détente. When the dissidents had entered the stage of Cold War international politics, their combination of anti-totalitarianism and peaceful resistance had been as deeply at odds with West European détente as with neoconservative Cold Warriordom. Yet as the West Europeans started to re-engage Warsaw in October 1984, at a time when Gorbachev was not yet in sight, when US–Soviet relations were at a low point and Western anxieties about a nuclear conflict were still running high, the dissidents had managed to transform their existence from an oddity into a group which West European visitors treated similarly to the legal opposition in a democratic country. In 1981, West European governments had still invoked "the principle of non-interference as laid down in the Helsinki Final Act" (see Chapter 3); 3 years later, Poland's penitentiary practice had become a legitimate concern for West European foreign policy. The West Europeans' actions in 1986 did not evolve organically out of previous policies. They had been brought about by how the opposition in Poland and elsewhere in the Soviet bloc had both benefitted from and accelerated a transformation of international politics in which human rights increasingly breached the wall of national sovereignty.

---

[57] X Plenum Komitetu Centralnego Polskiej Zjednoczonej Partii Robotniczej, część druga, 16–18 stycznia 1989 roku, stenogram, dated Jan. 1989, AAN, KC PZPR, III/190, Jaruzelski's speech on fol. 461–473, quotation on fol. 465–466.

The decisive blow to the People's Republic, moreover, was dealt by the opposition alone. In the run-up to the elections of 1989, the Polish activists won the support of a largely indifferent society over by running a highly effective election campaign. Drawing on the country's network of Catholic parishes, the campaign reached into virtually all corners of Poland, outdoing the PZPR's tight net of local organizations. The posters and leaflets showed the Solidarity candidates – unknown to the general public – standing next to Wałęsa. The campaign's most famous poster showed Gary Cooper in his role in *High Noon*, but rather than a gun he was carrying a ballot with the famous Solidarity logo in his holster. Western supporters, to be sure, had provided financial aid, but the creativity and organizational effort that made the campaign such a huge success had come from within Polish society.

Epilogue

On a hot summer day in late August 1988, shortly before the world of the Cold War started to unravel, the Polish peace and human rights activist Jan Maria Rokita addressed one of the turbulent and colorful sessions of the human rights conference in Nowa Huta.[1] Echoing the dissident thought of the 1970s, he described how the laws of the Soviet bloc, with their untruths and contradictions, perverted the very idea of the rule of law, reliant as it was on precise and unambiguous language.[2] The "Sovietized" societies of Eastern Europe, Leszek Kołakowski had written in 1974, were dominated by a deformed public language in which "there is nothing strange about the fact that a cockroach can be called a nightingale and a parsley called a symphony ..."[3] Fourteen years later, Rokita described how Polish labor law simultaneously guaranteed trade union pluralism and prohibited the legalization of Solidarity.[4]

The only way to make sure that legal institutions did protect human rights, Rokita continued, was to put them under social control. A major obstacle on the path to achieve this aim, he said to the meeting's thunderous applause, was "one of the most deeply ingrained myths of our time, the myth called state sovereignty ... In today's international conflicts, the famous 'interference in the internal affairs of a foreign state' has become the last argument of all tyrannies and dictatorships ... In the name of the principle of sovereignty, the civilized world turns its back on repression." In much of the rest of the speech, Rokita called upon social movements and non-governmental groups to join forces in order to overcome sovereignty in the name of human rights. But Rokita also mentioned – much to the consternation of many in his audience – what he saw as a successful example of human rights policies – the US invasion of Grenada in 1983.[5]

---

[1] See the introduction to this book.
[2] Jan Maria Rokita, speech manuscript, not dated, KARTA, AO IV/191.
[3] Kołakowski, "Sprawa," 6, 8.   [4] Rokita, speech manuscript, 2.   [5] Ibid., 3–4.

218 Poland's Solidarity Movement & the Politics of Rights

In the decade that followed the end of the Cold War so-called "humanitarian interventions" – overwhelmingly under American leadership – became the hallmark of an era in which the protection of human rights – or at least the claim to do so – trumped the principle of state sovereignty.[6] In the spring of 1991, the UN Security Council passed Resolution 688. Condemning Iraqi repression of Kurds and Shiites as a threat to "international peace and security in the region," it was the first time the Security Council had defined human rights violations occurring within the boundaries of a sovereign state as an international security problem.[7] The United States, Britain, and France saw Resolution 688 as legitimation for Operation Provide Comfort, a militarized humanitarian relief effort for the Kurdish population staged on Iraqi soil, and used their superior air forces to enforce no-fly zones in Iraq. Over the following years, the international community engaged in a series of similar operations, most notably in Somalia in 1993 and in Bosnia in 1995, militarily interfering in the domestic affairs of sovereign states to prevent human rights abuses.[8] Between March 24 and June 10, 1999, NATO undertook Operation Allied Force, a bombing campaign against the Federal Republic of Yugoslavia involving almost 10,500 air strike missions using 12,000 tons of ammunition to prevent ethnic cleansing in the Serbian province of Kosovo.[9]

Though the UN's stance on humanitarian interventions remained contested, the Security Council and General Assembly adopted a string of resolutions in their wake which further undercut the once ironclad principles of state sovereignty and territorial integrity for the sake of an obligation of the international community to protect human rights and

---

[6] Alex J. Bellamy, "The Changing Face of Humanitarian Intervention," *St Antony's International Review* 11 (2015), 1; Matthew Jamison, "Humanitarian Intervention since 1990 and 'Liberal Interventionism'," in Brendan Simms and D. J. B. Trim, eds., *Humanitarian Intervention: A History* (Cambridge et al.: Cambridge University Press, 2011); Fabian Klose, ed., *The Emergence of Humanitarian Intervention: Ideas and Practice from the Nineteenth Century to the Present* (Cambridge: Cambridge University Press, 2016); Jennifer M. Welsh, ed., *Humanitarian Intervention and International Relations* (Oxford: Oxford University Press, 2004).

[7] UN Security Council Resolution 688, April 5, 1991, available at https://documents-dds-ny.un.org/doc/RESOLUTION/GEN/NR0/596/24/IMG/NR059624.pdf?OpenElement (accessed January 2017). For the significance of this resolution see Nicholas J. Wheeler, "The Humanitarian Responsibilities of Sovereignty: Explaining the Development of a New Norm of Military Intervention for Humanitarian Purposes in International Society," in Welsh, ed., *Intervention*, 33–34.

[8] Ibid.; Jamison, "Humanitarian Intervention."

[9] Daniel R. Lake, "The Limits of Coercive Airpower: NATO's 'Victory,'" *International Security* 34 (2009), 1, 83; Mark Webber, "The Kosovo War: A Recapitulation," *International Affairs* 85 (2009), 3, 450. Webber's article is part of a special issue of *International Affairs* on the war in Kosovo.

Epilogue 219

prevent human suffering.[10] A global human rights conference held in Vienna in 1993 revised UN human rights policies and established the office of the UN High Commissioner for Human Rights to centralize and streamline existing procedures. Tribunals to investigate crimes committed in the former Yugoslavia and Rwanda were set up in 1993 and 1994 respectively and in 1998 the UN General Assembly adopted the Rome Statute to establish the International Criminal Court, a permanent tribunal to prosecute genocide, crimes against humanity, and war crimes. In that same year, a Spanish judge issued a warrant under which Chile's former dictator Augusto Pinochet was arrested in London.[11]

Following Operation Allied Force, in which NATO had acted without UN approval, UN General Secretary Kofi Annan called for a discussion to clarify the legal and political implications of humanitarian interventions. In response, the Canadian government appointed an expert body, the International Commission on Intervention and State Sovereignty, or ICISS. Its final report, published in December 2001 and titled *The Responsibility to Protect*, read like the fulfillment of the vision Rokita had sketched in August 1988. Once sovereign states failed to fulfill their responsibility to protect the human rights of its citizens, the ICISS argued, the international community was obliged to step in, with military means if necessary.[12]

The emergence of this post–Cold War world, where human rights have become so powerful and ubiquitous that they even justify military action, was the major impetus for historians to revisit and rewrite the history of human rights over the past decade.[13] It was certainly no accident that, in a seminal text of this historiography, Stefan Hoffmann quoted Geoffrey Barraclough's definition of contemporary history as beginning "when the problems which are actual in the world today first take visible shape ..."[14] In this sense, human rights history is contemporary history *par excellence*. Whether its practitioners look to antiquity, the enlightenment, the

---

[10] Adam Roberts, "The United Nations and Humanitarian Intervention," in Welsh, ed., *Humanitarian Intervention*.

[11] For a polemical, yet informative survey of these developments see Stephen Hopgood, *The Endtimes of Human Rights* (Ithaca, NY: Cornell University Press, 2013), 4–9.

[12] ICISS, *The Responsibility to Protect: Report of the International Commission on Intervention and State Sovereignty*, (Ottawa, 2001); on the document see Manuel Fröhlich, "The Responsibility to Protect," in Klose, ed., *Emergence*.

[13] For a review of this literature, see Robert Brier, "Beyond the Quest for a 'Breakthrough': Reflections on the Recent Historiography on Human Rights," *European History Yearbook* 16 (2015). For recent contributions to this debate see Hoffmann, "Human Rights"; Pamela Slotte and Miia Halme, eds., *Revisiting the Origins of Human Rights* (Cambridge, New York: Cambridge University Press, 2015).

[14] Quoted from his *Introduction to Contemporary History* from 1964 in Hoffmann, "Introduction," 2.

220 Poland's Solidarity Movement & the Politics of Rights

Universal Declaration of Human Rights, or the 1970s, their joint aim is to identify the roots of the human rights norms which, for better or worse, shape our contemporary world.[15]

To some extent this book, too, is contemporary history in this sense. The events and actors described in it were part of a global process in which many of the elements characterizing the post–Cold War era had first taken visible shape. Poland, to be sure, was never bombed by NATO, but the campaign on behalf of Solidarity and political prisoners, making economic cooperation dependent on cessation of human rights violations, anticipated the developments of the 1990s. Besides the more radical means of military force, economic conditionality became an important means of enforcing human rights compliance after 1989, especially by the EU. The human rights record of Central and Eastern European states, in fact, remained under international scrutiny even after the fall of Communism when both NATO and the EU made membership negotiations dependent on respect for individual rights.[16] Ironically, now that Poland and Hungary are established members of the EU, it became much more difficult to get their governments to comply with European legal standards.

The undermining of Poland's sovereignty, to be sure, was by no means a foregone conclusion of a human rights breakthrough in the 1970s, as the Western response to martial law had shown, but the result of social activism. Working to sustain international attention to the plight of Poland's political prisoners, Polish and Western activists had skillfully drawn on the "prisoner of conscience" – a symbolic figure central to a transformation of transnational activism away from campaigns driven by

---

[15] For sample of accounts, arguing from different perspectives, see Philip Alston, "Does the Past Matter? On the Origins of Human Rights," *Harvard Law Review* 126 (2013), 7; Bradley, *World Reimagined*, 1; Eckel, *Ambivalenz*, 9–11; Hoffmann, "Introduction," 1; Hoffmann, "Human Rights," 279–280, 282; Hunt, *Inventing*, 206–230; Keys, *Virtue*, 1; Lauren, *Evolution*, 3–4; Moyn, *Utopia*, 1.

[16] Broadly on human rights conditionality in EU external relations after 1989, see Elena Fierro, *The EU's Approach to Human Rights Conditionality in Practice* (The Hague, London: Martinus Nijhoff, 2003); Lorand Bartels, *Human Rights Conditionality in the EU's International Agreements* (Oxford: Oxford University Press, 2005); with regards to EU membership of post-Communist states see Frank Schimmelfennig, Stefan Engert, and Heiko Knobel, eds., *International Socialization in Europe: European Organizations, Political Conditionality, and Democratic Change* (Basingstoke: Palgrave Macmillan, 2005); Frank Schimmelfennig and Ulrich Sedelmeier, eds., *The Europeanization of Central and Eastern Europe* (Ithaca, NY: Cornell University Press, 2005); Antoaneta Dimitrova and Geoffrey Pridham, "International Actors and Democracy Promotion in Central and Eastern Europe: The Integration Model and its Limits," *Democratization* 11 (2004), 5; on the IMF and the World Bank see Daniel Bradlow, "The World Bank, the IMF, and Human Rights," *Journal of Transnational Law and Contemporary Problems* 6 (1996), 47–90.

Epilogue   221

ideology and solidarity toward a culture of empathy with distant suffering. During the 1990s – accelerated and made ubiquitous by the spread of cable news networks, satellite TV, and the Internet – this culture of compassion became a crucial condition of possibility for humanitarian interventionism. To be sure, the imagery of empathy seems to have changed during the 1990s as the sober human rights report of Amnesty International or the *Chronicle of Current Events* lost importance compared to a source that promised an even more immediate contact with suffering victims – often digital images and film coming directly from war zones. What remained constant, though, was the desire for an unambiguously altruistic activism on behalf of suffering strangers and the idea that "bare facts," now represented in powerful images, reveal a higher form of truth.[17]

Much like the discourse of the prisoner of conscience or the Nobel Prize ceremony for Lech Wałęsa, moreover, this culture was organized around a sacred core according to which some images, groups, or people, rather than others, were selected for "iconization." Much as had been the case with Adam Michnik in his prison cell or with Polish and Chilean emigres in the West, the human rights culture of the 1990s greatly empowered individuals to address the international community, but it also required them to pitch their cause in ways that resonated with the needs and desires – the ideas of "sanctity" – of an ever expanding human rights infrastructure.[18] Wałęsa is maybe one of the best examples of how much the making of icons had to do with the desire of the international community to see its own views reflected and how little with events on the ground. After a term as Poland's president characterized by an erratic leadership style, numerous gaffes, and streaks of authoritarianism, he lost the 1995 presidential election against the cosmopolitan ex-Communist Aleksander Kwaśniewski. Yet though he spent the following decade ostracized from Polish political life, the international community continued to celebrate him as a larger-than-life figure, a hero of the peaceful struggle for human rights.

With the notable exception of Václav Havel, who served as the Czech Republic's president until 2003, many former Soviet bloc dissidents

---

[17] For an illuminating, if polemical discussion, see Hopgood, *Endtimes*, 69–95. See also James Castonguay, "Representing Bosnia: Human Rights Claims and Global Media Culture," in Mark Bradley and Patrice Petro, eds., *Truth Claims: Representation and Human Rights* (New Brunswick, NJ, London: Rutgers University Press, 2002); Wendy Kozol, ed., *Distant Wars Visible: The Ambivalence of Witnessing* (Minneapolis, London: University of Minnesota Press, 2014).

[18] Clifford Bob, *The Marketing of Rebellion: Insurgents, Media, and International Activism* (Cambridge, New York: Cambridge University Press, 2005).

222   Poland's Solidarity Movement & the Politics of Rights

shared Wałęsa's fate. The heirs of East-Central Europe's former Communist rulers shaped the region's history for much of the 1990s. Despite their political misfortunes, however, many ex-dissidents remained influential public intellectuals, working as journalists or academics. Some of the former Commandos, most notably Adam Michnik, built on their experience as editors of illegal underground journals, independent trade union periodicals, and émigré newsletters to turn Solidarity's 1989 electoral newspaper – the *Gazeta Wyborcza* – into one of Central Europe's largest and most influential dailies. They also sustained and extended their contacts to other ex-dissidents, East European émigré circles in the West, and Western intellectuals and politicians. Drawing on their know-how in tapping Western financial support, the ex-dissidents thus established transnational networks of Central European intellectuals who used their clout as international icons to lobby for EU and NATO membership of their countries.[19]

From this position, many former dissidents endorsed armed humanitarian interventions as a continuation of the struggle they had been fighting during the 1970s and 1980s. In 1992, the UN Commission on Human Rights dispatched former Catholic dissident and advisor to Wałęsa Tadeusz Mazowiecki to the successor states of Yugoslavia as its special rapporteur. Understanding his role in a very active and political way, he filed a flurry of reports documenting atrocities and urging the international community to do something against them. In July 1995, a month before the first US bombings, he resigned to protest what he saw as Western inaction in the face of massive atrocities.[20]

Six weeks into the bombing of Serbia in 1999, President Havel addressed the Canadian parliament.[21] Central to his speech was an idea which his intellectual role model, the Czech philosopher Jan Patočka, had articulated in 1977 in an influential interpretation of the Charter 77: "The concept of *human rights* is nothing other than the conviction that states, too, and all of society are placed under the supremacy of moral feeling;

---

[19] Merje Kuus, "Intellectuals and Geopolitics: The 'Cultural Politicians' of Central Europe," *Geoforum* 38 (2007), 2; Kristina Mikulova and Michal Simecka, "Norm Entrepreneurs and Atlanticist Foreign Policy in Central and Eastern Europe: The Missionary Zeal of Recent Converts," *Europe-Asia Studies* 65 (2013), 6; Fredo Arias-King, "Orange People: Liberation Networks in Central and Eastern Europe," *St Antony's International Review* 2 (2007), 2; Jeffrey C. Isaac, "Rethinking the Legacy of Central European Dissidence," *Common Knowledge* 10 (Winter 2004), 1.

[20] Andrzej Brzeziecki, *Tadeusz Mazowiecki: Biografia naszego premiera* (Kraków: Znak Horyzont, 2015), 497–516.

[21] Václav Havel, "Kosovo and the End of the Nation-State," *New York Review of Books*, June 10, 1999.

Epilogue   223

that they recognize something unconditioned, above them ..."[22] Twenty-two years later, the Czech president described the war against Slobodan Milošević's regime as a harbinger of a new global order, an interconnected world in which nation-states gave way to local and global civil societies, for it was, Havel said, "probably the first war that has not been waged in the name of 'national interests,'" but placed "human rights above the rights of the state."[23] Other ex-dissidents, like Michnik, were more nuanced in their views; but overall there was robust support among them for military interventions in the name of human rights.[24]

★★★

Yet for all the continuities from the 1970s onward, it was, to say the least, a long and winding road that led from samizdat journals and letters smuggled out of prison, from American Cold War policies and French intellectual battles, and from trade union campaigns for freedom of association to the humanitarian interventionism of the 1990s. For one, if prominent ex-dissidents flourished in the post–Cold War world, many of their Western supporters did not. When Rokita called the invasion of Grenada a successful example of human rights policies, he was promptly thrown out of his peace organization. His views had upset not only his fellow Polish activists but also many Western guests at the conference, especially the West Germans. Many of them belonged to the Green party's radical left wing around the peace and environmental activist Petra Kelly. In 1982, Kelly had warned that the peace movements would forfeit their moral credibility if they failed to condemn events in Poland. Three years later, she called upon the Greens to imitate dissident anti-politics to transform Western consumer societies. At the time, Kelly had been the charismatic figurehead of the Green party. But as the 1980s wore on, her views were increasingly marginalized until they had become so irrelevant that when her husband killed Kelly in October 1992, it took her party and the German public several weeks to realize she was gone.[25]

The mastermind of the AFL-CIO's campaign for Solidarity, Tom Kahn, had passed away seven months before Kelly from complications resulting from AIDS. A memorial service for him, held in the AFL-CIO's headquarter and partly planned by himself, revived the imagery of his labor activism and struggle against Communism. East European emigres

---

[22] Quoted in Bolton, *Worlds*, 155.   [23] Havel, "Kosovo."
[24] Adam Michnik, "Mantra Rather than Discourse," *Common Knowledge* 8 (2002), 3, 516–525.
[25] Richter, *Die Aktivistin*.

224   Poland's Solidarity Movement & the Politics of Rights

gave eulogies and a trade unionist invoked Kahn's mentors – Bayard Rustin and Max Shachtman.[26] Yet with Kahn, this peculiar brand of social democracy, combining labor policies with a doctrinaire anti-Communism, was laid to rest. Three years later, internal rebels ousted Kahn's former boss Lane Kirkland as president of the AFL-CIO, charging that, having spent too much energy on international affairs, he had failed to halt labor's decline.[27] Freedom of association does not seem to have had a major impact on post–Cold War human rights debates as East European countries adopted the neoliberal consensus after 1989.

A less noticeable but similarly profound change occurred in France. Michel Foucault had died on June 25, 1984. Claude Lefort and Pierre Rosanvallon, meanwhile, both enjoyed academic success during the 1980s. Toward the end of the 1990s, in a book-length essay, Lefort reiterated his insistence that the totalitarian experience was central to modern political thought and history. Yet the threat he was writing against was not anymore the etatism of the traditional French Left, but the radical individualism of neoliberalism.[28] How precisely democracy was to be organized in opposition to totalitarianism, moreover, had long since ceased to be associated with the ideals of *autogestion*. Already in 1988, Rosanvallon had penned what Samuel Moyn and Andrew Jainchill fittingly describe as an autopsy of this idea.[29] "The word 'autogestion' crossed the political sky of the 1970s like a meteor," he wrote. Yet its "disappearance was as brutal as its ascension had been rapid." The "flag of 'socialisme autogestionnaire',," Rosanvallon explained, had helped the non-Communist Left to shed its negative, anti-totalitarian identity for something more positive.[30] But by 1988, this positive vision had little resemblance with what Rosanvallon had described as "the living practice of a true democracy" more than 10 years before.[31] *Autogestion*, he now shrugged, had helped socialists accept the market, by "putting in some way a left-wing label on issues of management [préoccupations managérials]" and it had rehabilitated individual rights for left-wing political thought. "That is not nothing."[32]

A year before Rosanvallon's article, Bernard Kouchner, the cofounder of Doctors without Borders whom Foucault had joined in 1982 to bring

---

[26] Horowitz, "Tom Kahn," 244–245; Elizabeth Kastor, "A Death in the Office: AIDS took Tom Kahn," *Washington Post*, Aug. 12, 1992.

[27] Puddington, *Kirkland*, 292–308.

[28] Claude Lefort, *Complications: Communism and the Dilemmas of Democracy* (New York, Chichester: Columbia University Press, 2007).

[29] Jainchill and Moyn, "French Democracy," 116.

[30] Pierre Rosanvallon, "Autogestion," *le débat* 50 (May–Aug. 1988).

[31] Rosanvallon, *L'âge*, 42–45.   [32] Rosanvallon, "Autogestion," 192.

Epilogue 225

food and medical supplies to Poland, co-organized a conference on morality and international law in Paris. Fourteen years before the *Responsibility to Protect*, Kouchner demanded at the meeting that the Universal Declaration of Human Rights be amended "in the name of a morality of extreme urgency, in the name of the duty to intervene. The *right of humanitarian intervention* has to be added to the Universal Declaration of Human Rights."[33]

In many ways, the conference evolved out of the 1970s anti-totalitarian moment: Alongside South African Bishop Desmond Tutu, Wałęsa had assumed the symbolic chairmanship over the meeting, which was attended by eminent anti-totalitarian intellectuals. The book in which the conference's proceedings were published, titled *The Duty of Interference: Can We Let them Die?*, featured as its motto a quote from Foucault saying that the work of NGOs like Amnesty International had created the "right of private individuals to intervene effectively in the order of international policies and strategies."[34]

But though drawing on the anti-totalitarian discourse, the conference signaled a profound change in the French imagery of human rights. Unlike Lefort in his seminal human rights article of 1980, Kouchner did not talk about courageous dissidents who taught French intellectuals how "to decipher the meaning of political practice."[35] He wrote about victims, "men, women, children crying out for help"; he did not write about intellectuals who might have something interesting to say, but those "who lack a voice of their own [n'ont pas de voix au chapitre]"; he did not see himself as someone's intellectual "brother in arms," as Lefort had done, but as a doctor of a suffering patient, as someone who, due to his superior knowledge, could assist an essentially helpless person.[36] Where Lefort had understood the "human" in human rights to mean an essentially social and political being, Kouchner – one of the world's most outspoken supporters of humanitarian interventions – looked upon humans in isolation with suffering as their sole characteristic.[37]

These changes in the French imagery of human rights may also point to ways in which the global culture of compassion changed after 1989.

---

[33] Mario Bettati and Bernard Kouchner, *Le devoir d'ingérence: Peut-on les laisser mourir?* (Paris: Denoël, 1987), 10.
[34] Kouchner. *Le devoir*, 7; Macey, *Lives*, 438.   [35] Lefort, *Forms*, 272.
[36] Bettati and Kouchner, *Le devoir*, 10–11.
[37] On Kouchner and humanitarian interventionism see Tim Allen and David Styan, "A Right to Interfere? Bernard Kouchner and the New Humanitarianism," *Journal of International Development* 12 (2000), 6; on this movement more broadly, see Davey, *Idealism*.

226   Poland's Solidarity Movement & the Politics of Rights

Amnesty International's focus on political dissent and the defense of individual conscience, embodied by heroic, largely male adults, gave way to a concern for suffering caused by war and ethnic cleansing, represented by images of women and especially children, symbols of innocent suffering and the need for protection.[38]

Maybe one of the most profound changes occurred in the thinking of the dissidents themselves. In the 1970s, they had discovered human rights as means to free human beings from the collective lie of the totalitarian system, a means of turning isolated individuals into citizens taking control of their collective fate. The occupied factories of August 1980, reimagined as a modern-day agora, seemed to put this vision into practice. But as they came to work with their compatriots, encountering visions of religion and nationhood deeply at odds with their own, many dissidents had second thoughts. By the end of the 1980s, they had come to believe that democracy required not only the political liberation from totalitarianism but also a collective psychotherapy of sorts in which, under the guidance of enlightened elites, Poland's *homines sovietici* would shed the habits and states of mind Communist rule had ingrained in them.[39]

Those Polish activists who had seen human rights as merely a continuation of Poland's historic struggle for independence, on the other hand, quickly came to rediscover the value of noninterference and sovereignty when international NGOs and the EU threatened the "natural social structures" necessary for human development – the nation, the Church, and the family. Chief among them was, alas, Rokita. After 2015, some of these former dissident activists came to power in Poland to implement policies curtailing the independence of the media and the judiciary.

But if the dissidents' understandings of human rights had changed by the 1990s, the same seems to be true for the human rights movement's standard bearer – Amnesty International. By the mid-1980s, Jan Eckel shows, Amnesty seemed to have run its course – its second campaign against torture did not catch on, it was incapable of solving its internal problems, and the gulf between its leadership and rank-and-file seemed to widen. If the organization made a spectacular comeback, it was only at the prize of organizing an actual spectacle – a tour of rock concerts called *Conspiracy of Hope* and *Human Rights Now!* By striking an alliance with the shrill world of 1980s pop culture, Amnesty was effectively turned into

---

[38] Hopgood, *Endtimes*, 69–73.

[39] See, for instance, Adam Michnik, "Three Kinds of Fundamentalisms" and "The Strange Epoch of Post-Communism: A Conversation with Václav Havel," both in Adam Michnik, *Letters from Freedom: Post-Cold War Realities and Perspectives* (Berkeley et al.: University of California Press, 1998).

Epilogue 227

a youth organization and entered a sphere that was worlds apart from the sternness and culture of suffering that had hitherto been the organization's hallmark.[40] How exactly this transformation of the organization's membership changed Amnesty remains to be explored. Yet the gulf between its pacifist letter writing campaigns of the 1960s and NATO's bombing campaigns of the 1990s seems rather obvious.

★★★

Where does all of this leave us with regards to the question of the origins of human rights? Given that there are as many differences, ruptures, and changes as there are similarities and continuities between the 1990s and previous decades, has the energy invested into the many studies of the 1970s been misspent? Should we concentrate our efforts on the post–Cold War era, the "real" age of human rights?[41] The fierce debate on the periodization of human rights history would suggest as much, given how it is dominated by presentations of clear-cut alternatives between competing decades as the origins of human rights. Solidarity's story suggests a different conclusion. For it is not one of how human rights acquired a precise meaning, came to be associated with one form of activism, and crowded out other social causes. It is, rather, the story of human rights as a contested source of authority which was associated with a wide variety of causes and mingled with different concerns. And this contestedness of human rights language, its adaptability to new circumstances and aims, is at least as important a continuity the 1990s share with previous times as the culture of compassion or the undermining of sovereignty.

For one, even after the end of the Cold War, human rights remained wedded to questions of citizenship, democracy, and national belonging. When the EU set out criteria for membership it did not make a difference between compliance with human rights norms and the adoption of democratic institutions – an approach well grounded in how the Universal Declaration of Human Rights or the human rights covenant of 1966 had enshrined democratic rights. The World Conference of Human Rights' Vienna Declaration of 1993, too, linked human rights to democracy, self-determination as well as to a host of other, group-specific causes such as a right to development or the rights of women.[42] Some of the most successful human rights campaigns of our own time,

---

[40] Eckel, *Ambivalenz*, 423–434.
[41] This seems to be the argument of Hoffmann, "Human Rights."
[42] "Vienna Declaration and Program of Action: Adopted by the World Conference on Human Rights in Vienna on 25 June 1993," available at www.ohchr.org/EN/ProfessionalInterest/Pages/Vienna.aspx (accessed February 2017).

moreover, focus on questions of gender and sexual orientation. As heavily as they draw on the vernacular of human rights, they evolved out of the discovery of group solidarity – complete with a collective identity celebrated on Christopher Street day, in gay pride parades, and LGBTQ history months – and they are primarily about the struggle for full citizenship and civil equality, most notably the right to enjoy the legal recognition and benefits of marriage. Foucault and Lefort would probably have abhorred of the LGBTQ movement's legalist strategy and celebration of a traditional institution like marriage, while the movement's view of sexuality would have clashed with the at times conservative views of many dissidents. But the approach of using human rights language to create and enlarge communities shows palpable similarities to the work of the dissidents and their French supporters.

Questions of national belonging, too, continued to play into human rights work after the end of the Cold War. The Yugoslav wars of succession, after all, were triggered by movements for national independence, and the bombing campaigns of 1995 and 1999 were followed by sustained and protracted projects of nation-building.[43] For someone like Rokita, national independence and human rights were but two sides of the same process. Even as he rejected the principle of noninterference as a sanctuary of tyranny, he was fiercely patriotic nonetheless. He and others sharing his view strongly believed that a government for and by the Polish people would enable them to claim and enjoy their rights. Only once an illegitimate group, like the Communists, had taken power would the international community need to step in. To some extent, this was also the core idea of the ICISS. The "responsibility to protect," it argued, fell primarily to national governments. Only once they failed to fulfill it or acted against it, was the international community supposed to step in.

In some ways, the human rights policies of the 1990s may have ended up strengthening the importance of nation-states. The resolutions and moral appeals of the global human rights community remained largely impotent if they were not enforced by economically affluent and militarily powerful states. Havel may have seen the bombing of Serbia as a harbinger of a world in which the nation-state gave way to global and local civil societies. Others saw the perceived need for humanitarian interventions as a confirmation that their nation-state was exceptional and had a historic mission to fulfill. "If we have to use force," US Secretary of State Madeleine Albright famously said in 1998, "it is

---

[43] James Dobbins, *America's Role in Nation-Building: From Germany to Iraq* (Santa Monica, CA: RAND, 2003), 87–128.

Epilogue 229

because we are America! We are the indispensable nation. We stand tall, and we see further into the future."[44]

A week before Havel spoke in Ottawa, British Prime Minister Tony Blair addressed the Economic Club in Chicago. Like the Czech president, he sketched an image of an "interdependent world" where everyone was an internationalist whether they liked it or not and the international community could not turn its back "on the violation of human rights within other countries."[45] Being the occupant of Downing Street 10, though, he hardly predicted the withering of the nation-state for the sake of a global civil society. In fact, a clear national interest was one of five criteria he believed could help decide if a humanitarian intervention should be undertaken.[46]

The very erosion of the principles of territorial integrity and sovereignty at the hands of human rights may thus have paradoxically reinforced the value of nation-states, at least of powerful ones. For what the actual practice of human rights drew into question was not so much sovereignty as such, but the sovereignty of small, weak, and poor states – a point driven home when Russian policies in Chechnya went largely unsanctioned and the United States refused to ratify the Statute of Rome to establish the ICC. In an era of global human rights policies and humanitarian law, statelessness may not be as problematic anymore as it was when Hannah Arendt equated the loss of citizenship with the loss of rights in her *Origins of Totalitarianism*.[47] Yet the impression many people around the world must have taken away from the actual application of human rights norms after 1989 must have been that the safest guarantee of their rights was still citizenship of a democratic, affluent, and militarily powerful nation-state under the rule of law.

If human rights continued to be intertwined with questions of citizenship and nationality, they may have become even more clearly associated with a specific political project after 1989 than they were in Amnesty International's 1970s activism or Jimmy Carter's human rights crusade. Blair's speech in Chicago was a seminal text of "liberal internationalism." Like Albright, he saw human rights as one building block, a crucial one to

---

[44] Quoted in G. John Ikenberry, *Liberal Leviathan: The Origins, Crisis, and Transformation of the American World Order* (Princeton, NJ: Princeton University Press, 2011), 278, nt. 35.
[45] Tony Blair, "Doctrine of the International Community," delivered at the Economic Club, Chicago, April 22, 1999, text available at www.globalpolicy.org/component/content/article/154/26026.html (accessed July 2020).
[46] On Blair, see Oliver Daddow, "'Tony's War'? Blair, Kosovo and the Interventionist Impulse in British Foreign Policy," *International Affairs* 85 (2009), 3.
[47] Hannah Arendt, *The Origins of Totalitarianism* (New York: Harcourt, 1968), 295–298; see also Natalie Oman, "Hannah Arendt's 'Right to Have Rights': A Philosophical Context for Human Security," *Journal of Human Rights* 9 (2010), 3.

be sure, for the construction what G. John Ikenberry calls a "liberal international order" – a global community of states organized around representative democracy, the rule of law, market economies, and global trade.[48] The expansion of the EU was a similar project. Unlike Willy Brandt and other postwar social democrats, who had seen democracy and human rights as the contingent outcomes of long-term processes of change, the architects of the liberal international order believed that Western economic and political institutions were transferable through the sophisticated design of political and economic institutions.[49]

Putting human rights into this context is not to say that they were mere tools in the hands of clever politicians or ideological fig leaves for hegemonic projects. They did exert normative constraints and shaped foreign policies and international institutions. Yet, for better or worse, they became part of a project which Ikenberry aptly describes as the externalization and attempted globalization of the West's internal order of the Cold War.[50] A month into its bombing campaign of Serbia, on April 23, 1999, NATO issued a statement describing the repression of the Albanian population of Kosovo as "a fundamental challenge to the values for which NATO has stood since its foundation: democracy, human rights, and the rule of law."[51] By enforcing human rights, NATO claimed, it had not left behind Cold War divisions to place itself under a universal set of values – it merely fought for what it had been fighting for all along. The interventionism of the 1990s, it seems, had less in common with Carter's human rights crusade, let alone Amnesty International's world-weariness, than with the views of Reagan and the Jackson Democrats on the link between human rights, democracy promotion, and Western military might.

★ ★ ★

This book, then, hopefully, helped understand how "some of the problems that are actual in the world today first took visible shape" – a global culture of compassion with distant suffering, an erosion of sovereignty, democracy promotion. But I would insist that understanding the projects and ideas that did *not* make it into "the world today" or appear as mere

---

[48] G. John Ikenberry, "Liberal Internationalism 3.0: America and the Dilemmas of Liberal World Order," *Perspectives on Politics* 7 (2009), 1; Ikenberry, *Liberal Leviathan*.

[49] Giuseppe Di Palma, *To Craft Democracies: An Essay on Democratic Transitions* (Berkeley et al.: University of California Press, 1990); Adam Przeworski and Fernando Limongi, "Modernization: Theory and Facts," *World Politics* 49 (1997), 2.

[50] Ikenberry, *Leviathan*, 222.

[51] William J. Clinton, Joint Statement on Kosovo, available www.presidency.ucsb.edu/ws/index.php?pid=57449 (accessed February 2020).

Epilogue

retrograde forces in it – social self-organization in a totalitarian state, nationalism, *autogestion*, freedom of association – may hold at least as important conclusions for the history of human rights. For what they show is that, if human rights were to become "actual in the world," they had to resonate with existing concerns, help reformulate them, and prove their usefulness in pursuing them.

Having explored various contexts in which human rights did resonate with existing concerns and proved useful, this book confirmed existing accounts that for many North Americans and Western Europeans of the 1970s, human rights proved useful and significant because they promised an *ersatz* for failed utopias and dried up sources of idealism. But it also showed that for many more people, human rights were useful only if they could prevail in the mundane world of social struggle and political conflict. And chief among those people were those who invoked human rights to protect themselves – the dissidents. As they did, they reinterpreted human rights and applied them to their own lifeworld, creating a specific human rights vernacular in the process. This specific human rights language may not have played a great role after 1989, but vernacularization itself is a constant feature of human rights history. The fact that "human rights" meant something different to early modern French revolutionaries than to the drafters of the Universal Declaration of Human Rights or to 1970s activists of Amnesty International than to Tony Blair does not show that some of these epochs and actors do not properly belong in the history of human right; it reveals something crucial about human rights – their malleability to different interpretations and their contested nature.

To some extent, this is true for all ideas that travel through time. Yet different ideas pose this problem in different ways. The semantic core of human rights since at least the late 1940s was the notion that there are some goods to which human beings are entitled simply and solely because they are human beings. What was thus left open was what these goods were, what hierarchy might exist among them, when and how they could be claimed, and – most crucially – what human beings were and what kind of world they inhabited. Different answers, especially to the latter questions, could make human rights more or less appealing and, crucially, also more or less plausible. In Willy Brandt's conceptual world, delineated as it was by broad time horizons and long historical processes, the moral absolutism of the dissidents' appeals was not morally wrong so much as unreasonable. A crucial context for the resurgence of human rights during and after the 1970s was how "History" ceased to provide a backdrop for political thought.

Once human rights claims did become plausible, they emerged as a powerful source of authority and "symbolic power" – the ability to control what can and cannot be said in political discourse. That was what made them uniquely attractive for Soviet bloc dissidents. Under the rule of a state seemingly capable of destroying truth itself, the categorical and absolute nature of human rights provided a firm grounding for the dissidents' quest for democracy. But this aspect also rendered human rights useful for people in less dramatic circumstances – French intellectuals looking for radical democratic alternatives to classic socialism, a US president seeking to revive American self-confidence, trade unionists trying to salvage Cold War liberalism. Precisely because human rights have the power to place certain aims – whether private property or freedom of association – beyond the grasp of politics will they continue to be contested sources of authority.

The history of human rights, it thus seems, is not about the quest for the moment or decade when they took on a definite meaning and established clear-cut social practices. It is about the conditions under which an idea, whose pedigree reaches back past the 1970s and probably also the 1940s, became plausible and useful and was reinterpreted as historical actors adapted it to their needs.

None of this entails a normative statement as to what place human rights should have in international affairs or domestic life. Historians are not in the business of defining what an idea or norm *ought* to mean. Our job is to delineate what it *did* mean to specific historical actors during specific times. Yet precisely in this might lie an important contribution history can make to political theory and debate. For by reconstructing the many ways in which ideas came to acquire new meanings and provide sources of hope and inspiration can historians help intellectuals and philosophers reimagine such ideas and turn them into sources of hope again.[52] Maybe, then, this book will have made a small contribution to sustaining human rights' ability to kindle hope the same way they did for a group of former student radicals as they were released from prison to make do in the inimical world of 1970s state socialism.

---

[52] Quentin Skinner, "Meaning and Understanding in the History of Ideas," *History and Theory* 8 (1969), 1, 52–53.

Bibliography

Archival Sources

AFL-CIO Unprocessed Records
  Free Trade Union Institute
  International Affairs Department
  Office of the President
Archiv der sozialen Demokratie (AdsD), Bonn
  Arbeitsgemeinschaft Dienste für den Frieden (AGDF)
  DGB-Archiv
  Nachlass Walter Polkehn (NL Polkehn)
  SPD-Parteivorstand/Internationale Abteilung (SPD-PV/Int. Abt.)
  Willy-Brandt-Archiv (WBA)
Archiv Grünes Gedächtnis (AGG), Berlin
  Bündnis '90/Die Grünen Bundestagsfraktion (B.II.2)
  Die Grünen im Bundestag 1983-1990 (B.II.1)
  Petra-Kelly-Archiv (PKA)
  Nachlass Rudolf Bahro (NL Bahro)
  Nachlass Wilhelm Knabe (NL Knabe)
Archives de la CGT-Force Ouvrière (CGT-FO), Centre de documentation Gabriel Ventejol, Paris
  Circulaires confederales
  Dossier Pologne I, 1974–1990
  Fond Marc Blondel
Archives du Secrétariat Confédéral CFDT (CFDT), Paris
  Direction Internationale et Europe (DIE)
  Fond Edmond Maire
  Secteur International (Sect. Int.)
Archiwum Akt Nowych (AAN), Warsaw
  Archiwum Komitetu Centralnego Polskiej Zjednoczonej Partii Robotniczej (KC PZPR)
  Polski Instytut Spraw Międzynarodowych (PISM)
Archiwum Instytutu Pamięci Narodowej (AIPN), Warsaw
  Akta Ministerstwa Spraw Wewnętrznych
Archiwum Opozycji, Ośrodek KARTA (KARTA), Warsaw
  "Solidarność" – Narodziny Ruchu
  Kolekcje osobiste, tematyczne i środowiskowe

234   Bibliography

Associations Solidarité France-Pologne (ASFP), Private Archive, Paris
Charles E. Young Research Library, University of California, Los
Angeles, CA
Susan Sontag Papers, 1933–2004
Committee in Support of Solidarity Records (CSS Records), accessed
at the Institute for Democracy in Eastern Europe, Washington, DC
George Meany Memorial Archive (GMMA), Silver Spring, Maryland
(in 2013 transferred to the library of the University of Maryland,
College Park, MD)
AFL-CIO Executive Council Minutes, 1955–1996 (RG4-006)
Information Department. CIO, AFL-CIO Press Releases, 1937–1995
(RG20-003)
Lane Kirkland Papers, 1863–1998 (RG95-007)
Hoover Institution Archives (HIA), Stanford, CA
Poland: Służba Bezpieczeństwa Departament III Collection
Romuald Spasowski Papers 1929–1995
Zdzisław Najder Papers 1959–1994
International Institute for Social History (IISH), Amsterdam
ETUC Archives (ETUC)
ICFTU Archives (ICFTU)
Patrick Serand Collection
The National Archives (TNA), London, United Kingdom
The Prime Minister's Office Records (PREM)
National Security Archives (NSA), George Washington University,
Washington, DC
FOIA Documents on U.S. Policies toward Poland Requested by
Gregory Domber
National Endowment for Democracy Collection
Soviet Flashpoints (Originals) Poland 1980-82-Incoming FOIAs
Soviet Flashpoints – Poland 1989 Cables
Ronald Reagan Presidential Library, Simi Valley, California (RRPL)
White House Office of Records Management (WHORM) Subject File
White House Staff Member and Office Files

Digital Collections

Amnesty International Annual Reports, accessed from www.amnesty.org/en/
latest/research/?contentType=2564&documentType=Annual+Report&sort=
date&p=5 (last accessed April 2017).
Documents on U.S. Neoconservatives, Compiled by Justin Vaïsse, accessed at
http://neoconservatism.vaisse.net/doku.php?id=start (last accessed June 2016).
NATO Archives, Documents Related to Events in Poland (1980–1984),
accessed at www.nato.int/cps/en/natolive/81233.htm (last accessed April
2017).
The Public Papers of Ronald Wilson Reagan, accessed at https://reaganlibrary
.archives.gov/archives/speeches/publicpapers.html#.V1WApZGLQ2w (last
accessed June 2016).

Bibliography   235

Soviet Archive, Collected by Vladimir Bukovsky, accessed at http://bukovsky-archives.net/ (last accessed April 2017).
U.S. Department of State, Virtual Reading Room, accessed at https://foia.state.gov/search/search.aspx (last accessed May 2016).
Wirtualna Czytelnia Bibuły – Encyklopedia Solidarności, accessed at www.encyklopedia-solidarnosci.pl/wiki/index.php?title=WCB_Strona_g%C5%82%C3%B3wna (last accessed April 2017).
Xronika tekuščix sobytij, accessed at http://old.memo.ru/history/diss/chr/index.htm (last accessed April 2017).

Published Collections of Documents

Akten zur Auswärtigen Politik der Bundesrepublik Deutschland, vols. 1980–1985. München: Oldenbourg, 2011–2016.
Dąbrowski, Franciszek, et al., eds. *Marzec 1968 w dokumentach MSW*, 2 vols. Warszawa: IPN, 2008.
"Document 1: The Note of Ministry of Foreign Affairs on Experiences So Far with the Model of Visits by Western Politicians," and "Document 2: 1987, October 19 Excerpt from the Protocol of the Session of the Secretariat of the CC of the PUWP." *Cold War History* 3, no. 3 (2003), 130–141.
"Dotyczy: działalności amerykańskich związków zawodowych AFL-CIO oraz kanałów wywierania wpływu na wydarzenia w Polsce." *Wolność i Solidarność* 4 (2012), 154–159.
Dudek, Antoni, ed. *Zmierzch dyktatury: Polska lat 1986–1989 w świetle dokumentów*, 2 vols. Warszawa: IPN, 2013.
Dudek, Antoni, and Andrzej Friszke, eds. *Polska 1986–1989: Koniec systemu*, vol. 3, Dokumenty. Warszawa: Trio/ISP PAN, 2002.
"The First Solidarity Congress." *World Affairs* 145, no. 1 (1982), 20–61.
Friszke, Andrzej, and Marcin Zaremba, eds. *Wizyta Jana Pawła II w Polsce 1979: Dokumenty KC PZPR i MSW*. Warszawa: Biblioteka "Więzi", 2005.
Hemmerling, Zygmunt, and Marek Nadolski, eds. *Opozycja demokratyczna w Polsce 1976-1980. Wybór dokumentow*. Warszawa: Wydawnictwo Uniwersytetu Warszawskiego, 1994.
Jastrzębski, Andrzej, ed. *Dokumenty Komitetu Obrony Robotników i Komitetu Samoobrony Społecznej 'KOR'*. Warszawa, London: Aneks, 1994.
Kamiński, Łukasz, and Paweł Piotrowski, eds. *Opozycja demokratyczna w Polsce w świetle akt KC PZPR (1976-1980): Wybór dokumentów*. Wrocław: Gajt, 2002.
Kamiński, Łukasz, and Grzegorz Waligóra, eds. *Kryptonim "Pegaz": Służba Bezpieczeństwa wobec Towarzystwa Kursów Naukowych 1978-1980*. Warszawa: Instytut Pamięci Narodowej, 2008.
Kryptonim "Wasale": Służba Bezpieczeństwa wobec Studenckich Komitetów Solidarnosci 1977-1980. Warszawa: Instytut Pamięci Narodowej, 2007.
Kryptonim "Gracze": Służba Bezpieczeństwa wobec Komitetu Obrony Robotników i Komitetu Samoobrony Społecznej "KOR". Warszawa: Instytut Pamięci Narodowej, 2010.
Kowalik, Tadeusz, ed. *Stanisław Gomułka i transformacja polska: Dokumenty i analizy 1968-1989*. Warszawa: Scholar, 2010.

236 Bibliography

Kubina, Michael, Manfred Wilke, and Reinhardt Gutsche, eds. *"Hart und kompromisslos durchgreifen": Die SED contra Polen 1980/81. Geheimakten der SED-Führung über die Unterdrückung der polnischen Demokratiebewegung.* Berlin: Akademie, 1995.

Lammich, Siegried. *Proces przeciwko zabójcom ks. Jerzego Popiełuszki: Relacja obserwatora i dokumenty.* London: Polonia, 1986.

Listy pasterskie episkopatu Polski 1945-1975. Paris: Éditions du dialogue, 1975.

Mastny, Vojtech, and Malcolm Byrne. *A Cardboard Castle? An Inside History of the Warsaw Pact, 1955-1991.* New York: Central European University Press, 2005.

"Notatka protokolarna z rozmowy Zespołu Dobrych Usług z 'jedenastką' 12 maja 1984 r." *Wolność i Solidarność* 4, no. 133–139 (2012).

Nowak, Jan, and Jerzy Giedroyc. *Listy 1952-1998.* Edited by Dobrosława Platt (Wrocław: Tow. Przyjaciół Ossolineum, 2001).

Pasierb, Bronisław, ed. *NSZZ "Solidarność" 1980-1981.* Wrocław: Wydawnictwo Uniwersytetu Wrocławskiego, 1990.

Paczkowski, Andrzej, and Malcolm Byrne, eds. *From Solidarity to Martial Law: The Polish Crisis of 1980-1981 - A Documentary History.* Budapest, New York: Central European University Press, 2007.

Perzkowski, Stanisław, ed. *Tajne dokumenty Biura Politycznego i Sekretariatu KC: Ostatni rok władzy 1988-1989.* London: Aneks, 1994.

Pleskot, Patryk, ed. *Solidarność, "Zachód" i "Węże": Służba Bezpieczeństwa wobec emigracyjnych struktur Solidarności 1981-1989.* Warszawa: IPN, 2011.

PZPR a Solidarność 1980-1981: Tajne dokumenty Biura Politycznego. Warszawa: IPN, 2013.

Raina, Peter, ed. *Arcybiskup Dąbrowski: Rozmowy z władzami PRL.* Warszawa: "Książka Polska", 1995.

Savranskaya, Svetlana, Thomas S. Blanton, and Vladislav Zubok, eds. *Masterpieces of History: The Peaceful Soviet Withdrawal from Eastern Europe, 1989.* New York, Budapest: CEU Press, 2010.

Skórzyński, Jan. "'List 59' i narodziny opozycji demokratycznej w Polsce." *Zeszyty Historyczne* vol. 163 (2008), 137–158.

Waligóra, Grzegorz, ed. *Dokumenty uczestników Ruchu Obrony Praw Człowieka i Obywatela w Polsce 1977-1981.* Kraków: Księgarnia Akademicka, 2005.

Włodek, Zbigniew ed. *Tajne dokumenty Biura Politycznego: PZPR a "Solidarność" 1980-1981.* London: Aneks Publishers, 1992.

Published Speeches and Political and Philosophical Writings

Aarvik, Egil. 1983. Lech Walesa Award Ceremony Speech. In *Nobelprize.org*, www.nobelprize.org/nobel_prizes/peace/laureates/1983/presentation-speech .html (accessed Jul. 21, 2012).

Albertz, Heinrich. "Es gibt nichts Wichtigeres als den Frieden: Ein Interview." In *Verantwortlich für Polen?*, edited by Heinrich Böll, Freimut Duve and Klaus Staeck. (Reinbek bei Hamburg: Rowohlt, 1982), 18–24.

Bibliography 237

Bahr, Egon . July 15, 1963. "Wandel durch Annäherung," speech given at the *Evangelische Akademie Tutzing*, available at http://www.fes.de/archiv/adsd_neu/inhalt/stichwort/tutzinger_rede.pdf (accessed May 2016).

Bell, Daniel. *The End of Ideology: On the Exhaustion of Political Ideas in the Fifties* (Glencoe, IL,: Free Press, 1960).

Bender, Peter. *Das Ende des ideologischen Zeitalters: Die Europäisierung Europas* (Berlin: Severin und Siedler, 1981).

Bettati, Mario, and Bernard Kouchner. *Le devoir d'ingérence: Peut-on les laisser mourir?* (Paris: Denoël, 1987).

Blumsztajn, Seweryn. *Je rentre au pays: Polonais, juif, membre du KOR et de Solidarité, Questions d'actualité* (Paris: Calmann-Lévy, 1985).

Bonhoeffer, Dietrich. *Wybór pism.* Translated by Anna Morawska (Warszawa: Biblioteka "Więzi", 1970).

Bourdieu, Pierre. "Die Intellektuellen und die Macht." In *Michel Foucault: Eine Geschichte der Wahrheit.* (München: Raben, 1987), 98–103.

Political Interventions: Social Science and Political Action, edited by Franck Poupeau and Thierry Discepolo (London, New York: Verso, 2008).

Brandt, Willy. *Berliner Ausgabe*, 10 vols., edited by Helga Grebing et al. (Berlin: J.H.W. Dietz, 2000–2009).

Koexistenz: Zwang zum Wagnis (Stuttgart: DVA, 1963).

Menschenrechte mißhandelt und mißbraucht (Reibeck bei Hamburg: Rowohlt, 1987).

The Ordeal of Coexistence. (Cambridge, MA: Harvard University Press, 1963).

Cywiński, Bohdan. *Rodowody niepokornych* (Warszawa: Biblioteka 'Więzi', 1971).

Foucault, Michel. *Dits et écrits : 1954-1988.* Vol. 4: 1980-1988 (Paris: Editions Gallimard, 1994).

Furet, François. *The Passing of an Illusion: The Idea of Communism in the Twentieth Century* (Chicago, London: University of Chicago Press, 1997).

Interpreting the French Revolution (Cambridge: Cambridge University Press, 1981).

Glucksmann, Andre. *La cuisinière et le mangeur d'hommes: Essai sur les rapports entre l'état, le marxisme et les camps de concentration* (Paris: Éditions du Seuil, 1975).

The Master Thinkers (New York: Harper & Row, 1980).

Hamon, Hervé, and Patrick Rotman. *La deuxième gauche: Histoire politique et intellectuelle de la CFDT.* 2nd ed. (Paris: Ramsay, 1984).

Havel, Václav. "The Power of the Powerless." *International Journal of Politics* vol. 15, no. 3/4 (1985), 23–96.

Moc bezmocných (Praha: Edice Ptelice [samizdat], 1979).

International Commission for Intervention and State Sovereignty. *The Responsibility to Protect: Report of the International Commission on Intervention and State Sovereignty.* (Ottawa: International Development Research Center, 2001).

Kelly, Petra. "Für eine Solidarność des Friedens." In *Politische Reden*, edited by Marie-Luise Recker. (Frankfurt am Main: Deutscher Klassiker Verlag, 1990), 738–743.

Kirkpatrick, Jeane J. *Legitimacy and Force: Political and Moral Dimensions*, 2 vols. (New Brunswick, NJ: Transaction, 1988).

238 Bibliography

Kołakowski, Leszek. *Leben trotz Geschichte*. (München: Piper, 1977).

Main Currents of Marxism: Its Rise, Growth, and Dissolution. Translated by P. S. Falla, 3 vols. (Oxford: Clarendon Press, 1978).

"Marxist Roots of Stalinism." In *Stalinism: Essays in Historical Interpretation*, edited by Robert C. Tucker and Włodzimierz Brus. (New York: Norton, 1977), 283–298.

"My Correct Views on Everything." *Socialist Register* 11 (1974): 1–20.

Kuroń, Jacek. *Opozycja: Pisma polityczne 1969-1989* (Warszawa: Wydawnictwo Krytyki Politycznej, 2010).

Kuroń, Jacek, and Karol Modzelewski. *An Open Letter to the Party* (London: Socialist Review Publishers, 1968).

Lefort, Claude. *Complications: Communism and the Dilemmas of Democracy*. (New York; Chichester: Columbia University Press, 2007).

Democracy and Political Theory (Cambridge: Polity, 1988).

"La première révolution antitotalitaire." In *1956: Varsovie-Budapest - La deuxième révolution d'Octobre*, edited by Pierre Kende and Krzysztof Pomian. (Paris: Seuil, 1978), 93–99.

L'invention démocratique: Les limites de la domination totalitaire (Paris: Fayard, 1981).

Éléments d'une critique de la bureaucratie. 2nd ed. (Paris: Gallimard, 1979).

The Political Forms of Modern Society: Bureaucracy, Democracy, Totalitarianism. Translated by John B. Thompson (Cambridge: Polity, 1986).

Un homme en trop: Réflexions sur "L'Archipel du Goulag" (Paris: Éditions du Seuil, 1976).

Lévy, Bernard-Henri. *Barbarism with a Human Face*. Translated by George Holoch (New York: Harper, 1979).

Testament of God (New York: Harper & Row, 1980).

Mazowiecki, Tadeusz. *Rozdroża i wartości* (Warszawa: Biblioteka "Więzi", 1970).

Michnik, Adam. *The Church and the Left*. Translated and ed. by David Ost (Chicago, London: Chicago University Press, 1993).

Kościół - lewica - dialog (Paris: Instytut literacki, 1977).

Letters from Freedom: Post-Cold War Realities and Perspectives, edited by Irena Grudzińska-Gross (Berkeley, Los Angeles, London: University of California Press, 1998).

Letters from Prison and Other Essays (Berkeley: University of California Press, 1985).

L'Église et la Gauche : le dialogue polonais (Paris: Éditions du Seuil, 1979).

"The Moral and Spiritual Origins of Solidarity." In *Without Force of Lies. Voices from the Revolution of Central Europe in 1989-1990*, edited by William M. Brinton and Alan Rinzler. (San Francisco: Mercury House, 1990), 239–252.

Penser la Pologne: Morale et politique de la résistance, edited by Zinaida Erard (Paris: La Découverte, 1983).

Szanse polskiej demokracji (London: Aneks, 1984).

Takie czase...rzecz o kompromisie (London: Aneks, 1985).

Z dziejów honoru w Polsce: Wypisy więzienne (Paris: Instytut Literacki, 1985).

Diabeł naszego czasu. Publicystyka z lat 1985-1994 (Warszawa: Oficyna Naukowa, 1995).

Bibliography 239

Novak, Michael. *The Spirit of Democratic Capitalism* (New York: Simon & Schuster, 1982).

Patočka, Jan. "Was die Charta 77 ist und was sie nicht ist." In *Zivilgesellschaft und Menschenrechte im östlichen Europa: Tschechische Konzepte der Bürgergesellschaft im historischen und nationalen Vergleich*, edited by Robert Luft, Miloš Havelka, and Stefan Zwicker (Göttingen: Vandenhoeck & Ruprecht, 2014), 384–389, at 387.

Powszechna Deklaracja Praw Człowieka: W językach polskim, białoruskim, czeskim, litewskim, rosyjskim, słowackim, ukraińskim. (Paris: Instytut Literacki, 1974).

Reagan, Ronald. *The Public Papers of President Ronald Wilson Reagan*, available at https://reaganlibrary.archives.gov/archives/speeches/publicpapers.html#.VztNuJGLQ2w (last accessed May 2016)

Rosanvallon, Pierre. *L'âge de l'autogestion* (Paris: Éditions du Seuil, 1976).

Rosanvallon, Pierre, and Patrick Viveret. *Pour une nouvelle culture politique* (Paris: Éditions du Seuil, 1977).

Sachs, Jeffrey, and David Lipton. "Creating a Market Economy in Eastern Europe: The Case of Poland." *Brookings Papers on Economic Activity* vol. 1 (1990), 75–145.

Sartre, Jean-Paul. *The Communists and Peace, with an Answer to Claude Lefort.* Translated by Irene Clephane (London: Hamilton, 1969).

Schell, Jonathan. "Introduction." In Adam Michnik, *Letters From Prison and Other Essays*, edited by Irena Grudzińska-Gross. (Berkeley: University of California Press, 1985), xvii–xlii.

Schlesinger Jr., Arthur M. *The Vital Center: The Politics of Freedom* (Cambridge, MA: Riverside Press, 1949).

Solzhenitsyn, Alexander. *Archipelag GUŁag* (Paris: Instytut Literacki, 1974).

Tischner, Józef. *The Spirit of Solidarity* (San Francisco, London: Harper & Row, 1984).

Wałęsa, Lech. 1983. Nobel Acceptance Speech. In *Nobelprize.org*, http://www.nobelprize.org/nobel_prizes/peace/laureates/1983/walesa-acceptance.html (accessed July 21, 2012).

1983. Nobel Lecture. In *Nobelprize.org*, http://www.nobelprize.org/nobel_prizes/peace/laureates/1983/walesa-lecture.html (accessed Jul. 21, 2012).

Wesołowski, Włodzimierz, ed. *Losy idei socjalistycznych i wyzwania współczesności.* (Warszawa: Polskie Towarzystwo Współpracy z Klubem Rzymskim, 1990).

Published Diaries and Memoirs

Balcerowicz, Leszek. *Trzeba się bić* (Warszawa: Wydawnictwo Czerwone i Czarne, 2014).

Błażejowska, Justyna. *Harcerską drogą do niepodległości: Od "Czarnej Jedynki" do Komitetu Obrony Robotników. Nieznana historia KOR-u i KSS "KOR"* (Kraków: Arcana, 2016).

Brandt, Willy. *Erinnerungen* (Zürich: Propyläen, 1989).

Geremek, Bronisław. "Doradcy i więźniowie." *Wolność i Solidarność* vol. 4 (2012), 113–130.

240 Bibliography

Kuroń, Jacek. *Autobiografia* (Warszawa: Wydawnictwo Krytyki Politycznej, 2011).

Modzelewski, Karol. "Włoski łącznik." *Wolność i Solidarność* vol. 4 (2012), 154–159.

Zajeździmy kobyłę historii: Wyznania poobijanego jeźdźca (Warszawa: Iskry, 2013).

Novak, Michael. *Writing from Left to Right: My Journey from Liberal to Conservative* (New York: Image, 2013).

Rakowski, Mieczysław F. *Dzienniki polityczne, 1976-1978* (Warszawa: Iskry, 2002).

Dzienniki polityczne, 1979-1981. Wyd. 1st ed. (Warszawa: Iskry, 2004).

Dzienniki polityczne, 1981-1983 (Warszawa: Iskry, 2004).

Dzienniki polityczne, 1984-1986 (Warszawa: Iskry, 2005).

Dzienniki polityczne, 1987-1990. Wyd. 1st ed. (Warszawa: Iskry, 2005).

Romaszewski, Zbigniew, Zofia Romaszewska, Agnieszka Romaszewska-Guzik, and Piotr Skwieciński. *Romaszewscy: Autobiografia* (Warszawa: trzecia strona, 2014).

Schmidt, Helmut. *Menschen und Mächte.* Vol. II: Die Deutschen und ihre Nachbarn (Berlin: Siedler, 1990).

Tischner, Józef, Adam Michnik, and Jacek Żakowski. *Między Panem a Plebanem* (Kraków: Znak, 1995).

Newspapers, Magazines, Journals

American Federationist
Aneks
Atlanta Constitution
Blätter für deutsche und internationale Politik
Boston Globe
CFDT Aujourd'hui
CFDT Syndicalisme Hebdo
CFDT Magazine
Chicago Tribune
Christian Science Monitor
Commentary
Democratyia
Dwadzieścia Jeden [samizdat]
Economist
Esprit
Foreign Affairs
Frankfurter Allgemeine Zeitung
Free Trade Union News
Freie Gewerkschaftswelt
Guardian
Karta [samizdat]
Kommune
KOS [samizdat]

Bibliography   241

Krytyka [samizdat]
Kultura
Le Débat
Le Matin
Le Monde
Le Nouvel Observateur
Les Temps Modernes
Neue Gesellschaft/Frankfurter Hefte
New America
New Republic
New York Times
Observer
Peace and Democracy News
Socialist Register
Socialisme ou Barbarie
Soho News
South China Morning Post
Spectator
Spiegel
Stern
Survey
Syndicalisme Hebdo
Telos
Times
Times of India
Tygodnik Mazowsze [samizdat]
Tygodnik Solidarność
Tygodnik Wojenny [samizdat]
Village Voice
Voice
Vorwärts
Wiadomości [samizdat]
Washington Post
Więź
World Affairs
Zeit

Interviews

Blumsztajn, Seweryn, Nov. 25, 2009, Warsaw, Poland.
Chenoweth, Eric, Feb.23, 2010, Washington, DC, USA.
Grudzińska, Irena, Nov. 21, 2010, Los Angeles, CA, USA.
Lasota, Irena, Mar. 9, 2010, Washington, DC, USA.
Sachs, Karol and Krystyna Vinaver, Dec. 7, 2009, Paris, France.
Smolar, Aleksandr, Dec. 8, 2009, Paris, France.
Weber, Elisabeth, Aug. 4, 2010, Cologne, Germany.

242   Bibliography

Secondary Sources

Alberska, Małgorzata. *Ośrodki emigracji polskiej wobec kryzysów politycznych w kraju (1976-1981)*. Wrocław: Arboretum, 2000.

Alberska, Małgorzata, and Rafał Juchnowski. "Z dziejów polskiej emigracji politycznej po II wojnie światowej." In *Polska i Polacy poza granicami kraju w polskiej polityce i myśli politycznej XX wieku*, edited by Małgorzata Alberska and Rafał Juchnowski. Wroclaw: Wydawnictwo Uniwersytetu Wrocławskiego, 2006, 11–54.

Alekseeva, Lyudmila. *Soviet Dissent: Contemporary Movements for National, Religious, and Human Rights*. Middletown, CT: Wesleyan University Press, 1985.

Allen, Tim, and David Styan. "A Right to Interfere? Bernard Kouchner and the New Humanitarianism." *Journal of International Development* 12, no. 6 (2000): 825–842.

Allitt, Patrick. *Catholic Intellectuals and Conservative Politics in America, 1950-1985*. Ithaca, NY, London: Cornell University Press, 1993.

The Conservatives: Ideas and Personalities Throughout American History. New Haven, CT: Yale University Press, 2009.

Alston, Philip. "The Commission on Human Rights." In *The United Nations and Human Rights: A Critical Appraisal*, edited by Philip Alston. Oxford: Clarendon Press, 1992, 126–210.

"Does the Past Matter? On the Origins of Human Rights." *Harvard Law Review* 126, no. 7 (2013): 2043–2081.

Altrichter, Helmut, and Hermann Wentker, eds. *Der KSZE-Prozess: Vom Kalten Krieg zu einem neuen Europa 1975 bis 1990, Zeitgeschichte im Gespräch*. München: Oldenbourg, 2012.

Anderes, Cord. "Neu gelesen: Auf der Suche nach dem roten Faden. Jürgen Habermas' Lesarten der europäischen Moderne in unübersichtlichen Zeiten." *Zeithistorische Forschungen/Studies in Contemporary History, Online edition* 7, no. 1 (2010). From: https://zeithistorische-forschungen.de/1-2010/4394 (last accessed January 2021).

Angster, Julia. "'Safe by Democracy': American Hegemony and the 'Westernization' of West German Labor." *Amerikastudien/American Studies* 46, no. 4 (2001): 557–572.

Arendt, Hannah. *The Origins of Totalitarianism*. New York: Harcourt, 1968.

Arias-King, Fredo. "Orange People: Liberation Networks in Central and Eastern Europe." *St Antony's International Review* 2, no. 2 (2007): 40–63.

Arndt, Agnes. *Rote Bürger: Eine Milieu- und Beziehungsgeschichte linker Dissidenz in Polen (1956-1976)*. Göttingen: Vandenhoeck & Ruprecht, 2013.

Bakuniak, Grzegorz, and Krzysztof Nowak. "The Creation of a Collective Identity in a Social Movement: The Case of 'Solidarność' in Poland." *Theory and Society* 16, no. 3 (1987): 401–429.

Bange, Oliver, and Gottfried Niedhart, eds. *Helsinki 1975 and the Transformation of Europe*. New York: Berghahn Books, 2008.

Barrera, Manuel, and J. Samuel Valenzuela. "The Development of Labor Movement Opposition to the Military Regime." In *Military Rule in Chile: Dictatorship and Oppositions*, edited by Manuel Barrera and J. Samuel

Bibliography 243

Valenzuela. Baltimore, MD: Johns Hopkins University Press, 1986, 230–269.

Bartels, Lorand. *Human Rights Conditionality in the EU's International Agreements*. Oxford: Oxford University Press, 2005.

Bartnik, Czesław. *Chrześcijańska nauka o narodzie według Prymasa Stefana Wyszyńskiego*. Lublin: Wydawnictwo KUL, 1982.

Bellamy, Alex J. "The Changing Face of Humanitarian Intervention." *St Antony's International Review* 11, no. 1 (2015): 15–43.

Bevan, Ruth A. "Petra Kelly: The Other Green." *New Political Science* 23, no. 2 (2001): 181–202.

Biernacki, Leszek. "Początki Wolnych Związków Zawodowych Wybrzeża." *Wolność i Solidarność* 5 (2013): 50–62.

Bob, Clifford. *The Marketing of Rebellion: Insurgents, Media, and International Activism*. Cambridge, New York: Cambridge University Press, 2005.

Boll, Friedhelm. "Zwischen politischer Zurückhaltung und humanitärer Hilfe: Der Deutsche Gewerkschaftsbund und Solidarność 1980-1982." In *Solidargemeinschaft und Erinnerungskultur im 20. Jahrhundert: Beiträge zu Gewerkschaften, Nationalsozialismus und Geschichtspolitik*, edited by Ursula Bitzegeio, Anja Kruke and Meik Woyke. Bonn: Dietz, 2009, 199–218.

Boll, Friedhelm, and Krzysztof Ruchniewicz, eds. *"Nie mehr eine Politik über Polen hinweg": Willy Brandt und Polen*. Bonn: J.H.W. Dietz, 2010.

Boll, Friedhelm, and Małgorzata Świder. "The FRG: Humanitarian Support without Great Publicity." In *Solidarity with Solidarity: Western European Trade Unions and the Polish Crisis, 1980-1982*, edited by Idesbald Goddeeris. Lanham: Lexington, 2010, 159–189.

Bolton, Jonathan. *Worlds of Dissent: Charter 77, the Plastic People of the Universe, and Czech Culture under Communism*. Cambridge, MA: Harvard University Press, 2012.

Bon, Tempo, and J. Carl. "Antikommunistische Menschenrechte: Die Republikanische Partei und die Menschenrechtspolitik in den späten 1970er Jahren." In *Moral für die Welt? Menschenrechtspolitik in den 1970er Jahren*, edited by Jan Eckel and Samuel Moyn. Göttingen: Vandenhoeck & Ruprecht, 2012, 290–315.

"From the Center-Right: Freedom House and Human Rights in the 1970s and 1980s." In *The Human Rights Revolution: An International History*, edited by Akira Iriye, Petra Goedde and William I. Hitchcock. Oxford, New York: Oxford University Press, 2012, 223–244.

Borstelmann, Thomas. *The 1970s: A New Global History from Civil Rights to Economic Inequality of America in the World*. Princton, NJ: Princeton University Press, 2011.

Bourdieu, Pierre. *Language and Symbolic Power*. Cambridge: Polity Press, 1991.

Bourg, Julian. *From Revolution to Ethics: May 1968 and Contemporary French Thought*. Montreal, et al.: Mc Gill-Queen's University Press, 2007.

Bradley, Mark Philip. "American Vernaculars: The United States and the Global Human Rights Imagination." *Diplomatic History* 38, no. 1 (2014): 1–21.

"Approaching the Universal Declaration of Human Rights." In *The Human Rights Revolution: An International History*, edited by Akira Iriye, Petra

244 Bibliography

Goedde and William I. Hitchcock. Oxford, New York: Oxford University Press, 2012, 327–343.

The World Reimagined: Americans and Human Rights in the Twentieth Century. Cambridge: Cambridge University Press, 2016.

Bradlow, Daniel. "The World Bank, the IMF, and Human Rights." *Journal of Transnational Law and Contemporary Problems* 6 (1996): 47–90.

Brands, H. W. *What America Owes the World: The Struggle for the Soul of Foreign Policy.* New York: Cambridge University Press, 1998.

Brands, Hal. *Making the Unipolar Moment: U.S. Foreign Policy and the Rise of the post-Cold War Order.* Ithaca, NY: Cornell University Press, 2016.

Bresselau von Bressensdorf, Agnes. *Frieden durch Kommunikation: Das System Genscher und die Entspannungspolitik im Zweiten Kalten Krieg 1979-1982/83.* Berlin, Boston, MA: de Gruyter, 2015.

Brier, Robert. "Beyond the Quest for a "Breakthrough": Reflections on the Recent Historiography on Human Rights." *European History Yearbook* 16 (2015): 155–174.

"Broadening the Cultural History of the Cold War: The Emergence of the Polish Workers' Defense Committee and the Rise of Human Rights." *Journal of Cold War Studies* 15 no. 4 (2013): 104–127.

"Tod eines Priesters: Der Erinnerungskult um Jerzy Popiełuszko aus global-historischer Perspektive." In *Osteuropäische Geschichte und Globalgeschichte,* edited by Julia Obertreis and Martin Aust. Stuttgart: Franz Steiner Verlag, 2014, 259–282.

"Entangled Protest: Dissent and the Transnational History of the 1970s and 1980s." In *Entangled Protest: Transnational Approaches to the History of Dissent in Eastern Europe and the Soviet Union,* edited by Robert Brier. Osnabrück: Fibre, 2013, 11–42.

Brier, Robert, ed. *Entangled Protest: Transnational Perspectives on the History of Dissent in Eastern Europe and the Soviet Union.* Osnabrück: Fibre, 2013.

Bright, Christopher. "Neither Dictatorships nor Double Standards: The Reagan Administration's Approach to Human Rights." *World Affairs* 153, no. 2 (1990): 51–80.

Brink, Cornelia. *Ikonen der Vernichtung: Öffentlicher Gebrauch von Fotografien aus nationalsozialistischen Konzentrationslagern nach 1945.* Berlin: Akademie, 1998.

Brown, Archie. *The Gorbachev Factor.* Oxford, England; New York: Oxford University Press, 1996.

Seven Years that Changed the World: Perestroika in Perspective. Oxford, New York: Oxford University Press, 2007.

Brown, Bernard E. *Socialism of a Different Kind: Reshaping the Left in France.* Westport, CT, London: Greenwood Press, 1982.

Brzeziecki, Andrzej. *Tadeusz Mazowiecki: Biografia naszego premiera.* Kraków: Znak Horyzont, 2015.

Buchanan, Tom. "'The Truth Will Set You Free:' The Making of Amnesty International." *Journal of Contemporary History* 37, no. 4 (2002): 575–597.

Buntman, Fran Lisa. *Robben Island and Prisoner Resistance to Apartheid.* Cambridge, UK; New York: Cambridge University Press, 2003.

Bibliography

Burke, Roland. *Decolonization and the Evolution of International Human Rights.* Philadelphia: University of Pennsylvania Press, 2010.

"Human Rights Day after the 'Breakthrough': Celebrating the Universal Declaration of Human Rights at the United Nations in 1978 and 1988." *Journal of Global History* 10, no. 01 (2015): 147–170.

Castonguay, James. "Representing Bosnia: Human Rights Claims and Global Media Culture." In *Truth Claims: Representation and Human Rights*, edited by Mark Bradley and Patrice Petro. New Brunswick, NJ, London: Rutgers University Press, 2002, 157–186.

Cenckiewicz, Sławomir, and Piotr Gontarczyk. *SB a Lech Wałęsa. Przyczynek do biografii.* Gdańsk: IPN, 2008.

Chappel, James. "Slaying the Leviathan: Catholicism and the Rebirth of European Conservatism, 1920-1950." Ph.D. thesis, Columbia University, 2012.

Chenoweth, Eric. "The Gallant Warrior: In Memoriam Tom Kahn." *Uncaptive Minds* 5, no. 2 (1992): 5–16.

"Poland Today: Democracy Aborning." *Freedom at Issue* 7 (1988): 10–13.

Chiampan, Andrea. "'Those European Chicken Littles': Reagan, NATO, and the Polish Crisis, 1981–2." *The International History Review* 37 (2014): 1–18.

Christofferson, Michael Scott. *French Intellectuals Against The Left: The Antitotalitarian Moment of the 1970s.* New York, Oxford: Berghahn Books, 2004.

Chwalba, Andrzej. *Czasy "Solidarności": Francuscy związkowcy i NSZZ "Solidarność" 1980-1990.* Kraków: Księgarnia Akademicka, 1997.

Chwalba, Andrzej, and Frank Georgi. "France: Exceptional Solidarity?" In *Solidarity with Solidarity: Western European Trade Unions and the Polish Crisis, 1980-1982*, edited by Idesbald Goddeeris. Lanham: Lexington, 2010, 191–218.

Ci, Jiwei. "Conscience, Sympathy, and the Foundation of Morality." *American Philosophical Quarterly* 28, no. 1 (1991): 49–59.

Ciżewska, Elżbieta. *Filozofia publiczna Solidarności: Solidarność 1980-1981 z perspektywy republikańskiej tradycji politycznej.* Warszawa: Narodowe Centrum Kultury, 2010.

Clark, Ann Marie. *Diplomacy of Conscience: Amnesty International and Changing Human Rights Norms.* Princeton, NJ, Oxford: Princeton University Press, 2001.

Cmiel, Kenneth. "The Emergence of Human Rights Politics in the United States." *The Journal of American History* 86, no. 3 (1999): 1231–1250.

Cohen, Jean L. "Rethinking the Politics of Human Rights with and beyond Lefort." In *Claude Lefort: Thinker of the Political*, edited by Martín Plot. Basingstoke: Palgrave-Macmillan, 2013, 124–135.

Critchlow, Donald T. *The Conservative Ascendancy: How the GOP Right Made Political History.* Cambridge, MA: Harvard University Press, 2007.

Cronin, James E. *Global Rules: America, Britain and a Disordered World.* New Haven, CT: Yale University Press, 2014.

Daddow, Oliver. "'Tony's War'? Blair, Kosovo and the Interventionist Impulse in British Foreign Policy." *International Affairs* 85, no. 3 (2009): 547–560.

246   Bibliography

Davey, Eleanor. *Idealism Beyond Borders: The French Revolutionary Left and the Rise of Humanitarianism, 1954-1988.* Cambridge: Cambridge University Press, 2015.

De Solidarność à l'entrée de la Pologne dans l'Union europénne: Un engagement citoyen. Paris: Association Solidarité France-Pologne, 2008.

Delton, Jennifer. "Rethinking Post-World War II Anticommunism." *The Journal of The Historical Society* 10, no. 1 (2010): 1–41.

Di Palma, Giuseppe. *To Craft Democracies: An Essay on Democratic Transitions.* Berkeley et al.: University of California Press, 1990.

Dietz, Hella. *Polnischer Protest: Zur pragmatistischen Fundierung von Theorien sozialen Wandels.* Frankfurt, New York: Campus, 2015.

Dimitrova, Antoaneta, and Geoffrey Pridham. "International Actors and Democracy Promotion in Central and Eastern Europe: The Integration Model and its Limits." *Democratization* 11, no. 5 (2004): 91–112.

Dobbins, James. *America's Role in Nation-Building: From Germany to Iraq.* Santa Monica, CA: RAND, 2003.

Doering-Manteuffel, Anselm, and Lutz Raphael. *Nach dem Boom: Perspektiven auf die Zeitgeschichte seit 1970.* Göttingen: Vandenhoeck & Ruprecht, 2008.

Doering-Manteuffel, Anselm, Lutz Raphael, and Thomas Schlemmer, eds. *Vorgeschichte der Gegenwart: Dimensionen des Strukturbruchs nach dem Boom.* Goettingen: Vandenhoeck & Ruprecht, 2016.

Domber, Gregory F. *Empowering Revolution: America, Poland, and the End of the Cold War.* Chapel Hill: University of North Carolina Press, 2014.

"Supporting the Revolution: America, Democracy, and the End of the Cold War in Poland, 1981-1989." PhD thesis, George Washington University, 2007.

"Transatlantic Relations, Human Rights, and Power Politics." In *Perforating the Iron Curtain: European Détente, Transatlantic Relations, and the Cold War, 1965-1985*, edited by Poul Villaume and Odd Arne Westad. Copenhagen: Museum Tusculanum Press, 2010, 195–214.

Donnelly, Jack. *Universal Human Rights in Theory and Practice.* 3rd ed. Ithaca, NY: Cornell University Press, 2013.

Dudek, Antoni. *Reglementowana rewolucja: Rozpad dyktatury komunistycznej w Polsce 1988-1990.* Warszawa: Arcana, 2004.

"Wstęp." In *Stan wojenny w Polsce 1981-1983*, edited by Antoni Dudek. Warszawa: IPN, 2003, 7–26.

Eckel, Jan. *Die Ambivalenz des Guten: Menschenrechte in der internationalen Politik seit den 1940ern.* Göttingen: Vandenhoeck & Ruprecht, 2014.

"The International League for the Rights of Man, Amnesty International, and the Changing Fate of Human Rights Activism from the 1940s through the 1970s." *Humanity* 4, no. 2 (2013): 183–214.

"'Under the Magnifying Glass': The International Human Rights Campaign Against Chile in the Seventies." In *Human Rights in the Twentieth Century*, edited by Stefan-Ludwig Hoffmann. Cambridge: Cambridge University Press, 2011, 321–342.

Eckel, Jan, and Samuel Moyn, eds. *The Breakthrough: Human Rights in the 1970s.* Philadelphia: University of Pennsylvania Press, 2013.

Bibliography

Ehrman, John. *The Rise of Neoconservatism: Intellectuals and Foreign Affairs, 1945-1994*. New Haven, CT: Yale University Press, 1995.

Eisler, Jerzy. *Polski rok 1968*. Warszawa: IPN, 2006.

English, Robert D. *Russia and the Idea of the West: Gorbachev, Intellectuals, and the End of the Cold War*. New York: Columbia University Press, 2000.

Ensalaco, Mark. *Chile under Pinochet: Recovering the Truth*. Philadelphia: University of Pennsylvania Press, 2000.

Falk, Barbara J. *The Dilemmas of Dissidence in East-Central Europe: Citizen Intellectuals and Philosopher Kings*. Budapest: Central European University Press, 2003.

Fantasia, Rick, and Kim Voss. *Hard Work: Remaking the American Labor Movement*. Berkeley: University of California Press, 2004.

Feldman, Burton. *The Nobel Prize: A History of Genius, Controversy, and Prestige*. 1st ed. New York: Arcade Pub., 2000.

Ferguson, Niall, et al., eds. *The Shock of the Global: The 1970s in Perspective*. Cambridge, MA: Harvard University Press, 2011.

Fierro, Elena. *The EU's Approach to Human Rights Conditionality in Practice*. The Hague, London: Martinus Nijhoff, 2003.

Flood, Patrick James. *The Effectivenes of UN Human Rights Institutions*. Westport, CT: Praeger, 1998.

Flynn, Bernard. *The Philosophy of Claude Lefort: Interpreting the Political*. Evanston, IL: Northwestern University Press, 2005.

Foot, Rosemary. "The Cold War and Human Rights." In *The Cambridge History of the Cold War*, vol. III, edited by Melvyn P. Leffler and Odd Arne Westad. Cambridge: Cambridge University Press, 2010, 445–465.

Friend, Julius Weis. *The Long Presidency: France in the Mitterrand Years, 1981-1995*. Boulder, CO.: Westview Press, 1998.

Friszke, Andrzej. *Anatomia buntu: Kuroń, Modzelewski i komandosi*. Kraków: Znak, 2010.

Czas KOR-u : Jacek Kuroń a geneza Solidarności. Kraków: Znak, ISP PAN, 2011.

Oaza na Kopernika : Klub Inteligencji Katolickiej, 1956-1989. Warszawa: Biblioteka "Więzi", 1997.

Opozycja polityczna w PRL 1945-1980. London: Aneks, 1994.

Polska Gierka. Warszawa: Wydawnictwa Szkolne i Pedagogiczne, 1995.

Rewolucja Solidarności 1980-1981. Kraków: Znak, 2014.

Friszke, Andrzej, ed. *Solidarność podziemna 1981-1989*. Warszawa: ISP PAN/ Stowarzyszenie "Archiwum Solidarności", 2006.

Fröhlich, Manuel. "The Responsibility to Protect." In *The Emergence of Humanitarian Intervention: Ideas and Practice from the Nineteenth Century to the Present*, edited by Fabian Klose. Cambridge: Cambridge University Press, 2015, 281–298 (2015/11/24).

Frybes, Marcin. "Solidarność-CFDT: L'expérience d'un dialogue Est-Ouest." *La Revue de la CFDT* 3 (1997): 9–26.

"Społeczne reakcje Zachodu na fenomen 'Solidarności' i rola emigracyjnych struktur związku 1980-1989." In *NSZZ Solidarność 1980-1989*, vol. 2: Ruch społeczny, edited by Łukasz Kamiński and Grzegorz Waligór. Warszawa: IPN, 2010, 505–574.

248   Bibliography

Furci, Carmelo. "The Chilean Communist Party (PCCh) and Its Third Underground Period, 1973-1980." *Bulletin of Latin American Research* 2, no. 1 (1982): 81–95.

Galenson, Walter. *The American Labor Movement, 1955-1995 of Contributions in Labor Studies,*. Westport, CT: Greenwood Press, 1996.

Garton Ash, Timothy. *The Magic Lantern: The Revolution of '89 Witnessed in Warsaw, Budapest, Berlin, and Prague.* New York: Random House, 1990.

Gawin, Dariusz. *Wielki zwrot: Ewolucja lewicy i odrodzenia idei społeczeństwa obywatelskiego.* Kraków: Znak, 2013.

Gebert, Konstanty. *Magia słów: Polityka francuska wobec Polski po 13 grudnia 1981 r.* London: Aneks, 1991.

Geenens, Raf. "Democracy, Human Rights and History: Reading Lefort." *European Journal of Political Theory* 7, no. 3 (2008): 269–286.

"'When I Was Young and Politically Engaged...': Lefort on the Problem of Political Commitment." *Thesis Eleven* 87, no. 1 (2006): 19–32.

Georgi, Frank. "Jeux d'ombres: Mai, le mouvement social et l'autogestion (1968-2007)." *Vingtième Siècle* 98 (2008): 29–41.

"Le monde change, changeons notre syndicalisme: La crise vue par la CFDT (1973-1988)." *Vingtième Siècle* 84 (2004): 93–105.

Glaessner, Gert-Joachim. *Die andere deutsche Republik: Gesellschaft und Politik in der DDR.* Opladen: Westdeutscher Verlag, 1989.

Gleason, Abbott. *Totalitarianism: The Inner History of the Cold War.* New York: Oxford University Press, 1995.

Glendon, Mary Ann. *A World Made New: Eleanor Roosevelt and the Universal Declaration of Human Rights.* New York: Random House, 2001.

Glucksmann, Andre. *La cuisinière et le mangeur d'hommes: Essai sur les rapports entre l'état, le marxisme et les camps de concentration.* Paris: Éditions du Seuil, 1975.

The Master Thinkers. New York: Harper & Row, 1980.

Goddeeris, Idesbald. "Lobbying Allies? The NSZZ Solidarność Coordinating Office Abroad, 1982–1989." *Journal of Cold War Studies* 13, no. 3 (2011): 83–125.

Goddeeris, Idesbald, ed. *Solidarity with Solidarity: Western European Trade Unions and the Polish Crisis, 1980-1982.* Lanham: Lexington, 2010.

Golder, Ben. "Foucault and the Unfinished Human of Rights." *Law, Culture and the Humanities* 6, no. 3 (2010): 354–374.

Grabowski, Tomek. "The Party That Never Was: The Rise and Fall of the Solidarity Citizens' Committees in Poland." *East European Politics and Societies* 10, no. 2 (1996): 214–254.

Graczyk, Roman. *Od uwikłania do autentyczności: Biografia polityczna Tadeusza Mazowieckiego.* Poznań: Zysk i S-ka, 2015.

Grant, Kevin. "British Suffragettes and the Russian Method of Hunger Strike." *Comparative Studies in Society and History* 53, no. 1 (2011): 113–143.

Habermas, Jürgen. "The New Obscurity: The Crisis of the Welfare State and the Exhaustion of Utopian Energies." *Philosophy & Social Criticism* 11, no. 2 (1986): 1–18.

Hatzfeld, Hélène. "Une révolution culturelle du parti socialiste dans les années 1970?" *Vingtième Siècle* 96 (2007): 77–90.

Bibliography

Haustein, Lydia. *Global Icons: Globale Bildinszenierung und kulturelle Identität.* Göttingen: Wallstein, 2008.

Hersh, Burton. *Edward Kennedy: An Intimate Biography.* Berkeley, CA: Counterpoint, 2010.

Heyde, Veronika. "Nicht nur Entspannung und Menschenrechte: Die Entdeckung von Abrüstung und Rüstungskontrolle durch die französische KSZE-Politik." In *Der KSZE-Prozess: Vom Kalten Krieg zum neuen Europa 1975 bis 1990*, edited by Helmut Altrichter and Hermann Wentker. München: Oldenbourg, 2012, 83–98.

Hoffmann, Stefan-Ludwig. "Human Rights and History." *Past & Present* 232, no. 1 (2016): 279–310.

"Introduction: Genealogies of Human Rights." In *Human Rights in the Twentieth Century*, edited by Stefan-Ludwig Hoffmann. Cambridge: Cambridge University Press, 2011, 1–28.

Hopgood, Stephen. *The Endtimes of Human Rights.* Ithaca, NY: Cornell University Press, 2013.

Keepers of the Flame: Understanding Amnesty International. Ithaca, NY: Cornell University Press, 2006.

Horowitz, Rachelle. "Tom Kahn and the Fight For Democracy: A Political Portrait and Personal Recollection." *Democratiya* 11 (2007): 204–251.

Horvath, Robert. "Breaking the Totalitarian Ice: The Initiative Group for the Defense of Human Rights in the USSR." *Human Rights Quarterly* 36, no. 1 (2014): 147–175.

The Legacy of Soviet Dissent: Dissidents, Democratisation and Radical Nationalism in Russia. London: Routledge, 2005.

"'The Solzhenitsyn Effect': East European Dissidents and the Demise of the Revolutionary Privilege." *Human Rights Quarterly* 29 (2007): 879–907.

Howard, Dick. "Claude Lefort: A Political Biography." In *Claude Lefort: Thinker of the Political*, edited by Martín Plot. Basingstoke: Palgrave-Macmillan, 2013, 15–22.

The Specter of Democracy. New York: Columbia University Press, 2002.

Hunt, Lynn. *Inventing Human Rights: A History.* New York: W.W. Norton & Co., 2007.

Ikenberry, G. John. "Liberal Internationalism 3.0: America and the Dilemmas of Liberal World Order." *Perspectives on Politics* 7, no. 1 (2009): 71–87.

Liberal Leviathan: The Origins, Crisis, and Transformation of the American World Order. Princeton, NJ: Princeton University Press, 2011.

Ingram, James D. "The Politics of Claude Lefort's Political: Between Liberalism and Radical Democracy." *Thesis Eleven* 87, no. 1 (2006): 33–50.

Isaac, Jeffrey C. "Critics of Totalitarianism." In *The Cambridge History of Twentieth Century Political Thought*, edited by Terence Ball and Richard Bellamy. Cambridge: Cambridge University Press, 2003, 181–201.

"Rethinking the Legacy of Central European Dissidence." *Common Knowledge* 10, no. 1 (2004): 119–130.

Jainchill, Andrew, and Samuel Moyn. "French Democracy between Totalitarianism and Solidarity: Pierre Rosanvallon and Revisionist Historiography." *The Journal of Modern History* 76, no. 1 (2004): 107–154.

250   Bibliography

James, Mel. "The Country Mechanisms of the United Nations Commission on Human Rights." In *The Universal Declaration of Human Rights: Fifty Years and Beyond*, edited by Yael Danieli, Elsa Stamatopoulu and Clarence J. Dias. Amityville, NY: Baywood, 1999, 75–84.

Jamison, Matthew. "Humanitarian Intervention since 1990 and 'Liberal Interventionism'." In *Humanitarian Intervention: A History*, edited by Brendan Simms and D. J. B. Trim. Cambridge: Cambridge University Press, 2011, 365–380.

Jarząbek, Wanda. "A Growing Problem: The Polish People's Republic and the Problem of Human Rights in the Context of the CSCE Process, 1975-1983." In *Entangled Protest: Transnational Perspectives on the History of Dissent Eastern Europe and the Soviet Union*, edited by Robert Brier. Osnabrück: Fibre, 2013, 129–149.

"Hope and Reality: Poland and the Conference on Security and Cooperation in Europe, 1964-1989," Cold War International History Project, no. Working Paper # 56 (2007), Woodrow Wilson Center, Washington DC.

Jaworski, Paweł, and Łukasz Kamiński, eds. *Świat wobec Solidarności 1980-1989*. Warszawa: IPN, 2014.

Jensen, Steven L.B. *The Making of International Human Rights: The 1960s, Decolonization and the Reconstruction of Global Values*. Cambridge: Cambridge University Press, 2016.

Jesse, Eckhard, ed. *Totalitarismus im 20. Jahrhundert: Eine Bilanz der internationalen Forschung*, 2nd ed. Bonn: Bundeszentrale für politische Bildung, 1999.

Johnstone, Diana. "How the French Left Learned to Love the Bomb." *New Left Review* I, no. 146 (1984): 5–36.

Judt, Tony. *Past Imperfect: French Intellectuals, 1944-1956*. Berkeley: University of California Press, 1992.

Postwar: A History of Europe Since 1945. New York: Penguin, 2005.

Kant, Immanuel. The Metaphysics of Morals. In *Cambridge Texts in the History of Philosophy*, edited by Mary J. Gregor. Cambridge, New York: Cambridge University Press, 1996.

Kaufman, Edy. "Prisoners of Conscience: The Shaping of a New Human Rights Concept." *Human Rights Quarterly* 13, no. 3 (1991): 339–367.

Kelly, Patrick William. "Sovereignty and Salvation: Transnational Human Rights Activism in the Americas in the Long 1970s." PhD thesis, University of Chicago, 2015.

Kemp-Welch, Anthony. *Poland under Communism: A Cold War History*. Cambridge: Cambridge University Press, 2008.

Kenna, Margaret E. "Icons in Theory and Practice: An Orthodox Christian Example." *History of Religions* 24, no. 4 (1985): 345–368.

Kenney, Padraic. *A Carnival of Revolution: Central Europe 1989*. Princeton, NJ: Princeton University Press, 2002.

"'I felt a kind of pleasure in seeing them treat us brutally.' The Emergence of the Political Prisoner, 1865–1910." *Comparative Studies in Society and History* 54, no. 04 (2012): 863–889.

Keys, Barbara. "Anti-Torture Politics: Amnesty International, the Greek Junta, and the Origins of the Human Rights 'Boom' in the United States." In *The*

Bibliography 251

Human Rights Revolution: An International History, edited by Akira Iriye, Petra Goedde and William I. Hitchcock. Oxford, New York: Oxford University Press, 2012, 201–222.

Reclaiming American Virtue: The Human Rights Revolution of the 1970s. Cambridge, MA: Harvard University Press, 2014.

Khilnani, Sunil. *Arguing Revolution: The Intellectual Left in Postwar France.* New Haven, CT: Yale University Press, 1993.

Kind-Kovács, Friederike. *Written Here, Published There: How Underground Literature Crossed the Iron Curtain.* Budapest, New York: Central European University Press, 2014.

Kind-Kovács, Friederike, and Jessie Labov, eds. *Samizdat, Tamizdat, and Beyond: Transnational Media During and After Socialism.* New York: Berghahn Books, 2013.

King, William. "Neoconservatives and 'Trotskyism.'" *American Communist History* 3, no. 2 (2004): 247–266.

Klose, Fabian. *Human Rights in the Shadow of Colonial Violence: The Wars of Independence in Kenya and Algeria.* Philadelphia: University of Pennsylvania Press, 2013.

Klose, Fabian, ed. *The Emergence of Humanitarian Intervention: Ideas and Practice from the Nineteenth Century to the Present.* Cambridge: Cambridge University Press, 2016.

Kołakowski, Leszek. *Leben trotz Geschichte.* München: Piper, 1977.

Komaromi, Ann. "Samizdat and Soviet Dissident Publics." *Slavic Review* 71, no. 1 (2012): 70–90.

Kosicki, Piotr H. "L'avènement des intellectuels catholiques: Le mensuel *Więź* et les conséquences polonaises du personanalisme mounierien." *Vingtième Siècle* 102 (2009): 31–47.

Kosinowa, Tatiana. *Polski mit: Polska w oczach sowieckich dysydentów.* Kraków, Warszawa: Instytut Książki, 2012.

Kotkin, Stephen. *Uncivil Society: 1989 and the Implosion of the Communist Establishment.* New York: Modern Library, 2009.

Kowal, Paweł. *Koniec systemu władzy: Polityka ekipy gen. Wojciecha Jaruzelskiego w latach 1986-1989.* Warszawa: ISP PAN/IPN/Trio, 2011.

Kowalczyk, Andrzej Stanisław. *Giedroyc i "Kultura."* Wrocław: Wydawn. Dolnośląskie, 1999.

Kowalski, Sergiusz. *Krytyka solidarnościowego rozumu: Studium z socjologii myślenia potocznego.* Warszawa: PEN, 1990.

Kozol, Wendy, ed. *Distant Wars Visible: The Ambivalence of Witnessing.* Minneapolis, London: University of Minnesota Press, 2014.

Kramer, Mark. "The Demise of the Soviet Bloc." *The Journal of Modern History* 83, no. 4 (2011): 788–854.

Kubik, Jan. *The Power of Symbols against the Symbols of Power: The Rise of Solidarity and the Fall of State Socialism in Poland.* Pennsylvania University Park: Pennsylvania University Press, 1994.

Kula, Marcin, Piotr Osęka, and Marcin Zaremba, eds. *Marzec 1968: trzydzieści lat później*, 2 vols. Warszawa: PWN, 1998.

Bibliography

Kunicki-Goldfinger, Marek. " Stowarzyszenie Solidarité France–Pologne i jego pomoc dla Polski w latach osiemdziesiątych XX wieku." In *Świat wobec Solidarności 1980-1989*, edited by Paweł Jaworski and Łukasz Kamiński. Warszawa: IPN, 2014, 307–334.

Kuroń, Jacek. *Autobiografia*. Warszawa: Wydawnictwo Krytyki Politycznej, 2011. *Opozycja: Pisma polityczne 1969-1989*. Warszawa: Wydawnictwo Krytyki Politycznej, 2010.

Kuus, Merje. "Intellectuals and Geopolitics: The 'Cultural Politicians' of Central Europe." *Geoforum* 38, no. 2 (2007): 241–251.

Laba, Roman. *The Roots of Solidarity: A Political Sociology of Poland's Working-Class Democratization*. Princeton, NJ: Princeton University Press, 1991.

Lake, Daniel R. "The Limits of Coercive Airpower: NATO's "Victory" in Kosovo Revisited." *International Security* 34, no. 1 (2009): 83–112.

Lauren, Paul Gordon. *The Evolution of International Human Right: Visions Seen*. Philadelphia: University of Pennsylvania Press, 1998.

Lebow, Katherine. *Unfinished Utopia: Nowa Huta, Stalinism, and Polish Society, 1949-56*. Ithaca, NY: Cornell University Press, 2013.

Lévesque, Jacques. *The Enigma of 1989: The USSR and the Liberation of Eastern Europe*. Los Angeles: University of California Press, 1997.

"Italian Communists versus the Soviet Union: The PCI Charts a New Foreign Policy," Policy Papers in International Affairs, no. Paper #34 (1987), Institute of International Studies, University of California, Berkeley.

Lewek, Antoni. *New Sanctuary of Poles: The Grave of Martyr - Father Jerzy Popiełuszko*. Warszawa: Parafia św. Stanisława Kostki, 1986.

Lipski, Jan Józef. *KOR: A History of the Workers' Defense Committee in Poland, 1976-1981*. Berkeley: University of California Press, 1985.

Luxmoore, Jonathan, and Jolanta Babiuch. "In Search of Faith: The Metaphysical Dialogue Between Poland's Opposition Intellectuals in the 1970s." *Religion, State and Society* 23, no. 1 (1995): 75–95.

Lyons, William. "Conscience – An Essay in Moral Psychology." *Philosophy* 84, no. 04 (2009): 477–494.

Macey, David. *The Lives of Michel Foucault: A Biography*. New York: Pantheon Books, 1993.

Machcewicz, Paweł, et al., eds. *Polska 1986-1989. Koniec systemu*, 3 vols. Warszawa: Wydawnictwo Trio, 2002.

Maynard, Patrick. "The Secular Icon: Photography and the Functions of Images." *The Journal of Aesthetics and Art Criticism* 42, no. 2 (1983): 155–169.

McCartin, Joseph Anthony. *Collision Course: Ronald Reagan, the Air Traffic Controllers, and the Strike that Changed America*. New York: Oxford University Press, 2012.

Mende, Silke. *"Nicht rechts, nicht links, sondern vorn": Eine Geschichte der Gründungsgrünen*. München: Oldenbourg, 2011.

Miedema, Christie. *Not a Movement of Dissidents: Amnesty International Beyond the Iron Curtain*. Göttingen: Wallstein, 2019.

Mikulova, Kristina, and Michal Simecka. "Norm Entrepreneurs and Atlanticist Foreign Policy in Central and Eastern Europe: The Missionary Zeal of Recent Converts." *Europe-Asia Studies* 65, no. 6 (2013): 1192–1216.

Bibliography 253

Milder, Stephen. "Thinking Globally, Acting (Trans-)Locally: Petra Kelly and the Transnational Roots of West German Green Politics." *Central European History* 43, no. 02 (2010): 301–326.

Militzer, Stefan. "Meinungsfreiheit und politischer Widerstand: Claude Leforts Menschenrechtskonzeption als Beitrag zu einer Ontologie der Demokratie." In *Am leeren Ort der Macht: Das Staats- und Politikverständnis Claude Leforts*, edited by Andreas Wagner. Baden-Baden: Nomos, 2013, 167–188.

Miller, Stefania Szlek. "Catholic Personalism and Pluralist Democracy in Poland." *Canadian Slavonic Papers/Revue Canadienne des Slavistes* 25, no. 3 (1983): 425–439.

Morley, Morris, and Chris McGillion. "Soldiering on: The Reagan Administration and Redemocratisation in Chile, 1983–1986." *Bulletin of Latin American Research* 25, no. 1 (2006): 1–22.

Moyn, Samuel. "Die neue Historiographie der Menschenrechte." *Geschichte und Gesellschaft* 38, no. 4 (2012): 545–572.

"Introduction: Antitotalitarianism and After." In *Democracy Past and Future: Selected Essays*. New York: Columbia University Press, 2007, 1–28.

The Last Utopia: Human Rights in History. Cambridge: Harvard University Press, 2010.

"Personalism, Community, and the Origins of Human Rights." In *Human Rights in the Twentieth Century*, edited by Stefan-Ludwig Hoffmann. Cambridge: Cambridge University Press, 2011, 85–106.

"The Politics of Individual Rights: Marcel Gauchet and Claude Lefort." In *French Liberalism from Montesqieu to the Present Day*, edited by Raf Geenens and Helena Rosenblatt. New York: Cambridge University Press, 2012, 291–310.

Mulcahy, Aogán. "Claims-Making and the Construction of Legitimacy: Press Coverage of the 1981 Northern Irish Hunger Strike." *Social Problems* 42, no. 4 (1995): 449–467.

Müller, Jan-Werner. *Contesting Democracy: Political Ideas in Twentieth-Century Europe*. New Haven, CT: Yale University Press, 2011.

Nathans, Benjamin. "The Dictatorship of Reason: Aleksandr Vol'pin and the Idea of Rights under 'Developed Socialism'." *Slavic Review* 66, no. 4 (2007): 630–663.

"The Disenchantment of Socialism: Soviet Dissidents, Human Rights, and the New Global Morality." In *The Breakthrough: Human Rights in the 1970s*, edited by Jan Eckel and Samuel Moyn. Philadelphia: University of Pennsylvania Press, 2013.

Nehring, Holger. "'Westernization': A New Paradigm for Interpreting West European History in a Cold War Context." *Cold War History* 4, no. 3 (2004): 175–191.

Neier, Aryeh. "Confining Dissent: The Political Prison." In *The Oxford History of the Prison: The Practice of Punishment in Western Society*, edited by Norval Morris and David J. Rothman. New York: Oxford University Press, 1995, 350-380.

The International Human Rights Movement: A History of Human Rights and Crimes against Humanity. Princeton, NJ: Princeton University Press, 2012.

254 Bibliography

Niedhart, Gottfried. "Deeskalation durch Kommunikation: Zur Ostpolitik der Bundesrepublik Deutschland in der Ära Brandt." In *Deeskalation von Gewaltkonflikten seit 1945*, edited by Corinna Hauswedell. Essen: Klartext, 2006, 99–114.

"Revisionistische Elemente und die Initiierung friedlichen Wandels in der neuen Ostpolitik 1967-1974." *Geschichte und Gesellschaft* 28, no. 2 (2002): 233–266.

"'The Transformation of the Other Side': Willy Brandt's Ostpolitik and the Liberal Peace Concept." In *Visions of the End of the Cold War in Europe, 1945-1990*, edited by Frédéric Bozo, Marie-Pierre Rey, N. Piers Ludlow and Bernd Rother. Oxford, New York: Berghahn, 2013, 149–162.

Nolan, Cathal J. "Jeane Jordan Kirkpatrick." In *Notable U.S. Ambassadors Since 1775: A Biographical Dictionary*, edited by Cathal J. Nolan. Westport, CT: Greenwood Press, 1997, 219–226.

Novak, Michael. *The Spirit of Democratic Capitalism.* New York: Simon & Schuster, 1982.

Writing from Left to Right: My Journey from Liberal to Conservative. New York: Image, 2013.

Oman, Natalie. "Hannah Arendt's "Right to Have Rights": A Philosophical Context for Human Security." *Journal of Human Rights* 9, no. 3 (2010): 279–302.

Ortner, Sherry B. "On Key Symbols." *American Anthropologist* 75, no. 5 (1973): 1338–1346.

Osa, Maryjane. *Solidarity and Contention: Networks of Polish Opposition.* Minneapolis: University of Minnesota Press, 2003.

Osęka, Piotr M. *Marzec '68.* Kraków: Znak, 2008.

Ost, David. *Solidarity and the Policits of Anti-Politics: Opposition and Reform in Poland since 1968.* Philadelphia, PA: Temple University Press, 1990.

Paczkowski, Andrzej. "Aneks 1973-1989." *Res Publica* 4, no. 9 (1990): 28–37.

"Boisko wielkich mocarstw: Polska 1980-1989. Widok od wewnątrz." *Polski Przegląd Dyplomatyczny* 2, no. 3 (2002): 165–210.

Paczkowski, Andrzej, and Malcolm Byrne, eds. *From Solidarity to Martial Law: The Polish Crisis of 1980-1981 - A Documentary History.* Budapest, New York: Central European University Press, 2007.

Patel, Kiran Klaus, and Kenneth Weisbrode. *European Integration and the Atlantic Community in the 1980s.* New York: Cambridge University Press, 2013.

Patman, Robert G. "Reagan, Gorbachev and the Emergence of 'New Political Thinking'." *Review of International Studies* 25, no. 4 (1999): 577–601.

"Some Reflections on Archie Brown and the End of the Cold War." *Cold War History* 7, no. 3 (2007): 439–445.

Paul, Gerhard. "Das Jahrhundert der Bilder: Die visuelle Geschichte und der Bildkanon des kulturellen Gedächtnisses." In *Das Jahrhundert der Bilder: 1949 bis heute*, edited by Gerhard Paul. Göttingen: Vandenhoeck & Ruprecht, 2008, 14–39.

Paus, Ansgar. "The Secret Nostalgia of Mircea Eliade for Paradise: Observations on the Method of the 'History of Religions'." *Religion* 19, no. 2 (1989): 137–149.

Bibliography

Perlman, Jason. "Terence MacSwiney: The Triumph and Tragedy of the Hunger Strike." *New York History* 88, no. 3 (2007): 307–319.

Peter, Matthias. *Die Bundesrepublik im KSZE-Prozess 1975 – 1983: Die Umkehrung der Diplomatie*. München: Oldenbourg, 2015.

Peterson, Christian. *Globalizing Human Rights: Private Citizens, the Soviet Union, and the West of Routledge Studies on History and Globalization*. New York: Routledge, 2011.

Pleskot, Patryk. *Kłopotliwa Panna "S": Postawy polityczne Zachodu wobec Solidarności na tle stosunków z PRL 1980-1989*. Warszawa: IPN, 2013.

"Potępić, nie obrazić: Reakcje zachodniej dyplomacji na zabójstwo ks. Jerzego Popiełuszki." In *Kościół w obliczu totalitaryzmów*, edited by Wojciech Polak, Waldemar Rozynkowski, Michał Białkowski and Jakub Kufel. Toruń: FINNA, 2010, 65–76.

Pleskot, Patryk, ed. *Solidarność, "Zachód" i "Wężę": Służba Bezpieczeństwa wobec emigracyjnych struktur Solidarności 1981-1989*. Warszawa: IPN, 2011.

Plot, Martín, ed. *Claude Lefort: Thinker of the Political*. Basingstoke: Palgrave-Macmillan, 2013.

Polak, Wojciech, ed. *Czas przełomu: Solidarność 1980-1981*. Gdańsk: ECS, 2010.

Porter-Szűcs, Brian. *Faith and Fatherland: Catholicism, Modernity, and Poland*. New York: Oxford University Press, 2011.

Probert, Thomas J. W. "The Innovation of the Jackson–Vanik Amendment." In *Humanitarian Intervention: A History*, edited by Brendan Simms and D. J. B. Trim. Cambridge: Cambridge University Press, 2011, 323–342.

Przeworski, Adam, and Fernando Limongi. "Modernization: Theory and Facts." *World Politics* 49, no. 2 (1997): 155–183.

Puddington, Arch. *Lane Kirkland: Champion of American Labor*. Hoboken, NJ: John Wiley & Sons, 2005.

Readman, Kristina Spohr. "National Interests and the Power of 'Language': West German Diplomacy and the Conference on Security and Cooperation in Europe, 1972-1975." *Journal of Strategic Studies* 29, no. 6 (2006): 1077–1120.

Reagan, Ronald. "Address to the Members of British Parliament, Westminster, 8 June 1982." *The Public Papers of President Ronald Wilson Reagan* (1982).

"Proclamation 5003 – Bill of Rights Day, Human Rights Day and Week, 1982, December 10, 1982." *The Public Papers of President Ronald Wilson Reagan* (1982).

Renouard, Joe. *Human Rights in American Foreign Policy: From the 1960s to the Soviet Collapse*. Philadelphia: Universiry of Pennsylvania Press, 2016.

Richter, Saskia. *Die Aktivistin: Das Leben der Petra Kelly*. München: DVA, 2010.

Roberts, Adam. "The United Nations and Humanitarian Intervention." In *Humanitarian Intervention and International Relations*, edited by Jennifer M. Welsh. Oxford: Oxford University Press, 2004, 72–97.

Rodgers, Daniel T. *Age of Fracture*. Cambridge, MA: Harvard University Press, 2011.

Rosen, Michael. *Dignity: Its History and Meaning*. Cambridge, MA: Harvard University Press, 2012.

Ross, Kristin. *May 68 and Its Afterlives*. Chicago, IL; London: University of Chicago Press, 2002.

256 Bibliography

Rother, Bernd. "Willy Brandts Besuch in Warschau im Dezember 1985." In *Versöhnung und Politik: Polnisch-deutsche Versöhnungsinitiativen der 1960er Jahre und ihre Bedeutung für die Entspannungspolitik*, edited by Friedhelm Boll, Wiesław Wysocki and Klaus Ziemer. Bonn: J. H. W. Dietz, 2008.

"Zwischen Solidarität und Friedenssicherung: Willy Brandt und Polen in den 1980er Jahren." In *"Nie mehr eine Politik über Polen hinweg"*: *Willy Brandt und Polen*, edited by Friedhelm Boll and Krzysztof Ruchniewicz. Bonn: J.H.W. Dietz, 2010, 220–264.

Rother, Bernd, ed. *Willy Brandt's Außenpolitik*. Wiesbaden: Springer VS, 2014.

Rowland, Robert C., and John M. Jones. *Reagan at Westminster: Foreshadowing the End of the Cold War*. College Station: Texas A&M University Press, 2010.

Rupnik, Jacques. "Le totalitarisme vu de l'Est." In *Totalitarismes*, edited by Guy Hermet. Paris: Economica, 1984, 43–71.

"The Legacies of Dissent: Charter 77, the Helsinki Effect, and the Emergence of a European Public Space." In *Samizdat, Tamizdat & Beyond: Transnational Media During and After Socialism*, edited by Friederike Kind-Kovács and Jessie Labov. New York: Berghahn Books, 2013, 316–332.

Ruzikowski, Tadeusz. *Stan wojenny w Warszawie i województwie stołecznym 1981-1983*. Warszawa: IPN, 2009.

Saal, Yuliya von. *KSZE-Prozess und Perestroika in der Sowjetunion: Demokratisierung, Werteumbruch und Auflösung 1985 – 1991*. München: Oldenbourg, 2014.

Sasanka, Paweł. *Czerwiec 1976 r: Geneza - przebieg - konsekwencje*. Warszawa: IPN, 2006.

Schimmelfennig, Frank, Stefan Engert, and Heiko Knobel, eds. *International Socialization in Europe: European Organizations, Political Conditionality, and Democratic Change*. Basingstoke: Palgrave Macmillan, 2005.

Schimmelfennig, Frank, and Ulrich Sedelmeier, eds. *The Europeanization of Central and Eastern Europe*. Ithaca, NY: Cornell University Press, 2005.

Schlesinger Jr., Arthur M. *The Vital Center: The Politics of Freedom*. Cambridge, MA: Riverside Press, 1949.

Schmidli, William Michael. *The Fate of Freedom Elsewhere: Human Rights and U.S. Cold War Policy toward Argentina*. Ithaca, NY: Cornell University Press, 2013.

Schmidt, Wolfgang. "Die Wurzeln der Entspannung: Der konzeptionelle Ursprung der Ost- und Deutschlandpolitik Willy Brandts in den fünfziger Jahren." *Vierteljahrshefte für Zeitgeschichte* 51, no. 4 (2003): 521–563.

Scott-Smith, Giles, and Hans Krabbendam, eds. *The Cultural Cold War in Western Europe, 1945-1960*. London: Frank Cass, 2003.

Selvage, Douglas. "The Politics of the Lesser Evil: The West, the Polish Crisis, and the CSCE Review Conference in Madrid, 1981-1983." In *The Crisis of Detente in Europe: From Helsinki to Gorbachev, 1975-1985*, edited by Leopoldo Nuti. London: Routledge, 2009, 41–54.

Sevinç, Murat. "Hunger Strikes in Turkey." *Human Rights Quarterly* 30, no. 3 (2008): 655–679.

Simpson, Bradley R. "Denying the 'First Right:' The United States, Indonesia, and the Ranking of Human Rights by the Carter Administration, 1976-1980." *The International History Review* 31, no. 4 (2009): 798–826.

Bibliography

Sirinelli, Jean-François. *Intellectuels et passions françaises: Manifestes et pétitions au XXe siècle.* Paris: Fayard, 1990.

Sjursen, Helene. *The United States, Western Europe and the Polish Crisis: International Relations in the Second Cold War.* Houndmills: Palgrave, 2003.

Skinner, Quentin. "Meaning and Understanding in the History of Ideas." *History and Theory* 8, no. 1 (1969): 3–53.

Skórzyński, Jan. "'List 59' i narodziny opozycji demokratycznej w Polsce." *Zeszyty Historyczne* 163 (2008): 137–158.

Od Solidarności do wolności. Warszawa: Trio, 2005.

Rewolucja Okrągłego Stołu. Kraków: Znak, 2009.

Siła bezsilnych: Historia Komitetu Obrony Robotników. Warszawa: Świat Książki, 2012.

Zadra: Biografia Lecha Wałęsy. Gdańsk: ECS, 2009.

Slotte, Pamela, and Miia Halme, eds. *Revisiting the Origins of Human Rights.* Cambridge, New York: Cambridge University Press, 2015.

Smolar, Aleksander. "History and Memory: The Revolutions of 1989-91." *Journal of Democracy* 12, no. 3 (2001): 5–19.

Snyder, Sarah. "The Defeat of Ernest Lefever's Nomination: Keeping Human Rights on the United States Foreign Policy Agenda." In *Challenging US Foreign Policy: America and the World in the Long Twentieth Century*, edited by Bevan Sewell and Scott Lucas. Basingstoke: Palgrave, 2013.

Snyder, Sarah B. "The CSCE and the Atlantic Alliance: Forging a New Consensus in Madrid." *Journal of Transatlantic Studies* 8, no. 1 (2010): 56–68.

Human Rights Activism and the End of the Cold War: A Transnational History of the Helsinki Network. Cambridge, New York: Cambridge University Press, 2011.

Söllner, Alfons, Ralf Walkenhaus, and Karin Wieland, eds. *Totalitarismus: Eine Ideengeschichte des 20. Jahrhunderts.* Berlin: Akademie Verlag, 1997.

Sowa, Andrzej Leon. *Historia Polityczna Polski 1944-1991.* Kraków: Wydawnictwo Literackie, 2011.

Srivastava, Pramod Kumar. "Resistance and repression in India: The Hunger Strike at the Andaman Cellular Jail in 1933." *Crime, Histoire & Sociétés/Crime, History & Societies* 7, no. 2 (2003): 81–102.

Suri, Jeremi. "Détente and Human Rights: American and West European Perspectives on International Change." *Cold War History* 8, no. 4 (2008): 527–545.

Sutor, Bernhard. "Katholische Kirche und Menschenrechte: Kontinuität oder Diskontinuität in der kirchlichen Soziallehre?" *Forum für osteuropäische Ideen- und Zeitgeschichte* 12, no. 1 (2008): 141–158.

Swartz, David. "Bridging the Study of Culture and Religion: Pierre Bourdieu's Political Economy of Symbolic Power." *Sociology of Religion* 57, no. 1 (1996): 71.

Symbolic Power, Politics, and Intellectuals: The Political Sociology of Pierre Bourdieu. Chicago, IL, London: The University of Chicago Press, 2013.

Sweeney, George. "Irish Hunger Strikes and the Cult of Self-Sacrifice." *Journal of Contemporary History* 28, no. 3 (1993): 421–437.

Bibliography

Szacki, Jerzy. *Liberalism after Communism*. Budapest, New York: Central European University Press, 1995.

Szarek, Jarosław. "Nim powstał SKS." *Biuletyn Instytutu Pamięci Narodowej* 5–6 (2007): 24–35.

Szporer, Michael. *Solidarity: The Great Workers Strike of 1980*. Lanham, MD: Lexington Books, 2012.

Szulecki, Kacper. "'Freedom and Peace are Indivisible': On the Polish and Czechoslovak Input to the European Peace Movement 1985-89." In *Entangled Protest: Transnational Perspectives on the History of Dissent in Eastern Europe and the Soviet Union*, edited by Robert Brier. Osnabrück: Fibre, 2013, 201–229.

"Hijacked Ideas: Human Rights, Peace, and Environmentalism in Czechoslovak and Polish Dissident Discourses " *East European Politics & Societies* 25, no. 2 (2011): 272–295.

Therborn, Göran, et al. "The 1970s and 1980s as a Turning Point in European History?" *Journal of Modern European History* 9, no. 1 (2011): 7–26.

Thomas, Daniel C. *The Helsinki Effect: International Norms, Human Rights, and the Demise of Communism*. Princeton, NJ: Princeton University Press, 2001.

Thomas, Johannes. *Engel und Leviathan: Neue Philosophie in Frankreich als nachmarxistische Politik und Kulturkritik*. München: Olzog, 1979.

Troy, Gil. *Moynihan's Moment: America's Fight against Zionism as Racism*. Oxford, New York: Oxford University Press, 2013.

Tychran, Mikołaj. "'Aneks': Pismo emigracji pomarcowej." *Studia medioznawcze* 2 (2009): 104–120.

Vaïsse, Justin. *Neoconservatism: The Biography of a Movement*. Cambridge, MA: Harvard University Press, 2010.

Valenzuela, J. Samuel, and Arturo Valenzuela. "Introduction." In *Military Rule in Chile: Dictatorship and Oppositions*, edited by J. Samuel Valenzuela and Arturo Valenzuela. Baltimore, MD: Johns Hopkins University Press, 1986, 1–12.

"Party Oppositions under the Authoritarian Regime: ." In *Military Rule in Chile: Dictatorship and Oppositions*, edited by J. Samuel Valenzuela and Arturo Valenzuela. Baltimore, MD: Johns Hopkins University Press, 1986, 184–229.

Vetter, Reinhold. *Polens eigensinniger Held: Wie Lech Wałęsa die Kommunisten überlistete*. Berlin: BWV, 2012.

Wagner, Andreas, ed. *Am leeren Ort der Macht: Das Staats- und Politikverständnis Claude Leforts*. Baden-Baden: Nomos, 2013.

Wald, Alan M. *The New York Intellectuals : The Rise and Decline of the Anti-Stalinist Left from the 1930s to the 1980s*. Chapel Hill: University of North Carolina Press, 1987.

Walicki, Andrzej. "Polish Conceptions of the Intelligentsia and its Calling." *Slavica Lundensia* 22 (2005): 1–22.

Waligóra, Grzegorz. *Ruch Obrony Praw Człowieka i Obywatela 1977-1981*. Warszawa: IPN, 2006.

Walker, Barbara. "Moscow Human Rights Defenders Look West: Attitudes toward U.S. Journalists in the 1960s and 1970s." In *Imagining the West in*

Bibliography 259

Eastern Europe and the Soviet Union, edited by György Péteri. Pittsburgh, PA: University of Pittsburgh Press, 2010, 237–257.

"Pollution and Purification in the Moscow Human Rights Networks of the 1960s and 1970s." *Slavic Review* 68, no. 2 (2009): 376–395.

Webber, Mark. "The Kosovo War: A Recapitulation." *International Affairs* 85, no. 3 (2009): 447–459.

Wehr, Ingrid. *Zwischen Pinochet und Perestroika: Die chilenischen Kommunisten und Sozialisten 1973-1994*. Freiburg i. Br.: Arnold-Bergstraesser-Inst., 1996.

Weigel, George. *The Final Revolution: The Resistance Church and the Collapse of Communism*. New York: Oxford University Press, 1992.

Weiss, Thomas G., David P. Forsythe, and Roger A. Coate. *The United Nations and Changing World Politics*, 3rd ed. Boulder, CO: Westview Press, 2001.

Welsh, Jennifer M., ed. *Humanitarian Intervention and International Relations*. Oxford: Oxford University Press, 2004.

Wentker, Hermann, and Matthias Peter, eds. *Die KSZE im Ost-West-Konflikt: Internationale Politik und gesellschaftliche Transformation 1975-1990*. München: Oldenbourg, 2012.

Wheeler, Nicholas J. "The Humanitarian Responsibilities of Sovereignty: Explaining the Development of a New Norm of Military Intervention for Humanitarian Purposes in International Society." In *Humanitarian Intervention and International Relations*, edited by Jennifer M. Welsh. Oxford: Oxford University Press, 2004, 29–51.

Wiegrefe, Klaus. *Das Zerwürfnis: Helmut Schmidt, Jimmy Carter und die Krise der deutsch-amerikanischen Beziehungen*. Berlin: Propyläen, 2005.

Wildenthal, Lora. *The Language of Human Rights in West Germany*. Philadelphia: University of Pennsylvania Press, 2013.

Wilson, James Graham. *The Triumph of Improvisation: Gorbachev's Adaptability, Reagan's Engagement, and the End of the Cold War*. Ithaca, NY: Cornell University Press, 2014.

Wohlforth, William C. "Realism and the End of the Cold War." *International Security* 19, no. 3 (1994): 91–129.

Wolin, Richard. *The Frankfurt School Revisited and Other Essays on Politics and Society*. New York, NY; London: Routledge, 2006.

Yurchak, Alexei. *Everything Was Forever, Until It Was No More: The Last Soviet Generation*. Princeton, NJ: Princeton University Press, 2006.

Zaremba, Marcin. "Propaganda sukcesu: Dekada Gierka." In *Propaganda PRL: Wybrane problemy*, edited by Piotr Semków. Gdańsk: IPN, 2004, 22–32.

Zubok, Vladislav. "Gorbachev and the Road to 1989." In *The End and the Beginning: The Revolution of 1989 and the Resurgence of History*, edited by Vladimir Tismaneanu and Bogdan Iacob. Budapest, New York: Central European University Press, 2012, 257–290.

Zubok, Vladislav M. "Gorbachev and the End of the Cold War: Perspectives on History and Personality." *Cold War History* 2, no. 2 (2002): 61–100.

Index

Aarvik, Egil 193
  speech at 1983 Nobel Peace Prize
    ceremony 178–179, 181–183
Abrams, Elliot 79, 138, 189
Afghanistan 71, 78, 88
AFL-CIO 9, 14, 16, 135, 139, 144–145,
    152, 212, 214, *see also* Jackson
    Democrats; Kahn, Tom; Kirkland,
    Lane
  adopting practices of Amnesty
    International 131–133
  and freedom of association 141–144
  and Reagan administration 134
  and situation in Chile 194–197
  fascination with Solidarity 128–129
  split with Jackson Democrats over Polish
    crisis 133
  support for Solidarity 130–133
  support for Soviet dissidents 129
  ties with Jackson Democrats 129–130
  views of totalitarian societies 127–128
Albright, Madeleine 228–229
Allende, Salvador 189
American Federation of Labor and
    Congress of Industrial Organizations,
    see AFL-CIO
Amnesty International 6, 8, 11, 16, 19,
    31–32, 39, 55, 57, 60, 68, 76, 98, 109,
    122, 148, 157, 159, 189, 209, 221,
    225–226, 229–231, *see also* Prisoner of
    conscience
  and emergence of Polish dissent 27
  awarded Nobel Prize 4
  development in the US 156
  evolution of since 1980s 226–227
  work on behalf of Bobby Sands 167
  work on behalf of prisoners of conscience
    155–156, 165–166
Annan, Kofi 219
Anti-Semitic campaign of 1968 24, 42, 47
Anti-Semitism 41, 46
Apartheid 143, 188

Arendt, Hannah 70, 229
Argentina 198
Autogestion 124, 224, 231, *see also* CFDT,
    French anti-totalitarian intellectuals;
    French Second Left; Maire, Edmond;
    Rosanvallon, Pierre
  Solidarity seen as example of 125–126

Bahr, Egon 92, 99–100, see also Bender,
    Peter; Brandt, Willy
  and concept of "change through
    rapprochement" 101
  position toward Polish crisis 102
Barraclough, Geoffrey 219
BBC 22, 25, 213
Benda, Václav 62
Bender, Peter 100–102, *see also* Bahr, Egon;
    Brandt, Willy
Berlinguer, Enrico 5, 84
Blair, Tony 229, 231
Blumsztajn, Seweryn 107–108, 110, 126,
    152, *see also* Commandos, *see also*
    Commandos
Bolton, Jonathan 21
Bonhoeffer, Dietrich
  as inspiration for Amnesty International
    157
  as inspiration for Polish intellectuals
    49–50
Bonn 73, 103, 185
Bosnia 218
Bourdieu, Pierre 14, 124, 150
Bradley, Mark 3, 12, 181
Brandt, Willy 16, 18, 73, 84, 89, 93–94,
    99–100, 102–103, 109, 128, 136, 145,
    206–207, 230–231, *see also* Bahr, Egon;
    Bender, Peter; CSCE; Détente;
    Ostpolitik; Socialist International
  1963 speech at Harvard University 94–95
  and dissidents 95–99
  and human rights 95, 97–99, 101,
    103–104

Index

position toward Polish crisis 73, 96, 102–103
social thought of 99–101, 103–106
view of CSCE 95
views on CSCE 104
Braniewo 153, 158
Brezhnev, Leonid 26, 30, 78, 123, 205
British Broadcasting Corporation *see* BBC
Buenos Aires 198
Bujak, Zbigniew 211–212
Bukovsky, Vladimir 129
Bush, George H.W. 132
1988 trip to Poland 212
Bussi, Hortensia 213
Bustos, Manuel 191

Carrington, Peter Lord 86–87
Carter, Jimmy 4, 31, 70, 75, 88–89, 93, 130, 229
Castoriadis, Cornelius 124
Catholic Church 22, 38, 47, 66, 171, 203, 210, 226, *see also* John Paul II; Wojtyła, Karol
and human rights 47
as actor in Poland 28, 30, 33, 203
personalist current in 51
support for dissidents of 47–48
support for political prisoners 171
supporting Solidarity internationally 133
Catholicism 60
Catholicism in Poland 46–47, 50
CDM 129, 135
CFDT 109, 113, 123, 127, 146, 152, 168, *see also Autogestion*; French Second Left; Lefort, Claude; Maire, Edmond; Rosanvallon, Pierre
adopting practices of Amnesty International 111
campaign in support of Solidarity of 107–108, 110–112
French politics and support for Solidarity of 125–126
Charter 77 7, 20, 62–63, 65, 95, 152, 157, 162, 222, *see also* Havel, Václav
as distinct from CSCE monitoring groups 69
meeting with members of KOR 61, 63
Charter of Workers' Rights 33, 57–58
Chechnya 229
Chérèque, Jacques 108
Chernenko, Konstantin 170–171, 205–206
Chile 10, 17–18, 100, 122, 164, 192, 219
as contested icon of human rights 190
as icon of global human rights culture 150

cooperation of trade unions with Solidarity 190–194
in global human rights discourses 186–187
repression in 4
seen as model for neoliberal policies 196
US conservatives and situation in 186–187
Christianity 46, 49
Christofferson, Michael Scott 108
Christopher Street day 228
Chronicle of Current Events 26–27, 29, 32, 45, 70, 221
Churchill, Winston 78
Club of Paris 214
Coalition for a Democratic Majority, *see* CDM
Cold War liberals 2, *see also* Jackson Democrats
Cologne 29
Commandos (Polish student radicals) 23–24, 27, 41–42, 46, 222, *see also* Blumsztajn, Seweryn; Michnik, Adam; Kuroń, Jacek
and theory of totalitarianism 45
quasi-religious views of 48–50
rapprochement with Catholicism of 47–48
Commentary 76–78
Committee against the Warsaw Trials 169
Committee for Social Self-Defense "KOR" (KSS KOR) 31, 57
Committee in Support for Solidarity, *see* CSS
Committee to Defend Human and Trade Union Rights 191
Committee to Defend Prisoners of Conscience 59, 157
Committee to Defend the Workers *see* KOR
Committees to Establish Free Trade Unions 32–33
Communist party in Poland, *see* PZPR
Confederation for an Independent Poland 56
Confédération française démocratique du travail see CFDT
Conference on Security and Cooperation in Europe, *see* CSCE
Conquest, Robert 41
Constitutional debate of 1975 27–28
Consumer socialism 41
Cooper, Gary 216
Cracow 1
Craxi, Bettino 208
CSCE 18, 25, 39, 86, 88, *see also* Détente; *Ostpolitik*
and dissent 66, 69–70

262 Index

CSCE (cont.)
  and fall of Communism 215
  and human rights 13, 39, 66–68
  and Polish crisis 66, 71–73, 88–89
  as based on postwar social thought 103
  as forum for human rights 69–71, 89
  as human rights forum 4
  Final Act of 4–5, 13, 25, 27, 29, 31–32,
    56, 59, 66, 69, 72, 78, 81, 88, 93, 103,
    110, 183
  follow-up conference in Belgrade 1977-
    1978 30–31, 70–71, 202
  follow-up conference in Madrid 1980-
    1983 5, 66, 71, 79, 87–88, 92, 112,
    131, 144, 146, 151–152, 163, 202
  principle of non-interference enshrined
    in 67, 73, 215
CSS 131, 152
Cuban missile crisis 148
Cywiński, Bohdan 177, 181–182
Czechoslovakia 26, 42, 62–63, 157, 162

Daniel, Jean 123–124
de Gaulle, Charles 98
Decter, Midge 76, 88
Détente 15, 69, 86, 98, 201, *see also* Brandt,
    Willy; CSCE; *Ostpolitik*
  and fall of Communism 215
  and human rights 12
  as based on postwar social thought 12–13
  as strategy to transform Communist
    societies 101–102, 105
Deuxième gauche see CFDT; French anti-
    totalitarian intellectuals; French
    Second Left
Dissent 3, 19–20, *see also* Dissidents
  as based on commitment to truthfulness 44
  as crucial for emergence of Solidarity
    Trade Union 58–61
  as political movement 6–7, 19–20, 39,
    55–57, 61–65
  as transnational movement 25
  as western label 21
Dissidence, *see* dissent
Dissidents 3, 10–11, 13, 15, 17, 39–40, 42,
    46, 79, 93, 109, 201, 203, 231–232, *see
    also* Dissent; Havel, Václav; Human
    rights; Kołakowski, Leszek; Kuroń,
    Jacek; Michnik, Adam; Prisoner of
    conscience; Solzhenitsyn, Aleksandr;
    Totalitarianism
  and détente 104
  and history of human rights 19
  and human rights 97
  and humanitarian interventions 222–223

and religion 46–50
  as actors in foreign policy 207
  as icons of human rights 8, 108
  as icons of human rightsr 216
  careers after 1989 221–222
  emergence of 25
  evolution of thought after 1989 226
  nationalism and 54–55
  personalist views of 20, 40, 52–55
  role in fall of Communism 200–202
  theory of human rights of 39–41, 60,
    64–65, 104
Dmowski, Roman 22
Doctorow, E. L. 85
Dolan, Anthony 137
Dole, Bob 132
Domber, Gregory 15, 210, 213
Dubček, Aleksandr 95

Eagleburger, Lawrence 74, 195
EC 66, 73, 82, 86–87
  demanding release of political prisoners
    (1986) 210
  policy toward Poland in late 1980s
    214–215
  policy towards Polish crisis 73
Eckel, Jan 226
Edward Gierek 41
Ehrman, John 135
El Salvador 77–78, 81, 85, 192
Ethics and Public Policy Center 184
EU 11, 222, 226–227
  and human rights 220
European Community, *see* EC
European Union, *see* EU

Federal Republic of Germany, *see* West
    Germany
Foucault, Michel 5, 16, 109, 115, 122, 126,
    224–225, *see also* French anti-
    totalitarian intellectuals
  and new philosophers 115
  French politics and support for dissidents
    of 123–124
  views on human rights of 121
  work in support of Solidarity 108, 112
Founding Committees for Free Trade
    Unions 35
  combining human rights with political
    and social aims 57–58
France 9, 71–72, 74–75, 86, 88–89, 122,
    126, 145, 168, 218
  government's response to Polish crisis
    87–88, 112–113, 123
  response to Polish crisis in 83, 109

Index

Free Trade Union Institute 133
Freedom House 2
Freedom of association 7, 14, 141–142, 168
French anti-totalitarian intellectuals 7,
   108–109, 146, 168, *see also* Bourdieu,
   Pierre; Castoriadis, Cornelius; CFDT;
   Daniel, Jean; Foucault, Michel; Lefort,
   Claude; Rosanvallon, Pierre
   and human rights 109
   and Polish dissidents 119–120
   concept of *autogestion* of 120–121
   emergence of 118–119
   evolution of views during 1980s 224
   fascination with dissent of 108, 119–120
   support for dissidents and French politics
      123–124
   support for Solidarity of 110–112
French Communist Party 114, 119–120
French new philosophers 115, 117, 137
French Second Left 128, 145, *see also*
   CFDT
French socialist party 74, 124
   government of formed in 1981 123
   position toward Polish crisis 73
Furet, François 114–115

Gdańsk 35, 97, 132, 179, 208
Gdańsk agreement 59
GDR 96
Geneva 186–188
Genscher, Hans-Dietrich 87, 213
George Meany Human Rights Award 143
Geremek, Bronisław 36, 152
German occupation of Poland 23
Gershman, Carl 135, 138
Gierek, Edward 30, 42
Ginsberg, Allen 85
Glucksmann, Andre 115
Gorbachev, Mikhail
   and situation in Poland 202–205, 215
   role in ending Cold War 200–202
Grabowski, Tomek 60
Great Britain *see* UK
Grenada 196, 217, 223
Gromyko, Andrei 170
Guatemala 77, 81
Guevara, Ernesto 174
Gulag Archipelago 13, 27, 70, 116
   reception of by French Left 108,
      114–115, 119–120

Habermas, Jürgen 94, 100, 105
Haig, Alexander 79, 82, 86, 88
Harvard 173
Hatmon, Hervé 125

Havel, Václav 21, 221, 228
   and humanitarian interventions 222–223
   theory of totalitarianism of 61–62
H-Blocks
   Irish republican protests in 166–167
Helsinki 56, 69
Helsinki Accords *see* CSCE, Final Act of
Helsinki Commission (US Congress) 131
Helsinki Committee 55
Helsinki effect 5, 69, 89, 201
Higgins, George 130
Hoffmann, Stefan 219
Honecker, Erich 214
Human dignity 40
   in dissidents' thought 40
Human rights
   1970s as crucial decade for 3–6, 89–90, 231
   and changing conceptions of time 94
   and crisis of postwar social thought 93–94
   and end of Cold War 15–16, 18, 215–216
   and liberal international order 229–230
   and Marxism 118
   and military interventions 217–218, 225,
      230
   and national sovereignty 228–229
   and religion 50
   and solidarity 122–123
   and western Cold War foreign policy 89
   as force shaping international politics
      146, 198–199, 208–213, 215–216
   as foundation for moral absolutism
      11–12, 40, 64, 145, 232
   as synonymous with civil rights 63
   breakthrough of 3, 66
   Claude Lefort's theory of 116–118,
      120–121
   enmeshed in political debates and social
      conflicts of early 1980s 84–86, 89–90,
      123–126, 128–129, 144–146
   French anti-totalitarian intellectuals
      vernacular of 122
   historiography of 2–4, 63, 219–220,
      224–225, 230–232
   in postwar social thought 103
   in world politics after 1989 217–219
   malleable nature of 3, 20, 38, 60, 68,
      231–232
   Polish dissident vernacular of 60–61,
      64–65
   political economy of symbolic power
      191–194, 198–199
   politics of 3, 6–8, 38–39, 55–57, 64, 68,
      117, 120, 122, 125–126, 139, 144–145,
      150, 156, 172, 182, 186–187, 191–194,
      198–199, 227–228, 231

264   Index

Human rights (cont.)
tenuous position after 1980 4–6, 67, 89, 148, 152–153, 198
Hungary 220
1956 uprising in 134

ICCPR 26, 57, 70
defining civil rights as human rights 63
invoking right to self-determination 63
ICESCR 33, 58
ICFTU 129, 142, 184, 195
and freedom of association 142–143
support for Solidarity of 142
Icon 8, 18, 172, *see also* Amnesty International; Dissidents; Prisoner of conscience; Michnik, Adam; Wałęsa, Lech
as contested source of symbolic power 185
depoliticization and 180–183
theory of 148–150, 166, 180–181, 183
Ikenberry, G. John 230
ILO 32–33, 112, 142, 151, 168
conventions of 32, 57–58
International Commission on Intervention and State Sovereignty 219
International Confederation of Free Trade Unions, *see* ICFTU
International Covenant on Civil and Political Rights *see* ICCPR
International Covenant on Economic, Social, and Cultural Rights *see* ICESCR
International Criminal Court 219, 229
International Helsinki Federation 2
International Labor Organization *see* ILO
International Union of Electrical, Radio, and Machine Workers 131
International Year of Human Rights 1, 27
Iraq 218
Irish Republican Army 166
Israel 188, 196
Italian Communist Party 83–84, 86, 92, 169
Italy 71, 74–75, 86, 88–89, 168
government's response to Polish crisis 87–88
response to Polish crisis in 83

Jackson Democrats 16, 84, 156, 189, 230, *see also* Decter, Midge; Kahn, Tom; Kirkland, Lane; Kirkpatrick, Jeane; Moynihan, Daniel Patrick; Neoconservatives; Podhoretz, Norman; Reagan, Ronald

and "liberalism of the vital center" 135–136
and Shachmanites 135
and Solidarity 127–128
ideological differences with Reagan administration 138
in Reagan administration 75, 88, 134
influence on US human rights policies 137
influence on US policies toward Polish crisis of 79
views of on human rights 75–77
views on human rights 79–80
views on Polish crisis 89
views on Polish crisis of 77–79
views on totalitarian societies 77
Jackson, Henry 75, 129, 136
Jaruzelski, Wojciech 72, 97, 99, 106, 123, 140, 160, 173, 175, 190, 205, *see also* Poland; PZPR
and Reagan administration 206
and Soviet leadership 170–171, 205–206
foreign policy during Polish crisis 102–103
likened to Augusto Pinochet 98, 197–198
relations with Western European politicians 206–207, 214–215
John Paul II 5, 38, 171, 181–182, 194, *see also* Catholic Church; Wojtyła, Karol
1983 visit to Poland 152, 167, 175–176
1987 visit to Poland 203
personalist philosophy of 52
visit to Poland, 1979 33–34
Johnson, Lyndon B. 136

Kahn, Tom 127, 129–135, 223–224, *see also* AFL-CIO; Jackson Democrats; Kirkland, Lane; Shachtman, Max
and freedom of association 143–144
conflict with Reagan administration of 138–139
evolution of political views of 134–135
Kant, Immanuel 159
Katyń massacre of 1940 22, 45
Kelly, Petra 5, 84, 185, 223
Kennedy, Edward 132
1987 trip to Poland 211–213
Kennedy, John Fitzgerald 94
Kenney, Padraic 154–155
Keys, Barbara 75, 128
KGB 152
Khrushchev, Nikita 26
King, Martin Luther, Jr. 178
Kirkland, Lane 5, 129–130, 133, 195–197, 224, *see also* AFL-CIO; Jackson Democrats; Kahn, Tom; Reagan, Ronald

as Cold War Liberal 135–136
conflict with Reagan administration
139–140
conflict with Reagan administration of
138–139
linking human rights and criticism of US
business 140–141
Kirkpatrick, Jeane 78, 80, 138, 140, 185,
188–189, *see also* Jackson Democrats;
Reagan, Ronald
on difference between authoritarian and
totalitarian governments 77
Kiszczak, Czesław 164–165, 171
Kołakowski, Leszek 23, 42, 54, 63–64, 217
concept of Sovietization 43
KOR 29–32, 44, 46, 48, 54, 56, 58, 70, 91,
107, 157, 161, 168–169, 172, *see also*
Commandos; Kołakowski, Leszek;
Kuroń, Jacek; Michnik, Adam
1984 trial of members of 147
amnesty for members of (1977) 30–31,
170
and creation of Solidarity 35
as distinct from CSCE monitoring
groups 55, 69
Catholic Church in Poland and 48
combining human rights with political
aims 57
creation of 27–29
meeting with members of Charter 77 61,
63
meeting with Soviet dissidents 32
prehistory of 21–28
KOS 151
Kosovo 218
Kouchner, Bernard 112, 224–225
Krauthammer, Charles 79
Kreisky, Bruno 169
Król, Marcin 44
Kubasiewicz, Ewa 160–161
Kuron, Jacek *see also* Commandos; KOR;
Michnik, Adam
Kuroń, Jacek 48–49, 147, 165
quasi-personalist views of 53–54
quasi-religious views of 49–50
Kwaśniewski, Aleksander 221

Labor unrest in Poland in 1976 28
Laborem exercens 181
Laqueur, Walter 78, 127
League for Industrial Democracy 135
Lefever, Ernest 75, 184
Lefort, Claude 7, 16, 114, 120, 122,
224–225, *see also* Gulag Archipelag;
Human rights; Rosanvallon, Pierre;

Solzhenitsyn, Aleksandr;
Totalitarianism
on Karl Marx 118
theory of human rights of 116–118,
120–121
theory of politics 7–8
theory of politics of 145
theory of totalitarianism of 116
views of Solidarity of 122
views on dissidents 116–117
Leipzig 200
Lenin shipyards 35, 59
Leninism 121
Levy, Bernard-Henry 115
Lewis, Anthony 198
London 29, 87, 103
Lublin 47
Luns, Joseph 74
Lutuli, Albert 178

Macierewicz, Antoni 50
view of totalitarianism of 44–45
Madrid 66–67, 69, 73, 88–89
Maire, Edmond 125–126, *see also*
Autogestion; CFDT
Mandela, Nelson 166
Martial law 4, 38, 67
Marx, Karl 118
Marxism 108, 115, 122
Mauroy, Pierre 113
Mazowiecki, Tadeusz 36, 59, 152
personalist views of 51, 53
UN envoy in former Yugoslavia 222
Meany, George 129, 194
Michnik, Adam 29, 48–49, 54, 62–64, 91,
93–94, 104, 120, 147, 171, 178, 180,
191, 193, 198, 204, 208, 212,
221–223, *see also* KOR; Icon; Prisoner
of conscience
addressing international audiences 91,
163–164
as human rights icon 165–167
awarded honorary degree 164
open letter to General Kiszczak of
164–165
prison writings of 161–162
theory of dissent of 62
Mickiewicz, Adam 24
Milewski, Jerzy 191–192
Milošević, Slobodan 223
Miłosz, Czesław 162, 164
Mitterrand, François 16, 92, 113, 119,
123, 163, 197, 206, 208, 213, *see also*
France
Moczulski, Leszek 56

266 Index

Montand, Yves
  work in support of Solidarity 112
Montevideo 188
Moscow 15, 26, 32, 82, 87, 92, 102, 170,
  188, 201, 203, 205
Movement to Defend Human and Civil
  Rights *see* ROPCiO
Moyn, Samuel 118
Moynihan, Daniel Patrick 76, 156

Nathans, Benjamin 26
National Endowment for Democracy, *see*
  NED
NATO 5, 11, 66, 78, 82, 87–89, 91,
  167–168, 186–187, 218–220, 222,
  227, 230
  and human rights 230
  demanding non-interference in Poland
  72–73
  members' policies toward Poland after
  1982 167–168
  response to Polish crisis 71–73, 86–88
Nazi Germany 164
NED 133, 135, *see also* AFL-CIO; Jackson
  Democrats; Kirkland, Lane; Reagan,
  Ronald
  financial support for Polish underground
  of 213–214
Neoconservatives (US) 7, 10, *see also*
  Jackson Democrats
Neue Ostpolitik see *Ostpolitik*
New Left 135
New School for Social Research 164
New York 85, 164
New York intellectuals
  and debate on Polish crisis 85
Newfoundland 78
Nicaragua 196
Nixon, Richard 134, 189
Nobel Committee 16
Nobel Peace Prize 198
  role in global human rights culture
  174
Novak, Michael 78, 188
Nowa Huta 1–3, 13–14, 34, 209, 217

Onyszkiewicz, Janusz 212–213
Operation Allied Force 218–219
Operation Provide Comfort 218
Orthodox Christianity 166
Orwell, George 41, 44, 61, 70
Ostpolitik 70, 92, 206, *see also* Bahr, Egon;
  Bender, Peter; Brandt, Willy; Détente
  as strategy to transform Communist
  societies 105

concept of 94–95, 100–102
French criticism of 110–111
Ottawa 151

Pacem in terris 47, 51, 70
Pacheco, Maximo 197
Paris 29, 107, 112–113, 225
PATCO 139
Patočka, Jan 222
Paus, Ansgar 180
People's Republic of Poland *see* Poland
Pérez Esquivel, Adolfo 178
Personalism 51–54, 70
  and Solidarity Trade Union 59
Piłsudski, Józef 22
Pinochet, Augusto 186, 189, 195, 219
Podhoretz, Norman 77, 88, 130
Poland 1, 3, 5, 10, 16–18, 21, 25, 27,
  29–30, 32, 35, 39, 41–42, 45, 62–63,
  67, 72, 77–78, 81–84, 86–89, 92, 99,
  102, 107, 111–113, 127, 131, 133,
  140–143, 145, 148, 150–152, 157,
  161–162, 164–165, 168, 170, 178,
  182, 186, 192, 195, 201–202, 204,
  209, 212, 214, 220, 223, 225, *see also*
  Jaruzelski, Wojciech; PZPR
  as contested icon of human rights 190
  Communist seizure of power in 21
  debates on at CSCE conference in
  Madrid 88–89
  German occupation of 21, 45, 50
  relations with US 206
  relations with Western Europe 206–207
Polish American Congress 132–133
Polish Catholic Left
  and human rights 47
  and KOR 48
  and personalism 53
Polish conservative intellectuals 21, 226
  and theory of totalitarianism 45
  personalist views of 52
Polish crisis 17, 102, 140
  and western civil societies 68, 82–86
Polish Helsinki Commission 32, 70, 151
Polish peace activists 208–209
Polish Round Table Talks 202–204
Polish underground army of WWII 21
Political economy of symbolic power: *see*
  Human rights
Political prisoners
  as central issue in Poland's foreign
  relations 162–163, 167–171, 207–208,
  210–211, 220
  history of 154–155
  in Poland in early 1980s 153–154

Index

Pope *see* John Paul II
Popiełuszko, Jerzy 207, 212
Prague 200
Prague spring 42
Prague Spring 98, 122
Prisoner of conscience 6, 8, 18, 27, 167, 220, *see also* Icon; Michnik, Adam; Political prisoners
and dissidents 156–157
and human dignity 160–161
and hunger strikes 158–159
and Polish prisoners 157–158
and politics of human rights 155–156, 172, 192
as reimagination of political incarceration 155–156
as symbolic figure of human rights culture 148, 165–166
concept of "conscience" of 159–160
in Adam Michnik's prison writings 161–162, 164–165
Puerto Rico 196
PZPR 28, 37, 169, 205, 210
policies in late 1980s 203

Radio Free Europe 22, 25, 213
Rakowski, Mieczysław 103, 173, 180
Reagan administration *see* Reagan, Ronald
Reagan, Nancy 208
Reagan, Ronald 5, 9, 16, 67, 77, 84, 86, 88–89, 103, 128–129, 132, 136, 142, 144, 167, 184, 192, 198, 200, 206, 230
1982 speech in London 80, 84, 136–138
and British position on Polish crisis 86–87
and changes in social imagery of US politics 128
and transformation of postwar social thought 136–138
approach to human rights 75, 133
conflict with West European allies over Polish crisis 82
message in honor of Lech Wałęsa 184
policies during Polish crisis 79–82, 140
policies toward Chile 195–198
policy toward Poland after 1983 152
response to Polish crisis 88
Responsibility to Protect 219
Revisionism (Polish Marxist current) 23
Rodgers, Daniel 13, 94, 136
Rokita, Jan Maria 217–219, 223, 226, 228
Romaszewski, Zbigniew 147, 172
Rome 29, 127, 130
Roosevelt, Franklin Delano 78
ROPCiO 29–30, 54, 70, 157

and Amnesty International 28
as combining human rights and political aims 56–57
as distinct from CSCE monitoring groups 55
creation of 32
split of 32
Rosanvallon, Pierre 120, 122, 224, *see also* *Autogestion*; CFDT; Lefort, Claude
views of Solidarity of 122
Rotman, Patrick 125
Rustin, Bayard 77, 135, 224
Rwanda 219

Sakharov, Andrei 27, 178, 213
Sands, Bobby 166–167
Schlesinger, Arthur M. 135
Schmidt, Helmut 16, 70, 96
Schneider, Romy 113
Seeger, Pete 85
Seguel, Rodolfo 190, 194
Serbia 228
Shachtman, Max 134–135, 138, 224
Signoret, Simone 112
Six-Day War 23
Snyder, Sarah 15
Social Defense Committees, *see* KOS
Social Democratic Party of Germany, *see* SPD
Social Democrats U.S.A. 135
Socialist International 73, 89, 93, 96, 100
debate on Polish crisis in 74
Society for Academic Courses 32
Solidarity 4, 9, 15–19, 37, 39, 66–68, 72, 77–79, 81–84, 89, 91, 102–103, 109, 112–113, 122–124, 127–128, 130–133, 141–143, 146–148, 150, 152, 158, 161, 163, 173, 175, 177–178, 180–182, 185, 203–204, 214, 220, 227
21 demands 35, 37
and Catholicism 46, 59
and CSCE Final Act 37
and human dignity 59
and western approaches to Cold War 89
as an icon of human rights 145–146
congress of 1981 59
cooperation with Chilean trade unions of 190–194
emergence of 34–36
first period of legal activities, 1980-1981 36–38
influenced by dissident movement 36, 58–61
members of in the West 107–108, 112

268   Index

Solidarity (cont.)
  organizing election campaign in 1989 216
  personalist views in 59
  program of 58, 60
  situation of in late 1980s 203
  strikes in 1988 203
  suppression of 38
  transnational coalition in support of 5–6,
    86, 151–152, 168–169
  underground activism of 150–151
  underground leadership of 162
Solidarity Eleven 147, 153, 168–169
  1984 amnesty for 170
Solidarity Trade Union see Solidarity
Solidarność see Solidarity
Solzhenitsyn, Aleksandr 13, 27, 61, 64,
    119, 123, 129, see also Gulag
    Archipelago; Soviet dissident movement
  influence on French anti-totalitarian
    intellectuals of 108, 114–115, 119–120
  view of life in totalitarian society 43
Somalia 218
Sontag, Susan
  and debate on Polish crisis 85
Sorbonne 173
South Africa 141, 143, 164, 166, 188, 193,
    196, 212
Soviet dissident movement 10, 15, 32, 39,
    60, 129, 152
  and Solidarity Trade Union 36
  emergence of 25–27, 69–70
  impact on Polish intellectuals 27, 29–30
  meeting with KOR member 32
Soviet Politburo 170
Soviet Union 22, 28, 42–43, 69, 86–89,
    132–135, 164–165, 201
SPD 92–93, 169
Stalinism 41–42, 134
Student unrest of 1968 24
Swartz, David 185
Symbolic power 14, 16, 149–150, 231

Tehran 1
Thatcher, Margaret 84, 167
  response to Polish crisis 86–87
The Worker of the Coast 32
Theobald, Thomas 140
Thomas, Daniel 5
Tischner, Józef 59
Totalitarianism 15, 17, 56, 60, 110, 127,
    231, see also Dissidents; Kirkpatrick,
    Jeane; Lefort, Claude
  Claude Lefort's theory of 116
  dissidents' theory of 20, 40–45, 54
  in rhetoric of Ronald Reagan 128

in thought of French anti-totalitarian
    intellectuals 108
theory of as sounding board for
    personalism 54
Touraine, Alain 124
Trade Union Advisory Committee 142
Trotsky, Leon 138
Turkey 85
Tutu, Desmond 225

Uganda 186
UK 72–73, 88, 166, 218
  response to Polish crisis 86
UN 30, 39, 196, 218
UN Charter 66, 72
UN Commission on Human Rights see
    UNCHR
UN General Assembly 218–219
UN High Commissioner for Human Rights
    219
UN human rights pacts 25, 29, 31–32, 57,
    59, 62, 227, see also ICCPR,
    ICESCR
UN Human Rights Pacts 29
UN Security Council 218
UNCHR 18, 112, 151, 186, 198, 222
  debates on Poland at 187–188, 190
Union of Soviet Socialist Republics (USSR)
    See Soviet Union
United Kingdom, see UK
United Nations 10, 183
United States, see US
United States of America 22
United States of America (US) 17
Universal Declaration of Human Rights 1,
    15, 27, 32, 52, 56, 66, 70, 80, 178,
    213, 220, 225, 227, 231
University in Exile 164
Uruguay 27
US 68, 72, 79, 85–86, 88–89, 107, 135,
    145, 164–165, 218, 229
  impact on events in Poland 215
  policy toward Poland in late 1980s
    214–215
US Democratic Party 135
US Department of State 147, 198
US Information Agency 78
Ustinov, Dmitry 170

Vance, Cyrus 164
Vatican 133, 176
Vidal, Gore 85
Vietnam 13, 75, 136, 156, 189
Volpin, Alexander 26
Vonnegut, Kurt 85

Index

Wałęsa, Bohdan 177
Wałęsa, Danuta 177, 179, 181
Wałęsa, Lech 1, 8, 15, 18, 33, 71, 97, 108,
  125, 143, 150, 152, 163, 172, 180,
  203–204, 212, 216, 225, *see also* Icon;
  Solidarity
  as icon of human rights culture 173–174,
  178–180, 211–212, 221
  as Solidarity leader 173
  awarded Nobel Prize 173
  in precarious situation in 1983 174–176
  Nobel lecture 177–178, 181
  Nobel Prize acceptance speech of
  177–178, 181
Warsaw 41, 52, 86–87, 146–147, 151–152,
  167–168, 178–179, 202
Warsaw Left 22–24, 46
  rapprochement with Catholicism
  47–48
Warsaw Pact 170
Washington 88–89, 127, 132, 139, 167,
  188, 190, 195–196, 198, 215
Watergate 75, 156
Weinberger, Caspar 81, 140

Weinstein, Allen 78
West Berlin 94
West German Green party 209, 223, *see also*
  Kelly, Petra
  and Polish crisis 85
West German peace movement 7, 86, 185,
  190, *see also* Kelly, Petra
  response to Polish crisis 82–83, 85
West Germany 72, 85, 113, 164, 206
  government's response to Polish crisis
  87–88, 91–92
  responses to Polish crisis in 82–83
Whitehead, John 211
Wojtyła, Karol 33–34, 48, personalist
  philosophy of *see* John Paul II
Wolin, Richard 109
World Conference of Human Rights 227
Wujec, Henryk 147, 172
Wyszyński, Stefan 33, 38, 48

Young People's Socialist League 135
Young Poland Movement 52
Yugoslav wars of succession 228
Yugoslavia 218–219

CPSIA information can be obtained
at www.ICGtesting.com
Printed in the USA
LVHW080920030821
694401LV00004B/308